Individuals and Institutions in Medieval Scholasticism

New Historical
PERSPECTIVES

New Historical Perspectives is a book series for early career scholars within the UK and the Republic of Ireland. Books in the series are overseen by an expert editorial board to ensure the highest standards of peer-reviewed scholarship. Commissioning and editing is undertaken by the Royal Historical Society, and the series is published under the imprint of the Institute of Historical Research by the University of London Press.

The series is supported by the Economic History Society and the Past and Present Society.

Individuals and Institutions in Medieval Scholasticism

Edited by Antonia Fitzpatrick and John Sabapathy

LONDON
ROYAL HISTORICAL SOCIETY
INSTITUTE OF HISTORICAL RESEARCH
UNIVERSITY OF LONDON PRESS

Published in 2020 by

UNIVERSITY OF LONDON PRESS
SCHOOL OF ADVANCED STUDY
INSTITUTE OF HISTORICAL RESEARCH
Senate House, Malet Street, London WC1E 7HU

Available to download free or to purchase the hard copy edition at https://www.sas.ac.uk/publications/.

ISBNs
978-1-912702-26-8 (hardback edition)
978-1-912702-27-5 (paperback edition)
978-1-912702-30-5 (PDF edition)
978-1-912702-28-2 (ePub edition)
978-1-912702-29-9 (.mobi edition)

DOI 10.14296/520.9781912702305

New Historical
PERSPECTIVES

Cover image: detail of Andrea da Firenze (Andrea Bonaiuti)'s 1366–8 *Allegory of the triumph of the Church* for the Dominican Order's Chapterhouse in S. Maria Novella, Florence.

Contents

Acknowledgements

Predictably enough there are a number of individuals and institutions we would like to thank. First, all our contributors for their patience with a project which has had a long gestation and for their commitment to it. Second, those contributors to the initial sunny conference in June 2015 at St John's College Oxford whom it was not possible to include in the volume: Charles Burnett, Magnus Ryan and Juhana Toivanen. Those who chaired and commented on our discussions were also enormously helpful: Mary Carruthers, Jean Dunbabin, Kantik Ghosh, Stephen Mossman, Sandy Murray, Lucy Sackville, Cecilia Trifogli and Ian Wei. Third – if we may – each other. This has been an enormously enjoyable and collaborative project from the start. Antonia Fitzpatrick remembers John Sabapathy proposing the idea but the undertaking has been entirely collaborative from beginning to end. The project's structure was generated together; its introduction written and revised collaboratively; and its articles proofed alongside one another.

There are a number of institutions we would like to thank, not at all distinct from the individuals involved. First, St John's College, Oxford and University College London, both of which have provided us with physical and intellectual homes for important periods and which have played instrumental roles in the genesis of this project. We hope that Sir Richard Southern would look favourably on this book. Certainly, his presidential portrait at St John's seemed to. Neither of us knew Southern but he has had an important influence on our thinking. More materially, St John's and UCL History Department provided the financial support for the ridiculously fun conference which brought everyone together in the first place. John Sabapathy would also like to thank the Leverhulme Trust for granting a research fellowship on thirteenth-century institutionalization during which this project was completed. This was very much appreciated. Second, the Warburg Institute, where we co-ran a scholasticism reading group for several years, including with some contributors to this volume. The Warburg is one of the best places in the world to work on scholasticism and the book was proofed in its spiritual home on the third floor. Third, the Royal Historical Society and the Institute of Historical Research whose New Historical Perspectives series welcomed our proposal for this book and have supported its production so helpfully.

Finally, this book only apparently lacks a dedication since its efficient cause is an individual who so entirely pervades it that acknowledgment would be as gratuitous as it would be unwanted. In all honesty and gratitude, *ceci n'est pas une Festschrift.*

Antonia Fitzpatrick and John Sabapathy
Eton and Bloomsbury, July 2019

List of abbreviations

BNF	Bibliothèque nationale de France
Brit. Libr.	British Library, London
CCCM	*Corpus Christianorum Continuatio Mediaevalis*
CCSL	*Corpus Christianorum Series Latina*
CSEL	*Corpus Scriptorum Ecclesiasticorum Latinorum*
lat.	Latin
MGH	Monumenta Germaniae Historica
MGH SRG	Monumenta Germaniae Historica. Scriptores rerum Germanicarum in usum scholarum
MGH SS	Monumenta Germaniae Historica. Scriptores (in Folio)
ODNB	*Oxford Dictionary of National Biography* (https://www.oxforddnb.com)
PL	*Patrologia Latina*

Notes on contributors

Peter Biller is emeritus professor at the University of York. His earlier research was on medieval thought about population and 'race' in medieval science. Now he is a member of a group editing a large tranche of the earliest inquisition records from southern France – specifically, those that survive only in seventeenth-century copies.

Emily Corran is lecturer in medieval history at University College London. Her research focuses on practical ethical thought and casuistry in the later middle ages, with a particular interest in manuals for confessors. Her monograph *Lying and Perjury in Medieval Practical Thought: a Study in the History of Casuistry* was published in 2018.

David d'Avray is emeritus professor of history at University College London. He is a fellow of the British Academy and of the Medieval Academy of America.

Blaise Dufal is associated researcher to the University of Sydney and the Ecole des hautes études en sciences sociales (Paris). He is a specialist in medieval scholasticism (late thirteenth century – early fourteenth century), with a focus on the classical and patristic traditions. His research interests include the historiography and epistemology of the humanities and social sciences. He co-edited *L'historien et les fantômes. Lectures (autour) de l'œuvre d'Alain Boureau* (Paris, 2017) and *Une histoire au présent. Les historiens et Michel Foucault* (Paris, 2013).

Antonia Fitzpatrick is a Bedingfield scholar and Residential Scholar at the Honourable Society of Gray's Inn. She is studying the bar professional training course at the City Law School and will begin pupillage at Monckton Chambers in October 2020. Before retraining as a barrister, she held a junior research fellowship and a departmental lectureship in medieval history at St John's College, Oxford, during which time she published a monograph, *Thomas Aquinas on Bodily Identity*, with Oxford University Press (2017).

Isabel Iribarren is professor of medieval church history and philosophy at Strasbourg University, and director of the Master of Medieval Studies programme. She has published a number of papers on medieval angelology, scholastic intellectual traditions and the history of medieval Thomism, which led to a monograph: *Durandus of St Pourçain: a Dominican Theologian in the Shadow of Aquinas* (Oxford, 2005). More recently, her research has focused on Jean Gerson's work. She is the author of an annotated and widely commented French translation of Gerson's epic poem *Josephina. L'épopée de saint Joseph* (2 vols, Paris, 2019).

Matthew Kempshall is Cliff Davies Fellow and Clarendon associate professor in history at Wadham College, University of Oxford. He works on the transmission and transformation of aspects of the classical tradition within medieval and early Renaissance Europe. He is the author of *The Common Good in Late Medieval Political Thought* (Oxford, 1999) and *Rhetoric and the Writing of History 400–1500* (Manchester, 2011).

Cornelia Linde studied medieval Latin, classical Latin and auxiliary sciences of history at the universities of Göttingen, Bologna and Freiburg im Breisgau. She holds an MA in cultural and intellectual history and a PhD in combined historical studies from the Warburg Institute, University of London. From 2009 to 2012 she was a British Academy postdoctoral fellow at the Department of History, University College London, after which she joined the German Historical Institute London as a research fellow in medieval history. In April 2020 she took up the professorship of medieval history at the University of Greifswald.

John Marenbon is a fellow of Trinity College, Cambridge (since 1978), and honorary professor of medieval philosophy in the University of Cambridge (since 2010). His most recent books are *Pagans and Philosophers: the Problem of Paganism from Augustine to Leibniz* (Princeton, N.J., 2015) and *Medieval Philosophy: a Very Short Introduction* (Oxford, 2016).

Gert Melville is senior professor and director of the Research Center for Comparative History of Religious Orders (FOVOG) at the University of Dresden. He researches the functioning of institutions, the organization and spirituality of medieval monasteries, and has published on this topic, among others, the books *Charisma und religiöse Gemeinschaften im Mittelalter* (Münster, 2005) and *The World of Medieval Monasticism* (Collegeville, MN, 2016). He is editor of the series *Vita regularis* (81 vols, Münster, 2019) and co-editor of *Brill's Encyclopedia of the Middle Ages* (Leiden, 2016). He is a member of the Pontifical Committee of Historical Sciences, Rome, and a member of the programming committee of the International Medieval Congress, Leeds.

Sylvain Piron is directeur d'études at the Ecole des hautes études en sciences sociales in Paris. His research deals with various aspects of medieval intellectual history, with particular interests in Franciscan radicals, mystics and prophets, and the history of economic thought. His latest monograph is entitled *L'occupation du monde* (Brussels, 2018).

John Sabapathy is associate professor of medieval history at University College London. *Officers and Accountability in Medieval England* (Oxford, 2014) won the Royal Historical Society's Whitfield Prize 2015. He is currently working on *The Cultivation of Christendom: Europe 1187–1321*, the thirteenth-century volume in the new Oxford History of Medieval Europe series, as well as *Emergency History: a Natural History of Humanity for the Present*.

Introduction: individuals and institutions in medieval scholasticism[*]

Antonia Fitzpatrick and John Sabapathy

This volume has three purposes. It gathers together a wide range of current approaches analysing the relationship between individuals, institutions and medieval scholasticism; it sets them in a broad historiographical frame; and through these it suggests an agenda for future work in relation to these subjects. It does that by bringing together a range of important perspectives, including many not well known within Anglophone circles. This introduction sets a number of them out at length. An afterword by David d'Avray offers suggestions for agendas to be extended. The editors offer suggestions themselves below.

A miniature portrait in a landscape: Richard Southern

A very helpful way of opening out the issues and problems in which we are interested can be provided by considering the work of one of the greatest medieval historians of the twentieth century, partly because his distinctive interpretations remain of great interest, partly because he exemplified a number of wider currents. Sir Richard Southern (1912–2001) began and ended his intellectual life writing about scholasticism, both in relation to specific individuals' thinking and in relation to wider patterns of thought and the social structures underlying them.[1] In particular, Southern's work helpfully reflects a wider tendency to separate phenomena which in this volume we wish to connect. These are: work on the substance of *individuals'* thought (e.g., Southern's work on Anselm or Grosseteste's thought); work

* Our thanks to David d'Avray for comments on a earlier draft of this.

1 See the last quarter of R. W. Southern, *The Making of the Middle Ages* (London, 1953), *St. Anselm and His Biographer* (Cambridge, 1963); and the unfinished trilogy on *Scholastic Humanism and the Unification of Europe* (2 vols, Oxford, 1995–2001). For Southern see A. Murray, 'Richard William Southern', *Proc. Brit. Academy*, cxx (2003), 413–42; A. Boureau, 'Richard Southern: a landscape for a portrait', *Past and Present*, clxv (1999), 218–29; and R. Bartlett's introduction to *History and Historians: Selected Papers of R. W. Southern*, ed. R. J. Bartlett (Oxford, 2004), pp. 1–10.

A. Fitzpatrick and J. Sabapathy, 'Introduction: individuals and institutions in medieval scholasticism', in *Individuals and Institutions in Medieval Scholasticism*, ed. A. Fitzpatrick and J. Sabapathy (London, 2020), pp. 1–49.

on wider intellectual *practices* and also schools and intellectual *groupings* (e.g., his work on 'scholastic humanism'; his argument that there was no school of Chartres); and, finally, work on the administrative *organization* which structured, enabled and/or constrained this thought (e.g., his work on ecclesiastical government; his argument that Grosseteste's writings are incompatible with an Oxford/Paris formation and therefore prove an English provincial education). All these we sketch below.

Southern's writings, then, present a nuanced picture of how he thought individuals and institutions interacted in medieval scholasticism and can provide the point of departure for our wider consideration of the recent historiography. It is a mark of their interest, weight and force that sixteen years after his death they remain one of the great syntheses with which it is worth engaging. Southern alternated between the close-up and the panorama. On the one hand, there are the portraits of the ecclesiastics and thinkers Anselm of Aosta/Bec/Canterbury (*c.*1033–1109) and Robert Grosseteste (*c.*1170–1253). On the other, there are the much larger landscapes in which such writers thrived: first, *Western Society and the Church in the Middle Ages* (1970) and the unfinished project on scholastic humanism. It is these latter which are most 'institutional' – but they are such only in some respects and, in part, negatively so. *Western Society* was the book Southern said he enjoyed writing least. Not coincidentally, it is also the most conventionally 'institutional', dealing with the development of ecclesiastical organization between *c.*700 and *c.*1520 (it was a volume in the 'Penguin History of the Christian Church', definitionally 'Institutional'). There is discussion of 'thought' here, but it is diffused through the whole or sneaks in through individual pen portraits (of Archbishop Eudes Rigaud or Grosseteste). 'Administering' and 'thinking' appear as oil and water in consequence. The two volumes of *Scholastic Humanism and the Unification of Europe* establish a more comfortable 'institutional' register. If *Western Society* is institutional largely in an (ecclesiastical) *organizational* sense, *Scholastic Humanism* is institutional in the sense of describing the intellectual *practices* its protagonists developed. It is these that are orientated towards exploring and asserting the fundamental dignity of human nature, its right ordering and its enrichment through the cultivation of human and divine friendship. The overwhelming focus is on the intellectual disciplines developed for these purposes: institutions-*qua*-practices. Here is the canonist Gratian's 'integration of doctrine and law'; the exegete Anselm of Laon's move 'from glosses to *sententiae*'; the subsequent 'stumbling' 'from sentences to system'; the 'great achiever' Peter Lombard's re-organizing of theological commentary.[2] Institutions-*qua*-organizations *are* here, but somewhat negatively. Some inhibit thought, others do not exist, a select few enable. The school of Laon's inability to expand, given its finite hill-top location, is described; the existence of any 'school of Chartres' is given a final savaging (a long-running debate between Southern, Peter Dronke and others); the practical problems with cathedral schools are described; the need for curriculum organization at Paris is analysed. A core narrative is the institutional clearing of the ways which led to the eventual ascendancy of Paris, an ascendancy Southern sadly never fully described since it would have formed a pivot in the never-completed third volume. That absence inadvertently contributes to the absence of institutions-*qua*-organizations, since chronologically this volume would have contained Southern's account of how universities regulated themselves and were regulated from Robert of Courson's 1215 rules, Gregory IX's 1231 bull *Parens scientiarum*, to the 1277 condemnations of various Aristotelian teachings in the arts faculty.[3] It is fair to say, however, that (a) comments about such organizational underpinnings could already have been made for twelfth-century Bologna in earlier volumes; and (b) their absence may point partly towards Southern's thematic, disciplinary and geographical preferences: namely, intellectual practices, theology and Paris. Nevertheless, it is clear that volume three would have stressed the organizational institutionalization which produced the dominance of Paris, even if only to argue for its negative intellectual effects. A core of that criticism is clear from *Robert Grosseteste*, in which a key argument is that Grosseteste's 'provincial' English education accounts for his innovative work across multiple fields, work which could not have been well countenanced by the disciplinary silos of Paris (or Oxford). Parisian hegemony entailed intellectual conservatism, in Southern's account. If that critique relates to scholastic *organizational* institutionalization, our great loss is that we lack Southern's full case for it as well as his case for the failure of his scholastic system as a set of institutionalized *intellectual practices*.

We stress 'his' because that narrative was sharp and particular. It had three stages: innovation, application, then disintegration.[4] From *c.*1080 to 1160 was the first period of heroism, 'the essential period of innovation', when 'the scholastic method of absorbing, elaborating, Christianizing and systematizing the whole intellectual deposit of the Greco-Roman past to produce a complete body of doctrine about both the natural and

[2] The quotations are taken from subheadings in the books.

[3] I. P. Wei, *Intellectual Culture in Medieval Paris: Theologians and the University, c.1100–1330* (Cambridge, 2012), ch. 3.

[4] It would also have included a final, post-medieval 'renewal' of scholasticism.

the supernatural worlds took place'.[5] Scholastic theology then entered a 'placid phase in which it put on weight and grew in importance ... without making any spectacular new advance or asking any new fundamental questions'.[6] This period up to variously 1215 or 1250 saw 'the theoretical work of scholars in the schools [turned] to practical use in government'.[7] Thereafter Southern's history of scholastic humanism was one of 'increasing difficulties encountered, especially from the middle of the thirteenth century onwards, by those who aimed to make the system complete in substance and operation'.[8] Central to these difficulties was scholars' compulsion for both completeness and order, since 'systematization requires selection, selection requires omission, and omission impairs completeness'.[9] Implicit anyway in even early scholastic sophistication was a tendency towards over-elaboration, impenetrable private languages and the picking at ostensibly innocuous threads which would ultimately unravel the whole.[10] This was so, furthermore, before the Aristotelian and Arabic textual influx of the later twelfth and thirteenth centuries which 'opened up many new problems on which no generally agreed solutions appeared to be attainable'.[11] Even at the very apex of their 'comprehensive serenity' – Southern suggested – it is not clear that the scholars' confidence in their enterprise was well-founded.[12] This characterization has not carried universal assent by any means. One might look to Alain Boureau for an alternative, much less negative account of the later chronology; or to John Marenbon for both a critique of Southern's idea of 'scholastic *humanism*' *per se* and of his unitary model of scholasticism.[13]

This is not the moment to seek to resolve such issues. Scholasticism itself can, of course, be defined in different ways, as much to do with how a group validates itself as the holders of knowledge as with the intellectual practices

[5] Southern, *Scholastic Humanism*, i. 6.

[6] Southern, *Scholastic Humanism*, ii. 145.

[7] Southern, *Scholastic Humanism*, ii. 152. A synecdoche for what would have been Southern's later judgement on the happiness of the marriage between learning and government in the 13th century can be found in his *Robert Grosseteste: the Growth of an English Mind in Medieval Europe* (2nd edn, Oxford, 1992), pp. 270–81, 285–91.

[8] As volume 3 was previewed on the hardback cover of *Scholastic Humanism*, ii.

[9] *Scholastic Humanism*, ii. 54.

[10] Respectively: *Scholastic Humanism*, ii. 23, 130, 118.

[11] R. W. Southern, 'The changing role of universities in medieval Europe', *Hist. Research*, lx (1987), 133–46, at p. 138.

[12] Southern, *Scholastic Humanism*, ii. 47, on the biblical *Glossa ordinaria*.

[13] A. Boureau, *La Raison scolastique* (4 vols, Paris, 2006–16); J. Marenbon, 'Humanism, scholasticism and the school of Chartres', *Internat. Jour. Classical Tradition*, vi (2000), 569–77.

they then carry out.[14] We find the following definition by Riccardo Quinto helpful, which focuses on scholasticism as a set of intellectual practices. Scholasticism following Quinto's 'ideal type' is a 'certain way of reading texts'. This 'way' [*modo*], Quinto suggested, comprised the following: (1) an 'objective' engagement with texts 'independent of the subjective conditions of the commentator', that is, not primarily concerned with a 'subjective' personal, spiritual engagement – as in monastic texts; (2) texts are subject to an analytical reading, with 'individual statements' compatibility established though dialectical means'; (3) the text's value comes wholly from its truth-value and not from its 'own' interest or purpose – to that degree it produces knowledge (*scientia*), 'an ensemble of propositions guaranteed by their conformity to an authoritative text, yet integrated in a new ensemble in which their legitimacy and reciprocal connection shines in an even clearer way'.[15] We wonder about the first proposition insofar as it seems there are scholastic texts (e.g., Bonaventure's *Journey into the Mind of God*) which are both 'scholastic' and meditative, but we nevertheless find this 'ideal type' dynamically useful. (Isabel Iribarren's chapter on Jean Gerson's poem the *Josephina* in this volume also raises important questions about this facet of the ideal type.) We would stress two further aspects.[16] First, scholasticism's *modo* was conspicuously world-facing as well as revealed-truth-reconciling. Scholastic thinking was not cloistered in an ivory tower. On the contrary, its influence was a function of its utility and applicability well outside the schools.[17] This volume, then, pointedly emphasizes the extension of scholasticism's institutional role far beyond academic 'disputed questions'. Second, and correlated, the range of subject matter and fields of action addressed by scholasticism was accordingly vast and certainly not restricted to theology or philosophy. The chapters which follow deliberately reflect this. Without aiming to be comprehensive, our chapters show the place of scholastic 'trouble-shooting' in law and inquisition, for instance, just as much as in theology; in poetry as well as history; and in targeting problems ranging from the concrete and particular to the abstract and general. In what follows we now review important relevant historiographical trends

[14] C. König-Pralong, *Le bon usage des savoirs* (Paris, 2011), pp. 290–4.

[15] Summarizing R. Quinto, *Scholastica. Storia di un concetto* (Subsidia Mediaevalia Patavina, ii, Padua, 2001), pp. 416–17. See further D. L. d'Avray, *Medieval Religious Rationalities: a Weberian Analysis* (Cambridge, 2010), pp. 70–6. Translations in this chapter are by the authors unless otherwise specified.

[16] See also Emily Corran's comments on Quinto in her chapter in this volume at pp. 220, 233–4; and David d'Avray's comments in his afterword at pp. 271–2.

[17] D'Avray's comments on preaching in the afterword to this volume at p. 276 may also be thought of in this context.

and then return to those areas marked out above – namely individuals, schools and, finally, institutions as both practices and organizations.

Perspectives and premises

What is one interested in?

This book is interested in the back-and-forth relationship between individual thinkers and the various institutional contexts in which their thought was produced and by which it may have been inflected. It is obvious that the parameters of one's interests and axioms radically predetermine and alter the history one writes. In the history of philosophy alone, for example, there are a variety of possible approaches.[18]

A particularly insightful way of encapsulating this plurality was suggested by David d'Avray over thirty years ago. He suggested that, among the subjects grouped under 'the history of ideas and attitudes', one could differentiate between history which was principally interested in (1) the history of original ideas; (2) ideology and social development; (3) 'ordinary' beliefs.[19] This schema remains very helpful – though one might want to make explicit that (1) also contains the history of philosophy as a set of disciplinary interests.[20] Of course, historians have sometimes interested themselves in more than one in the same instance. However, part of our point in using Southern as a point of departure is that more often than one might expect these interests have been canalized in a rather artificial way. We may, say, be interested in Dominican thought, but what we want to do with that thought may vary. We may be mostly interested in how theological ideas played out in identity formation for a group; why Dominican organizational life seemed so much less painful than the Franciscans'; how to isolate those aspects of inquisitorial procedure which are intellectually 'Dominican' in order to differentiate what, within inquisitorial depositions, may be 'Dominican' and what may be 'irreducibly' heretical. Three contributors to this volume have addressed each of these respective questions (Fitzpatrick, Melville, Biller), but it is an obvious truth that the complexity of Dominican life as

[18] C. König-Pralong, 'L'histoire de la philosophie médiévale depuis 1950: méthodes, textes, débats', *Annales*, lxiv (2009), 143–69; É. Anheim, A. Lilti and S. van Damme, 'Quelle Histoire de la philosophie?', *Annales*, lxiv (2009), 5–11.

[19] D. L. d'Avray, *The Preaching of the Friars: Sermons Diffused from Paris Before 1300* (Oxford, 1985), pp. 258–9.

[20] Given its most 'institutional' form in Anglophone historiography in *The Cambridge History of Later Medieval Philosophy: from the Rediscovery of Aristotle to the Disintegration of Scholasticism, 1100–1600*, ed. N. Kretzmann, A. Kenny, J. Pinborg, with E. Stump (Cambridge, 1982); and in a slightly different way in its successor volume *The Cambridge History of Medieval Philosophy*, ed. R. Pasnau with C. van Dyke (2 vols, Cambridge, 2010).

it was experienced by medieval Dominicans intertwined all these facets of institutional and intellectual life and more.

These are not either/or alternatives: all are important. Accordingly, we have not sought to even out differences of approach so much as to showcase what each offers. This volume seeks to think further about these interconnections, the reciprocal relationship between individual and institution and the thinking the latter produced. As Nathalie Gorochov said apropos the University of Paris, 'no text without context then, but equally [scholastic] works themselves are liable to reflect the institutional, political, social, and religious stakes which galvanize the history of the university'.[21]

The history of medieval thought on whose terms?

The moment for undertaking such an exercise seems propitious across a range of historiographies which are different both in geographical origin and historiographical style. We have already alluded to the obvious fact that the sorts of ambition one has for an intellectual history very significantly alter the resulting account. Peter Biller has recently argued that it is worth thinking again about Antonio Gramsci as a mediator in connecting intellectuals with their various contexts.[22] Biller suggests there was a road not taken after the 1970s with respect to constructing stronger analytical models which put intellectuals in a better-rooted, sociological context; and the present seems a good time to review this.[23] Gramsci certainly furnished some of the moving parts which drive the engine of what is still one of the most stimulating essays on the subject of 'intellectuals in the middle ages': Jacques Le Goff's book of 1957, revised in 1985.[24] That argument – elegantly compressed by Alain Boureau and compatible with Southern's – was a three-act tragedy of individuals devoured by the institution which also empowered them, the university:

[21] N. Gorochov, *Naissance de l'université: les Écoles de Paris d'Innocent III à Thomas d'Aquin (v. 1200–v. 1245)* (Paris, 2012), p. 23.

[22] P. Biller, 'Intellectuals and the masses: oxen and she-asses in the medieval Church', in *The Oxford Handbook of Medieval Christianity*, ed. J. H. Arnold (Oxford, 2014), pp. 323–39, at pp. 335–6. See also J. L. Nelson, 'Organic intellectuals in the Dark Ages?', *History Workshop Jour.*, lxvi (2008), 1–17 (on Gramsci).

[23] There is plainly work which does this (e.g., R. I. Moore's), but it seems to us there remains room for further differentiation of intellectuals with respect to different forms of power.

[24] J. Le Goff, *Les Intellectuels au Moyen Âge* (Paris, 1957). For Gramsci's further influence here see G. Tabacco, 'Gli intellettuali del medioevo nel giuoco delle istituzioni e dalle preponderanze sociali', in *Storia d'Italia, Intelletuali e potere*, ed. R. Romano and C. Vivanti (Annali, iv, Turin, 1981), pp. 7–46.

> [T]he twelfth century, full of promise and disinterested enthusiasm, sees the birth of the hero of the intellect; the thirteenth century sees a twist in the plot: the intellectual falls into the trap of the institution of the university, encountering the constraints of authority, which he does not always resist. The 'internal contradictions' of the university intellectual harden, at the end of the century, into the 'double truth', philosophical and theological. The play, in the fourteenth century, ends badly: internal conflicts produce patent divorces, between faith and reason, between knowing and teaching, between the critical spirit and careerist flattery.[25]

The immediate point is this: Le Goff's (and Biller's) sociological history of intellectuals is only one possible frame which could be chosen for something which contributed to 'a history of medieval thought'. The degree to which Le Goff privileged the university as the relevant space in which such an intellectual history played itself out is made clear by the vigorous 'counter'-thesis and paradox of Alain de Libera in 1991: intellectuals as intellectuals could only freely and properly develop once university activities were extended outside the university, since there intellectual activities and identities could flourish independently of that institutionalized setting. Condemnations such as Étienne Tempier's 1277 censure of various Aristotelian positions being taught in the Paris arts faculty acted as a goad to thought. Censure ultimately played a useful role; and the leaking of intellectual activity outside universities ultimately produced 'the intellectual'.[26] (One notes that here universities are still given a very privileged space in terms of the sheer possibility of thinking *at all* in these middle ages.) 'Intellectuals' as a category – argued de Libera – were therefore closely connected with the deprofessionalization of philosophy.

Such a critique indeed takes many of Le Goff's starting premises for granted.[27] However, historians of philosophy might critique the 'ideas in context' of *Les Intellectuels au Moyen Âge* for being long on context and personalities and short on ideas.[28] Historians of philosophy might be more interested in the ideas than their authors.[29] The history of philosophy, however, can be written with different accents. The history *of philosophy*

[25] A. Boureau, 'Intellectuals in the middle ages, 1957–1995', in *The Work of Jacques Le Goff and the Challenges of Medieval History*, ed. M. Rubin (Woodbridge, 1997), pp. 145–55, at p. 147. For a variant stressing earlier 'colour' and plasticity, see F. Rexroth, *Fröhliche Scholastik. Die Wissenschaftsrevolution des Mittelalters* (Munich, 2018).

[26] A. de Libera, *Penser au Moyen Âge* (Paris, 1991), pp. 12–13, 349–51. For the role of censure and self-policing in shaping Parisian thought between 1200 and 1250, see Gorochov, *Naissance de l'université*.

[27] Pointed out by Boureau, 'Intellectuals in the middle ages', pp. 150–1.

[28] See de Libera, *Penser au Moyen Âge*, p. 75.

[29] König-Pralong, 'L'histoire de la philosophie médiévale'.

stresses a continuous history of philosophical interests as validated by contemporary philosophers (ethics, metaphysics, philosophy of language etc.). It may also seek to show the ongoing resonance of medieval philosophical formulations as a resource for contemporary philosophy. This, however, may require taking it some considerable distance from its medieval setting-in-life (*Sitz im Leben*). The *history* of philosophy might be denatured by such an enterprise. Thus John Marenbon (another contributor here), while sympathetic to and practitioner of such methods, has nevertheless argued that the re-tooling of medieval philosophical formulations so as to make them fit for modern philosophical use may cause significant problems from a historian's perspective. Damage may be done to the *history* of philosophy. One may give a precision to a medieval argument which was lacking, unnecessary, in its medieval formulation. Restating medieval formulations using the symbols of modern propositional logic produces a 'deformation of the historical truth'. Finally, applying the interpretative principle of charity to such thought, whereby the most coherent and least problematic interpretation is always preferred, is 'not a good method to arrive at a fair understanding of that which a past philosopher actually thought'.[30]

Elsewhere, Marenbon has helpfully suggested one might study 'antiquated philosophy' for at least six reasons which sometimes intertwine (this intersects with and extends d'Avray's model above). In summary, these are: (1) because its philosophical content may help the progress of contemporary philosophers; (2) because, as history, intellectual history is as interesting as the next sort of history; (3) this, however, requires a division of labour in which the history of philosophy provides an 'internal history' for philosophers while the history of ideas offers a more 'external' history of wider interest; (4) really great philosophers perennially merit study as exemplars of thinking philosophically, though arguably few medieval philosophers would make the canon; (5) like great works of literature, anyone interested in understanding the heights of human culture should read its great philosophical works (again the question of what counts is begged); (6) reading antiquated philosophy challenges what we might conceive of as valid philosophy precisely because it operated differently from what we hold philosophy to be.[31]

[30] J. Marenbon, *Le temps, l'éternité et la prescience de Boèce à Thomas d'Aquin* (Paris, 2005), ch. 6. The quotations are from pp. 164, 168.

[31] Summarizing J. Marenbon, 'Why study medieval philosophy?', in *Warum noch Philosophie? Historische, systematische und gesellschaftliche Positionen*, ed. M. van Ackeren, T. Kobusch and J. Müller (Berlin/New York, 2011), pp. 65–78, at pp. 66–72.

The 'return' of institutions and organizations

If it is to introduce the historiographical context of the present volume as it relates to intellectuals, this introduction should do something similar with respect to 'institutions', which have been less fashionably the focus of post-war historical study, be those institutions constitutional, legal and ecclesiastical, administrative or economic. Such institutions saw a waning of an influence which had waxed strongest in the nineteenth and early twentieth centuries and whose dominance itself largely evoked movements such as the *Annales* 'school'. Southern himself acknowledged that *Scholastic Humanism* was in part a reaction against older institutional models.[32]

Southern's rather negative approach to the role institutions played in constraining individual thought is best exemplified in his arguments about Grosseteste's intellectual formation. Grosseteste was an extraordinarily wide-ranging thinker across a range of different intellectual, linguistic, scientific, mathematical, philosophical and theological traditions. In what institutional matrix should he be placed? A long-standing tradition suggested a Parisian and an Oxford one. Southern argued for a provincial English one. To look in Paris's direction was to see Grosseteste 'as a precursor of Albert the Great [d. 1280]; and I [Southern] look on him as an enlargement of Adelard of Bath', the equally skilled interdisciplinary English intellectual of an earlier generation (d. *c.*1150).[33] This remains a somewhat controversial interpretation and Southern restated it forcefully in the book's second edition. Southern's arguments are detailed and specific but his conclusion is this:

> We can say that Grosseteste's pre-1225 works were scientific; that, with the possible exception of his Commentaries on Aristotle's *Posterior Analytics* and *Physics*, which probably belong to the years after 1220, they show no sign of having been written in or for the schools; that several seem to be written to clear his own mind. These works also show a progression from the calendar to astronomy and astrology, and then to the study of the great texts on scientific method (Aristotle's *Posterior Analytics*) and the origin of motion in the universe (Aristotle's *Physics*). So the evidence of his writing from 1200 to 1225 suggests the development of a scientist in the tradition of Adelard of Bath turning into a philosopher of science ... Such evidence as we have, therefore, both about his physical whereabouts and about his writings, places him in the line of English scientists working in relatively humble administrative position in some kind of

[32] Southern's 'author response' to D. L. d'Avray, 'Review of *Scholastic Humanism and the Unification of Europe. Volume I: Foundations*', *Reviews in History*, xiii (1996) <http://www.history.ac.uk/reviews/review/13> [accessed 13 June 2016]. Cf. Gorochov's reflections in *Naissance de l'université*, pp. 15–22.

[33] Southern, *Robert Grosseteste*, p. lvi.

> association with the diocesan administration of Hereford, which was also an outstanding centre of scientific study at the time when Grosseteste went there.[34]

In other words, one apparently marginal institutional setting (Hereford) enabled an interdisciplinary creativity which would have been quite impossible within the ostensibly obvious places for such study (Paris, Oxford). Grosseteste's work before 1220 'showed no clear signs of a scholastic background and give no indication of theological study or training'.[35]

In this case, the institutional margins are where this important and innovative work can happen, not the centre. This is no rule, however, demonstrating the iron inflexibility of university syllabuses, a black mark against scholasticism's institutions; it is simply what happened in this case. Indeed arguments have been made that Grosseteste could have had a Parisian intellectual formation.[36] This would be interesting not because Southern would then be wrong, but because of how he would be wrong. Southern's axiomatic argument was that Grosseteste's interdisciplinary freewheeling was incompatible with a highly regulated, scholastic milieu (Paris). If Grosseteste can be shown to have had Parisian formation, it makes Southern's underlying argument about institutional formation highly overdetermined.[37]

Southern's reaction against an over-privileging of institutions can be usefully connected with more recent approaches which stress the variability of what particular institutional spaces enable or constrain. Étienne Anheim, for instance, has called for better 'topographies of institutions'.[38] He argues that not all positions in an institutional space are equivalent and they change over time. The intellectual pope Clement VI (1342–52) can prove a decisive figure in reconfiguring papal authority at the centre of the papacy because he is at the centre of the papacy.[39] This sounds obvious, but it need not be. The history of the western Church suggests that after the Gregorian reforms 'the closer one is to the centre the greater one's capacity to transgress or innovate becomes … – Franciscanism takes off when Pope

[34] Southern, *Robert Grosseteste*, pp. lix–lx.

[35] Southern, *Robert Grosseteste*, p. xxviii.

[36] N. Schulman, 'Husband, father, bishop? Grosseteste in Paris', *Speculum*, lxxii (1997), 330–46.

[37] John Marenbon's article in this volume is an especially subtle exploration of the limits and promise of 'institutional' explanations in this spirit.

[38] É. Anheim, 'Le pape et les artistes au milieu du XIVe siècle. Réflexions sur les notions d'actueur et d'institution', *Circé*, i (2012) <http://www.revue-circe.uvsq.fr/le-pape-et-les-artistes-au-milieu-du-xive-siecle-reflexions-sur-les-notions-dacteur-et-dinstitution/> [accessed 11 July 2019].

[39] É. Anheim, *Clément VI au travail. Lire, écrire, prêcher au XIVe siècle* (Paris, 2014), p. 352.

Innocent III (1198–1216) decides to protect it, and one could suggest that Boniface VIII (1295–1303) was the best placed, paradoxically, to doubt the Christian faith'.[40] Anheim suggested that the situation with respect to the court is the opposite: 'peripheral positions in relation to the court, where the dependence [on the institution] is relative, as for Petrarch [at Avignon], are the topographical positions with the strongest innovative capacity':

> Not all institutions, each in relation to the other, give the same space to actors' practices [i.e., scope for action]; furthermore, at the heart of each institution not all the positions for the actors give the same possibilities in terms of the game [i.e., the rules of the game]. To produce a repertoire of these internal and external differences would be to imagine in general a topography of institutions, taking into account the fact that the relationship between actor and institution is not fixed. This would help to historicize these two notions where generalities sometimes risk enclosing the historian in proofs which are all too predictable.[41]

What institutions do is neither constant nor a given: they both enable and constrain, but how they do so always requires analysis and attention to time, place and individuals. The complexity of the dialectic between individual and institution may be vertiginous. One forceful example is the Avignonese papal penitenciary Opicino de Canistris (1296–*c.*1354), whose idiosyncratic psychosexual Mediterranean maps and registers, Sylvain Piron has argued, are an inverted response to the institutions which shaped him. Like Kafka's 'K', he is the 'unhappy bureaucrat who cannot stop himself from loving the institution which destroys him'.[42] Opicino, for all his idiosyncrasies – *because* of all his idiosyncrasies – is in some sense a symptom of his own institutions.[43]

An inverse pendant to Opicino's exceptional idiosyncrasy, stressing intellectual anonymity, is Ulla Kypta's recent account of the agency of countless nameless, literate and numerate clerks of the English royal exchequer in the twelfth century.[44] This is, in fact, as 'intellectual' an

[40] Anheim, 'Pape et les artistes', developing an idea of Jean Coste.

[41] Anheim, 'Pape et les artistes'.

[42] S. Piron, *Dialectique du monstre. Enquête sur Opicino de Canistris* (Brussels, 2015), p. 174.

[43] Cf. K. Achams's statement: 'We are always already in institutions' (Wir sind immer schon in Institutionen), cited in G. Melville, 'Institutionen als geschichtswissenschaftliches Thema', in *Institutionen und Geschichte. Theoretische Aspekte und mittelalterliche Befunde*, ed. G. Melville (Norm und Struktur, i, Cologne, 1992), pp. 1–24, at p. 17.

[44] U. Kypta, *Die Autonomie der Routine. Wie im 12. Jahrhundert das englische Schatzamt entstand* (Historische Semantik, xxi, Göttingen, 2014). What follows draws on J. Sabapathy, 'Review, Ulla Kypta, *Die Autonomie der Routine. Wie im 12. Jahrhundert das englische Schatzamt entstand*', *German Hist. Institute London Bull.*, xxxviii.1 (2016), 40–6.

institution as more recognizable ones and Kypta's argument is as follows: it is fundamentally mistaken to think of kings and high-level administrators as the guiding hands and minds behind the innovative administrative development of the exchequer as a government department. They played no such role. Rather, agency belongs anonymously to the humble clerks who, through their many, small, repeated actions and modifications, created the exchequer-as-department, the unintended longer-term consequence of those same actions and their development of the technical language needed to articulate it to one another. This is the autonomy of exchequer routine, which develops its own agency à la genetic mutations which are at once random and preserved as a function of their fit within their environmental context. The resulting interpretation is effectively one about a kind of 'automatic government': unconscious, impersonal, anonymous. The institution is the (anonymous) practice. However, between Opicino and the anonymous exchequer clerk, who was the more 'institutionalized', who the more 'individualized'? Are idiosyncratic 'one-offs' more 'individual' by definition than 'orthodox' contributors to institutional practices? Might a 'conservative' institutional enforcer such as Étienne Tempier not be both?[45]

In recent decades European historians have found new ways to return to those older, important concerns, all the better for the collective time spent away from them.[46] One might point to the Dresden-based 'Forschungsstelle für Vergleichende Ordensgeschichte' (FOVOG, Research Network for the Comparative History of Religious Orders), led by Gert Melville (another contributor), which has focused comparatively on the rationality and constitutional logics of a wide range of religious orders. The project 'Power and Institutions in Medieval Islam and Christendom' (PIMIC) focused on medieval institutional similarities and differences between western and Islamic countries.[47] FOVOG has focused on recognizably 'hard' institutional

[45] F.-X. Putallaz, *Insolente liberté. Controverses et condamnations au XIIIe siècle* (Paris, 1995), pp. 58–64, 82–91. For the intellectual coherence of Tempier's 1277 condemnations, see S. Piron, 'Le plan de l'évêque. Pour une critique interne de la condamnation du 7 mars 1277', *Recherches de théologie et philosophie médiévales*, lxxviii (2011), 383–415.

[46] J. Sabapathy, *Officers and Accountability in Medieval England 1170–1300* (Oxford, 2014), with wider historiographical comment on the 'new administrative history' at pp. 10–19. Important reflections on institutions and intellectuals include É. Anheim, 'L'histoire intellectuelle du moyen âge, entre pratiques sociales et débats doctrinaux. Revue critique de la collection 'Vestigia' (Éditions du Cerf)', *Médiévales*, xxxvii (1999), 151–63; and É. Anheim and S. Piron, 'Le travail intellectuel au moyen âge', *Revue de Synthèse*, cxxix (2008), 481–84, part of a special issue which we have found very helpful.

[47] One product was: *Diverging Paths? The Shapes of Power and Institutions in Medieval Christendom and Islam*, ed. J. Hudson and A. Rodríguez (The Medieval Mediterranean, ci, Leiden/Boston, 2014).

forms – religious orders; PIMIC on 'structures or processes performed by social regularities, which do not simply flow from an addition of individual behaviours, but rather as the outcome of power struggles among multiple actors who shape institutions as arenas of social conflict and dispute'.[48] Kypta's work on the exchequer comes out of a distinctive German tradition of historical semantics and conceptual history (*Begriffsgeschichte*).[49] Art historians have analysed the institutional 'content of the form', examining the connections between corporate identity, memory and bureaucracy in images in charters, as well as in cartularies and charters themselves.[50] Such work takes diplomatic (the history of formal texts and their rules) into new fields, building importantly on Michael Clanchy's seminal contribution to the history of literacy and the written word.[51] Many fields remain (we still need an intellectual history of registers and cartularies, for instance).[52]

An especially vivid proof of the importance of these issues is that one of the most controversial medieval disputes of recent years has focused on institutionalization. The issue is heresy; and the core of the dispute is whether Cistercian and Dominican, as well as other, 'secular', theologians articulated so compelling a set of intellectual grids for perceiving heresy that inquisitors internalized them and projected them from the schools onto the world, reality notwithstanding, from the late twelfth century on. 'Cathars', by this account, were the institutionalized *tromp l'oeil* produced by intellectual inquisitors. Whether or not one accepts these arguments, the issue concerns intellectuals' creation of institutions which change reality.[53] Institutionalization plainly matters. We have, so far, briefly introduced intellectuals and institutions, key categories in this book. We turn now to unpacking the 'question' of individuals before thinking about how these elements can be understood to interlock and interact.

[48] As was defined on the project website <http://pimic.eu/what/>. This is no longer live. For one successor development see the St Andrews Institute of Legal and Constitutional Research <https://ilcr.wp.st-andrews.ac.uk> [accessed 11 July 2019].

[49] Kypta, *Autonomie der Routine*.

[50] J. Berenbeim, *The Art of Documentation: Documents and Visual Culture in Medieval England* (Toronto, 2015).

[51] M. T. Clanchy, *From Memory to Written Record: England, 1066–1307* (3rd edn, Chichester, 2013 [1979]).

[52] A valuable recent contribution is *L'art médiéval du registre: Chancelleries royales et princières*, ed. O. Guyotjeannin (Paris, 2018).

[53] The debate and positions are set out in *Cathars in Question*, ed. A. Sennis (Woodbridge, 2016).

Individuals

Impersonal individualism

The history of 'individuals' and individualism in western liberal historiography has been extraordinarily shaped by somewhat uncritical contemporary valuations of 'the individual' and individualism, whether that historiography belongs to the 1860s or the 2010s.[54] This is, perhaps, as unsurprising as it has become unhelpful – but its contradictions are interesting. On the one hand, the roll-call of named medieval intellectuals includes a clutch who might even today muster a trace of popular recognition (just about): Augustine, Abelard, Aquinas, Dante, Ockham, Petrarch. These are unmistakably significant figures. On the other hand, there is a forceful argument that our 'standard' accounts of medieval thought are almost fatally reliant on a wildly distorted, partial picture of what the most important intellectual texts of the period were. A misplaced, 'literary' privileging of authorship means we seek to write a personalized history of this thought when, in fact, we must learn to write a history of influential texts about whose authors we often know nothing personal. The 'death of the author' is resurrected. In some cases much editing of manuscripts remains to be done. We have lists of works without authors and lists of authors without works, to paraphrase Alain de Libera.[55] Texts are often individual *and* impersonal. Further, this is not something we must rectify, 'not an accident or external catastrophe but the very essence of the matter': the anonymous manner of copying manuscripts was a fundamental feature of such thinking and needs to be built into our accounts. (Recall Kypta above.) 'To understand the history of thought as an anonymous history, such is, in our view, the first task of the medievalist', de Libera argued.[56] Yet – to join this with his other argument – as 'thought' escaped from the universities it produced that egoist, the intellectual. The resulting paradox, according to de Libera, is that 'the middle ages of the "intellectuals" was marked simultaneously by the invention of egoism and the effacement of the ego'.[57]

The point can be exemplified through Peter Abelard (*c.*1079–1142), intellectually famous for his contribution to dialectic, individually famous

[54] For the 1860s see, of course, J. Burckhardt's *The Civilization of the Renaissance in Italy*, trans. S. G. C. Middlemore (London, 1990), on which see below; for the 2010s see, e.g., L. Siedentop, *Inventing the Individual: the Origins of Western Liberalism* (London, 2014). One exception to this general rule is J. Seigel, *The Idea of the Self: Thought and Experience in Western Europe since the Seventeenth Century* (Cambridge, 2005).

[55] de Libera, *Penser au Moyen Âge*, pp. 65–8.

[56] de Libera, *Penser au Moyen Âge*, p. 67.

[57] de Libera, *Penser au Moyen Âge*, p. 356.

for seducing his pupil Heloise and the castration and flight which followed. Abelard is arguably a curious amalgam of excess and absence with respect to his individualism. Institutions play a non-accidental role. His *History of My Calamities* has been described as dramatizing a 'conflict between the individual and the surrounding world, the institutions of the church to which the individual belongs'.[58] The *History* is indeed a sequence of battles against intellectual antagonists (William of Champeaux, Anselm of Laon, Bernard of Clairvaux), nothing if not individualistic. Something of this mutability or volatility was sensed at the time. Bernard of Clairvaux said Abelard was 'a man dissimilar from himself'.[59] Nonetheless, Aron Gurevich suggested, behind these antagonisms, Abelard's 'personality remains hidden behind a mask, or rather, behind several different masks, following on from another, which the philosopher saw fit to don'.[60] One of Abelard's teachers, Roscelin, said he did not know what to call Abelard since he was neither a cleric, a layman or a monk. Indeed, Abelard's modern biographer Michael Clanchy persuasively constructed his life according to the sequence of roles Abelard assumed (master, logician, knight, lover, man, monk, theologian, heretic).[61] To Roscelin's retort Clanchy suggested the riposte that Abelard 'fitted none of these [Roscelin's] roles because they were too restrictive'.[62] More positively, Caroline Walker Bynum said (at least of the *History*) that it 'is really the story of the rise and fall of a type: "the philosopher"'.[63] Gurevich offered a more sociological solution: '[B]ecause of his new social status, which he tried to create for himself, [Abelard] was unable to integrate himself into any group'. Abelard exemplified a new type of individual, 'the autonomous individual'.[64]

Nevertheless, in Gurevich's account one cannot help but feel he is disappointed that Abelard did not do better at fully expressing himself beyond his masks. Did institutions, therefore, enable or inhibit Abelard? Historians of individualism sometimes seem unsure whether individuals'

[58] A. Gurevich, *The Origins of European Individualism*, trans. K. Judelson (Oxford, 1995), p. 130.

[59] Discussed in Gurevich, *Origins of European Individualism*, p. 143; M. T. Clanchy, *Abelard: a Medieval Life* (Oxford, 1997), pp. 18, 339–40.

[60] Gurevich, *Origins of European Individualism*, p. 142.

[61] Clanchy, *Abelard*; see also J. Marenbon, *The Philosophy of Peter Abelard* (Cambridge, 1997), p. 36.

[62] Clanchy, *Abelard*, p. 332.

[63] C. W. Bynum, 'Did the twelfth century discover the individual?', *Jour. Eccles. Hist.*, xxxi (1980), 1–17. See also C. Morris, *The Discovery of the Individual 1050–1200* (Toronto, 1972), with which Bynum partly disagreed. Morris responded in 'Individualism in twelfth-century religion: some further reflections', *Jour. Eccles. Hist.*, xxxi (1980), 195–206.

[64] Gurevich, *Origins of European Individualism*, p. 144.

institutional contexts are the grit which produces the pearl or simply a stone inside the shoe. Much of the time interpretative problems arise precisely because of this idea of 'free' individuation, excessively idealized apart from a specific social context.[65] Indeed, this, ultimately, is the problem with Gurevich's wider history of the origins of European individualism (whence his account of Abelard). Gurevich was torn between historically relativistic and specific ways of expressing individualism (for him, e.g., the Icelandic Sagas) and a teleological, developmental model through which individuals are increasingly, absolutely, expressing themselves (where Abelard disappoints). By this yardstick, the middle ages are ultimately found wanting: 'The system of values substantiated by medieval Christianity did not encourage men and women to proclaim and assert their individualities'. Gurevich's assumption of how free such an assertion can ever be appears as remarkably unproblematized as his argument that medieval Christianity provided so necessary and restrictive an armature.[66] In so far as Gurevich's middle ages had individual high points, Augustine figures as the overwhelming peak, with Petrarch at the other end.[67] Yet if even (!) *Abelard* somehow failed fully to discover his personality; if, between Augustine (d. 430) and Petrarch (d. 1376!!) the landscape of European individualism appears uninhabited, perhaps we are looking at a *question mal posée*? As many historians have pointed out, this way of thinking about discovering personality and a particular way of being individual imposes a highly static expectation of what ways of being individual 'count'.

The mirage of the complete individual

One can critique the older argument which elevated the individual in other ways. Important and still influential presumptions were set out in Jacob Burckhardt's hymn to the renaissance individual in *The Civilization of the Renaissance in Italy* (1860). Burckhardt's deeply sociological account offered an explanation of why Italian city-states allegedly produced the individual. The argument can be compressed as follows: particularly in despotic city-states but also in republics, the cult of the individual extended well beyond leaders who used it as a means of gripping power more tightly. Fostered by competition for favour and patronage, the renaissance state accordingly provided both space and stimulus for individual self-cultivation. This

[65] See Bynum, 'Did the twelfth century discover the individual?'.

[66] The point about reductive and essentializing characterizations of what Christianity inherently represses or enables is also made by J.-C. Schmitt, 'La "découverte de l'individu": une fiction historiographique', in J.-C. Schmitt, *Le corps, les rites, les rêves, le temps. Essais d'anthropologie médiévale* (Paris, 2001), pp. 241–62, at p. 246.

[67] Gurevich, *Origins of European Individualism*, p. 150.

individuation was not necessarily political since its articulation spread into private spheres, but in republics the effect was the same since competition for power and its subsequent exercise also provided a platform for individualism and self-differentiation.[68] By contrast, in the middle ages both inward and outward aspects of self-consciousness were 'dreaming or half-awake' beneath a veil:

> woven of faith, illusion and childish prepossession, through which the world and history were seen clad in strange hues. Man was conscious of himself only as a member of a race, people, party, family or corporation – only through some general category. But at the close of the thirteenth century Italy began to swarm with individuality; the ban laid upon human personality was dissolved; and a thousand figures meet us each in its own special shape and dress.[69]

In this negative stress on restrictive categories and groupings which inhibit the full articulation of individuality one sees the interpretation which had left its clear trace elements in Gurevich's account and many others. One way of identifying what goes wrong here is to suggest that the historiographical ideal of what the individual ought to look like has not progressed very far beyond the model of nineteenth-century realist fiction, capable of dramatizing the relationship between inner and outer worlds.

If, by contrast, Virginia Woolf's *The Waves* is a modernist literary account of consciousness, perhaps it is then interesting to ask what a modernist historiographical equivalent might look like. In many ways the dominance of traditional biography as the mode of studying the individual probably contributes to the conservatism analysed here. A modernist stress on permeability and flux is, of course, very much more in sympathy with modern brain science but also with more recent approaches to understanding specific forms of identity, such as gender.[70] Piron's reading of Opicino de Canistris, stressing his multiple, interpenetrating identities, might then be seen as a much more responsive development of such approaches (and contrasting with Gurevich, who also wrote on Opicino).[71]

[68] This is to compress Burckhardt, *Civilization of the Renaissance in Italy*, pp. 98–119. See also Schmitt, '"Découverte de l'individu"', pp. 242–4.

[69] Burckhardt, *Civilization of the Renaissance in Italy*, p. 98.

[70] Contrast the reading of the 'Montaillou' deposition material of J. Fournier (e.g., on Arnaud de Verniolles) in J. H. Arnold, *Inquisition and Power: Catharism and the Confessing Subject in Medieval Languedoc* (Philadelphia, Pa., 2001), ch. 5; and E. Le Roy Ladurie, *Montaillou. Village occitan, de 1294 à 1324* (Paris, 1975).

[71] Piron, *Dialectique du monstre*.

Beyond false oppositions

A second critique of the 'old' elevation of individuals was made by Caroline Walker Bynum – discussing twelfth-century religious and spiritual groups – and is worth revisiting. (Southern's individualistic scholastic humanism, we should note, is one of the interpretations she critiqued for their privileging of internal mental space over external group.) Bynum's argument had several key turns.

First, it is worth stressing Bynum's focus on *religious* groups as a basis for individuals' sense of selfhood. In modern, secularizing accounts religion often figures as a feature which must be sublimated before a more or less explicitly 'full' individualism can be achieved.[72] This can be seen in the tendency (encouraged by Burckhardt) to align 'secular' with 'renaissance' in analyses of intellectual development.[73] Yet, as Étienne Anheim has pointed out in relation to the impeccable renaissance and anti-scholastic figure of Petrarch, he could only articulate his individuality 'on condition of having the humility to accept the Other (God, death) in himself'. Petrarch's version of self-expression is not a Cartesian *cogito ergo sum* but *credo ergo sum*. As Anheim suggested, one could write an equally true, parallel history of self-knowledge and the philosophy of conscience to the conventional, secularizing one which took full account of the role of religion.[74]

Second, a 'Burckhardt-style' opposition between group and individual is unhelpful. Medieval 'individualism' did not go hand-in-hand with declining group identity. On the contrary, the proliferation of reflections about the former was sharply aligned with the proliferation in number and form of the latter: '[I]t was characterized by the one *because* it was characterized by the other'.[75] The individual understands him-her-self as such through a group's

[72] L. Dumont, *Essais sur l'individualisme. Une perspective anthropologique sur l'ideologie moderne* (Paris, 1983), stresses the modern form and its medieval origins. See also D. Iogna-Prat, 'Introduction générale: la question de l'individu à l'épreuve du Moyen Âge', in *L'individu au Moyen Âge. Individuation et individualisation avant la modernité*, ed. B.-M. Bedos-Rezak and D. Iogna-Prat (Paris, 2005), pp. 7–32.

[73] E.g., R. G. Witt, *The Two Latin Cultures and the Foundation of Renaissance Humanism in Medieval Italy* (Cambridge, 2012).

[74] É. Anheim, 'Une lecture de Pétrarque. Individu, écriture, et dévotion', in Bedos-Rezak and Iogna-Prat, *L'individu au Moyen Âge*, pp. 187–209, at pp. 206–7.

[75] Bynum, 'Did the twelfth century discover the individual?', p. 3. See also Schmitt, '"Découverte de l'individu"', p. 255. Bynum was partly responding to Morris, *Discovery of the Individual*. Morris's response in 'Individualism in twelfth-century religion' (esp. pp. 199–205) generally accepted the importance of thinking about groups. Cf. Rexroth, *Fröhliche Scholastik*, for stress on group relations and their instrumental affinities in transforming early scholasticism.

projection and validation of this.[76] Further, the articulation of individualism was very frequently connected directly to fulfilment of a model and/or fulfilment of a type ('fulfilment', not 'conformity', since the question of how to fulfil the type was to be contested, as with the Franciscans on whom more below). A central insight of Bynum was that these models and types provided the means to articulate individuality with increasing granularity. Corporate and individual identity do not need to be opposed in this way. Institutionalization in different ways was how the groups gave shape to individuals.[77] The medieval use and importance of models and types (those 'enemies' of individual character!) can, in fact, provide an answer to what a modernist historiographical analogue of Woolf's *The Waves* might look like. It might, that is, look something like Jacques Le Goff's *Saint Louis* (1996), a book which deconstructed the notion of the individual apart from the typological models (king, warrior, etc.) in relation to which he validated himself. This is a book, after all, which (in)famously asked: 'Saint Louis – did he really exist?' How, that is, can he be said to exist for us as a historical individual apart from the grids and characters through which he was expressed in the medieval sources?

Exemplarity was central to Louis (as with the advice he gave to his children). Exemplarity-through-typology is also central to two of the greatest individualistic works of medieval literature: Dante's *Commedia* (the categorization of damned to redeemed; the sorting by moral qualities; the mirroring of this by fitting *contrapasso* punishment); and Chaucer's *Canterbury Tales* (the exploration and testing of character/vocational types; the exploration of their *personae* and their fallibilities). In terms of lived life, however, perhaps no more powerful or problematic model of exemplarity is available than Francis of Assisi. The whole *purpose* of Francis's order was to exemplify the apostolic life and *imitatio Christi*, an exemplification which Francis's stigmatization took to extremes. Francis was a man whose concern with being a model, being an example, being a pattern, is stressed again and again in texts close to his earliest entourage, such as the *Writings of Brother Leo*. It is present in Francis's *Testament*, the unexploded bomb he left behind which would go on to blow up in the faces of a series of friars and popes in the later thirteenth and fourteenth centuries. The *Testament*, the rule-that-was-not-a-Rule, would blow up so repeatedly precisely because it provided the nexus for conflict between Francis's own exemplary manifestation and definition of what being a Franciscan meant in practice on the one hand

76 Iogna-Prat, 'La question de l'individu à l'épreuve du Moyen Âge'.

77 For an interesting demonstration, see G. Rosser, *The Art of Solidarity: Guilds in England 1250–1550* (Oxford, 2015).

and what the Rule's institutionalized version seemed to say on the other. The chapters by Sylvain Piron and Gert Melville look at the problem of religious orders (specifically mendicant ones) from these quite distinct angles. The Franciscans' problem with their own institutionalization can, then, be reconnected to the problem which Bynum raised in her article but which, like Southern's, remains unanswered:

> No period was ever busier creating structures for its own piety than the twelfth century. My analysis therefore suggests that in order to understand the relationship between twelfth-century religion and the fifteenth-century 'Renaissance' we need to ask more clearly than we have so far not only how twelfth-century attitudes lead into the self-awareness often associated with later periods but also how and why the twelfth-century equilibrium between self and community, interior and exterior, falters in the later Middle Ages.[78]

There are presumptions here one might want to question. Is the twelfth-century's equilibrium quite as clear as assumed here? Are later disequilibria quite as apparent as assumed? However, even if one wished to qualify the axioms, the fundamental grounds of Bynum's question still demand answers. It is hoped that our focus on precisely this period – from the later twelfth century (Corran, Melville, Sabapathy) into the thirteenth (Corran, Sabapathy, Biller, Dufal, Fitzpatrick, Piron), fourteenth (Dufal, Kempshall, Linde) and fifteenth centuries (Iribarren, Marenbon) – will help to do so. Indeed, it is precisely this period's proliferation of thought and practice regarding individuals and institutions which provides the rationale for our chronological focus. The chapters in this volume are intended to take us beyond unnecessary oppositions in general as well as taking forward a range of more detailed questions and problems.

'Schools' and beyond

Richard Southern was keenly aware of the role of intellectual 'schools' in his own life. In his sensitive memoir of his friend Beryl Smalley Southern wrote that 'she wanted to be remembered as a member of a group'.[79] The importance of filiation extended to Southern's own work. Michael Clanchy recalls talking to him near the end of his life about the origins of *Scholastic Humanism*. Of Southern's two great teachers, Vivian Galbraith and Maurice Powicke, Clanchy suggested to Southern that Powicke must have been

[78] Bynum, 'Did the twelfth century discover the individual?, p. 16.

[79] R. W. Southern, 'Beryl Smalley (1905–1984)', *Proc. Brit. Academy*, lxxii (1986), 455–71, including the photo of that group; repr. in Bartlett, *History and Historians*, pp. 235–9, at p. 238.

more influential on the project, given his own interest in scholasticism, as in his work on the theologian and archbishop Stephen Langton. Southern, however, was vehement in saying that it was all down not to Powicke but Galbraith, whom he praised elsewhere for unravelling 'the significance of documents of modest size' and throwing 'light on the thoughts, circumstances, and difficulties in which they had their origin'.[80] In fact, it is hard to see a better 'model' for Southern's work on 'scholastic humanism' in its connecting of intellectual and 'real world' concerns than Powicke's *Stephen Langton*, but Southern's disavowal is nonetheless notable. Positive or negative, intellectual filiation – and its (mis)remembrance – mattered.

Problems with schools

The genealogical master-pupil relationship provides one way of framing intellectual filiation for the period from the twelfth to the fifteenth centuries, but the question of what, if anything, constituted a medieval intellectual school is complex. Answers could range from a more or less loose network of shared interests, such as Peter the Chanter's 'biblical-moral' Parisian tendency, to a Dominican *studium* in which a particular set of intellectual positions are sometimes assumed as a corollary of that membership. Within twentieth-century historical, and historical-theological, continental scholarship on scholasticism there was also a distinctive investigative thread which effectively confined itself to an ideological plane, searching for thirteenth-century intellectual schools as defined by individuals' common subscription to discrete sets of doctrine. Much work was framed by researchers' own beliefs; and while we would not want to be reductive about that, equally it seems foolish to ignore it.

Southern took no part in this doctrinal approach to intellectual schools. We have already seen that he approached the medieval institutionalization of thought from a different angle. He also thought that 'as a general rule, medieval historians do well to avoid words ending in "-ism"',[81] the exception being his own 'scholastic humanism'. This continental tradition nevertheless left deep marks on historiography. The key questions here were taxonomic: what were the branches of intellectual affiliation and influence one should induce? How determinative were differences shaped by readings in Aristotle, Avicenna, Platonic texts, or Augustine, for that

[80] Personal information from Michael Clanchy and R. W. Southern, 'Vivian Hunter Galbraith (1889–1976)', *Proc. Brit. Academy*, lxiv (1978), 397–425; repr. in Bartlett, *History and Historians*, pp. 168–92, at p. 191. See also R. I. Moore, 'Southern and the sinews of power' <http://rimoore.net/wp-content/uploads/2016/12/R.W.-Southern.pdf> [accessed 11 July 2019].

[81] R. W. Southern, *Medieval Humanism and Other Studies* (Oxford, 1970), p. 29.

matter? In the decades following the classic studies by Karl Werner and Franz Ehrle in the late 1880s – which first divided Aquinas's 'Aristotelianism' from Franciscan 'Augustinianism' – there was much debate over where exactly the intellectual fault lines between these apparent, great, ideological tectonic plates should be drawn. The resulting historiographical confusion sprung from an attempt to codify individuals' thought according to a vast taxonomy of '-isms'. One automatically associates this tendency with Etienne Gilson, but equally indicative is the work of Maurice de Wulf, for instance, who argued for a complex five-fold taxonomy within thirteenth-century thought: Augustinianism vs. Thomism vs. Scotism vs. Averroism (all as mutually divergent sub-species of Aristotelianism) vs. Neoplatonism (as a separate current of thought altogether). Such complexity tells its own story, perhaps to the long-term detriment of medieval intellectual history.

Nevertheless, school labels ending in '-ism' have proved surprising durable as shorthand terms in historical writing on scholasticism, even though the general approach to medieval thought to which they used to be tethered has somewhat fallen out of fashion. If doctrinally focused schemata bear critiquing from several angles, then two problems are particularly important for us. First, these schemata assume that doctrinally defined intellectual schools established themselves only in the thirteenth century. Like Bynum's question about the balance between individual and group, this is a chronological issue and raises the question 'So what?' in either case. Fernand Van Steenberghen's solution, while implicitly critiquing De Wulf and Gilson for failing to give a convincing explanation for diachronic change, exemplified his targets' tendency to privilege a doctrinally focused approach. According to van Steenberghen, the twelfth century's characteristic philosophy was too pluralistic, literary and subjective to admit of systematic differentiation into schools.[82] It was only from *c.*1250, when a new Aristotle stripped of Arabic and Neoplatonic interpolations became available and could underpin a rigorous, constraining, objective and shared approach to philosophy, that schools attuned to doctrinal difference could emerge. To complicate matters further, historians of fourteenth- and fifteenth-century thought have kicked against the entire bulk of this writing on the thirteenth century to argue that doctrinally defined schools can be detected only from the late fourteenth century (the clash of philosophical and theological 'ways', 'nominalists' vs. 'realists', etc.), if at all.[83]

[82] F. Van Steenberghen, *La Philosophie au XIIIe siècle* (2nd edn, Louvain, 1991), pp. 169–76, 405–11.

[83] This paragraph and the last compress S. P. Marrone, *The Light of Thy Countenance: Science and Knowledge of God in the Thirteenth Century* (Studies in the History of Christian Thought, 2 vols, Leiden, 2001), i. 1–10.

The second problem lies at a deeper level and goes to the heart of some of the questions addressed by this volume. When talking of intellectual schools in the middle ages (as in any period) we run the risk of reification in thinking of schools as intellectual communities defined by total mutual agreement on doctrine. The artificial imposition of uniformity upon the original and creative thinking of individuals simply does not stand up against a close, hard look at the evidence. The diffuseness of the so-called contemporary 'Cambridge School' of intellectual history illustrates the difficulty of such labels today, let alone the 'Annales School'.[84] This lies at the heart of the critique of Southern's 'scholastic humanism' by Marenbon, for whom it offers too monochromatic a view of very colourful twelfth- and thirteenth-century scholastic worlds.[85] To agree with Marenbon's rejection of Southern's formulation would entail abandoning any general co-ordinating 'word ending in "-ism"' (saving scholasticism) for these groups and thinkers. That may be no bad thing, especially if one thinks the designation 'scholastic humanism' is indeed fallacious. It would produce a much more multi-polar set of configurations (again, good so far as they are true). It does, however, leave unresolved the problem of how to describe their undeniable structure, influence and effects accurately and adequately.

The suggestion is not that evacuating 'intellectual schools' of all explanatory power whatsoever provides a satisfactory solution to either problem. Sensitivity to one's own and others' membership of an intellectual group evidently could shape scholars' self-identification and political outlook. This is most readily explored by looking at recent analysis of Parisian intellectual groupings, on which much recent work has focused. For instance, William Courtenay's study of the seals of Parisian theology masters between 1190 and 1308 analyses master William of Bardenay's 1211 seal bearing the slogan 'ex impossibili quidlibet', a logical position identifying him as a member of the 'Parvipontani', that is to say, as a pupil of Adam of Balsham (or Petit Pont) or of one of his disciples.[86] This is

[84] For reflection by members of the 'Cambridge School', see *Rethinking the Foundations of Modern Political Thought*, ed. A. Brett, J. Tully and H. Hamilton-Bleakley (Cambridge, 2006); for Annales see, e.g., S. Clark, 'The Annales school', in *The Return of Grand Theory in the Human Sciences*, ed. Q. Skinner (Cambridge, 1990 [1985]), pp. 177–98.

[85] Marenbon, 'Humanism, scholasticism and the school of Chartres'. Rexroth's *Fröhliche Scholastik* is an interesting recent interpretation stressing a more colourful, flexible, 'joyful' scholasticism between *c.*1070 and 1250, in contrast to the straitjacketing 'conservative revolution' which made a golden cage for university scholasticism (Rexroth, *Fröhliche Scholastik*, pp. 20, 320–50).

[86] W. J. Courtenay, 'Magisterial authority, philosophical identity, and the growth of Marian devotion: the seals of Parisian masters, 1190–1308', *Speculum*, xci (2016), 63–114, at pp. 75–7.

both an intellectual position and a group affiliation: the inscription refers to the logical position that from an impossible premise any conclusion may follow. Mews and Zahora, meanwhile, have drawn attention to two early fourteenth-century anonymous treatises on the last things, of mendicant origin and probably produced in the French royal court, which evince a meticulous attempt to synthesize Bonaventure's and Aquinas's approaches to the intellect, will and grace, in order to overcome mendicant factionalism[87] – hardly worthwhile if 'school' divisions had no concrete importance in informing individuals' actions beyond the *studia*.

We think the solution to these problems lies instead in a re-framing of intellectual schools, grounded in questioning the ways in which the politics of group identification, and institutions more generally, did, or did not, constrain, enable and inflect the substantive thinking of individuals, rather than in attempting to track doctrine primarily and *per se*. Two relatively recent major studies deserve particular attention for suggesting just such an agenda for further work on medieval intellectual schools, namely Steven Marrone's *The Light of Thy Countenance: Science and the Knowledge of God in the Thirteenth Century* (2001); and Russell Friedman's *Intellectual Traditions at the Medieval University: the Use of Philosophical Psychology in Trinitarian Theology among Franciscans and Dominicans* (2013). Both Marrone and Friedman reconstruct intellectual schools as traditions of thought which were shaped first and foremost by the politics of group identification rather than rigid adherence to distinct sets of doctrinal details and which kept their integrity in spite, or perhaps because, of the creativity of the individuals within them.

Tracing thirteenth-century theologians' various metaphysical and epistemic interpretations of the notion of 'divine illumination' derived from Augustine, Marrone argued for an 'Augustinian school', which is primarily politically rather than doctrinally defined. According to Marrone's model, which he evidently intends to be applicable more generally, one's particular political affiliation or group identification would in practice restrict the range of stances one could take for or against a particular theoretical position just enough to result in an 'intellectual consanguinity' between thinkers over the decades, although within 'an especially elastic set of formal boundaries or constraints'. Such affiliations, Marrone argued, would have been perceptible to contemporaries, whether evoked and expressed 'in a tendency to call upon a common fund of models and metaphors for

[87] C. J. Mews and T. Zahora, 'Remembering the last things and regulating behaviour in the early fourteenth century: from the *De consideratione novissimorum* to the *Speculum morale*', *Speculum*, xc (2015), 960–94. See also B. Kent, *Virtues of the Will: the Transformation of Ethics in the Late Thirteenth Century* (Washington, D.C., 1995).

analysis' consciously or unconsciously by scholars themselves.[88] In this way, theologians almost a century apart and as divergent in the fine-grained detail of their thought as Robert Grosseteste and John Duns Scotus emerge equally as members of Marrone's 'Augustininan school'.

Where Marrone focused mostly but not exclusively on Franciscans, Friedman examined the oppositional politics of the Dominican and Franciscan orders (*c.*1250–*c.*1350). Friedman conceived of intellectual traditions in a way which is broadly compatible with Marrone, but goes much further in drawing out the implications of such an approach. The cut and thrust of scholastic debate at precise moments of intense opposition between the orders could shape the content of individuals' arguments in quite an exact way. Franciscan and Dominican mutual opposition thus worked as a motor, pushing philosophical and theological debate along for scholars both within and outwith the two orders themselves. The history of scholastic theology in this hundred-year period, it emerges, cannot be understood without taking into account ways in which the thinking of individuals at the cutting edge of debate was inflected by the politics of these rival intellectual traditions and the internal politics of these orders:

> By tradition I want to denote that a general approach to certain philosophical and theological problems was handed down from one scholarly generation to the next, and solutions to these problems were developed and discussed on the basis of a shared approach. These approaches were general enough to leave room for internal development and disagreement within each of the traditions, but they were also developed in conscious opposition to the other tradition ... they developed together inasmuch as their mutual criticism was a motive force in the way that debate evolved. Criticism by one tradition of the other was neither ignored or flatly denied; rather it frequently elicited a change of some kind in the original position with the purpose of countering the critique. In this sense we can say that the mutual criticism of the two traditions led to improvements in the original position, with each step laying the groundwork for a new round of criticism.[89]

Taking Marrone and Friedman together, then, membership of an intellectual school or tradition would consist not in the mere recapitulation of the thinking of one's intellectual antecedents, but in the *use* made of it, specifically its positioning to reaffirm one intellectual identity within one tradition precisely in opposition to another tradition. Fitzpatrick's chapter

[88] Marrone, *Light of Thy Countenance*, ii. 571–2.

[89] R. L. Friedman, *Intellectual Traditions at the Medieval University: the Use of Philosophical Psychology in Trinitarian Theology among the Franciscans and Dominicans, 1230–1350* (Leiden, 2013), pp. 21–2.

in the present volume is a case study of the effect of these oppositional dynamics in thirteenth-century theological discussions of the central philosophical problem of the composition of human nature. Hence, Dominicans in the 1280s came up with interpretations of the theory which diverged quite far in their detail from Aquinas's own, precisely to counter Franciscans' inaccurate caricature of his thought.

While Marrone and Friedman offer models for intellectual schools which are both doctrinally sensitive and politically astute, they both still propose a certain hardening of intellectual lines *c.*1250 at the universities of Paris and Oxford. Recent work by Constant Mews strikes at this assumption, questioning whether the acceptance of a full Aristotelian curriculum at the faculty of arts in 1255 in itself had any radical effect at all on patterns of intellectual affiliation. Mews's argument, in short, is this: the twin tendencies in historical writing on scholasticism – to treat Aquinas as the quintessence of scholastic thinking; and to place an implicit emphasis upon the basic curricular unity of Paris in the mid thirteenth century – stem ultimately from the papal encyclical of *Aeterni patris* (1879) and have been seriously distorting of both scholasticism's institutional and its intellectual history. Mews does concede, along lines suggested by Van Steenberghen, that the various 'Logico-Theological Schools' (*nominales*, *reales*, *Porretiani*, *Meludinenses* and *Montani*, as well as the *Parvipontani* mentioned above) appearing in Parisian records from *c.*1150 well into the thirteenth century were probably relatively unsystematically defined, or 'as slippery as "deconstructionists" and "post-modernists" today'.[90] Up to 1255 there was a low degree of uniformity in the study of arts and theology.[91] The point, however, is that Parisian intellectual pluralism lasted beyond Courson's decree of 1215, and even beyond 1255, precisely as a function of complex institutional politics.

The university of Paris was not a single, centralized institution and at no point did its scholars actually study one uniform, coherent curriculum. Rather, the university's intellectual life was characterized by 'the competition between different communities of learning', struggling 'to define a vision of synthesis', of their own, underpinned by their own curriculum and serving

[90] C. J. Mews, 'Communities of learning and the dream of synthesis: the schools and colleges of thirteenth-century Paris', in *Communities of Learning: Networks and the Shaping of Identity in Europe, 1150–1500*, ed. J. N. Crossley and C. J. Mews (Turnhout, 2011), pp. 109–35, at p. 112. See also Y. Iwakuma and S. Ebbesen, 'Logico-theological schools from the second half of the 12th century: a list of sources', *Vivarium*, xxx (1992), 173–210.

[91] S. E. Young, *Scholarly Community at the Early University of Paris: Theologians, Education and Society 1215–1248* (Cambridge, 2014) makes this point and affirms the significance of master–pupil intellectual filiation in the theology faculty.

as a symbol of their group's identity.[92] Here, Mews is indebted to Boureau's use of Brian Stock's notion of a 'textual community' as defined by a group's interpretation of a particular text.[93] Yet, crucially, Paris's rival 'communities of learning' were shaped just as much by parameters of place and loyalties associated with precise political networks as they were by their selection of their own specific range of texts for study.

After 1255 it is not the competition between the mendicants as such but rather the competition between the secular college of the Sorbonne (1257) and the College of the Treasurer (1266) which best exemplifies the complex political dynamics in which Mews is interested. The former was established for students of theology of any nation and no religious order, under the authority of the bishop of Paris and with close connections to the royal court.[94] The latter was regional, established for poor students from Rouen for the study of both arts and theology, enabling Norman students to study theology free of the bishop's supervision. However, for Mews the 'Averroist Crisis' of 1272 to 1275 in the faculty of arts is best explained by the politics surrounding Siger of Brabant's bid for the rectorship of the faculty rather than by his supposed 'heterodox Aristotelianism' and commitment to Averroes' belief in humans sharing a single external intellect.[95]

Marrone, Friedman and Mews all emphasize the primacy of 'political' factors in delineating communities of learning and intellectual frameworks of endorsement and critique in the late thirteenth century. Even so, there would still appear to have been a particular quality of thought among the mendicants which *demanded* self-definition and counter-definition with respect to doctrinal minutiae, such as was not produced by other clusters of interests within faculties. If, therefore, it is the opposition of the Franciscan and Dominican religious orders which provides the crucial stimulus to this

[92] Mews, 'Communities of learning', p. 135. Cf. Alasdair MacIntyre on modern intellectual disagreements and affiliations: 'It is always important not to confuse the consequences of intellectual positions with those of institutional arrangements. What appears to be an *impasse* resulting from theoretical commitments of those involved in debate may sometimes, in part at least, be one brought about by institutional arrangements and social habits' (A. MacIntyre, *Three Rival Versions of Moral Enquiry: Encyclopaedia, Genealogy, and Tradition* (London, 1990), p. 6).

[93] B. Stock, *The Implications of Literacy: Written Language and Models of Interpretation in the Eleventh and Twelfth Centuries* (Princeton, N.J., 1983); A. Boureau, *L'Empire du livre. Pour une histoire du savoir scolastique (1200–1380)* (La Raison scolastique, ii, Paris, 2007).

[94] On the Sorbonne's group identity see J. Sabapathy 'Regulating community and society at the Sorbonne in the late thirteenth century', in *Legalism: Justice and Community*, ed. F. Pirie and J. Scheele (Oxford, 2014), pp. 151–76; and D. Gabriel, *La 'Maison des pauvres maîtres' de Robert de Sorbon. Les débuts de la Sorbonne (1254–1274)* (Paris, 2014).

[95] Mews, 'Communities of learning', *passim*.

quality of thought, then what is it about religious orders that produces this result? The institutional similarities between the Franciscan and Dominicans, and their resulting (and ever increasing) direct competition for benefactions, chairs and recruits, might go some way towards explaining the dynamics involved, along with contingent facts about the way in which regent masterships develop, so that the mendicants appear to gain a de facto monopoly *c.*1250. Whichever way one looks at it, the formation of theological traditions and intellectual schools in Paris after *c.*1250 appears as a function of organizational development.

Other ways of grouping: constellations and networks

Schools in themselves are an important but limited analytical prism through which to tell the whole story of patterns of learning and thought in the period which our essays address. Shaped by contextual factors other than curricula and extending beyond the theology faculties of the major universities, there were complex regional and temporal patterns of intellectual debate, influence, approbation and disapprobation. Thus, Blaise Dufal's chapter in this volume argues that the self-conscious use of Augustine as an authority, in particular in commentaries on *De civitate Dei*, could extend beyond the mere exigencies of positioning oneself in live academic debate and become a means of self-identification in relation to a range of institutions from religious order to kingdom.

This wider insight that ideas can never be properly understood apart from the places, spaces and located networks in which they emerge has been well-taken.[96] The idea of *Konstellationsforschung* (constellation research) in German historiography, meanwhile, has developed a more granular set of axes for thinking about the networks linking individuals both in terms of external organizational links, affiliations, social groups, shared publishers, patrons and the like. The metaphor of constellation does not imply fixity but stresses fluidity and development over time.[97] From other quite different disciplinary perspectives have come deep mappings of the sociologies of particular intellectual cadres – such as Pierre Bourdieu's account of the fields structuring Parisian *homo academicus* at the time of the student rebellions in 1968.[98] Another sociologist, Randall Collins, has sought to map literally

[96] E.g., *Lieux de savoir*, ed. C. Jacob (2 vols, Paris, 2007–11), i: *Espaces et communautés* (Paris, 2007); ii: *Les mains de l'intellect* (Paris, 2011). For a medieval application with this model partly in mind, see C. J. Mews, 'Communautés de savoirs. Écoles et collèges à Paris au xiiie siècle', *Revue de synthèse*, cxxix, 6th ser., iv (2008), 485–507.

[97] M. Mulsow, 'Qu'est-ce qu'une constellation philosophique? Propositions pour une analyse des réseaux intellectuels', *Annales*, lxiv (2009), 81–109, at pp. 84–8.

[98] P. Bourdieu, *Homo Academicus*, trans. P. Collier (Cambridge, 1988). In so far as it is

the sociology of *all* philosophy, stressing the 'interaction rituals' between individuals whose friction produces new thought.[99] However, it is hard for historians to see how, for example, this produces new insights into Franciscan and Dominican rivalries between 1200 and 1335.[100] There are obvious limits to how far one can reconstruct past networks anyway.[101] Nevertheless, it is perfectly possible to point towards rich studies of medieval intellectual networks and patterns in the development of ideas which do not burnish especial methodological credentials.[102] This is not to imply that there are no useful heuristics through which our understanding of intellectual groupings in our period can be deepened. We analyse below some which seem especially helpful (some have influenced contributors here). These comprise: Alasdair MacIntyre's 'traditions'; Weberian 'conviction rationalities' and d'Avray's extension of them; and Niklas Luhmann's 'systems thinking'.

Traditions

Collins's *Sociology of Philosophy* includes, but is not especially galvanized by, consideration of medieval thought. By contrast, the philosopher Alasdair MacIntyre has for decades placed medieval philosophy – specifically Aquinas's – at the heart of his project to re-describe the terms on which viable (modern) ethical thought might be constructed. Our interest here, however, is not so much in the accuracy of MacIntyre's account of that medieval thought as in the model he develops to account for its integrity – the idea of 'tradition'.[103] For MacIntyre a:

sociological, Bourdieu's analysis is less personal and more structural than the historical reconstitution of particular intellectual constellations Mulsow has in mind.

[99] R. Collins, *The Sociology of Philosophies: a Global Theory of Intellectual Change* (Cambridge, Mass., 1998), sketches the approach and key terms at pp. 1–53, esp. at pp. 20–4, 28–9, 35–6.

[100] For Collins's map of Franciscan/Dominican rivalries, see *Sociology of Philosophies*, p. 470. Cf. Mulsow's comments on Collins's *Sociology of Philosophies* in Mulsow, 'Qu'est-ce qu'une constellation philosophique?', pp. 90–3.

[101] Mulsow, 'Qu'est-ce qu'une constellation philosophique?', pp. 98–9.

[102] E.g., J. Marenbon, *From the Circle of Alcuin to the School of Auxerre* (Cambridge, 1981); D. E. Luscombe, *The School of Peter Abelard* (Cambridge Studies in Medieval Life and Thought, n.s., xiv, Cambridge, 1969); M. S. Kempshall, *The Common Good in Late Medieval Political Thought* (Oxford, 1999), E. Coccia and S. Piron, 'Poésie, sciences et politique. Une génération d'intellectuels italiens (1290–1330)', *Revue de synthèse*, cxxix, 6th ser., iv (2008), 549–86.

[103] For a critique, see J. Coleman, 'MacIntyre and Aquinas', in *After MacIntyre: Critical Perspectives on the Work of Alasdair MacIntyre*, ed. J. Horton and S. Mendus (Cambridge, 1994), pp. 65–90.

> living tradition then is an historically extended, socially embodied argument, and an argument precisely in part about the goods which constitute that tradition. Within a tradition the pursuit of goods extends through generations, sometimes through many generations ... Once again the narrative phenomenon of embedding is crucial: the history of a practice in our time is generally and characteristically embedded in and made intelligible in terms of the larger and longer history of the tradition through which the practice in its present form was conveyed to us; the history of each of our own lives is generally and characteristically embedded in and made intelligible in terms of the larger and longer histories of a number of traditions.[104]

Traditions here are construed very much as practices or 'crafts' within a magisterial context: that is, an apprentice is instructed in the terms of a craft by a master. The rationality and excellence of the craft (furniture making, philosophy) is internal to the craft and also directed out to its worldly purpose (*telos*). This emphatically Aristotelian model is also emphatically based in a group (a 'moral community') and placed in time (the tradition develops itself under the impetus of successive generations):[105] 'The craft is justified by its history so far, which has made it what it is in that specific time, place, and set of historical circumstances, such rationality is inseparable from the tradition through which it was achieved'.[106] The rationality of the tradition, that is, is relativistic within the overall arc of the tradition but also an objective achievement at any single point in time. Matthew Kempshall's chapter in this volume explores this in relation to the very discipline of history itself, arguing that as historiographically sophisticated a thinker as the Dominican Nicholas Trevet produced surprisingly annalistic histories, not because of any inherent limitation in his analytical abilities but rather as a function of an epistemological tradition which drew sharp barriers around what he thought history was competent to explain.

MacIntyre counterpointed traditions against 'encyclopaedic' and 'genealogical' modes of enquiry. The latter two, he argued, give poor accounts of how knowledge is both social and develops over time. For the former, the 'external', social aspects of its intellectual content are in fact part and parcel of its intellectual standing.[107] By contrast, the encyclopaedist

[104] A. MacIntyre, *After Virtue: a Study in Moral Theory* (2nd edn, London, 1985), p. 222. J. Porter argued he does not define the term, but this seems a de facto definition (J. Porter, 'Tradition in the recent work of Alasdair MacIntyre', in *Alasdair MacIntyre*, ed. M. C. Murphy (Contemporary Philosophy in Focus, Cambridge, 2003), pp. 38–69, at p. 38).

[105] These ideas are developed in MacIntyre, *Three Rival Versions of Moral Enquiry*, pp. 59–66.

[106] MacIntyre, *Three Rival Versions of Moral Enquiry*, pp. 65, 116.

[107] MacIntyre, *Three Rival Versions of Moral Enquiry*, p. 117.

wishes to elevate thinking for him-her-self and to assert that knowledge rests on generally accepted (commensurable) grounds in a way which no longer seems credible. The genealogist, meanwhile, wishes to unearth the disreputable descent of all intellectual knowledge since knowledge is always compromised by the ulterior wilfulness it masks (as Nietzsche argued in *The Genealogy of Morals*).[108] Yet how can the genealogist sustain any sequence of unmaskings over time which are not equally open to having their own disreputable genealogies unearthed (and hence their case undermined)? If they avoid this implosion, how can they do so without implying an unacknowledged tradition of truthfulness to give sense and continuity to their claims as a whole, thus undermining the premises of their entire genealogical model?[109] Traditions, then, are MacIntyre's alternative model, offering an approach with which historians can think in many ways, especially medieval historians. His central medieval exemplification is Aquinas, whom he takes to exemplify the thirteenth-century reconciliation of two apparently immiscible and contradictory traditions, an indigenous Augustinian one and a recently interpolated Aristotelian one.[110]

Whether one wishes to amend or reconstruct MacIntyre's account of this conflict, his three characteristic models of enquiry raise interesting questions. First, Southern, we have seen, stressed the unitary ambitions of what he called scholastic humanism, the desire for a complete 'system' of knowledge. That sounds more similar to MacIntyre's encyclopaedic enquiry than his tradition-based one, yet for MacIntyre it is *scholastic* practices which pre-eminently exemplify the open-ended, moral-community learning of tradition. MacIntyre is insistent that Aquinas's method of intellectual progression was inherently provisional: '[W]hen Aquinas has reached his conclusion, the method always leaves open the possibility of a return to that question with some new argument'.[111]

One might wonder whether Southern (b. 1912) was back-projecting a nineteenth-century encyclopaedic model onto his scholastic humanists. MacIntyre's quintessential exemplification of encyclopaedic knowledge is, after all, the ninth edition of the *Encyclopaedia Britannica* (1873–88).

[108] F. Nietzsche, *'On the Genealogy of Morality' and Other Writings*, ed. K. Ansell-Pearson, trans. C. Diethe (Cambridge, 1994).

[109] For these arguments, see MacIntyre, *Three Rival Versions of Moral Enquiry*, pp. 32–57. B. Williams, *Truth and Truthfulness: an Essay in Genealogy* (Princeton, N.J., 2002) is a very sophisticated genealogist's case.

[110] MacIntyre's successive accounts of this conflict and the reconciliation of it are found in *After Virtue*, pp. 165–80; A. MacIntyre, *Whose Justice? Which Rationality?* (London, 1988), pp. 164–208, but also chs. VII–IX; and *Three Rival Versions of Moral Enquiry*, pp. 82–126.

[111] MacIntyre, *Three Rival Versions of Moral Enquiry*, pp. 124–5.

However, second, one might wonder whether MacIntyre's account of encyclopaedism is sufficient in the first place. There was, after all, a massive *medieval* tradition of encyclopaedism, well before either this Victorian one or, indeed, Diderot and D'Alembert's. It is hard not to see how Vincent of Beauvais's (d. *c.*1264) still-unedited encyclopaedia, the *Speculum maius*, could *not* be considered an encyclopaedia which was *also* part of a tradition in MacIntyre's terms.[112] Genealogy, third, may unmask intellectual affiliations less straightforwardly as well. In scholastic thought more than anywhere else one might expect to unearth unedifying intellectual genealogies in which institutional affiliation pre-determines intellectual/credal positions. Yet, *pace* Mews, as several chapters here show (notably Linde's and Fitzpatrick's) the positions taken might be quite different from what one would expect given institutional affiliations. That is to say: MacIntyre's three versions of moral enquiry are particularly instructive for specialists on scholasticism to think about even – perhaps especially – when they appear *not* to work or call their own categories of analysis into question. Whether that has any bearing back on MacIntyre's own ethical thought may be a question more for philosophers than historians.

Conviction rationalities and thought styles

MacIntyre's account is philosophical and historical, but not especially sociological. In fact, it describes a semi-permeable style of thinking similar to the account of 'conviction rationalities' which David d'Avray has developed from Max Weber.[113] Like Macintyre's traditions, conviction (or value) rationalities are socially embedded modes of reasoning with internal standards of rational justification, but, unlike Macintyre's traditions, conviction rationalities encompass any world-view or system of conviction. As an 'ideal type' of rationality, systems of conviction have two principal

[112] See *Vincent de Beauvais et le Grand Miroir du monde*, ed. M. Paulmier-Foucart and M.-C. Duchenne (Turnhout, 2004); and *Atelier Vincent de Beauvais* <https://ateliervdb.hypotheses.org> [accessed 11 July 2019]. See, more widely, *Die Enzyklopädie im Wandel vom Hochmittelalter bis zur frühen Neuzeit. Akten des Kolloquiums des Projekts D im Sonderforschungsbereich 231 (29.11.–1.12.1996)*, ed. C. Meier-Staubach (Munich, 2002); B. Ribémont, *Littérature et encyclopédies du Moyen Âge* (Orléans, 2002); B. Ribémont, *La 'Renaissance' du XIIe siècle et l'encyclopédisme* (Paris, 2002); and the *SourcEncyMe* project <http://sourcencyme.irht.cnrs.fr> [acccessed 11 July 2019].

[113] D. L. d'Avray, *Rationalities in History: a Weberian Essay in Comparison* (Cambridge, 2010); and *Medieval Religious Rationalities: a Weberian Analysis* (Cambridge, 2010). The first volume develops the analytical model which the second volume applies. D'Avray noted the similarity of MacIntyre's traditions with his conviction rationalities in *Rationalities in History*, p. 100.

features.[114] First, there is interconnectedness. The individual values or convictions which comprise the system form a logically interlocking web, a unique *Gestalt*. Individual components can take the form of 'is'-, as well as 'ought'-convictions when the former are phenomenologically very similar to the latter (to use one of d'Avray's own examples, the conviction 'there is a God' is phenomenologically similar to the belief 'polygamy is wrong'). Each individual conviction is thus rendered rational in the context of the system; and the interconnectedness of values strengthens the structure as a whole. Different value systems may overlap, but cannot be simultaneously correct. What it is crucial to note is that they can all be rational by their own internal standards.

Second, there is concreteness. Social practices, emotional experience and strong mental images bear out, reinforce and justify values and beliefs, functioning as 'concrete' arguments which enter into and cement the overall structure of the system. Medieval Christianity provides an excellent example of how value rationalities work. As d'Avray explains, one could illustrate *ad infinitum* the thickly and precisely interconnected and interdependent nature of various doctrinal convictions (the Trinity, Christ's suffering humanity, the resurrection) and the institutions, rituals and other practices and experiences in which they were embodied and which gave them force (the liturgy; the mass; prayer; interaction with images of Christ's passion; confession; penance; and the apostolic penitentiary; and so on).[115]

Conviction rationalities have considerable explanatory as well as illustrative power. When systems of values compete, individuals rarely abandon their convictions when confronted with logical counter-arguments they cannot easily answer. The model just outlined explains why it may be rational for individuals to hold onto their values in this way, even when they basically understand one another's positions and share a great deal of overlap in their general world-view.[116]

The example of competing Franciscan and Dominican intellectual traditions illustrates this point. We have met the work of Russell Friedman, which explains the resilience of these traditions as a matter of the politics of group identification. This leaves fairly open the question of any deeper intellectual conviction. It is true that, even following the mendicant legislation of the 1280s which sought to direct their scholars' output either for or against Aquinas, it was possible for Franciscans and Dominicans

[114] Following d'Avray, *Medieval Religious Rationalities*, pp. 21–3.

[115] d' Avray, *Medieval Religious Rationalities*, ch. 2: 'Medieval values: structures'.

[116] A philosophical presentation is G. A. Cohen, 'Paradoxes of conviction', in G. A. Cohen, *If You're an Egalitarian, How Come You're so Rich?* (Cambridge, Mass., 2001), pp. 7–19, discussed by d'Avray in *Rationalities in History*, pp. 66, 73.

either to dissent from the 'party line' on any one issue or range of issues, or just to appear less than fully convinced of it.[117] Still, there is enough of a pattern discernible in the later middle ages of Franciscans and Dominicans consistently failing to convince one another on a whole variety of issues to suggest that competing systems of intellectual conviction were in play and that these systems, even if internally flexible, remained fundamentally resistant to attack by one another over time.[118]

The tenacity of convictions can be explained in part by their interconnectedness: one axiom cannot be easily extricated from the set; rather, several, perhaps all, stand or fall together.[119] This applies in the case of the mendicants. Scholastic theology was a purposefully holistic mode of thinking; and the basic theses about which Franciscans and Dominicans argued were embedded in thick webs of interlocking positions on fundamental metaphysical issues about which the two traditions also disagreed. Although positions within each tradition could be developed, it would have had hugely disruptive consequences for a scholar's entire metaphysical apparatus suddenly to change his mind with respect to any individual major thesis. There was little motivation, then, to be convinced by objections from the other tradition targeted against any one basic metaphysical position. Rather, the support provided for any disputed thesis by the supposed truth of several related theses would have reduced the perceived likelihood that the individual thesis under attack was false; while thoroughly debating all the relevant theses at once would have been impracticable: according to the internal standards of the tradition it was rational to be unconvinced by individual objections.

Furthermore, the intellectual convictions associated with their tradition would have derived psychological support from mendicant scholars' concrete, everyday experiences as members of their order: self-identification as Franciscan or Dominican; material dependence on the order; the interrelated sentiments of loyalty towards order, minister general and schoolmaster; and so on. In light of this it becomes less difficult to

[117] E.g., I. Iribarren, *Durandus of St. Pourçain: a Dominican Theologian in the Shadow of Aquinas* (Oxford, 2005). On the Franciscan Richard de Mediavilla, see S. Piron, 'Franciscan *quodlibeta* in southern *studia* and at Paris, 1280–1300', in *Theological Quodlibeta in the Middle Ages: the Thirteenth Century*, ed. C. Schabel (Leiden, 2006), pp. 403–38, at pp. 417–18.

[118] Alongside Friedman, *Intellectual Traditions*, see B. Gaspar, 'The immaculate conception, 1100–1700: para-magisterial powers and their politics' (unpublished University College London PhD thesis, 2012) on Franciscan and Dominican disputes over the immaculate conception; and A. Fitzpatrick on the issue of the unicity versus plurality of forms in Franciscan and Dominican thought (A. Fitzpatrick, 'Mendicant order politics and the status of Christ's shed blood', *Hist. Research*, lxxxv (2012), 210–27).

[119] See d'Avray, *Rationalities in History*, pp. 70–7.

understand why Franciscans and Dominicans appeared prone to argue so fiercely about the orthodoxy of abstract metaphysical details as well as the more concrete issue of the correct definition of apostolic poverty.

Systems thinking

A final powerful, universally applicable set of tools for thinking about the dynamics involved in the patterning of social action is Niklas Luhmann's systems theory. Of particular relevance here is Luhmann's theory of social systems, which offers a way of understanding how individuals can change wider institutions. A basic introduction to the central ideas is as follows.[120] The function of all social systems, which are all systems of communication (including action as a form of communication), is to reduce complexity, fulfilling humans' need to orientate themselves in the world in a suitably planned and structured way. A taxonomy of social systems takes in not just social organizations but time-limited interactions and conversations (teacher-pupil; doctor-patient; students in a classroom; partners in a household) and whole societies (comprehensive social systems which contain functionally differentiated sub-systems).[121] Any social system defines itself with reference to what is outside it, namely its environment, which, from the perspective of the system, is unstructured and exceedingly complex. The system stabilizes expectations regarding the range of communications or actions which can take place within it through channelling communication between social actors. This channelling maintains the boundaries between communication system and uncontrolled environment. Pietro Pomponazzi, working within the arts faculties of Paris and Bologna universities, is accordingly enabled to present what appears to be a highly sceptical Aristotelian account of the mortality of the soul. As John Marenbon shows in his chapter in this volume, however, one risks seriously misunderstanding Pomponazzi's wider position by extracting from within one social system of communication arguments which are not intended to be viable within other social systems of communication. Marenbon does not frame his account in Luhmann's terms, but the usefulness of the framework is demonstrated precisely by the fact that Pomponazzi's position can be explicated by it.

To view social systems as static and/or closed would be to miss the fundamental point about the relationship between system and environment.

[120] Useful studies are: N. Luhmann, *Social Systems*, trans. J. Bednarz Jr., with D. Baecker (Stanford, Calif., 1995); N. Luhmann, 'Differentiation of Society', *Canadian Jour. Sociology*, ii (1977), 29–53; R. Muench, *Sociological Theory* (3 vols, Chicago, Ill., 1994), iii: *Development since the 1960s*, pp. 273–95.

[121] Luhmann, *Social Systems*, p. 2 for a diagram of the taxonomy of systems.

The continuing, stabilizing operations of a system involve constant reference to the system itself and to that extent entail continual reference to what lies outside it. The environments relative to systems are continually changing; and changes in the external environment of a system (which includes other sub-systems to which it will be necessary to react, for instance) will introduce changes into that system. This is where individual agents come in. Insofar as they subsist *between* individual agents, systems have a life of their own, but changes and adaptations in social systems are driven by the individuals who connect with and make use of them, who continually recreate the boundary between system and environment by actively selecting and/or rejecting new operations as pertaining to the system. John Sabapathy's interpretation of the master of theology Robert of Courson (d. 1219) can be seen in this light. His focus is the internal logic of Courson's attitude to the pastoral problems which he addressed in his *Summa*. This was systematic – but not really in Southern's sense of a complete and formalistically consistent set of answers. Rather, what unites Courson's solutions seems to be a pragmatic, relativistic system which asked what was spiritually damaging for particular communities in specific contexts. Courson's systematic logic seems keyed to a relative sense of what would damage community X specifically. It can itself be seen as the articulation of a particular idea of a 'social system' in the period. The particular tradition stemmed from the 'school' of Peter the Chanter itself and seemed rather short-lived – perhaps as a consequence of the difficulty of extending such an approach on any scale. As such, it exemplifies the need to grasp the sometimes quite rapid ways in which particular social systems, and ways of institutionalizing them, wax and wane. Cornelia Linde's chapter offers an analogous example over one hundred years later when she argues that the Dominican Robert Holcot's (d. *c.*1349) writings regarding the 1215 Fourth Lateran Council's rule on confession were strongly influenced not only by the glosses of Aquinas and Albertus Magnus on this rule, but also by the need to respond to contemporary Parisian intellectual debates and practical social concerns. The social system continued to draw on its 'rule base' while remaining responsive to contemporary context.

Groups may generate their social systems in quite distinct ways using quite distinct tools, however. In his work on the Dominicans (and in his chapter here) Gert Melville has explored how monastic rules interact with other means of creating social groups. In an early essay Melville suggested three striking hypotheses in relation to institutions-as-organizations which still reward reflection. They will, first, seek to perfect themselves through an increasingly precise and detailed set of procedural and proscriptive rules, a process which may very well be self-destructive through hypertrophy or impossible demand setting. Second, the principle of guaranteeing institutional stability provides grounds against change, thus external changes can threaten the organization's arrangement, either its functions or its meaning. As a result, it may develop a new role and become a new organization. Internal change within an organization may, third, also seek to re-stabilize it by either seeking to return to an earlier state or an adjustment to present needs.[122] All this will need to be legitimized in relation to the organization's own history and values. For religious orders, how this plays out will depend on whether the originating norms came from a founding text or the words of a charismatic leader.[123] Even in the latter case, however, there will need to be some written routinization of that charisma (in Weberian terms) for the institution to endure beyond the first generation. The balance between rules and a charismatic legacy can produce very different outcomes for religious orders. 'Rules' may be usefully differentiated between a rule itself (the articulation of a binding message for right-living), customs (self-ratifying descriptions of established practice glossing the rule) and statutes (in principal consensual documents generated by a community for engineering its self-regulation to a greater degree).[124] The Dominicans are a key example for Melville of religious order as institutional system – both in terms of the practices and organization. The case exemplifies his approach. What is striking about the Dominicans, he argues, is their 'total fixation' on their preaching purpose. The Paris-educated Dominican master general Humbert of Romans's commentary on the order's *Constitutiones* illustrates this. Other values were subordinated to securing its preaching purpose through dispensations or re-orientated to strengthen it. Hence fasting could be dispensed with if it was hindering preaching; and poverty was endorsed because a poor preacher was likely to get a better reception than a rich one. The relative relation of religious values, authoritative regulations and charismatic totem-founder played out in a very different way for the Franciscans, whose later thirteenth century was riddled with disputes precisely about their founding values, rules and the meaning of their founder. Whether, however, the Franciscans as an institution were any less successful in the long run for all that remains an interesting question. In his chapter Sylvain Piron offers a very different – almost antithetical – approach to that of the Dominican Humbert of Romans by analysing the Franciscan Peter John Olivi. For Olivi it is not the Franciscans' *Regula bullata* which is central

[122] Melville, 'Institutionen als geschichtswissenschaftliches Thema', pp. 18–20.

[123] G. Melville, *Die Welt der mittelalterlichen Klöster. Geschichte und Lebensformen* (Munich, 2012), pp. 294–6; trans. now by J. Mixson as *The World of Medieval Monasticism: its History and Forms of Life* (Collegeville, Penn., 2016), pp. 343–5.

[124] Melville, *Welt der mittelalterlichen Klöster*, pp. 290–4, summarizing his earlier work (= Melville, *World of Medieval Monasticism*, pp. 338–42).

to being a Franciscan but the individual Franciscan's vow – a vow constantly and perpetually renewed in action and which simply cannot be settled by a prescriptive stipulation. Melville's chapter in this volume offers a further way of reading how the founders of religious orders made use of themselves as symbols to construct a more enduring legal authority for their organizations. Both chapters show a plurality of ways through which institutions may express their social systems.

Institutions and institutionalization

These reflections on traditions, rationalities and systems-thinking have already led us into a consideration of institutions. To be sure, these 'institutions' do not look like the traditional objects of institutional history. That is the point. 'Institutional history' from its heyday up to the first half of the twentieth century generally concerned itself with organizations and their rules, often within a more or less Whiggish teleological framework (parliamentary developments were perhaps the British acme of this historiography). Today the landscape is refreshingly altered, both because historians have re-evaluated their hierarchy of historical 'objects' and because they have revised how to think about institutions, notably under the influence of philosophy, sociology and anthropology.

The historian Jacques Revel rightly argued that institutionalization can be treated as a spectrum. At one end lies the institution as the 'juridical-political reality' of traditional institutional history; at the other lie institutions at their most diffuse: 'every form of social organization which links values, norms, models of relation and conduct, roles'. Here 'every social form that presents some regularity can be subject to an institutional analysis'. In the middle of the spectrum Revel places 'every organization functioning in any regular way within a society, according to explicit and implicit rules, and where one assumes that it responds to a particular collective demand' (family, school, hospital, etc.).[125] Revel thus argued for an 'open definition of the institution that is plastic and relational. It [the institution] formalizes an ensemble of conventions which are the regularized forms of exchange [*formes réglées de l'échange*] (whence constraint and conflict play a role). At the same time one needs to understand the relationship which actors sustain with them as being based in practice'.[126]

[125] J. Revel, 'L'Institution et le social', in J. Revel, *Un Parcours critique. Douze exercices d'histoire totale* (Paris, 2006), pp. 85–110, at p. 86. For a parallel analysis, see Melville, 'Institutionen als geschichtswissenschaftliches Thema'.

[126] Revel, 'Institution et le social', p. 106.

As mentioned above, we are principally interested in the relationship between the softer and harder forms, between institutions-as-practices and institutions-as-organizations and the role of individuals within this. Institutions-as-organizations are simply the hardest form humans ever give to the social practices they most want to protect and mark off – but they must always contain institutions-as-practices: these are their content. The metaphor of slugs and snails may show what we mean: the snail's extruded shell is the structure of traditional institutional analysis, but still requires the organism within to give it life. The shell has to be understood as an expression, an outgrowth, of those practices. Likewise, while the shell *per se* structures and protects the organism, it is neither impregnable nor a sufficient explanation for that life. Slugs, after all, lack shells. One has to go further. A good illustration of this is Dominique Iogna-Prat's analysis of the medieval Church, the quintessential medieval institution marrying both hard and soft forms as a 'total institution'.[127] On the one hand, we naturally today think of the Church as its buildings and human hierarchies. Iogna-Prat argued, however, that it was only between *c.*800 and *c.*1040 (esp. 800–880) that there occurred, within medieval thinking, a basic conflation of churches (*ecclesiae*) with an idea of The Church (*Ecclesia*) itself, when *Ecclesia* as a body could stand for the whole of rightly ordered European society by definition, becoming both 'container and content'.[128] From 1050 to 1200 further micro-institutionalizations occurred whereby the Church itself became a person and clearly thought-through answers were offered to *how* Christians were contained in their churches.[129] This happened above all, he argued, through the re-ordering of sacramental practices which were increasingly rendered valid by their attachment to physical churches.[130] Both 'hard' and 'soft' institutionalization occurred but they had a history which was not at all inevitable.

[127] The phrase partly originates in M. Mauss, 'Essai sur le don forme et raison de l'échange dans les sociétés archaïquès', *L'Année Sociologique*, n.s., i (1923–4), 30–186, at p. 179. It was developed further by Erving Goffman (*Asylums: Essays on the Social Situation of Mental Patients and Other Inmates* (New York, 1961); see also Blaise Dufal's comments in 'The fathers of scholasticism' in this volume). Dominique Iogna-Prat borrows the phrase from Anita Guerreau-Jalabert (D. Iogna-Prat, *La Maison Dieu. Une histoire monumentale de l'Église au Moyen Âge (v. 800–v. 1200)* (Paris, 2006), p. 265). See A. Guerreau-Jalabert, 'L'*ecclesia* médiévale, une institution totale', in *Les tendances actuelles de l'histoire du Moyen Âge en France et en Allemagne. Actes des colloques de Sèvres (1997) et Göttingen (1998)*, ed. J.-C. Schmitt and O. G. Oexle (Paris, 2002), pp. 219–26. For religious orders as total institutions, see G. Melville, 'L'institutionalité médiévale dans sa pluridimensionalité', in Schmitt and Oexle, *Les tendances actuelles de l'histoire du Moyen Âge*, pp. 243–64.

[128] Iogna-Prat, *Maison Dieu*, *passim*, esp. pp. 107–8, 155, 309–14, 613–15.

[129] Iogna-Prat, *Maison Dieu*, pp. 314, 323 and ch. 6.

[130] Iogna-Prat, *Maison Dieu*, chs. 8–9.

As noted, much work on medieval intellectual thought and 'institutionalization' has invariably and intelligibly denoted the formal organizational structures within which that thought was produced: universities and their faculties above all, but also monastic schools, mendicant *studia* and their attendant organizational structures. As is clear, here we wish to expand, differentiate and integrate 'institutionalization' in order to accommodate *both* organizational forms (universities; faculties; colleges; *studia*; legal courts) *and* intellectual practices (dialectic; syllogistic reasoning; quodlibets; disputed questions; commentaries; *summae*; as well as disciplinary forms). It was the latter which gave intellectual substance and *raisons d'être* to the former. It was the former which provided a protected, constraining environment for the latter's development. Even in cases in which intellectual practices developed at arm's length or free from such organizational-institutional influence, they developed in ways deeply inflected by them (as with the notable generations of lay, multi-disciplinary, politically active Italian scholars of the late thirteenth and fourteenth centuries).[131] Understanding their differences and the relationships between these two different senses of 'institutional' seems to us only to increase our understanding of both.[132]

One of the aims of this book is to encourage historians to think harder about how these forms shape one other. It is encouraging that important recent works in English, French and German are convergent in doing so.[133] Still, it remains a gross, but generally valid, observation that much work on scholasticism has tended to stress either the content (the thought) or the form (the organizational setting in which it was produced) and sometimes the practice (particular intellectual techniques, such as the disputed question), but seldom how one informed the others. We have already argued that this can be illustrated in relation to Southern's work. Other great historians of scholasticism illustrate the same division of labour. Palémon Glorieux wrote on the 'hard' institution of the Sorbonne and on the 'soft' institution of quodlibets, and on the ideas of an individual, Jean Gerson, but the levels of

[131] E.g., de Libera, *Penser au Moyen Âge*; Coccia and Piron, 'Poésie, sciences et politique'.

[132] Interesting analyses of medieval social and religious life in a parallel vein are being developed by I. Forrest, 'The transformation of visitation in thirteenth-century England', *Past and Present*, cci (2013), 3–38; 'Power and the people in thirteenth-century England', *Thirteenth Century England*, xv (2015), 17–33; *Trustworthy Men: how Inequality and Faith Made the Medieval Church* (Princeton, N.J., 2018).

[133] Respectively, Wei, *Intellectual Culture in Medieval Paris*; Gorochov, *Naissance de l'université*; and, most recently – as this volume was being edited – Rexroth, *Fröhliche Scholastik*. A mould-breaking work of cross-thinking remains A. Murray, *Reason and Society in the Middle Ages* (Oxford, 1978).

analysis tended to separation not integration.[134] By focusing on the figure of Gerson, Isabel Iribarren demonstrates, in fact, how deeply in Gerson's own thought intellectual practices meshed with institutional ones through her close reading of his epic poem the *Josephina*, composed during and at the council of Constance as both a devotional text and a political work of reform. It is necessary now, therefore, to turn to ways of explaining how institutions work.

Articulating institutions

Many analysts of institutionalization risk dizzying heights of abstraction, so it is helpful to start with John Searle's approach, which does not.[135] A philosopher, his is an ordinary language tradition via J. L. Austin, not a sociological or anthropological one, although he engages with some of this material.[136] Searle argues that the fundamental logic underlying all human institutions can be clearly stated. He begins with language as the foundation of institutionalization. 'Innocent III is a man', describes a reality (what Searle calls 'word-to-world fit ↓') – we describe a world with words. 'Let us go on crusade' describes a reality Innocent III hopes to achieve through his words (what Searle calls a 'world-to-word fit ↑') – he wants to change the world to match the word. Institutions are different: they point in both directions. With institutions we collectively agree to grant certain functions to certain practices in certain contexts. By allowing this we actually create these powers. Our words change our world. This can be put as 'X counts as Y in context C'. 'The Albigensian Crusade is a crusade' is a nice medieval example (because the standing of non-Holy Land crusades were argued about). To use one of Searle's, 'playing chess is constituted in part by acting in accord with the rules [of chess]'.[137] These sets of constitutive rules are fundamental in his explanation: the functions to which we put X (the chess piece) only exist within the constitutive terms

[134] E.g., P. Glorieux, *Aux origines de la Sorbonne* (2 vols, Paris, 1965–6); P. Glorieux, *La littérature quodlibétique* (2 vols, Paris, 1925–35); J. Gerson, *Oeuvres complètes*, ed. P. Glorieux, (10 vols, Paris, 1960–73).

[135] Particularly useful are J. R. Searle, *Intentionality: an Essay in the Philosophy of Mind* (Cambridge, 1983), pp. 141–59; *The Structure of Social Reality* (London, 1995); 'What is an institution?', *Jour. Institutional Economics*, i (2005), 1–22; *Making the Social World: the Structure of Human Civilization* (Oxford, 2010). For discussion of Searle, see Searle, *Making the Social World*, pp. xi–xii; the whole issue of the journal *Anthropological Theory*, vi (1) (2006); *Tracés*, xvii (2009), the issue entitled *Que faire des institutions?*, esp. the interview at pp. 243–58. We sketch here only those parts most relevant for historical analysis.

[136] J. R. Searle, 'Lukes and "substantive social scientific work"', *Anthropological Theory*, vi (2006), 122–5.

[137] Searle, *Structure of Social Reality*, p. 28.

of those rules (what counts as a crusade or chess).[138] Hence Searle defines an institution as 'a system of constitutive rules, and such a system creates the possibility of institutional facts'.[139] What seems especially powerful in Searle's account is the role which social assertion plays ('X counts as Y') within a particular context ('in context C'). As noted, these sorts of speech act combine both word-to-world fit ↓ and world-to-word fit ↑: '[T]hese are cases where we change reality to match the propositional content of the speech act and thus achieve world-to-word direction of fit. But, and this is the amazing part, we succeed in so doing because we represent the reality as being so changed'. Such 'declarations' (Searle's name for such speech acts) 'change the world by declaring that a state of affairs exists and thus bringing that state of affairs into existence': 'this is a church', 'this is a valid marriage', 'this is a quodlibet', 'this is a religious order's rule' are all examples of this.[140] Searle further states: 'The phenomena in question are what they are in virtue of being represented as what they are'.[141] Searle nicely captures the circular, problematic social nature of this through a quotation from Marx: 'One man is king only because other men stand in the relation of subjects to him. They, on the other hand, imagine that they are subjects because he is king'.[142] Explaining the ostensibly circular logic through which concrete historical institutions are formed, persist, mutate and die is one of the historian's great tasks (we suggest). It is, indeed, as the historian John Bossy put it, a 'social miracle'.[143] Further (says Searle), all these institutions entail obligations, duties or powers – reasons for doing things which do not depend on our desires. Indeed, Searle suggests, their owning such powers is how to tell whether a phenomenon is actually institutional: it should carry those consequences socially for it to count as such.[144] Emily Corran's chapter

[138] For functions and the status we assign them, see Searle, *Making the Social World*, pp. 58–60, 94–5; *Structure of Social Reality*, pp. 13–23.

[139] Searle, *Making the Social World*, p. 10; *Structure of Social Reality*, pp. 54–5.

[140] Searle, *Making the Social World*, pp. 11–12 (the examples are ours); this can only be done with language, according to Searle (pp. 68–9). On the deontology internal to language for which Searle argued, see *Making the Social World*, pp. 80–6. It was a criticism of Austin's approach to speech acts that it did not attend to their social context (P. Bourdieu, *Le sens pratique* (Paris, 1980), p. 54).

[141] Searle, *Making the Social World*, p. 85. For parallel lines of medieval thought which had implications for phenomena such as the sacraments, see I. Rosier-Catach, *La parole efficace. Signe, rituel, sacré* (Paris, 2004).

[142] K. Marx, *Capital: a Critique of Political Economy*, trans. B. Fowkes (3 vols, London, 1976), i. 149 n. (the section on the commodity and the relative form of value); quoted by Searle, *Making the Social World*, p. 107.

[143] J. Bossy, *Christianity in the West, 1400–1700* (Oxford, 1985), pp. 57–75; see also J. Bossy, 'The mass as a social institution 1200–1700', *Past and Present*, c (1983), 29–61.

[144] These are known as 'deontic' powers in the jargon (Searle, *Making the Social World*,

in this volume offers an exemplary instance in the way the institution of private confession produced sophisticated and practical moral thought in trying to systematize and rationalize the issues arising from concrete pastoral problems.

For a historian there are several attractions to Searle's approach. First, and fundamentally, it makes very clear just how basic institutions are to social life and how important its histories should be. Second, and analytically, it recognizes the role of both power and group consent or acceptance of the institutions. Being able to represent 'X as Y' is a fact of power and communication (not of truth) and one which is contingent on others accepting (willingly or not) that it is such. It also enables a group to have a church, or a crusade, or a quodlibet, all of which do jobs within the societies which have them.[145] However, because the status of these things as churches, crusades, or quodlibets is constructed through social acceptance, that status can be gradually acquired, lost, contested, ignored or become redundant (like MacIntyre's traditions). The institutions do make claims on us – but those claims are not necessarily efficacious; they depend on our recognition of them and the possibilities they offer.[146] Explaining the process of how this happens – and stops happening – is the business of historians; being clearer about what is going on institutionally makes clearer what the general shape of this historical task is.[147] Peter Biller's chapter in this volume is an exemplary case study of how theological, legal and medical thinking from Paris and Montpellier was transmitted and instrumentalized by Rolando of Cremona into the Dominican *studium* at Toulouse, where it seems to have played a key role in the early institutionalization of inquisitorial practices against heretics. This occurred through the sorts of 'declarations' Searle analyses, although how such processes begin is something theory struggles to clarify.

Establishing institutions: habits, practices, games

Is this only relevant for those institutional objects which are at the 'hardest' end of Revel's spectrum? Not really, since the 'received' norms of institutions

pp. 91–2, 105–6). On desire-independent reasons, see Searle, *Making the Social World*, pp. 123–32.

[145] Searle, *Making the Social World*, pp. 105–6, 118–19, 123–32.

[146] Searle, *Making the Social World*, pp. 140–1; Searle, *Construction of Social Reality*, pp. 117–19.

[147] In *Making the Social World* Searle does go on to explain certain 'big' institutions like the state (pp. 160–98), but as he becomes more concrete his examples – to a historian – seem to include more value judgements (from a modern, secular, liberal, democratic perspective) and therefore become less historically useful, generally speaking.

should be statable at a push ('Abelard does not behave as an early twelfth-century teacher ought because ...').[148] How does this explain, however, how a group acquires or follows rules when they do not do so consciously? One answer is Ludwig Wittgenstein's language games (*Sprachspiele*). Another is anthropologist-sociologist Pierre Bourdieu's *habitus* (see below). Yet another is Searle's own idea of the 'background'.[149] Although it has been the least influential on historians it is also the clearest one with which to start.

Abelard had a background understanding of how to cope with his world and apply his intentions in it: what, in the twelfth century, a city was; what a school was; what private tutoring was; what marriage was; what humiliation was, etc. Like us, he had a background 'of all those abilities, capacities, dispositions, ways of doing things, and general know-how that enable us to carry out our intentions and apply our intentional states generally'.[150] *Rule*-following at this level, Searle suggests, is an unhelpful way of thinking about what is going on: '[W]e should not say that the man who is at home in his society ... is at home because he has mastered the rules of the society, but rather that the man has developed a set of capacities and abilities that render him at home in the society; and he has developed those abilities because those are the rules of his society'.[151] This looks like a problem but it is precisely what makes institutions so invaluable socially. They enable order and reduce effort. (This is also why it is enormously easy to take them for granted.) The mathematician Alfred North Whitehead's arguments about mathematical notation seem exactly applicable to institutions:

> It is a profoundly erroneous truism ... that we should cultivate the habit of thinking of what we are doing. The precise opposite is the case. Civilization advances by extending the number of important operations which we can perform without thinking about them. Operations of thought are like cavalry charges in a battle – they are strictly limited in number, they require fresh horses, and must only be made at decisive moments.[152]

[148] Searle, *Making the Social World*, pp. 158 and 167.

[149] Searle argued that he, Bourdieu and Wittgenstein mean the same thing (*Construction of Social Reality*, p. 132). Wittgenstein himself talks about the background (*Hintergrund*) but Searle means something much wider in their affinity. For the *Hintergrund*, see L. Wittgenstein, *Über Gewissheit/On Certainty*, ed. G. E. M. Anscombe and G. H. von Wright, trans. D. P. and G. E. M. Anscombe (Oxford, 1974 [1969]), §§ 94, 461; *Philosophische Untersuchungen/Philosophical Investigations*, ed. P. M. S. Hacker and J. Schulte, trans. G. E. M. Anscombe, P. M. S. Hacker and J. Schulte (4th edn, Chichester, 2009), §§ 102, 422.

[150] Searle, *Making the Social World*, pp. 31, 155–60; Searle, *Construction of Social Reality*, pp. 127–47.

[151] Searle, *Construction of Social Reality*, pp. 143–7.

[152] A. N. Whitehead, *An Introduction to Mathematics* (Oxford, 1948 [1911]), pp. 41–2; in the same vein but a different discipline, see M. Douglas, *How Institutions Think* (Syracuse, N.Y.,

This runs in tandem, too, with Luhmann's thinking, which stresses the role of social systems in reducing the white noise of human life into some sort of bounded, manageable order.

Searle's stress on intuited background understanding meshes very well with the ideas of Pierre Bourdieu, especially the latter's ideas of practice and *habitus*. Bourdieu's *habitus* operates at the same level as Searle's background and, while more sociologically concrete, can be analytically diffuse. It is the internal logic produced and shared within a given social group, a reflex logic which springs from and reproduces the social structures which have produced it and in turn produces a set of social practices whose logic it structures (e.g., marriage, inheritance, kin relations). For its adherents this shared subjective logic produces an ostensible objectivity in the norms and practices they apply. It is a shared subjective grid through which the world is objectively and practically ordered.[153] To seek to represent the resulting social practices theoretically is to misunderstand their essentially practical, concrete nature for those enacting them. The practice is the only theory one needs. Hence the religion of medieval knights was a practical, corporal one of ritual practices – and such logic is best 'seized in the act'.[154]

The example of the medieval knights is one Bourdieu himself borrowed from historians; and, in fact, he ostensibly derived his central idea of *habitus* from Erwin Panofsky's argument that there was a deep underlying concordance behind the logic of both gothic architecture and scholastic thought and that this derived from the shared *habitus* of those who thought this architecture and reason.[155] *Habitus* itself was a technical, but straightforward, term of scholastic art, defined by Aquinas as 'principally bringing order to an act'.[156] Panofsky applied this. Scholastic thought sought clarification; gothic architecture, transparency. Scholastic thought

1986), pp. 76–7 on energy-saving.

[153] Bourdieu, *Sens pratique*, pp. 87–109; and in relation to Béarnaise inheritance practices, p. 270.

[154] Bourdieu, *Sens pratique*, pp. 152–65, quotation at p. 155. The example of the knights is borrowed by Bourdieu from G. Duby, *Temps des cathedrals* (Paris, 1976), p. 155 n. There are useful comments on ritual at pp. 161–4. The stress on practice is entirely consonant with Searle's. Practices are also important in MacIntyre's thinking but they enact particular virtues for him: MacIntyre *After Virtue*, pp. 187–91, 275–7. Cf. also Wittgenstein, *Über Gewissheit*, § 601; *Philosophische Untersuchungen*, §§ 150–5.

[155] E. Panofsky, *Architecture gothique et pensée scolastique*, trans. and afterword P. Bourdieu (Paris, 1967), pp. 142, 151–67 (Bourdieu's gloss). On Panofsky's thesis today, see P. Binski, *Gothic Wonder: Art, Artifice and the Decorated Style 1290–1350* (New Haven, Conn., 2014), *passim* and particularly pp. 43–4, 50, 142, 278.

[156] Aquinas, *Summa theologiae*, Ia IIae, q. 4, a. 3c., cited by Panofsky, *Architecture gothique*, p. 83, although in a slightly different form. Panofsky did not invest the term with the same explanatory power as Bourdieu (Panofsky's original English was 'mental habitudes').

sought definitional differentiation and distinction; gothic architecture spatial differentiation of form. Scholastic thought sought the reconciliation of received authorities; gothic architecture sought that of authoritative buildings and motifs.[157] It is this underlying logic which led thinkers and architects to say of their institutions, 'this counts as a *summa*', 'this counts as a church' ('X counts as Y in context C'). While striking and evocative, Panofsky's parallelisms risk oversimplification.

A powerful and still useful way of thinking about how this happens comes from Wittgenstein. Wittgenstein might say there was a match here between the pattern of the 'language game' (*Sprachspiel*) played by scholastics and gothic architects. He, too, famously thought about these issues with a medieval (or late antique) example: Augustine's account of how children acquire language from the *Confessions*, which Wittgenstein found far too narrow. Wittgenstein suggested that languages are communicative, social games of plural types whose tacit rules can be extraordinarily complicated yet navigable. 'The limits of my language', he had argued, 'mean the limits of my world': the games construct the world's meaning for its participants.[158] Language games only makes sense within their own terms and as an ensemble rather than a linear series: the elements of the game hang together. Language, like institutions, builds a cumulative, enveloping world:[159]

> Not only rules, but also examples are needed for establishing a practice [*Praxis*]. Our rules leave loop-holes open, and the practice has to speak for itself. We do not learn the practice of making empirical judgments by learning rules: we are taught *judgments* and their connexion with other judgments. *A totality* of judgments is made plausible to us. When we first begin to *believe* anything, what we believe is not a single proposition. It is a whole system of propositions. (Light gradually dawns over the whole.) It is not single axioms that strike me as obvious, it is a system in which consequences and premises give one another *mutual* support.[160]

[157] Panofsky, *Architecture gothique*, pp. 83–7, 102, 117–21.

[158] Wittgenstein, *Tractatus Logico-Philosophicus*, § 5.6.

[159] Wittgenstein, *Philosophische Untersuchungen*. Specifying these general features in the work is almost pointless but see §§ 25–32, 150–5. A critique of the transposition of such terms to topics such as religion or science is G. Graham, *Wittgenstein and Natural Religion* (Oxford, 2014), ch. 3, esp. pp. 35–42. Graham's critique of this over-interpretation seems more justified in relation to the uses made of *Lebensform* [form of life] compared to *Sprachspiele*. However, since, following Bernard Williams, Wittgenstein's use of 'language game' was 'notoriously generous', it does seem to permit the application of Wittgenstein's philosophy to historical/empirical material (B. Williams, 'Wittgenstein and idealism', in B. Williams, *Moral Luck* (Cambridge, 1981), pp. 144–63, at pp. 154 and 155–6).

[160] Wittgenstein, *Über Gewissheit*, §§ 139–142; discussed by d'Avray in *Rationalities in History*, p. 175 n. 19

The coherence of Wittgenstein's language-game institutions comes from how they hang together and we are entirely justified in scaling them up into institutional registers (just as Searle does).[161] Anthropologists argue that social institutions work in precisely this way, too. Mary Douglas suggested that the reliability of social institutions arose from strong connections between groups' ideas of their world and those institutions themselves: 'for a convention [say a form of worship] to turn into a legitimate social institution [say a church] it needs a parallel cognitive convention to sustain it [say, 'this idea of right worship confirms and conforms to this idea of a church]'.[162] Returning to Panofsky, his account of gothic architecture and scholastic thought suggested that the homology between two quite distinct traditions can derive from a hidden water table they both share. The logic of one language game (scholastic thought) informed another one (gothic architecture) in that society. This is, in practice, a version of what David d'Avray has elsewhere called the 'weak Zeitgeist principle': without projecting a singular spirit of the age one can perfectly respectably examine actual structural similarities between historical phenomena.[163]

***

[161] Wittgenstein says so: *Philosophische Untersuchungen*, § 7.

[162] Douglas, *How Institutions Think*, p. 46. The square brackets are the editors'; see above the discussion of Iogna-Prat's *Maison Dieu*.

[163] Since this very useful idea of d'Avray has been insufficiently noted, it is worth quoting (it refers to E. H. Gombrich's 1967 lecture 'In search of cultural history'): 'Taken in this strong sense, the Zeitgeist is a sort of central principle to which the various aspects of a period's culture all lead back – an essence, as it were, in which art, religion, customs, politics, etc. all really participate. If one is not a conscious or unconscious Hegelian there seems no reason why this should be the case, and Gombrich suggested that cultural historians would do better to look for cultural "syndromes", such as the association at a particular time of anti-realistic painting with Catholicism. Since there is no intrinsic relation between the style and the religion this is quite different from the search for essential structural similarities between apparently diverse phenomena … Gombrich remarked that to criticize the Zeitgeist principle proper is not "to deny that such structural likenesses between various aspects of a period may be found to be interesting"; and by the "weak Zeitgeist principle" I mean no more than this. There is no "iron law of such isomorphism" (that is, of structural similarity), and of course "ages" do not have "essences". So far as periods are concerned, almost everyone now believes in a plurality of forms. When a structural similarity emerges empirically, however, it need not be ignored, and there is indeed a sort of "isomorphism" between the relation of secularity to eschatology in the sermons and in the political world around 1300' (D. L. d'Avray, *Death and the Prince: Memorial Preaching before 1350* (Oxford, 1994), pp. 223–4).

Panofsky's analysis brought together institutions 'hard' (church) and 'soft' (scholastic textual practices) – two very different ends of the institutional spectrum. Thus it fits entirely with our argument in this introduction and the volume as a whole that institutional history should occupy itself with the full range of the institutional spectrum. Without re-summarizing ourselves, what we have sought to do here is to offer an introduction to major, useful ideas about how institutionalization, individualization and intellectual grouping happen. Some are individually familiar to historians, but showing how they can connect with one another helps to strengthen the historian's analytical arsenal. The chapters which now follow illustrate the explanatory benefits of thinking about the relationship between individuals and institutions more widely.

I. Individuals and intellectual traditions: construction and criticism

1. The fathers of scholasticism: authorities as totems*

Blaise Dufal

Individual thinkers and institutions of meaning

As a social institution, medieval scholasticism was a historical moment of *moyenne durée* in the *longue durée* of medieval societies, lasting from the beginning of the twelfth century to the end of the fourteenth century. As a place of activity, medieval scholasticism was located in Latin western Europe, in the schools, in the universities and in the monasteries. As knowledge, it was defined in the thirteenth century as a *scientia* within the Aristotelian philosophical principles applied to Christian culture. As a method, medieval scholasticism originated with Anselm of Canterbury and his attempt systematically to ally the Augustinian sentence 'faith seeking understanding' (*fides quaerens intellectum*) with the logical method of 'by reason alone' (*sola ratione*).[1] Anselm also introduced the positive conviction that knowledge could be a way of salvation for humankind. This conviction found its role in the institution of medieval scholasticism, the 'empire of the book',[2] as an institution for the production of meaning over which it had the official monopoly in western medieval societies. Medieval scholasticism was the major apparatus of the process of veridiction – determining the truth – as a social and cultural activity, an institution which organized the production, circulation and consumption of the truth. It was an arm of the Church, an institution of faith, of adhesion to belief, an institution focused on the will-to-truth which was also a self-fulfilling prophecy (in that the knowledge produced by its truthful procedures would be true).[3] However, more than any complete institution, medieval scholasticism was itself a long and complex process of institutionalization.[4]

* I thank John Sabapathy for his important help in the writing of this paper.

[1] In general, M. Grabmann, *Die Geschichte der scholastischen Methode* (2 vols, Freiburg, 1909–10). Translations are by the author unless otherwise specified.

[2] A. Boureau, *L'empire du livre. Pour une histoire du savoir scolastique (1200–1350)* (La Raison scolastique, ii, Paris, 2007).

[3] G. Leclerc, 'Histoire de la vérité et généalogie de l'autorité', *Cahiers Internationaux de sociologie*, cxi (2001), 205–31, esp. p. 221 on self-fulfilling prophecies.

[4] See V. Tournay, *Sociologie des institutions* (Paris, 2011).

Applying the idea from canon law that formally defined an institution (*institutio*) as an act of recognition of a religious community by an ecclesiastical superior shows us medieval scholasticism as a grouping of institutions:[5] the universities founded by papal acts of recognition which gave them their specific missions and privileges.[6] Here, as in Catholic monastic moral conduct, individualism is reprehensible. The community of monks – the model for university communities – was founded on the renunciation of individual character. Following John Cassian and Benedict of Nursia, Bernard of Clairvaux defined an institution as the rules which organized a community, 'a rule accepted by everyone'.[7] Adopting this formula from the 'last Father of the Western Church',[8] we can say that medieval scholasticism was a social structure defined by rules of social relationships (juridical statues, legal exceptions, internal rules); rules of teaching (graduations, teaching programmes, reading lists); and rules of thinking and writing (censure, controversies). Medieval scholasticism was a discipline (*disciplina*) in the monastic ascetic conception and in its scholarly application. This discipline was the way to guarantee the regulation of the controversies and dogmatic order. These rules assured the proper functioning of scholasticism and guaranteed the legitimacy of knowledge. The scholastic world, then, was an institution governed by an idea of establishing truth, the necessity of providing sense in a Christian world and the requirement to boost the Church's doctrinal foundations. Thus, while the medieval scholastic world was not a 'total institution' in some modern senses,[9] it was an institution

[5] Y. Thomas, *Los artificios de las istituciones. Estudios de derecho romano* (Buenos Aires, 1999); E. Coccia, '"Qu'est-ce que la vérité?" (Jean 18,38). Le christianisme ancien et l'institution de la vérité', in *Aux origines des cultures juridiques européennes. Yan Thomas entre droit et sciences socialesi*, ed. P. Napoli (Rome, 2013), pp. 207–30; R. Chéno, 'La pertinence ecclésiologique de la théorie de l'institution de Maurice Hauriou', *Revue sciences religieuses*, lxxxii (2008), 225–43.

[6] For Paris, see I. P. Wei, *Intellectual Culture in Medieval Paris: Theologians and the University, c.1100–1330* (Cambridge, 2012), ch. 3.

[7] Bernard of Clairvaux, *Liber de Praecepto et Dispensatione* (*PL*, clxxxii), col. 861 (cap. I, 'An monasticae Regulae instituta praecepta sint, an consilia duntaxat'). See also letters 7 and 221 in the same volume. Commentary in J. Dubois, 'Ce qu'étaient pour saint Bernard la *Regula* et l'*Institutio* dans les monastères de son temps', *Bull. Société Nat. des Antiquaires de France* (1980 for 1977), 162–5; E. Coccia, 'Regula et vita. Il diritto monastico e la regola francescana', *Medioevo e Rinascimento*, xx (2006), 97–147.

[8] J. Mabillon, 'Préface', in Bernard of Clairvaux, *Liber de Praecepto*, cols. 25–6; O. Rousseau, 'S. Bernard. Le "dernier des Pères"', *Analecta Sacri Ordinis Cisterciensis*, ix (1953), 300–8.

[9] E. Goffman, *Asylums: Essays on the Social Situation of Mental Patients and Other Inmates* (New York, 1961); *Erving Goffman et les institutions totales*, ed. C. Amourous and A. Blanc (Paris, 2001); M. Foucault, *Surveiller et punir. Naissance de la prison* (Paris, 1975).

for producing a total interpretation of reality, an institution of totalized meaning with much variety within and many extensions into other cultural systems.[10] Bernard of Clairvaux's conceptualization of institutions finds echoes in contemporary sociological definitions of institutions as collective beliefs and behaviours.[11] For him, institutions were ways to act and think used by individuals. However, if the monastic model played an important role in the construction of the university and medieval scholarly self-representations, the scholastic institution was in practice more open and inclusive, more plastic and dynamic. The scholastic institution stretched the tension of an institutional formulation originally designed to produce conformity; and its extension to include the individuality of scholars created an ambiguous paradox.[12]

In a parallel way the historiography of medieval scholasticism has been torn between a focus on some of the most important figures of western thought, such as Thomas Aquinas, and an insistence on the collective aspect of academic and religious groups, especially between the universities and the mendicants. The dialectical movement of this historical analysis between individuals as writers and institutions as producers of archives properly reflects, in this case, the paradigmatic image of the tension which structured the world of medieval scholasticism. The historiographical narration of medieval scholasticism tends constantly to try to articulate these twinned dimensions.[13] It also reflects the internal tension within a strong institution which produced and expressed strong personalities. Medieval scholasticism was a world dominated by a *habitus* of humility and dogmatic normativity, two strong forms of domination in which individuals could find collective justifications for their own activities. The medieval scholastics were obsessed with the notion of individual and of person – it was placed in the centre of their investigation – but in connection with the question of individuals' community – the central place of their reflection.[14] The specificity of scholastics as individuals, and as social actors, was to produce highly developed theories of their own activity and of their own institution.

[10] See A. de Libera, *Penser au Moyen Âge* (Paris, 1991).

[11] 'One can … call institutions all the beliefs and all the patterns of conduct established by a collectivity. Sociology can thus be defined as the science of institutions, of their genesis and of their functioning', cited in E. Durkheim, *Les règles de la méthode sociologique* (Paris, 1871), pp. xxii–xxiii.

[12] Y. Thomas, 'Les artifices de la vérité en droit commun médiéval', *L'Homme*, clxxv–clxxvi (2005), 113–30.

[13] See the comments on the work of Southern and Glorieux in the introduction to this volume.

[14] A. Boureau, *De vagues individus. La condition humaine dans la pensée scolastique* (Paris, 2008).

In a way the institution often remained the unspoken but ubiquitous *moule* (mould) within which the theories of their activity were articulated.[15] In this context, examining the distinctive individuals used by scholastic thinkers as models for thinking about their own particular identities is both a paradoxical and a fitting activity.

Reconciliation and fathers in the twelfth century

The Church Fathers were models who offered a way to articulate the individual in the Christian community and unite authoritative groups of intellectuals. In medieval societies based on a globalizing conception of kinship,[16] especially spiritual kinship,[17] the figures of the Church Fathers were at the centre of the practices of communication by different social agencies from the twelfth century on. In spiritual kinship, they guaranteed the institution of charity, the link which unifies the Church. Scholasticism became an institution at a symbolic level by establishing a universal heredity from these (past) thinkers through the (present) textual memorialization of them. Building on patristic thought – for example, through commentaries, that 'idiom of scholastic thought'[18] – was a way to articulate the individual thinker and the institution as a past and as a present through intertextuality. If medieval divine kinship could be understood as an anti-genealogical kinship[19] – it was the place where everything was amassed and where the difference between filiation and alliance was abolished – all the scholastics' work on patristic texts was a way of reintroducing genealogy and history into this kinship. Thus, scholasticism raised itself by cutting the patristic knot and unrolling the exegetical string. The rise of medieval scholasticism was a dialectical movement both identifying with, and distinguishing itself from, the models of the Church Fathers.

During the twelfth century the theologians and philosophers of the medieval schools began to have the same attitude towards patristic texts as toward biblical texts. This was the result of a long, prior process of incorporating patristic explanations (*expositiones*) onto the biblical sacred page (*sacra pagina*) itself. For Lanfranc (*c.*1020–89), the Church Fathers

[15] E. Marmursztejn, *L'autorité des maîtres. Scolastique, normes et société au XIIIe siècle* (Paris, 2007).

[16] A. Guerreau-Jalabert, 'Sur les structures de parenté dans l'Europe médiévale', *Annales*, xxxvi (1981), 1028–49.

[17] D. Boquet, *L'ordre de l'affect au Moyen Âge. Autour de l'anthropologie affective d'Aelred de Rievaulx* (Caen, 2005).

[18] As Alexander Murray said at Oxford during the original conference for this volume.

[19] See P. Legendre, *Leçons IV, suite. Le dossier occidental de la parenté. Textes juridiques indésirables sur la généalogie* (Paris, 1988).

were under the 'stronghold of authority' (*arx auctoritatis*).[20] They became a specific sort of authority. Later debates around the work of Rupert of Deutz (*c.*1075–1129/1130) were also focused on the intellectual and religious status of the Church Fathers – especially Augustine in *De omnipotentia Dei* – and Rupert was one of the first to make a clear distinction between apostolic authority and that of the Church Fathers.[21] Nevertheless, by the beginning of the twelfth century patristic writings had gained a quasi-scriptural status. In the work of Hugh of St Victor (d. 1141) the Church Fathers were associated with the apostles and the evangelical texts.[22] Patristic writings gained an increasingly quasi-juridical status equivalent to the founding texts of Christianity itself. From now on this group of exegetes became the point of reference for intellectual production, the source of intellectual legitimacy and the model for scholastics. That influence is seen in criticism of it, such as that by the canonist Stephen of Tournai at the end of the twelfth century, when he complained about contemporary masters who produced 'little books' (*summulae*) 'as if the works of the holy fathers were insufficient'.[23]

The question of patristic authority was at the centre of some of the most important controversies of the twelfth century, especially around Peter Abelard (1079–1142).[24] His *Sic et non* was an enormous collection of patristic contradictions and a methodical attempt to overcome them.[25] In his preface Abelard summarized the way to reconcile the different religious and intellectual authorities,[26] providing a way to synthesize the evolution of the doctrinal issues inspected by the theologians and canonists from the beginning of the twelfth century.[27] Following the school of Laon,[28]

[20] Lanfranc of Bec, *Liber de corpore et sanguine Domini* (*PL*, cl), col. 408; see also cols. 428–9, 435.

[21] Rupert of Deutz, *Expositio in Apocalypsim* (*PL*, clxix), cols. 10–17.

[22] Hugh of St Victor, *De scripturis et scriptoribus sacris* (*PL*, clxxv), col. 15 (c. 6).

[23] 'quasi non suffecerint sanctorum opuscula patrum', *Epistola Stephani Tornacensis episcopi, ad Romanum quemdam Pontificem* (*Chartularium universitatis Parisiensis*, ed. H. Denifle and E. Chatelain (4 vols, Paris, 1889–99), i. 47–8 (no. 48)).

[24] B. Pranger, '*Sic et non*: patristic authority between refusal and acceptance: Anselm of Canterbury, Peter Abelard and Bernard of Clairvaux', in *The Reception of the Church Fathers in the West from the Carolingians to the Maurists*, ed. I. Backus (2 vols, Leiden, 2001), i. 165–93, at p. 169.

[25] D. E. Luscombe, *The School of Peter Abelard: the Influence of Abelard's Thought in the Early Scholastic Period* (Cambridge, 1969), pp. 214–22.

[26] Peter Abailard [*sic*], *Sic et non: a Critical Edition*, ed. B. B. Boyer and R. McKeon (Chicago, Ill., 1976), p. 96.

[27] J. Jolivet, 'Le traitement des autorités contraires selon le *Sic et non* d'Abélard', in J. Jolivet, *Aspects de la pensée médiévale: Abélard. Doctrines du langage* (Paris, 1987), pp. 79–92.

[28] E. Bertola, 'I precedenti storici del metodo del Sic et non di Abelardo', *Rivista di filosofia neo-scolastica*, liii (1961), 266–76; N. M. Häring, 'The interaction between canon law

Abelard built his scholastic method as a dialectical way of reconciling biblical and patristic writings. Medieval scholasticism was based on the effort of integrating the diverse excerpts and different authorities which were, moreover, historically and geographically remote from medieval European societies. With similar goals but different methods, the school of St Victor in Paris developed a conception based on the principle of reason as the handmaid of faith (*ratio ancilla fidei*).[29] For Richard of St Victor (d. 1173) the most important intellectual test was the ability to confront patristic authority itself.[30] Patristic authority became the invaluable test of scholastic authority by its proponents' willingness to conform to the high threshold of its reasoning.[31] For scholastic thinkers this validated; it did not restrict. Based on attempts to resolve the dissonances and discrepancies of a millennium of Latin Christian writing, early scholasticism evolved out of institutions of concord producing dialectical harmonies following the model of canonists' work.[32] In a way we can say that scholastic thought was this effort of reconciliation itself. The two works which effectively founded medieval scholasticism were Gratian's legal *Decretum* (by 1140), whose original title was the *Concordia*, and the theological *Sentences* of Peter Lombard (*c.*1100–60) with an analogous goal. Medieval scholasticism appeared thereafter as an institution for the resolution of conflicts: religious, dogmatic, doctrinal and intellectual.[33]

The distinction of a major group of four principal Fathers of the Latin Church (Augustine of Hippo, Ambrose of Milan, Jerome of Stridon and Pope Gregory I) appeared only in the second half of the twelfth century in the Latin world.[34] These choices were the result of a long process in which the intellectual value of their writings had been important but

and sacramental theology in the twelfth century', in *Proceedings of the Fourth International Congress of Medieval Canon Law*, ed. S. G. Kuttner (Monumenta Iuris Canonici, series C, Subsidia, xv, Vatican City, 1976), pp. 483–93; G. Makdisi, 'The scholastic method in medieval education: an inquiry into its origins in law and theology', *Speculum*, xlix (1974), 640–61.

[29] E. Michaud, *Guillaume de Champeaux et les écoles de Paris au XIIe siècle* (Paris, 1867).

[30] Richard of St Victor, 'Prologue', in *In visionem Ezechiel* (*PL*, lcvi), cols. 527–34.

[31] A. Boureau, 'L'usage des textes patristiques dans les controverses scolastiques', *Revue des Sciences Philosophiques et Théologiques*, xci (2007), 39–49, at p. 43.

[32] S. G. Kuttner, *Harmony from Dissonance: an Interpretation of Medieval Canon Law*, ed. R. M. Kollar (Latrobe, Pa., 1960); S. G. Kuttner, 'On *auctoritas* in the writing of medieval canonists: the vocabulary of Gratian', in S. G. Kuttner, *La Notion d'Autorité au Moyen Age. Islam, Byzance, Occident* (Paris, 1982), pp. 69–81; C. Munier, *Les sources patristiques du droit de l'Église du VIIIe au XIIIe siècle* (Mulhouse, 1957).

[33] Marmursztejn, *L'autorité des maîtres*, p. 17.

[34] On Ambrose's multiple afterlives, see P. Boucheron, *La trace et l'aura. Vies posthumes d'Ambroise de Milan (IVe–XVIe siècle)* (Paris, 2019).

not superordinate. The model of the Church Fathers became Augustine of Hippo (354–430), who wrote his own biography. The importance of those *Confessions* in medieval Latin societies was extraordinary, especially in the twelfth century.[35] Rupert of Deutz built a compilation of excerpts from it and Ivo of Chartres (*c.*1040–1115/16) tried to fill the gaps in the Augustinian biography. The Gregorian reforms had emphasized the place of the lives of the Fathers (*Vitae patrum*) and these became very important for preaching, a trend which assured the place of Jerome as a Father by virtue of his embodiment of Christian language, time and memory.[36] Medieval scholastic thinkers were part of the ecclesiastical movement which built up this group of Church Fathers and in return their codification of them ensured the collective affirmation of the scholastics as an institution themselves. The movement opened the possibility for theologians and philosophers to find models for their own social activity. In the case of Hugh of St Victor, the Fathers provided a model for defining different intellectual attitudes and the place of each scholastic thinker in the history of Christian intellectualism.[37] The Church Fathers became the benchmark system of medieval scholasticism.

The institution of a specific past in the thirteenth century

The Church Fathers and the symbols of the primitive Church became the official Christian past for many thirteenth-century groups more generally, as well as for the founders of the scholastic movement. The Fathers articulated the past for the present of scholasticism, the latter defined by its temporal distance from it.[38] Medieval scholasticism affirmed itself by creating a past through a group of thinkers and textual compilations which provided a mirror for its own historical identity. The medieval scholastics upheld the Fathers as a common culture and identified commonalities of collective models of behaviour. The Fathers worked as a referential past which scholasticism interpreted and vivified to assert its own powers of interpretation. As a novel institution, scholasticism needed a past; and to

[35] P. Courcelle, *Les Confessions de saint Augustin dans la tradition littéraire: antécédents et postérité* (Paris, 1963).

[36] J. Lössl, 'Hieronymus – ein Kirchenvater?', in *Väter der Kirche. Ekklesiales Denken von den Anfängen bis in die Neuzeit. Festgabe für Hermann Josef Sieben SJ zum 70. Geburtstag*, ed. J. Arnold et al. (Paderborn-Munich, 2004), pp. 431–64.

[37] D. Poirel, '"Alter Augustinus – Der zweite Augustinus". Hugo von Sankt Viktor und die Väter der Kirche', in Arnold et al., *Väter der Kirche*, pp. 643–68.

[38] See Lévi-Strauss's dictum that 'a myth is always related to a past event' (C. Lévi-Strauss, 'La structure des mythes', in C. Lévi-Strauss, *Anthropologie structurale* (2 vols, Paris, 1956–73), i. 227–55, at p. 231.

have permanent links to and foundations in that past. The intellectual and spiritual mobilization of the Church Fathers afforded a link to the primitive Church which avoided the possibility of rupture, as unmasked in earlier Christian anthropology. Thus, scholasticism's interaction with the Fathers could be defined as a process of making them sociably 'memorable' – a 'knowledge for the present'.[39]

At the beginning of the thirteenth century the translation into vernacular languages, especially French, of the *Lives of the Fathers* spread patristic images to all medieval Latin societies.[40] This vernacularizing movement was reinforced by a strong interest in Greek patristics throughout the thirteenth century, supported by the Dominican and Franciscan orders.[41] The building of a strong, specific conception of the *Latin* Church tradition was also a weapon in the struggle against the Greek Church, an attempt to marginalize this Church which defined itself as the first Church of the Fathers. The Latin Church and its scholastic theologians therefore tried to affirm a similar anteriority for their institution of knowledge. In the thirteenth century the explosion of iconographic representations of the Church Fathers went alongside a declining representation of earlier 'ancestors': Abraham, for example.[42] Augustine of Hippo and Abraham had the same function of double kinship, maternal and paternal, which characterized the paternity of the Christian divinity. The stronger affinity between the Fathers and the scholars is, however, self-evident. The iconic status of the four Church Fathers also diversified. The locating of the Church Fathers in the paradisal court and in the Church militant evolved considerably. This movement was reinforced by the diffusion from the late thirteenth century of the Dominican Jacobus da Voragine's (*c.*1230–98) collection of saints' lives, the *Golden Legend* (*Legenda aurea*), which reinforced the Fathers' liturgical recognition and distinction.[43] In 1298

[39] M. Détienne, *L'invention de la mythologie* (Paris, 1981), p. 79.

[40] Wauchier de Denain, *L'histoire des moines d'Égypte suivie de la Vie de Saint Paul le Simple*, ed. M. Szkilnik (Geneva, 1993); E. Schwan, 'La vie des anciens pères', *Romania*, xiii (1884), 233–63.

[41] N. Lewis, 'Robert Grosseteste and the Church Fathers', in Backus, *Reception of the Church Fathers*, i. 197–229; G. Bardy, 'Sur les sources patristiques grecques de saint Thomas dans la Iere partie de la *Somme théologique*', *Revue des sciences philosophiques et théologiques*, xii (1923), 493–502.

[42] J. Baschet, *Le Sein du Père. Abraham et la paternité dans l'Occident médiéval* (Le temps des images, Paris, 2000), pp. 308–9.

[43] B. Fleith, 'The Patristic sources of the *Legenda aurea*. A research report', in Backus, *Reception of the Church Fathers*, i. 231–87; A. Boureau, '*Vitae Fratrum, Vitae Patrum*. L'ordre dominicain et le modèle des Pères du désert au XIIIe siècle', *Mélanges de l'École française de Rome*, xcix (1987), 79–100.

a decretal of pope Boniface VIII instituted the feast of the four Church Fathers. This ecclesiastical decision had important liturgical consequences. The feast of each became a double celebration, meaning that the antiphon (sung response) was doubled between each psalm during celebrations of the office. The four Fathers were now officially distinguished in the Christian community's liturgical celebration of itself. They became the mirror of the four evangelists. This papal decision registered the ongoing evolution of cultural, religious and intellectual practices which became, from that time onwards, a canonical command throughout Christendom. This feast symbolized the link between past and present: it was a social and ritual construction which also promoted an institutional pattern for the future of scholastic individuals.

Scholastic thinkers increasingly differentiated between grades of past and present exegetical authority. At the beginning of the thirteenth century Alexander of Hales (d. 1245) developed, in his *Gloss on the Sentences* (*Glossa super Sententias* (1227)), a distinction between the authority of the Church Fathers and the authority of the French Victorine school, particularly of Anselm of Laon, who inherited some attributions of patristic authority as a specified father of contemporary scholasticism.[44] Philip the Chancellor's *Summa de bono* (1225–8) distinguished three forms of intellectual authority: the Fathers, the pagan philosophers and contemporary Latin thinkers.[45] This conception stressed the differences between the world of scholasticism and the world of the classical Christian Fathers. The scholasticism of the thirteenth century was conscious of being very different in time and place to that of the early Church. In the middle of the thirteenth century scholastic thinkers, therefore, produced both an important, self-conscious movement with regard to the historicity of knowledge, and historical self-reflection on the ecclesiastical institutionalizing process. Thomas Aquinas, who gave an important place to doxography in his work, considered the first five ecumenical councils as historical sources and textual context for the patristic canon.[46] Scholasticism was moving to become dominant over, and independent of, patristic thought by enclosing its textual corpus and base within a discrete historical period. Aquinas developed a very high degree of attention to the diversity of texts he could use and the diversity of the knowledge to which he had access. He often quoted the patristic

[44] A. Horwoski, *La Visio Dei come forma della conoscenza umana in Alessandro di Hales* (Rome, 2005), p. 16; H. P. Weber, *Sünde und Gnade bei Alexander von Hales. Ein Beitrag zur Entwicklung der theologischen Anthropologie im Mittelalter* (Innsbruck, 2003).

[45] Philip the Chancellor, *Summa de bono*, ed. N. Wicki (Bern, 1985).

[46] L. J. Elders, 'Thomas Aquinas and the Fathers of the Church', in Backus, *Reception of the Church Fathers*, i. 337–66, at p. 344.

authority before the biblical text in his demonstrations. His enterprise to reconcile Aristotle and Plato with the Fathers, especially Augustine, became the model for a medieval intellectualism in which biblical exegesis would orbit away from the centre of intellectual gravity.

Throughout the thirteenth century we see an explosion of patristic compilations which continued the trend initiated in the twelfth century. Those compilations, such as the *Liber florum*, or *Liber florigenus*, were very important for scholarly learning and scholastic works, becoming the major point of access to patristic writings.[47] These compilations certainly reinforced the authority of patristic thought. In compilations and encyclopaedias the Church Fathers began to be treated as original sources (*originalia, documenta*).[48] Early encyclopaedias, such as Vincent of Beauvais's *Speculum maius* (1240s–50s), were also important secondary sources for scholastic knowledge of the Fathers. In the encyclopaedias, begun and developed in the thirteenth century, they became sources of knowledge, but without specific differentiation in their level of authority as distinct from other sources. During the thirteenth century, then, patristic texts were often used outside the frame of theology as a discipline, with its focus on preaching and liturgical debate.[49] The trend of specialization in scholastic production also impacted on the representations of the Church Fathers. It is striking, however, that by the end of the thirteenth century – at precisely the point they are singled out liturgically – we also see a disintegration of their actual theological distinctiveness. The omnipresence of the Church Fathers in scholastic texts, especially Augustine of Hippo, also marked a sort of dissolution. They began to be nowhere by being everywhere. The diluting of the individuality of patristic writings was one of the logical consequences of the scholastic 'washing machine'. The scholastic institution became too powerful and spun the Church Fathers to the side for its own development. The dialectic between the dissolution of the individuality of the Fathers' writings and the consolidation of their descendants' authority became a far more general phenomenon in many later medieval intellectual contexts.

[47] E. Dekkers, 'Quelques notes sur des florilèges augustiniens anciens et médiévaux', *Augustiniana*, xl (1990), 27–44, at pp. 36–7; T. Falmagne, 'Le *liber Florigerus*: recherches sur l'attribution d'un florilège augustinien', *Revue d'études augustiniennes et patristiques*, xlv (1999), 139–81, at p. 160.

[48] R. H. Rouse, 'La diffusion en Occident au XIIIe siècle des outils de travail facilitant l'accès aux textes autoritatifs', *Revue des études islamiques*, xliv (1976), 115–47, at pp. 142–3.

[49] Boureau, 'Usage des textes patristiques'.

Collective identities through patristics in the fourteenth century

As a past for a world, as the memory of an institution, the Fathers needed to be studied with the building of specific tools of knowledge as well. Scholastic work on the patristic *corpus* in the second part of the thirteenth century evolved to become more intensive, with new forms of critical textual approach. At the beginning of the fourteenth century, medieval theologians were involved in very deep, extensive work around the writings of the Church Fathers, fashioning new sorts of tools for it. In 1306 the theologian Thomas of Ireland wrote the *Manipulus florum*, which contained thousands of references to patristic sources.[50] His works, and those produced by the Dominican Robert Holcot (*c.*1290–1349), the Franciscan Walter of Bruges (*c.*1225–1307) and many others, tried to order the ocean of patristic writings and were characterized by an erudite approach, especially in the construction of tables (*tabulae*), which proved very useful for the scholars.[51] It was an attempt at classification and indexing and a mark of the evolution of the scholastic analysis in complete autonomy from the older structures of knowledge.[52] Simply put, the scholastic writers re-composed patristic texts according to their own interest and their own methods. Popes, notably John XXII, supported and sometimes provided impetus to this movement, as well as discouraging misunderstanding and misuse of patristic sources.[53] In the middle of the fourteenth century Bartolomeo of Urbino composed the *Milleloquium veritatis Augustini*, dedicated to Pope Clement VI, and perhaps the *Milleloquium Sancti Ambrosii*.[54] These big compendia, and the *Vidarium Gregorianum*[55] and the *Hieronymianus* of Jacques Fouquier, were organized alphabetically. The scholastics of the first part of the fourteenth century built textual monuments for the Church Fathers. Those monuments celebrated their authority but also relegated them to the status of intellectual tools and references.

[50] R. H. Rouse and M. A. Rouse, *Preachers, Florilegia and Sermons: Studies on the Manipulus Florum of Thomas of Ireland* (Toronto, 1979), pp. 311–407; R. H. Rouse, 'The list of authorities appended to the *Manipulus florum*', *Archives d'histoire doctrinale et littéraire du Moyen Âge*, xxxii (1965), 243–50.

[51] Walter of Bruges, *Tabula originalium*, in *Répertoire des maîtres en théologie de Paris*, ed. P. Glorieux (2 vols, Paris, 1933–4), ii. 84–6.

[52] J. de Ghellinck, 'Une édition ou une collection médiévale des *Opera omnia* de saint Augustin', *Liber Floridus. Mittellateinische Studien Paul Lehman gewidmet*, ed. B. Bischoff and S. Brechter (St Ottilien, 1950), pp. 63–82.

[53] F. Ehrle, *Historia bibliothecae romanorum pontificum tum bonifatianae tum avenionis* (Rome, 1890), i. 151–4, 180–1.

[54] Paris, BNF, MS. lat. 2120, offered to Pope Clément VI; Rome, Biblioteca Apostolica Vaticana, MS. Urb. Lat. 81 and MS. Vat. Lat. 518.

[55] J. Fouquier, *Vidarium Gregorianum* (Paris, Bibliothèque Mazarine, MS. 687).

These different, somewhat countervailing, currents can be interestingly explored in attitudes towards one Church Father, dogmatically the most important but also the most global figure to mix the figures of pastor and theologian: St Augustine. The uses made of Augustine were multiple. During the first four decades of the fourteenth century a few scholastics from the mendicant orders composed commentaries on Augustine's monumental *City of God* (413–26), written as a riposte to learned pagan criticism of Christianity after the Goths' sack of Rome in 410. These commentaries showed a variety of different views and representations of Augustine.[56] For these commentators *The City of God* provided an opportunity to define their conceptions of Augustine and develop their own conception of what the scholastic thinker should be, drawing on his model and the common patristic references and distinctions. For the Dominican Nicolas Trevet (*c.*1258–1335), Augustine's *City of God* became an 'old' text whose cultural references needed explanation, something which Trevet provided in his commentary on pagan religion and classical literature by focusing on the first ten books of the *City of God*. For the Dominican Thomas Waleys (*c.*1287–1349) and the Franciscan John Ridevall (d. after 1340), the Augustinian text needed to be used for preaching as well as explanation.[57] For these scholastic writers the patristic text did not need *theological* explanation; and they accordingly developed a conception of scholastic thought which encompassed erudite knowledge about *all* the texts from the past. The Franciscan theologian François of Meyronnes (*c.*1280–1328), by contrast, tried to organize the theological aspects of *The City of God* and composed a text which put in order the religious and doctrinal developments of Augustine's thought. He proposed a 'scholastization' of Augustine's text to make it comprehensible for students and young monks. The Carmelite John Baconthorpe (*c.*1290–1348) used scholastic logic and Aristotelian tools to establish the superiority of the theology of Augustine. He defended the conception of scholasticism's focus on theology and tried to avoid what he saw as excesses in philosophical trends. These commentaries expressed the intellectual and cultural concerns of contemporary commentators and illustrate how, by the fourteenth century, the Church Fathers and their texts had become polysemous figures. All wanted to defend Augustine's text but not in the same way or with the same goals; and in so doing they proposed various conceptions of Augustine – and of patristic figures more widely. Thus, for example, employing the four Aristotelian causes (material, formal,

[56] B. Dufal, 'Repenser l'autorité du Père Saint Augustin et le *De civitate Dei* au XIVe siecle' (unpublished University of Paris PhD thesis, 2014).

[57] B. Smalley, *English Friars and Antiquity in the Early Fourteenth Century* (Oxford, 1960).

efficient, final), Trevet divided the four exegetical meanings of scripture across each of the four Church Fathers (the division became current in the fourteenth century). Jerome represented the historical level of meaning; Gregory the allegorical; Ambrose the tropological/moral; and Augustine the anagogical/mystical level of meaning. The Church Fathers each embodied one technique of exegesis and represented different traditions of interpretation. This typological schematization nicely exemplifies the scholastic subordination of these superordinate patristic figures within their descendants' intellectual frameworks.

These different appropriations of St Augustine testify to a diffraction of the scholastic world, a world which by the beginning of the fourteenth century appeared as an institution co-ordinated by the constellation of authorities. Thus scholasticism, a written world inked by speculative distinctions and a social world built by classification struggles, was dividing into multiple communities and identities. From the fourteenth century specific schools and groups of thinkers appeared which distinguished themselves with reference to specific contemporary authorities (Averroes, Thomas Aquinas, Duns Scotus). This competition over identification was further stressed by the question of Aristotle's place, still seen as a pagan Father, but perhaps also a *scholastic* Father in the manner of Augustine.[58] The Church Fathers became demultiplicate bodies: they were limbs of the Church and the scholastic institution and they were specific figureheads for certain groups. Their texts, as specific bodies for specific questions, functioned as ambiguous masks for these different groups. The various appropriations and mobilizations of patristic figures in the fourteenth century were a de facto way of inscribing new forms of dispositive authority and of re-composing the system of scholastic self-representation. In this connection, the patristic author, as a source of authority, became an individual because of his existence as a historical figure. He moved from saintly to human.[59] Through St Augustine, groups which affirmed their own identity found a way to attach that specificity to a normative intellectual pedigree, something which contemporary institutionalization required. For the mendicant orders, Augustine's writings in particular became a forge on which to make – individually and collectively – proofs for their own institutions and a way to be a part of the glorious history of the Church. The Augustinian orders themselves also had an enormous impact on the cultural production of this

[58] C. König-Pralong, *Avènement de l'aristotélisme en terre chrétienne. L'essence et la matière entre Thomas d'Aquin et Guillaume d'Ockham* (Études de philosophie médiévale, Paris, 2005).

[59] A. J. Minnis, *Medieval Theory of Authorship: Scholastic Literary Attitudes in the Later Middle Ages* (2nd rev. edn, Philadelphia, Pa., 2012).

patristic figuration, likewise the Carmelite order.[60] The important diffusion of *De origine et progressu ordinis fratrum eremitarum Sancti Augustini et vero ac proprio titulo eiusdem* (1334) by Henry of Friemar throughout the fourteenth century showed the polysemy and ambiguity of medieval conceptions of the Fathers.[61] Its success nursed new evolutions in patristic attitudes at the end of the fourteenth century. The mendicant orders, to reinforce themselves, built patristic figures who mixed ascetic behaviours and intellectual aptitudes. Doing so brought them back as religious and devotional figures in the second part of the fourteenth century, qualifying their earlier dominance as primarily scholastic intellectual figures.

The Church Fathers as 'totems' of medieval scholasticism

As a world of coexistence between naturalist and analogist anthropology, Latin medieval societies participated in some totemic representations. Anthropologically, western medieval societies were characterized by a mix between a naturalist ontology and an analogic ontology, following Descola's typology.[62] Briefly, Descola has suggested that it is useful to think about societies in terms of the four ways of relating themselves to the world which, he argues, they adopt, adapt and mix to different degrees: animistic (perceiving continuities between humans and other living systems/ creatures); totemistic (perceiving particular shared attributes between humans and other particular species); analogistic (perceiving multiple parallels and correspondences across created substances); and naturalistic (perceiving the world and its entities as belonging to a single generalizable order of material logic but where internal worlds are separate, in contrast

[60] D. Blume and D. Hanssen, 'Agostino pater e praeceptor du un nuovo religioso (considerazioni sulla propaganda illustrata degli eremiti agostiniani)', in *Arte et spiritualità degli Ordini Mendicanti. Gli Agostiniani et il cappello di S. Nicola a Tolentino* (Tolentino, 1992), pp. 77–92; S. Dale, 'I veri figli di Agostino e gli affreschi della chiesa di Sant'Agostino a Gubbio', in *Arte et spiritualità degli Ordini Mendicanti*, pp. 151–64.

[61] R. Arbesman, 'Henry de Friemar's treatise on the origin and development of the order of the hermits friars and its true and real title', *Augustiniana*, vi (1956), 37–145; P. Courcelle, 'Les romans de propagande développés par les ermites de saint Augustin', in P. Courcelle, *Les Confessions de saint Augustin dans la tradition littéraire. Antécédents et Postérité* (Paris, 1963), pp. 324–7.

[62] P. Descola, *Par-delà nature et culture* (Paris, 2005); F. Coste, 'Philippe Descola en Brocéliande', in *Faire l'anthropologie historique du Moyen Âge*, ed. E. Brilli, P.-O. Dittmar and B. Dufal (= *Atelier du Centre de Rechercher Historique*, vii (2010)) <https://journals.openedition.org/acrh/1911> [accessed 15 Feb. 2019]; P.-O. Dittmar, *L'invention de la bestialité. Une anthropologie du rapport homme-animal dans les années 1300* (Paris, 2010). An accessible English summary by Descola of his typology is 'Modes of being and forms of predication', *HAU: Journal of Ethnographic Theory*, iv (2014), 271–80 <https://www.haujournal.org/index.php/hau/article/view/hau4.1.012> [accessed 15 Feb. 2019].

to animism). The scholastic world dealt with the principle of Christian transcendence and earthly material embodiment with a discursive structure dominated by analogical principles. The ambiguity of the ontological background of medieval societies was fixed by the gravity of the Church Fathers as institutional embodiments of an individual figure, abstracting the individual into a general understanding of their *personae* (following the classical theatrical term for a dramatic character). The Church Fathers accordingly became mythological figures, the products of culture[63] and collective representation,[64] at a moment when scholastics became aware of the temporal difference between antiquity and their modernity.[65] The Church Fathers represented the past of the scholastic world, but this past needed to be managed if the present was to remain self-sufficient and not be overwhelmed by it. The Fathers needed to be connected, but not too connected, to their contemporary successors. On the one hand, these mythologized figures were formulated to function in a genealogy of scholasticism which connected medieval societies to the early and classical Christian world. On the other hand, too great a distancing from them would have risked a break between the Church's legitimating late antique roots and the ecclesiastical institution of the thirteenth and fourteenth centuries which claimed those roots as its warrant. The Church Fathers were given a double structure, historic and a-historic: they belonged to the inscribed word but also to the living language.[66] They were a way for scholastics to build a continuity between two worlds which had become different. Scholastic interpretations of the Church Fathers could be seen as different versions of a mythological story.[67] They appeared in the scholastic texts as names, where they were put forward as emblems.[68] These emblems were social characteristics for groups and for individuals, embodying and operating as tutelary authorities.[69] These 'totems' gave the name of the

[63] *Pensée mythique et représentations sociales*, ed. D. Jodelet and E. Paredes (Paris, 2010).

[64] According to R. Barthes, '[m]yth, closely related to what Durkheimian sociology calls a collective representation, can be heard to speak in the formulations of newspapers, advertising, mass-market goods, is that which is determined socially, a reflection. This reflection however, conforming to the celebrated image of Marx, is inverted – myth consists in overturning culture into nature, or at least, the cultural, ideological, historical into the natural' (R. Barthes, *Mythologies* (Paris, 1957), pp. 181–2).

[65] According to Lévi-Strauss , '[a] myth is always related to a past event' (Lévi-Strauss, 'La structure des mythes', p. 231).

[66] F. Saussure, *Cours de linguistique générale* (Paris, 1995).

[67] Lévi-Strauss, 'La structure des mythes', p. 240.

[68] A. Boureau, *L'aigle. Chronique politique d'un emblème* (Paris, 1985).

[69] According to E. Durkheim, '[t]he use of emblems, necessary for a society to become conscious of itself, is no less indispensable in assuring the continuity of that conscience' (E.

social groups; fixed the identity; named and appointed their purpose; and guaranteed the harmony of their society.[70] Monastic orders, as brotherhoods and similar to clans,[71] also built their identities on the paternal reference to a spiritual father, again operating as institutionalizing totems.[72] As a specific cult, the Church Fathers supported a more general cult of the late antique patristic past which instituted and reinforced the identifies of medieval intellectual groupings and of the Church itself.[73]

The Church Fathers, as paradigmatic, instrumental figures, provided a way to think both of the collective past and the present world; and a way to conceive the genealogies between individuals and scholastic culture. As figures of mediation between individuals and institutions, the Church Fathers worked as totemic forms for the medieval scholastic world,[74] in a process of institutionalization which aimed to organize and control the links between individuals and social models.[75] In a dialectical process of self-recognition, medieval intellectuals defined themselves relative to these 'ideal types'. Scholastic thinkers built their own Fathers as a way to describe themselves and to recognize their relative intellectual ancestors. The Patristic Fathers worked as social models, exemplary figures, cultural prototypes, ideal types, for their scholastics sons. Those very polysemous 'ideal types' played a decisive part in the construction of scholasticism as an institution. Between individuals and institution, the Church Fathers were

---

Durkheim, *Les formes élémentaires de la vie religieuse. Le système totémique en Australie* (2nd rev. edn, Paris, 1925), p. 331).

[70] Barthes writes: 'Myth correctly has a double function: it designates and it notifies, it creates understanding and imposes it' (Barthes, *Mythologies*, p. 202).

[71] Durkheim writes: 'The clan is moreover, a society which can, less than any other, dispense with emblems and symbols, since there is hardly another so lacking in coherence. The clan cannot define itself through its chief, since even if all central authority is not absent, it is at least uncertain and unstable. It cannot, furthermore, define itself through the territory which it occupies, since the population, being nomadic, is not tightly tied to a specific locality ... The unity of the group then is only apprehensible thanks to the collective name which all its members bear and the emblem, also equally collective, which reproduces the thing designated by this name' (Durkheim, *Formes élémentaires*, pp. 333–4).

[72] D. Donadieu-Rigaut, *Penser en images les ordres religieux (XIIe–XVe siècles)* (Paris, 2005), p. 2.

[73] According to Durkheim, '[t]he different cults specific to each clan merge and complement one another by forming an interdependent whole [*un tout solidaire*]' (Durkheim, *Formes élémentaires*, pp. 423–4).

[74] Descola asserts that '[t]he Lévi-Straussian principle of conceiving of discontinuities in the natural world [as a means of explaining discontinuities in humans' social world] is inoperable here and one has to turn therefore towards mythical ontogenesis [i.e., the way humans stage their narrative of mythical development] in order to understand the reasons for totemic rearrangements' (Descola, *Par-delà nature et culture*, p. 228).

[75] M. Weber, *Économie et société* (2 vols, Paris, 1995), i: *Les catégories de la sociologie*, p. 94.

social figures, cultural intermediaries and subtle intellectual mediators who allowed the building of representations of individual intellectuals linked to a collective identity. In order to objectify and stabilize itself, scholasticism as an institution needed the Church Fathers to circumscribe the social *habitus* which embodied its own social standards, to put a limit on the hubris of theologians and philosophers.[76] The referential system of scholasticism needed permanently to reconcile its internal tensions and external social injunctions. The resolution of this conflict between individuals and scholasticism lay in the institutional reconfiguration of patristic authors as common cultural references which each Christian thinker could appropriate. As they were figures of intellectual and religious authority in the medieval world, talking and writing about the Fathers was an important contribution to the strengthening of scholasticism as a set of institutions. Commentaries on their works and the different uses of their authority were ways for scholastics to distinguish themselves and connect internal groupings, expressed by specific conceptions of what they were reading, writing and arguing. The uses of these figures showed, in fact, how an institution was not a common way to realize common purposes but a common way to realize different ends.[77] The Church Fathers represented the possibility of plural expressions in a unified context which included the possibility of individual self-affirmation. Together, these different intellectual attitudes produced a large pantheon; and the patristic tradition was employed as a founding agency for scholasticism as an institution which gathered together all the symbolic structures for each group and intellectual individuality.[78] They represented kinship as a shared fatherhood, a conception of the generational transmission of sacred knowledge; and they embodied love and charity (*caritas*) as the spiritual link which unified the Church and sought to protect it from the dangers of misinterpretation.

[76] P. Bourdieu, 'Les rites comme actes d'institution', *Actes de la recherche en sciences sociales*, xliii (1982), 58–63.

[77] J. Rawls, *A Theory of Justice* (Cambridge, Mass., 1971), ch. 2.

[78] M. Douglas, *How Institutions Think* (Syracuse, N.Y., 1986); M. Calvez, 'L'analyse culturelle de Mary Douglas: une contribution à la sociologie des institutions', *SociologieS* (2006) <http://journals.openedition.org/sociologies/522> [accessed 15 Feb. 2019].

2. The unicity of substantial form in the *Correctoria corruptorii fratris Thomae* of Richard Knapwell, Robert Orford and John of Paris

Antonia Fitzpatrick

The Dominican general chapter of June 1286 demanded that each and every individual friar (*omnes et singuli*) familiarize himself with, promote and defend the teachings of Thomas Aquinas.[1] This was a response to certain events of 30 April that year. The archbishop of Canterbury, John Peckham, a Franciscan, had condemned as heretical Aquinas's theory of human nature, according to which there is one and only one substantial form in a human being: the rational soul.[2] The condemnation followed – without being the inevitable conclusion of – the thirteenth century's most acrimonious and significant scholastic debate.[3] Was there one substantial form alone in a human being, as Aquinas's (mostly Dominican) defenders argued;[4] or was there more than one, or a plurality of forms,[5] as his (mostly Franciscan)

[1] *Acta capitulorum generalium Ordinis Praedicatorum*, ed. B. M. Reichert (9 vols, Rome, 1898–1904), i. 235.

[2] *Registrum epistolarum fratris Johannis Peckham archiepiscopi cantuariensis*, ed. C. T. Martin (RS, 3 vols, 1882–5), iii. 922–3.

[3] See A. Boureau, *Théologie, science et censure au XIIIe siècle* (Paris, 1999); and R. Zavalloni, *Richard de Mediavilla et la controverse sur la pluralité des formes* (Louvain, 1951). In English see: A. Fitzpatrick, *Thomas Aquinas on Bodily Identity* (Oxford, 2017), pp. 5–11, 175–80; J. F. Wippel, *The Metaphysical Thought of Godfrey of Fontaines: a Study in Late Thirteenth-century Philosophy* (Washington, D.C., 1981), pp. 314–47. For the later history of the debate: R. Pasnau, *Metaphysical Themes 1274–1671* (Oxford, 2011), pp. 574–605.

[4] The Augustinian Giles of Rome, additionally, was an important defender of the theory of the unicity of form. See his *De gradibus formarum*/ *Contra gradus et pluralitatem formarum* (Venice, 1500).

[5] The secular Henry of Ghent, an early critic of Aquinas's thought, proposed a duality (not plurality) of forms in humans. See esp. his *Opera omnia*, ed. R. Macken et al. (multiple vols, Leuven, 1979–), v–viii (*Quodlibets*, I.4, II.2, III.6 and IV.13). For commentary: Boureau, *Théologie, science et censure*, pp. 118–34; Wippel, *The Metaphysical Thought of Godfrey of Fontaines*, pp. 329–35.

critics maintained?[6] The deep philosophical and theological importance of this question will become clear shortly. At the centre of the conflict was another Franciscan's contentious 'corrective' to Aquinas's thought, William de la Mare's *Correctorium fratris Thomae* (Paris, *c.* March 1277),[7] mandatory reading for Franciscans studying Aquinas's *Summa theologiae* following their own general chapter of 1282.[8] For their part, Dominican leaders encouraged a deepening connection between Aquinas's theology and Dominican group identity before 1286, even if early legislative measures emphasized discipline over doctrine: in 1278 and 1279 general chapters empowered visitators, provincial and conventual priors to punish any friar bringing scandal to the order by openly criticizing Aquinas's writings.[9] There were five Dominican responses to William de la Mare, each a *Correctorium corruptorii fratris Thomae*. Three of these will be discussed here.

The *Correctoria corruptorii*, self-evidently, hold out an opportunity for a case study in the formation of individuals' thinking in relation to the institution of which they were a part. Yet it would hardly be worth returning to these texts and to the debate over the unicity of form, mapped out so well by others, were there not the possibility of revealing something new, or at least underappreciated. It is not the argument of this chapter that the *Correctoria corruptorii* of Richard Knapwell (*Quare*, Oxford, *c.* 1278), Robert Orford (*Sciendum*, Oxford, 1282–3) and John of Paris (*Circa*, Paris, 1283–4)[10] yield a straightforward study in the homogenization and institutionalization of Dominican thought on the basis of Aquinas's philosophy. The last study

[6] For one version of the doctrinal case against the unicity of form argument, see the 1278 apologia by John Peckham's predecessor as archbishop of Canterbury, the Dominican Robert Kilwardby, edited in F. Ehrle, 'Der Augustinismus und der Aristotelismus in der Scholastik gegen Ende des 13. Jahrhunderts', *Archiv für Literatur- und Kirchengeschichte des Mittelalters*, v (1889), 603–35, at pp. 614–32; and A. Birkenmajer, *Vermischte Untersuchungen zur Geschichte der mittelalterlichen Philosophie* (Münster, 1922), pp. 60–4. This apologia was one of the targets in July 1278 of the Dominican Giles of Lessines' *De unitate formae*, ed. M. de Wulf (Louvain, 1902). For commentary, see Boureau, *Théologie, science et censure*, pp. 36–8, 63–70, 76, 80–1; Fitzpatrick, *Thomas Aquinas on Bodily Identity*, pp. 8–9 and n. 24. All translations are by the author.

[7] For this dating: Boureau, *Théologie, science et censure*, p. 75.

[8] 'Definitiones Capituli Generalis Argentinae, Celebrati anno 1282', ed. P. Geroldus Fussenegger, *Archivum Franciscanum historicum*, xxvi (1933), 127–40, at p. 139.

[9] Reichert, *Acta capitulorum generalium*, i. 199, 204.

[10] Each is named after the first word of its incipit. For an overview of the 5 *Correctoria corruptorii*, see M. D. Jordan, 'The controversy of the *Correctoria* and the limits of metaphysics', *Speculum*, lvii (1982), 292–314, esp. pp. 292–8 and n. 3, with bibliography detailing the previous 70 years of research on these texts, notably works by Hödl, Mandonnet, Ehrle, Glorieux, Creytens and Pelzer. Jordan's dating of the *Correctoria* is challenged by Boureau, *Théologie, science et censure*, p. 79. Here this chapter follows Boureau.

devoted to the cast of characters and the range of issues with which this chapter is concerned, Frederick J. Roensch's *Early Thomistic School* (1964) – also published as *The Unicity of Substantial Form and its Implications in the Early Thomistic School* – presented things in exactly that way. Noting that 'the doctrine of unicity of substantial form … constituted the most basic yardstick by which to judge the character of any early Thomist', Roensch intended to show that our three Dominicans were 'true and loyal Thomists' who 'not only defended St. Thomas, but understood his teaching in exactly the same way as he did himself'.[11] Here Roensch missed something significant. Read closely, the *Correctoria* instead provide a case study in individual thinking deeply marked by the politics of group opposition – in this case, the institutional rivalry between the two major mendicant orders. It emerges, furthermore, that this partisan process of critical re-evaluation could have a radically disintegrative effect, generating wildly divergent renderings of Aquinas's theory of the composition of a human being.

Admittedly, one does not have to look far to find discussions of 'Thomism' which suggest less stringent criteria for membership of a 'Thomistic school' than Roensch's study of 1964. Still, an assumption often encountered is that this supposed intellectual school or '-ism', grounded in Aquinas's writings, has possessed, from the thirteenth century until now, an unchanging essence of 'basic doctrines … commonly recognized as characteristic', even if the 'problems and polemics of their day' have influenced the range of questions which different Thomists, as individuals or generations, have asked of Aquinas's works and the answers they have looked to defend.[12] It may appear obvious, then, that Roensch's concept of an 'Early Thomistic School' should have failed to capture the real diversity of the earliest Dominican interpretations of Aquinas: we might immediately suppose that individuals should have found themselves at least slightly adapting, rather than merely replicating, what Aquinas said, in order to keep pace with the development of debate.[13] What is too infrequently recognized, however, and what it is crucial to understand, is that Aquinas's 'basic doctrines', as set out over the range of his works, could themselves appear fundamentally underdetermined, especially

[11] F. J. Roensch, *The Unicity of Substantial Form and its Implications in the Early Thomistic School* (Dubuque, Iowa, 1964), pp. ix, 19.

[12] Quotations from J. A. Weisheipl, 'Thomism', in *New Catholic Encyclopedia* (18 vols, New York, 1967–88), xiv. 126–35, at pp. 126–7 (20 'basic doctrines' are listed at pp. 127–8).

[13] On the impossibility of reconciling the evolution of scholastic debate with the notion of intellectual schools defined by doctrine, see S. P. Marrone, *The Light of Thy Countenance: Science and Knowledge of God in the Thirteenth Century* (Studies in the History of Christian Thought, 2 vols, Boston, Mass., 2001), i. 13–15.

when subjected to the pressure of questions which Aquinas himself (d. 1274) did not (or could not) foresee.[14]

This was just the case with the theory of the unicity of substantial form in humans. In some aspects, it was clear and uncompromising. In others, especially the theory's implications for the continuity of the body after death (or the composition of the corpse), Aquinas's thinking appeared muddled. Many different views could consequently follow. As we shall see, it was no accident that William de la Mare chose to focus his critique of the unicity of form upon the issue of post-mortem bodily continuity, or that discussion of the theory's alleged consequences in this area could provide ample material for an increasingly complex and heated scholastic debate. It followed, too, that, while the Dominican authors of the *Correctoria* wrote on Aquinas's behalf, countering de la Mare '*secundum Thomam*' [according to Thomas], the act of constructing an effective defence of Aquinas on the subject of the composition of a human being was a case of setting out creatively and originally what Aquinas *must have* intended or *would have* said. Finally, and most importantly, it could follow that these Dominicans' readings of the 'basic doctrine' of the unicity of form, profoundly shaped by the need to find a reply to a distorting Franciscan caricature of Aquinas's thought on human nature, were just as likely (if not more) to replicate critical aspects of de la Mare's misrepresentation as they were to attempt to rectify them.[15]

The political-intellectual dynamics in play can be explained much more readily with reference to what Russell Friedman has identified as rival Franciscan and Dominican intellectual 'traditions' at the medieval university[16] than by the language of '-isms' or 'schools'. First, however, we need to return to the issue at stake. Scholastic theologians held that the two most basic components of composite things were matter and substantial form. A substantial form was a form which determined something's nature – as a human, an animal, or a body, for instance. The question of the unicity or plurality of substantial forms in a human, then, was fundamental: a theologian's answer would determine, *inter alia*, his account of how a

[14] An emphatic appreciation of this point may be the key to understanding Aquinas's reception more broadly. Cf. H. de Lubac: '[C]e grand docteur ... apparaît plutôt comme un auteur de transition, et l'ambivalence de sa pensée en équilibre instable, rançon de sa richesse même, explique qu'on ait pu dans la suite l'interpréter en des senses si opposés' (H. de Lubac, *Surnaturel: Études historiques* (Paris, 1946), pp. 435–6).

[15] Here this discussion respectfully parts ways with elements of I. Iribarren's crucial article '*Responsio secundum Thomam* and the Search for an Early Thomist School', *Vivarium*, xxxix (2001), 255–96, at pp. 281, 295.

[16] R. L. Friedman, *Intellectual Traditions at the Medieval University: the Use of Philosophical Psychology in Trinitarian Theology among the Franciscans and Dominicans, 1250–1350* (2 vols, Leiden, 2013).

single being could arise from the union of matter and soul; his theory of embryogenesis;[17] his understanding of which of a human's components were essential to a person's continuing identity over his or her lifetime;[18] and – as just indicated – his judgement of what continued, and what perished, at the moment of death.

Aquinas's account of human nature was innovative.[19] One substantial form alone, the rational or human soul, was to be the source of all a human's defining characteristics and to give to it the totality of its existence (*esse*). 'In one individual, there is only one substantial form [*forma substantialis*]', Aquinas says, and 'through this substantial form, which is the human soul [*anima humana*], this individual is not only human, but an animal, one thing, a body, a substance, and a being [*ens*]'.[20]

This intervention was neither random nor arbitrary. Like the majority of the most significant philosophical theories developed by medieval universities' most important thinkers,[21] the theory of the unicity of substantial form in humans was motivated by theological considerations. Aquinas had the doctrine of the bodily resurrection in mind. If the soul were a human's only substantial form, then the union between soul and matter in each human would be intimate and essential. It would make sense to say, as the Fourth Lateran Council's declaration of faith proposed, that, at the resurrection, each person's soul would be reunited to a body recovered from their own matter, so that the whole person, sinning flesh included, could be judged justly.[22] Additionally, the theory (like the Council's doctrinal pronouncement), was distinctively shaped by Catholic polemic with dualist

[17] Studies include F. Amerini, *Aquinas on the Beginning and End of Human Life*, trans. M. Henninger (Cambridge, Mass., 2013); and M. A. Hewson, *Giles of Rome and the Medieval Theory of Conception* (London, 1975).

[18] An indispensable study of medieval debates on personal identity over time, relating them to analogous discussions in modern philosophy and science fiction, is C. W. Bynum, 'Material continuity, personal survival and the resurrection of the body: a scholastic discussion in its medieval and modern contexts', in C. W. Bynum, *Fragmentation and Redemption: Essays on Gender and the Human Body in Medieval Religion* (New York, 1991), pp. 239–97 and 393–417.

[19] S. de Boer, *The Science of the Soul: the Commentary Tradition on Aristotle's De anima, c. 1260–c. 1360* (Leuven, 2013), p. 40.

[20] Thomas Aquinas, *Opera omnia*, ed. Leonine (multiple vols, ongoing, Rome and Paris 1882–), xxiv. 2. 40 (*Quaestio disputata de spiritualibus creaturis*, 3c). This and other translations are the author's own.

[21] J. Marenbon, *Later Medieval Philosophy (1150–1350)* (London and New York, 1987), p. 190.

[22] All were to rise in the 'bodies which they now wear' (*Qui omnes cum suis propriis corporibus resurgent, quae nunc gestant*) (*Decrees of the Ecumenical Councils*, ed. N. P. Tanner S.J. (2 vols, Washington, D.C., 1990), i. *Nicaea I to Lateran V*, pp. 230–230*).

heresy.[23] Aquinas thought that if there were another substantial form in a human being intervening between the soul and matter, for instance a corporeal substantial form which gave definition and existence to the body independently of the soul, then the union of a human soul to any particular body would be merely incidental. Body and soul would be substances arranged next to one another, like a woman and the clothes she wears, but not complementary components of one naturally unified thing. Reincarnation would become conceivable, a heretical opinion which Aquinas understood to have been taught 'continuously down to today [*usque hodie*]', from Plato to Origen to, now, certain 'Manichees [*Manichaei*]'.[24] Indeed, for Aquinas, soul and body are more than just complementary components of the human being. They overlap: the soul, as the body's substantial form, is an intrinsic component of the body. Strictly, for Aquinas *matter* (the body's other component) and soul, not *body* and soul, come together to compose the human being.[25]

The *Correctorium fratris Thomae* is dominated by a critique of the theory of the unicity of form.[26] Of the 117 theses de la Mare selects for 'correction', at least twenty-one are related to the theory, even if the central claim 'that in a human being there is one substantial form alone' is attacked only in article 31.[27] Tying together all de la Mare's criticisms of the theory is a basic assertion: Aquinas places such great emphasis on the essential unity of body and soul, the Franciscan argues, that his theory effectively denies the autonomy of the body, or of the material part of human nature, relative to the soul. If the soul were the body's only substantial form, what was the body just in itself? As de la Mare makes clear, several points of Catholic doctrine, not least transubstantiation, the incarnation and the contraction of original sin, appear to require a strong account of the body's autonomy.

[23] For historiographical debate, see *Cathars in Question*, ed. A. Sennis (York, 2016), including an important discussion by D. d'Avray, 'The Cathars from non-Catholic sources', pp. 177–84.

[24] Aquinas, *Opera omnia*, xiii. 520 (*Summa contra Gentiles*, II.83).

[25] For further discussion, see Fitzpatrick, *Thomas Aquinas on Bodily Identity*, pp. 84–5, 89–91.

[26] For biography and bibliography, see J. Marenbon, 'Mare, William de la [William de Mara] (*fl.* 1272–1279)', *ODNB* <https://doi.org/10.1093/ref:odnb/18025> [accessed 26 Aug. 2018].

[27] De la Mare's text is transmitted as incorporated into Knapwell's reply, *Quare*, and edited accordingly: *Le Correctorium Corruptorii 'Quare'*, ed. P. Glorieux (Kain, 1927). Article 48 of *Quare* bears the same heading as article 31, but adds no new arguments from de la Mare, containing simply Knapwell's extended defence of the unicity of form. The number of theses targeted is thus not actually 118, as is often claimed, but 117. Articles 8, 10, 11, 12, 27, 28, 29, 30, 32, 52, 85, 86, 88, 90, 98, 100, 102, 107, 113, 114 and 115 also relate to Aquinas's thought on the union of body and soul.

The theological issue he places in primary position (which would also provide the focus of Peckham's condemnation of Aquinas's theory in 1286), however, is the continuity and identity of Christ's corpse during the three days of His death:

> [I]f however there had not been some substantial form other than the intellective soul belonging to the body of Christ, then after the soul was separated prime matter [*prima materia*] alone remained, or another substantial form was introduced. From this it follows that it was not the same body in number [*idem corpus numero*] dead on the crossbar and buried in the sepulchre. For if matter alone remained, it was not a body; nor, therefore, was it the same body in number, for prime matter is not a body ... But if ... some other substantial form ... was introduced, it follows from this ... that the body of Christ living and dead was not the same in number; for where there is a different substantial form there is another body. In the three days [*in triduo*], therefore, it would not have been the body that He assumed.[28]

That the hypostatic union between Christ's divinity and each component of His human nature, His body and His soul, once forged, could not be dissolved, was taken as an article of faith. This implied that the corpse in the tomb (somehow, its death notwithstanding) had remained 'the same in number' (the selfsame individual thing) as Christ's living body.[29] William de la Mare's point is that, assuming the unicity of form, there is no bodily continuity. For when it comes to the composition of the corpse ('body' with soul removed), there are only two options. If all that crosses over from living body to corpse is mere *prime* matter, then the corpse is no body at all: scholastic theologians understood prime matter, posited as the ultimate substratum of all cases of natural change, to be completely raw and featureless, such that it was not a 'this', nor 'this much', nor 'this way', nor otherwise determined in any manner whatsoever.[30] If, however, we decide that the matter in the corpse must have a substantial form, this must be a new form altogether.[31] Then, although we do have a body, it is a different body entirely.

[28] William de la Mare, *Correctorium fratris Thomae*, pp. 129–30 (a. 31).

[29] See discussion in J.-L. Solère, 'Was the eye in the tomb? On the metaphysical and historical interest of some strange quodlibetal questions', in *Theological Quodlibeta in the Middle Ages: the Thirteenth Century*, ed. C. Schabel (Brill's Companions to the Christian Tradition, Leiden, 2006), pp. 526–58, esp. at p. 530.

[30] 'Materia prima nec est quid, nec est quantum, nec quale, nec aliquid aliorum quibus ens est determinatum' (*Les 'Auctoritates Aristotelis': un florilège médiéval*, ed. J. Hamesse (Louvain, 1974), p. 128).

[31] This possible consequence of the theory of the unicity of substantial form for Christ's corpse was identified earlier, by Henry of Ghent in his *Opera omnia*, v. 14–17 (*Quodlibet* I.4c (dated 1276)).

For de la Mare, therefore, the faith demands a plurality of substantial forms in a human being, especially an additional bodily form giving the body existence independently of the soul and remaining after the soul's separation. The human being's essential unity, meanwhile, can be maintained if this subsidiary bodily form is understood to be intrinsically incomplete, bestowing an incomplete act of existence, in such a way that it is in potency to and perfected by the soul (*esse … est incompletum et in potentia ad esse completum*).[32]

With what conceptual resources could Aquinas's Dominican defenders respond to William de la Mare? Though it has not been very well understood, Aquinas did develop an account of the body's autonomy relative to the soul. If we take seriously his concern for the correct understanding of the bodily resurrection, a point of doctrine which clearly implies that the material part of human nature makes its own contribution to the person, then this should come as no surprise. Aquinas specifies, for instance, that the human essence ('what it is to be' human) comprises not only form, or the soul, but matter too.[33] Furthermore, Aquinas pointedly explains that the matter which enters into human nature is not mere prime matter, 'common to all things', but a differentiated material arrangement which is the intrinsically appropriate subject for a rational soul. He calls this the '*proper* matter' (*materia propria*) of the human being.[34] Finally, although he holds that the soul is the body's only substantial form, Aquinas does not think that the soul is a shape or a physical structure. For Aquinas, there is another form in a body which gives it its physical structure and proportions, spreading out its organic parts into particular positions relative to one another and marking out and particularizing its matter. Importantly, this bodily form is not a substantial form, but an 'accidental' form, or a property of the bodily substance, meaning that it depends, for its existence, on the continued union between matter and soul. Aquinas calls this structuring accidental form 'dimensive quantity' (*quantitas dimensiva*).[35]

[32] William de la Mare, *Correctorium fratris Thomae*, p. 133 (a. 31).

[33] Aquinas, *Opera omnia*, iv. 330 (*Summa theologiae*, I, q. 29, a. 2, ad 3). For further discussion, see Fitzpatrick, *Thomas Aquinas on Bodily Identity*, pp. 83–91.

[34] Thomas Aquinas, *In Metaphysicam Aristotelis commentaria*, ed. M.-R. Cathala (Turin, 1935), p. 503 (VIII. lect. 4, § 1735), beginning 'Quia vero, licet materia prima sit communis omnibus, tamen materiae propriae sunt diversae diversorum'. For further discussion, see Fitzpatrick, *Thomas Aquinas on Bodily Identity*, pp. 88–91.

[35] Aquinas, *Opera omnia*, xii. 183 (*Summa theologiae*, III, q. 76, a. 3, ad 2), beginning: 'determinata distantia partium in corpore organico'; and v. 207 (*Summa theologiae*, I, q. 75, a. 7c), beginning: 'nec poterit dici materia haec alia ab illa'. Constraints of space prevent further discussion of the pivotal role which dimensive quantity has to play in Aquinas's account of the human body's composition, individuality and identity over time. For a full

Aquinas's statements on the subject of post-mortem bodily continuity, however, could be deeply ambiguous and were never brought together in one place, let alone in a discussion of Christ's corpse. Aquinas asks whether Christ's body was the same in number living and dead at *Summa theologiae*, III, q. 50, a. 5, answering simply as follows:

> [A] body that ceases to be alive does not remain totally the same ... The dead body of any other human being does not remain united to any abiding hypostasis, as Christ's dead body did. And therefore the dead body of any other human is not the same absolutely [*simpliciter*], but only relatively [*secundum quid*], because it is the same according to its matter [*secundum materiam*], but not according to form. But the body of Christ remains the same absolutely, because of the identity of the *supposit* [*propter identitatem suppositi*].[36]

Here, Aquinas confirms there is physical continuity across bodily death, including Christ's. This continuity is not on the level of substantial form, or else the body would not have died at all, but rather on the level of matter. Aquinas does not actually say a new form is introduced into Christ's corpse, nor does he explain what continuity 'according to matter' really means. Instead, at the crux of his argument is the corpse's continued union to the same ultimate metaphysical subject, namely the divine hypostasis, *supposit* (*suppositum*), or person of Christ. The (presupposed) continuing hypostatic union of the divinity to the components of Christ's human nature guarantees the absolute identity of living body and corpse in this unique case.

Elsewhere, it is true, Aquinas suggests that a new substantial form is introduced into a dead body, albeit an imperfect form, as here in his commentary on Aristotle's *De generatione et corruptione*, I.3:

> [F]or it is not that, with the soul separated, the body of the animal is resolved immediately into the elements; but this happens through several intermediate corruptions, as several imperfect forms succeed one another in matter [*succedentibus ... formis imperfectis*], like the form of the dead body [*forma corporis mortui*], and afterwards the form of the decomposed body.[37]

Again, how should the material continuity Aquinas posits between living body and corpse be construed? Aquinas nowhere suggests that all that persists is prime matter. Moreover, his general insistence on the importance of proper matter ('the proper matters of different things are different'[38]) dovetails with his deep commitment to the Aristotelian idea of material

account, see Fitzpatrick, *Thomas Aquinas on Bodily Identity*, esp. pp. 96–103, 118–27, 135–41.

[36] Aquinas, see, *Opera omnia*, xi. 484 (*Summa theologiae*, III, q. 50, a. 5c and ad 1).

[37] Thomas Aquinas, *Opera omnia*, iii. 292 (*In De gen. et corr.*, I, lect. 8, § 3(60)).

[38] Aquinas, *In Metaphysicam*, VIII. lect. 4, § 1735 (Latin text above, n. 34).

causation (that in order for a certain form to manifest itself, certain material conditions must necessarily be present[39]). This makes it *a priori* unlikely that Aquinas would have conceded that the substratum persisting in Christ's dead body was mere prime matter, as opposed to, say, the proper matter of a corpse. Aquinas even says that in the generation and corruption of substances material resolution never proceeds as 'far down' as prime matter: prime matter is rather peripheral to Aquinas's account of substantial change.[40]

One model for post-mortem bodily continuity could be found in Aquinas's commentary on *Metaphysics* VII.16, in which Aristotle stated that the material parts of substances were not substances in their own right, but in a state of potentiality. Aquinas explains:

> When those things which are posited as parts are separated from one another with the dissolution of the whole, then they are beings in act [*entia in actu*], not as parts, but as matter existing under the privation of the form of the whole [*forma totius*]. This is evident of earth and fire and air, which, when they are parts of the mixed body, are not existents in act, but are in potency ... but when they are separated, then they are things existing in act, and not parts ... one might suppose that the parts of animated things, especially ... are ... so as to be in a state of potency close to act [*potentia propinqua actui*] ... because animated bodies are organic bodies possessing parts that are formally distinct [*distinctas secundum formam*]; hence those most of all are close to act ... nonetheless they are all in potency when the whole is one and continuous by nature.[41]

Perhaps this applied to a human being. One could say that the living body's complex material constituents, falling on the side of matter and potentiality when in composition with the soul (corresponding here to the 'form of the whole'), were so 'close to act' that they could take on an actuality or existence of their own once the human being corrupted (or died) at the soul's separation.

If his commentary on *Metaphysics* VII.16 contains obscurities (what exactly is the relationship between the body's material constituents which

[39] Aristotle, *Metaphysics*, VIII.4, 1044a 15–30; Aristotle, *Physics*, II.9, 200a24–b4. For commentary, see Fitzpatrick, *Thomas Aquinas on Bodily Identity*, pp. 31–8.

[40] Aquinas, *Opera omnia*, xii. 165 (*Summa theologiae*, III, q. 75, a. 3c): 'praeiacens autem materia in quam corpora mixta resolvi possunt, sunt quatuor elementa, non enim potest fieri resolutio in materiam primam, ita quod sine forma existat, quia materia sine forma esse non potest'. For further discussion, see Fitzpatrick, *Thomas Aquinas on Bodily Identity*, pp. 108–12, 156–8. This chapter disagrees with the discussion in R. Pasnau, *Thomas Aquinas on Human Nature: a Philosophical Study of Summa Theologiae 1a 75–89* (Cambridge, 2002), in particular that 'Aquinas's theory of matter is eliminative' (p. 131).

[41] Aquinas, *In Metaphysicam*, pp. 472–3 (VII., lect. 16, §§ 1633–1634, 1636).

are 'close to act' and any new substantial form?), then other passages in which Aquinas discusses post-mortem material continuity appear positively inconsistent. Analysing the general resurrection, Aquinas claims that traces of a body's structural form, its dimensive quantity, can remain to mark out its matter even after death. 'The matter which was subject to the soul remains', he says, 'under the same dimensions from that which it had it when it was individual matter'.[42] How could this be possible? Unlike Averroes, by whom this argument is inspired,[43] Aquinas consistently holds, elsewhere at least, that a substance is ontologically prior to its accidents:[44] if the human body corrupts at death, its accidents should go too.

Let us now turn to our Dominican *Correctoria*. Of the five responses to de la Mare, only three deal directly with article 31 of the *Correctorium fratris Thomae*.[45] The earliest, and least conceptually developed, is Richard Knapwell's *Quare*:[46]

> [B]rother Thomas responds in the final part of the *Summa*, saying that the body of Christ dead and living is the same in number absolutely [*idem numero simpliciter*] ... and this is because of the unity of the *supposit* of the divine person ... in which it subsisted. But it was not the same ... totally [*totaliter*], for then it would not have changed [*mutatum*], nor ... died, which it is heretical to say. And although the body changed through death, it does not follow that in death Christ assumed a new nature [*novam naturam*], both because the substantial form induced in death is not assumable in itself [*per se assumptibilis*], and because such a nature, a mutable and mortal one, was assumed in the beginning of His incarnation, at length to be changed through death and repaired through the glory of resurrection.[47]

Much here recalls Aquinas's *Summa theologiae*, III.50.5. Of course, Knapwell says, there is a sense in which Christ's corpse cannot have been totally the same as his living body: to claim otherwise would be to deny Christ's true

[42] Aquinas, *Opera omnia*, xv. 252 (*Summa contra Gentiles*, IV.81). For commentary, see Fitzpatrick, *Thomas Aquinas on Bodily Identity*, pp. 159–65.

[43] Fitzpatrick, *Thomas Aquinas on Bodily Identity*, pp. 69–78.

[44] E.g., Thomas Aquinas, *In quattuor libros Sententiarum* (Thomas Aquinas, *Opera omnia*, ed. R Busa (7 vols, Stuttgart-Bad Cannstatt, 1980), i. I.8.5.2c), *Summa theologiae*, I, q. 76, a. 6c. Cf. Aristotle, *Metaphysics*, VII.1, 1028a21–b2.

[45] The remaining two are William of Macclesfield's *Quaestione* (*c.*1284) (*Le correctorium corruptorii 'Quaestione': texte anonyme du ms. Merton 276*, ed. J.-P. Müller (Rome, 1954)); and Ramberto dei Primadizzi of Bologna's *Apologeticum veritatis* (1286–8) (*Apologeticum veritatis contra corruptorium*, ed. J.-P. Müller (Vatican, 1943)).

[46] For biography and bibliography, see S. Tugwell, 'Knapwell [Clapwell], Richard (*fl.* 1284–1286)', *ODNB* <https://doi.org/10.1093/ref:odnb/5434> [accessed 26 Aug. 2018].

[47] Richard Knapwell, *Quare*, in *Le Correctorium Corruptorii 'Quare'*, ed. P. Glorieux (Kain, 1927), p. 135 (a. 31).

death and tantamount to heresy.[48] However, for Knapwell, as for Aquinas, the absolute identity of the body, grounded on the hypostatic union, overrides any natural substantial mutation in the body's composition.

Note that Knapwell is ready to concede de la Mare's point that a new substantial form must have been introduced into Christ's corpse on the grounds that the Franciscan's objections are thereby neutralized. The new form does not imply a new nature was absorbed into the hypostatic union: the form is not assumed in its own right by the divinity; rather, the divinity originally assumed a mortal human nature, destined always to be transformed in death. Here, however, the analysis stops. Knapwell appears to assume concrete material continuity between living body and corpse (the entombed body is evidently the very same one which is to be resurrected), but he sidesteps the question of what this physical continuity consists in, be it prime matter or anything else.

In *Circa*, John of Paris,[49] like Richard Knapwell, grants that a new substantial form was introduced into Christ's corpse and denies this altered the hypostatic union: Christ voluntarily assumed a mortal body, death and all that followed from the separation of matter and soul.[50] John emphasizes, as 'the response of brother Thomas', that 'numerical identity is the identity of the supposit':[51] the unbroken hypostatic union guarantees the absolute identity of Christ's body living and dead. What is striking, however, is quite how much further than Knapwell John of Paris is willing to go in conceding de la Mare's interpretation of Aquinas. Crucially, John clarifies that, taking the hypostatic union out of the equation, the body in the tomb was a totally new, individual body: not only did it have a new substantial form, but all that remained on a material level was prime matter. Glossing Psalm XV: 10 ('nor will you give your holy one to see corruption'), John says: 'The body of Christ did not suffer complete dissolution ... not because in death it was not resolved into prime matter, but because the forms of the simple elements did not succeed the rational soul immediately, but rather the form of a mixed body [*forma mixti corporis*], which was never corrupted further'.[52] This picture of bodily corruption as involving a succession of ever lower forms is recognizable from Aquinas's commentary on *De generatione et corruptione* I.3. In John of Paris's hands, however, every other significant

[48] Cf. Aquinas's *Quodlibets* III.2.2c and IV.5c.

[49] For biography and bibliography, see R. L. Friedman, 'John of Paris', in *A Companion to Philosophy in the Middle Ages*, ed. J. J. E. Gracia and T. B. Noone (Oxford, 2003), pp. 382–3.

[50] John of Paris, *Le Correctorium Corruptorii 'Circa'*, ed. J.-P. Müller (Rome, 1941), p. 172 (a. 30 (31)).

[51] John of Paris, *Circa*, p. 170 (a. 30 (31)).

[52] John of Paris, *Circa*, p. 173 (a. 30 (31)).

aspect of Aquinas's thought on the composition of the corpse (notably, as we have said, his concern for concrete material continuity) has fallen away sharply. Why? It cannot be discounted out of hand that pure intellectual impulse was responsible. Yet, read closely, *Circa*'s argument indicates a more complex and interesting possibility. Not only, in John's view, could much of the Franciscan reading of Aquinas be safely conceded: it could also be positively instrumentalized to reinforce the unicist position, while simultaneously undermining the pluralist line.

First, John of Paris is happy to allow radical discontinuity between living body and corpse, at least in part because he is able to argue that even pluralists have to fall back on the corpse's union with the divinity in order to preserve bodily identity. The corporeal form which pluralists say remained in the corpse could hardly have remained in a generic way, John says. That form would have to establish the body in an entirely new species,[53] yielding nothing short of a new individual body:

> And it should not seem unfitting to the adversary that a new individual body [*novum singulare corporis*] and a new corporeity [*nova corporeitas*] were substantified [*substantificata*] in the divine *supposit* ... because they necessarily have to concede this, if they posit in Christ both a form of corporeity and a form of life, and that, with soul separated from body, the same corporeity remains as before ... That there should remain an individual of a subaltern genus, without a species ... is against reason in every way. Therefore it is necessary that this remaining corporeity gave the body of Christ ... an act of existence [*esse*] of a new species ... And so the adversary ought ... to concede that there was not the same species [or form] of the body in the body of Christ living and dead, but one and then another.[54]

Here, the pluralist position on bodily continuity is made to appear just as feeble as de la Mare's construal of Aquinas's position: in either case there was in effect a new form, and hence a new body, in the tomb.

Second, John of Paris evidently saw a particular theological advantage in taking up a reading of unicity theory which thoroughly diminished any meaningful autonomy of the material part of human nature relative to the soul. If everything essential to human nature, including everything essential to the body, 'radically remained [*radicaliter remansit*]' within the immortal soul as the one and only substantial form (and especially as the body's substantial form), then, when it came to explaining how the bodily

[53] This represents a significant hardening of the position found in Aquinas's commentary on *De generatione et corruptione*, I.3, where it was permitted that *formae imperfectae* could succeed the soul in matter.

[54] John of Paris, *Circa*, pp. 172–3 (a. 30 (31)).

resurrection could happen, the knotty problem of post-mortem material continuity could be circumvented entirely:

> [Christ] did not abandon the corporeity assumed in the incarnation, because this always remained in its root [*in radice*], namely in the separated soul, from which the divinity was not separated. It this sense, the Psalm [XV: 9] says: *My flesh shall rest in hope*, because the same flesh radically remained in the separated soul where it waited to be resurrected.[55]

John intends this not merely as an innovative solution to a theological problem, but as an anti-Franciscan attack on pluralist theory. As we know, the Dominican thinks he has been able to deduce that the pluralists' corporeal form effectively falls out of existence at Christ's death. How, then, could the very same form return at his resurrection?[56] Pluralist theory, John suggests, has heretical implications. In construing the theory of the unicity of form in this particular way, however, he ends up undermining one of the exact points of doctrine Aquinas intended the theory to preserve: the bodily resurrection literally understood.[57]

Robert Orford's[58] encounter with de la Mare's arguments pushed him to test the limits of the theory of the unicity of form in a completely different way. In article 31 of *Sciendum*, looking to bolster bodily autonomy relative to the soul, Orford alters Aquinas's metaphysical framework so significantly that he threatens the human being's intrinsic unity. Orford begins by clarifying his terms: regarding everything composed of matter and form, we must consider 'what it is' (*quod est*), namely a composite of matter and form; and 'that by which it is' (*quo est*), or that which gives it its existence, namely form.[59] So far, so straightforward. Then, however, Orford appears to advance a pluralist account of human composition:

[55] John of Paris, *Circa*, p. 172 (a. 30 (31)), editor's emphasis, my insertions.

[56] In their discussions of resurrection, scholastic theologians of the late 13th century tended to assume that continuity was necessary for identity, taking it as axiomatic that 'Quorum substantia deperit, non redeunt eodem numero, sed specie' (Hamesse, '*Auctoritates Aristotelis*', p. 171). Cf. Aristotle, *De generatione et corruptione*, II.11, 338b14–18.

[57] *Pace* Bynum, who traces this theory of 'form as identity' back to Aquinas himself ('Material continuity, personal survival', pp. 258–60). John of Paris was criticized for denying a literal understanding of the resurrection when his *Sentences* commentary was censured in 1295. His *apologia* is edited in P. Glorieux, 'Un mémoire justificatif de Bernard de Trilia', *Revue des sciences philosophiques et théologiques*, xvii (1928), 407–15, at p. 411.

[58] For biography and bibliography, see S. F. Gaine, 'Orford, Robert [Robert of Orford] (fl. c.1280–c.1293)', *ODNB* <https://doi.org/10.1093/ref:odnb/20827> [accessed 26 Aug. 2018].

[59] 'in omni re composita ex materia et forma est duo considerare, scilicet quod est et quo est. Quod est, est ipsum suppositum subsistens compositum ex utroque; quo est, est forma' (Robert Orford, *Correctorium corruptorii 'Sciendum'*, ed. P. Glorieux (Paris, 1956), pp. 137–8 (a. 31)).

> But to give an absolute act of existence [*esse simpliciter*], namely substantial existence [*esse substantiale*], happens in two ways, either partially, or totally. Now, for there to be several forms in a thing which give partial substantial existence is not unfitting, more precisely it is necessary ... and according as the form of the whole [*forma totius*] is more noble, a greater plurality of partial forms [*pluralitas formarum partialium*] is required ... because ... according as it is more powerful in its operations, it requires a greater diversity in the parts [of the body].[60]

Recognizing the danger, Orford tries to distance himself from pluralist theory, explaining that none of the 'partial' substantial forms necessary in a complex organism like a human actually give existence in their own right: rather, they passively participate in the act of existence communicated by the soul as 'form of the whole [*forma totius*]'.[61] This 'total' act of existence, meanwhile, is the metaphysical glue binding soul to body:

> These [partial forms] ... do not give an act of existence impeding the form of the whole, but they participate in the form of the whole [*participant formam totius*] ... If we should speak of ... the form that gives total substantial being [*esse substantiale totale*], thus it is impossible for there to be several forms in a single thing ... such a substance would be not one whole but several ... From a single form, as from the rational soul, which contains in itself whatever the inferior forms, like the vegetative and the sensitive soul, contain, a human being is human and an animal and living and a body.[62]

Note, in particular, that although the rational soul gives existence to the body, it virtually contains only two 'inferior forms': the sensitive and the vegetative souls. The 'partial substantial forms' composing the body, in contrast, appear to be essentially distinct from the soul, even if they participate in the act of existence which the soul communicates. Orford even says that body and soul 'differ according to their essence', although they 'come together [*conveniunt*] in a single act of existence'.[63]

This is a startling interpretation of Aquinas's theory of the unicity of form. For Aquinas, the soul did enter into what the body essentially was, as its only nature-determining form. That was rather the point. For Orford,

[60] Orford, *Sciendum*, p. 138 (a. 31).

[61] Cf. the Franciscan pluralist Peter John Olivi, who posited a theory of 'formal parts' (*partes formales*), each actively communicating a grade of being (*gradum essendi*) (not per se but *qua* parts of a whole), from which, collectively, a 'total form' (*forma totalis*) 'arose' (*consurgit*) (*Petrus Iohannis Olivi Quaestiones in secundum librum sententiarum*, ed. B. Jansen (3 vols, Ad Claras Aquas, 1922–6), ii. 36 (II.50 ad 1)).

[62] Orford, *Sciendum*, pp. 138–9 (a. 31).

[63] Orford, *Sciendum*, pp. 132–3 (a. 29).

the body has its own (albeit partial) form and the soul does not enter into what it is at all. Even the Franciscan de la Mare argued that the soul entered into the body's essence, intrinsically perfecting it. As Orford sees it, however, there is none of this essential overlap between body and soul: a single act of existence, again, is all that connects the two. Yet now, of course, Orford can argue that *what* the body of Christ is (*quod est*) survives in its entirety across his death:

> [T]he body of Christ can be understood in two ways: with regard either to what it is [*quod est*] or that by which it is [*quo est*]. That by which it is, according as the soul makes the human being, is the form of the whole; and the body loses this form when the soul, through death, is separated ... But if we should speak of the body of Christ as regards that which it is [*quantum ad id quod est*], it is a body composed of matter and the form corresponding to it, and thus it remains the same in number living and dead.[64]

In contrast to Richard Knapwell and John of Paris, Orford can also avoid conceding de la Mare's suggestion that there must have been a new substantial form introduced into Christ's corpse, accurately noting that 'Thomas can never be found to have said this *about the body of Christ*'.[65] Instead, citing Aristotle's *Metaphysics*, VII.16, Orford explains that the body's form (or 'partial forms' or, here, 'form(s) of the parts'), although falling on the side of potency while in the composite, take on an act of existence of their own upon the soul's separation, emerging thereby as a new form of the whole:

> [W]ith the form of the whole removed, the form of the part [*forma partis*] ... becomes the form of the whole ... for the form of the part, with the form of the whole remaining, was in potency that it be the form of the whole ... hence just as when a worm [*anguilla*] is divided no new form is introduced, but souls which were in a state of potency close to act [*potentia propinqua actui*] advance into act [*vadunt in actum*], the same is to be understood of the forms of the parts which are similarly in a state of potency close to act, according to the Philosopher in *Metaphysics* VII.[66]

Along with some of the language in which this account of post-mortem bodily continuity is couched – the departure of the soul as removal of the form of the whole; the material parts of the body subsisting in a state of potency close to act – the analogy of the divided worm, whose latent forms (here souls) spring forth into act, also recalls Aquinas's commentary on Aristotle's *Metaphysics*, VII.16.[67] Again, it is Orford's insistence on an

[64] Orford, *Sciendum*, p. 139 (a. 31).
[65] Orford, *Sciendum*, p. 141 (a. 31), my emphasis.
[66] Orford, *Sciendum*, p. 142 (a. 31).
[67] Aquinas, *In Metaphysicam*, VII. lect. 16, § 1635.

essentially distinct corporeal form (or forms) which significantly distances his thought from Aquinas's.

Orford's divergence from Aquinas (and Richard Knapwell and John of Paris), is exposed again in how he handles the question of the hypostatic union. Having just shown that the body of Christ was the same in number across death as regards what it is [*quod est*], Orford adds that 'besides this identity, there is the identity of the *supposit* [*suppositum*], which gives a greater unity [*maior unitas*]'.[68] What was the crux of the argument for the other Dominicans is plainly an afterthought here. If Orford's claim is that Christ's living body and corpse were the same in number anyway, then what possible greater identity can be guaranteed by the hypostatic union? Orford's reference to the divine *supposit* makes sense as an indication of intellectual allegiance to his Dominican brothers, a marker of what Stephen Marrone would call 'intellectual consanguinity',[69] but not as a necessary stage in his argument.

What happened next?[70] Richard Knapwell made another, more decisive, intervention with his *Quaestio disputata de unitate formae* (1285), now as regent master in theology at Oxford. He picked up John of Paris's anti-pluralist argument with regard to the resurrection, developing it with the help of the Averroan theory of a quantitative structure in matter to which Aquinas had been so attracted. The pluralists' corporeal form would eventually disintegrate as the corpse decayed, Knapwell argued: only if matter had its own 'nature of dimensive quantity' (*natura quantitatis dimensivae*) could the material belonging to each individual body be marked out between their death and the general resurrection.[71] This line of argument aggravated the Franciscans Roger Marston, also regent in theology at Oxford,[72] and John Peckham at Canterbury: Knapwell's *Quaestio disputata* was the proximate target of the condemnation of 1286, whose terms made particular reference to 'dimensions' and 'quantity' in the matter of dead bodies.[73]

Knapwell, eventually, came the closest of our three Dominicans to capturing what Aquinas was trying to say about postmortem bodily

[68] Orford, *Sciendum*, p. 141 (a. 31).

[69] Marrone, *The Light of Thy Countenance*, ii. 571.

[70] Some Dominicans' thought on these issues can be found in in A. Fitzpatrick, 'Dominican theology at the early fourteenth-century universities: bodily identity in the quodlibets of Nicholas Trivet, Hervaeus Natalis, and John of Naples', in *King's Hall, Cambridge and the Fourteenth-Century Universities: New Perspectives*, ed. J. Marenbon (forthcoming).

[71] Richard Knapwell, *Quaestio disputata de unitate formae*, ed. F. E. Kelley (Paris, 1982), pp. 67–8 (*responsio* section). For commentary, see Fitzpatrick, *Thomas Aquinas on Bodily Identity*, pp. 178–9.

[72] R. Marston, *Quodlibeta Quatuor*, ed. G. Etzkorn and I. Brady (Grottaferrata, 1994), p. 427 (IV.27 ad 1).

[73] John Peckham, *Registrum*, iii. 922–3, cf. also 866.

continuity, but that is not the point this chapter wishes to make.[74] Neither is the point simply that William de la Mare distorted Aquinas's thought, nor that, in responding to the Franciscan, Aquinas's earliest Dominican defenders distorted it too – even in ways which were mutually incompatible. The purpose of examining the *Correctoria* so closely has been to show just how deliberate, and just how precisely and inextricably embedded within the institutional context of inter-order rivalry, were Richard Knapwell's, John of Paris's and Robert Orford's very distinct readings of Aquinas.

Russell Friedman has identified the competition between Franciscan and Dominican 'intellectual traditions' as a, even *the*, principal factor which not simply drove scholastic debate forward in a general way but also shaped quite specifically the way in which debate surrounding critical concepts and ideas developed. Those oppositional dynamics apply here. Our three Dominicans 'neither ignored nor flatly denied' de la Mare's critique.[75] Rather, in order to respond effectively, they conceded and incorporated parts of that critique, either neutralizing it or proceeding to show how unicist theory remained superior. Plainly, these individuals were intellectuals wholeheartedly committed to their institutions and deeply motivated by the politics of group opposition, even though they were certainly not a 'school', and barely even 'Thomistic', in the exact way Roensch would have liked them to be.

[74] See, further, Fitzpatrick, *Thomas Aquinas on Bodily Identity*, pp. 159–65, 178–9.

[75] Friedman, *Intellectual Traditions at the Medieval University*, i. 22.

3. Italian universities, arts masters and interpreting Pomponazzi's *De immortalitate animae*

John Marenbon

This study of Pietro Pomponazzi in relation to the institutions which shaped his work is intended to contribute to the wider discussion of the historiography of institutions and individuals in medieval scholasticism opened up by the editors in their substantial, thought-provoking introduction. It concentrates on the most famous and interpretatively controversial feature of Pomponazzi's thought, the position he takes on the immortality of the human soul in his *De immortalitate animae*. The first section gives a neutral summary of the argument of Pomponazzi's treatise and the different interpretations which have been proposed. The second section looks at how considering Pomponazzi's institutional background as an arts master in the north Italian universities helps to solve the interpretative problem. However, Pomponazzi was far from a simple representative of a type: the third section will consider some of the ways in which he defied institutional norms and how they relate to interpreting his views about the soul.[1]

De immortalitate animae*: the argument and its interpretation*

De immortalitate sets out to answer two questions put to Pomponazzi by his one-time pupil, the Dominican Girolamo Natale of Ragusa.[2] What does

[1] The very inclusion in a book about *medieval* scholasticism of Pomponazzi, who did his most important work in the early 16th century, points to an interesting problem. The methods and practices characteristic of medieval scholasticism flourished from *c.*1050 to *c.*1700, a period which only partially coincides with what most historians identify as the middle ages. Related problems of chronology and the relation between 'medieval' and 'renaissance' philosophy are discussed in J. Marenbon, 'When was medieval philosophy?' (inaugural lecture, University of Cambridge, 2011) <https://www.repository.cam.ac.uk/handle/1810/240658?show=full> [accessed 24 Oct. 2019]; 'Latin philosophy, 1350–1550', in *The Oxford Handbook of Medieval Philosophy*, ed. J. Marenbon (Oxford and New York, 2012), pp. 222–44; 'When did medieval philosophy begin?', in *Ingenio facilis. Per Giovanni Orlandi (1938–2007)*, ed. P. Chiesa, A. M. Fagnoni and R. E. Gugliemetti (Florence, 2017), pp. 149–62.

[2] P. Pomponazzi, *Traité de l'immortalitate de l'âme/ Tractatus de immortalitate animae*, ed.

J. Marenbon, 'Italian universities, arts masters and interpreting Pomponazzi's *De immortalitate animae*', in *Individuals and Institutions in Medieval Scholasticism*, ed. A. Fitzpatrick and J. Sabapathy (London, 2020), pp. 89–106.

Pomponazzi think about the immortality of the human soul 'putting all revelation and miracles aside, and without going beyond the boundaries of nature [*pure infra naturales limites*]'; and what does he think about Aristotle's view of this matter? Starting (chapter 1) from the generally accepted view that the nature of human beings is ambiguous (*anceps*), in between mortality and immortality, and from the logical truth that nothing can be mortal and immortal at the same time, Pomponazzi spells out (chapter 2) six possibilities. Either (A) humans have two different natures, by one of which they are mortal, by the other of which they are immortal; or (B) they are at once mortal and immortal by one and the same nature. In the first case, either (Ai) each human has his/her own mortal and his/her own immortal nature; or (Aii) there is one immortal nature for all humans, but each has his/her own mortal natures; or (Aiii) vice versa, there is one mortal nature for all, but an immortal nature for each. In the second case, since it would be contradictory for anything to be mortal without qualification and immortal without qualification, the one nature by which each human is both mortal and immortal must be either (Bi) immortal without qualification (*simpliciter*) and mortal with qualification (*secundum quid*); or (Bii) mortal without qualification and immortal with qualification; or (Biii) both mortal and immortal with qualification. (Aiii) and (Biii) are both merely theoretically possible positions, held by no one. The four remaining positions, however, correspond to the main views held in Pomponazzi's day about the immortality of the human soul.

(Ai) is the Platonic view, as expounded by Ficino (not mentioned by name, but clearly in Pomponazzi's mind). It is recounted and dismissed briefly (chapters 5–6). (Aii) is the view of Averroes, who held that there is one immortal, incorporeal intellect shared by all humans, whose individual souls are themselves mortal. Many of Pomponazzi's contemporaries in the Italian universities subscribed to this interpretation as the correct reading of Aristotle.[3] Here, however, he begins by declaring (chapter 4) that he has nothing himself to add to Aquinas's exposition of the falsity of this opinion which 'leaves nothing intact, nor any reply that might be made on Averroes's behalf unrefuted'.[4] Pomponazzi confines himself, therefore, to an extended discussion of how Averroes is not merely wrong, but unfaithful to Aristotle's text.

T. Gontier (Paris, 2012), p. 5 (Proem 5). Gontier's long introduction is one of the best recent studies of the treatise, as is that in *Pietro Pomponazzi. Trattato sull'immortalità dell'anima*, trans. V. Perrone Compagni (Florence, 1999).

3 See G. di Napoli, *L'immortalità dell'anima nel Rinascimento* (Turin, 1963), pp. 179–226.

4 Pomponazzi, *De immortalitate animae*, p. 21 (4.24).

(Bi) is Aquinas's view. It is expounded in chapter 7; and Pomponazzi begins chapter 8 by declaring he has no doubt about the truth of this position 'since Holy Scripture, which should be preferred to any human reasoning or experience, since it has been given by God, endorses this position'.[5] However, he continues, reiterating his description in the preface of the scope of his discussion, he *does* think that it is questionable whether the position, as Aquinas thought, is in accordance with Aristotle's texts and whether it can be rationally established or, rather, makes presuppositions based on revelation or belief. There follows a long sequence of arguments against both the fidelity to Aristotle and the rational coherence of Aquinas's view. (Bii) is Pomponazzi's own view: it can be called 'mortalism' because according to it the human soul is unqualifiedly mortal and immortal only with qualification. Since this view is the mirror-opposite of Aquinas's, it is not surprising that Pomponazzi's arguments against Aquinas and his defence of his own position against possible objections follow the same lines.

Despite the intricacy of this discussion, Pomponazzi's central point, to which he returns again and again, is straightforward. For Aristotle, intellection itself is an incorporeal action and Pomponazzi follows him and the whole medieval tradition in regarding it as such. However, in *De anima* Aristotle adds that the human soul does not engage in intellection without having imaginative images (*phantasmata*).[6] In Aristotelian psychology, imaginative images belong to the corporeal sensible soul: to its inner senses, which are situated in specific parts of the brain. Aristotle himself, in a phrase often quoted by Pomponazzi, comments that 'if intellection [*intelligere*] either is imagination [*phantasia*] or is not without imagination, then it cannot be separated' (that is, from the body).[7] Pomponazzi puts the position in terms of subject and object. The human intellect does not require the body as a subject: that is to say, it does not need anything bodily in order to function as such; but it does require something bodily as an object, because it cannot in fact function without forming some corporeal image (*idolum*).[8] As a result the human soul is without qualification inseparable and so mortal, even though – because it participates in the incorporeal action of intellection – it is immortal with qualification.

After four chapters (9–12) setting out this position and defending it from counter-arguments, Pomponazzi moves, in chapter 13, to objections of a different sort. These objections are not based on attacking the coherence of Pomponazzi's theory of the soul, or its fidelity to Aristotle, but on the

5 Pomponazzi, *De immortalitate animae*, p. 57 (8.94).

6 Aristotle, *De anima*, III, 431a16–17; 432a8–9.

7 Aristotle, *De anima*, I, 403a8–10.

8 Pomponazzi, *De immortalitate animae*, pp. 89–91 (9.150).

unacceptability of mortalism in general and its consequences. They include, among others, the arguments that, if humans are mortal, then self-sacrifice for a friend or the common good will be irrational; that, since the good and evil are frequently not fittingly rewarded or punished in their earthly lives, God either does not govern the universe or is wicked; and that all the religious laws (*leges*) say the soul is immortal and those who have denied its immortality were impious and wicked. Pomponazzi's replies (chapter 14) are even bolder than his earlier arguments. The essential reward for virtuous actions, he contends, is simply that of being virtuous; and the prospect of other 'accidental' rewards, even heavenly ones, reduces the essential reward gained by acting well. From this perspective, not only are God's goodness and justice vindicated simply by virtuous people being virtuous – the implication is also that the pagan mortalist is able to be more virtuous than any Christian. Pomponazzi is able to assemble a list of great and worthy figures who, it seems, were mortalists, among them Homer, Simonides, Galen, Hippocrates, Pliny, Seneca, al-Farabi and Ibn Gabirol.[9] As for the point that all the laws support human immortality, Pomponazzi remarks that 'since there are just three laws – that of Christ, or Moses and of Mohammed – either they are all false, and so everyone is mistaken, or at least two of them are false, and so the greater part of the world is mistaken'.[10] He then goes on to suggest that, in any case, many of those who have taught there is an afterlife have done so not because they thought it was true, but so as to produce good conduct. Only a very few people, he argues, will act well for the sake of virtue alone; and for most the threat of punishment in an afterlife is the only way to restrain their wickedness.[11]

Yet, in the final chapter, Pomponazzi declares that the immortality of the soul is 'a neutral problem', like that of the eternity of the world. Problems were considered to be neutral when no proof could be found for either of their contradictory sides. This was exactly how Aquinas thought about the eternity of the world, but not, of course, about the immortality of the soul. Pomponazzi goes to say both that on such a question, on which many are in doubt, only God can be certain; and yet that we cannot afford not to be certain about such a matter, since this uncertainty means we do not know our end or goal and so cannot decide how to act: 'If the soul is immortal we should despise earthly things and seek eternal ones; but if it is mortal, we should follow the opposite path'.[12]

[9] Pomponazzi, *De immortalitate animae*, pp. 203–5 (14.308).
[10] Pomponazzi, *De immortalitate animae*, p. 185 (14.279).
[11] Pomponazzi, *De immortalitate animae*, pp. 185–7 (14.280–1).
[12] Pomponazzi, *De immortalitate animae*, p. 211 (15.317).

However, we need not remain in doubt. The question is resolved, Pomponazzi declares, by the statements of revelation in the Old and New Testaments; and there are overwhelming reasons, because of the way in which the revelation has been made, to accept its truth. Pomponazzi does not go into these reasons himself, but he refers readers to the expositions by both Aquinas and Scotus.[13] The immortality of the soul is, indeed, an article of faith and, as such, it should be proved through arguments proper to matters of faith, that is to say, through revelation and the Bible.[14]

Clearly, the *De immortalitate* poses an interpretative problem. Given the length and power of the arguments for mortalism, to which no replies are developed, and the absence of arguments left unrefuted for immortalism, it is hard to see how the preceding chapters bear out the view, announced in chapter 15, that the immortality of the soul is a neutral problem. Some interpreters, therefore, hold that Pomponazzi really thought that the soul was mortal; and that chapter 15 and the other places where he professes his personal adherence to the Church's teaching are dissimulations, included in order to allow the book to be published and save its author from trial as a heretic. Others accept the sincerity of these professions.

These differences over how to interpret Pomponazzi arose from the very beginning.[15] Some of his opponents, such as Ambrogio Fiandino and Bartolomeo Spina, treated him as unqualifiedly denying the immortality of the soul or as writing in such a way as to undermine people's faith.[16] In Venice Pomponazzi was declared a heretic and it was ordered that copies of *De immortalitate* should be burned;[17] and in Rome the master of the apostolic palace, Silvestro Mazzolini, applauded this decision, considering

[13] Pomponazzi, *De immortalitate animae*, p. 213 (15.318). He refers to Aquinas's *Summa contra Gentiles*, Prologue, p. 6; and to Scotus's *Ordinatio*, Prologue, pt. 2, q. unica (a very long and detailed discussion).

[14] Pomponazzi, *De immortalitate animae*, p. 213 (15.319).

[15] On the controversy provoked by *De immortalitate*, which produced many books and lasted beyond Pomponazzi's own life, see E. Gilson, 'Autour de Pomponazzi. Problématique de l'immortalité de l'âme en Italie au début du XVIe siècle', *Archives d'histoire doctrinale et littéraire du Moyen Âge*, xxxvi (1961), 163–279, at pp. 196–277; di Napoli, *L'Immortalità dell'anima*, pp. 277–338; and M. L. Pine, *Pietro Pomponazzi: Radical Philosopher of the Renaissance* (Padua, 1986), pp. 124–234.

[16] On Ambrogio, see Gilson, 'Autour de Pomponazzi', pp. 230–6; di Napoli, *L'Immortalità dell'anima*, pp. 300–1; Pine, *Pietro Pomponazzi*, pp. 133–4 (and in the following, synthetic, discussion); on Spina, see Gilson, 'Autour de Pomponazzi', pp. 196–206; di Napoli, *L'Immortalità dell'anima*, pp. 302–9; Pine, *Pietro Pomponazzi*, pp. 134–5 (and in the following, synthetic, discussion).

[17] See P. Pomponazzi, *Apologia*, in *Pietro Pomponazzi. Tutti i trattati peripatetici*, ed. F. P. Raimondi and J. M. García Valverde (Milan, 2013), pp. 1107–537, at pp. 1492–4 (III, 2). References to the *Apologia* are to this edition.

that Pomponazzi's book weakened and destroyed the faith in the minds of the young.[18] However, his most considered opponents, Gasparo Contarini, a one-time pupil, Venetian diplomat and future cardinal, and Agostino Nifo, a colleague and rival, accepted that Pomponazzi was discussing just what could be established by arguments based on natural reason, although they differed from his conclusions; while the Dominican Chrysostom Javelli publicly affirmed Pomponazzi's religious sincerity.[19] Pietro Bembo appears to have stopped a papal call for a retraction in its tracks and declared he found nothing heretical in the treatise.[20]

Later reactions are similarly divided. In the seventeenth century *De immortalitate* was frequently cited, though rarely directly, by 'atheists' – those who questioned aspects of Christian doctrine, including post-mortem survival.[21] However, in his *Dictionnaire historique et critique* Bayle fully accepted that Pomponazzi wished simply to say that rational proof of the soul's immortality is impossible; and Bayle's discussion was influential in many circles.[22] Recent scholars, too, are split. Giovanni di Napoli and, more stridently, Martin Pine and Burkhard Mojsisch see Pomponazzi as dissimulating a disbelief in personal immortality.[23] However, the opposite view, put polemically by Kristeller half a century ago, is shared, with more nuance, by most of the leading scholars today.[24] All, however, would agree that the problem is not, as some earlier historians thought, one of deciding whether or not Pomponazzi is a herald of modernity; but rather one of reconstructing the framework within which he worked and thought so that the elusive, and probably complex, intention behind his text can be identified. How far does investigating Pomponazzi's institutional background help towards this aim?

[18] See *Pietro Pomponazzi. Apologia*, trans. V. Perrone Compagni (Florence, 2011), p. 254, n. 17, quoting from Mazzolini's own *De strigmagarum demonumque mirandis* (1521). Pomponazzi himself gives a completely different account, in which Mazzolini laughs and says he approves of the book (*Apologia*, p. 1494 (III, 2)).

[19] See Gilson, 'Autour de Pomponazzi', p. 265; on Javelli, see below, p. 100.

[20] Pomponazzi, *Apologia*, p. 1494 (III, 2); cf. B. Nardi, *Studi su Pietro Pomponazzi* (Florence, 1965), pp. 25–7.

[21] See Gontier's comments in *De immortalitate*, introduction, pp. lxi–lxii.

[22] See P. Bayle, *Dictionnaire historique et critique* (4 vols, Amsterdam, 1740), iii. 777–83; cf. M. Longo, 'L'immagine di Pomponazzi nella "prima Aufklärung"', in *Pietro Pomponazzi. Tradizione e dissenso*, ed. M. Sgarbi (Florence, 2010), pp. 407–34.

[23] di Napoli, *L'Immortalità dell'anima*, pp. 274–5; Pine, *Pietro Pomponazzi*, *passim*; *Pietro Pomponazzi. Abhandlung über die Unsterblichkeit der Seele*, trans. B. Mojsisch (Philosophische Bibliothek, ccccxxxiv, Hamburg, 1990), pp. ix–xiv.

[24] P. O. Kristeller, 'The myth of renaissance atheism and the French tradition of free thought', *Jour. Hist. Philosophy*, vi (1968), 233–43; cf. the introduction to Gontier's edition of *De immortalitate* and, though her view does not fit neatly into either alternative, Perrone Compagni, *Trattato*, pp. lxxxv–xcvi.

Pomponazzi the institutional insider

Pomponazzi is more clearly and closely tied to a particular sort of institution than most thinkers. No philosopher of the long middle ages was more a creature of the university system, a true academic insider. Born in Mantua in 1462, he studied at Padua university, one of the two most prestigious in Italy. When his studies were finished in 1487, he became a teacher there, staying – except for a three-year break at the court in Ferrara at the very end of the century – until 1509, when the university was closed due to Padua's rebellion and the Venetian reconquest. Then, from 1511 until his death in 1525, Pomponazzi taught at Bologna, the other leading Italian university.[25] Pomponazzi did not merely work within the system: he used the celebrity he gained to play the system to his own advantage, in a way that some of today's academic superstars would be happy if they could emulate. When the temporary closure of the universities at Padua and then Ferrara left Pomponazzi without a job, Bologna took the opportunity to poach him. At first he had to take a cut in salary, though he was still paid more than twice as much as the professorial average, but then, in the face of counter-bids from Pisa, by 1518 the university had to pay him three times the original sum in order to retain him.[26]

Pomponazzi's writings are mostly closely linked to his university teaching. Many of them are, indeed, not properly speaking his *writings* at all, but *reportationes* of his lectures on exactly the texts which a professor of arts would have been expected to teach – especially Aristotle's physical works, with a particular concentration on the *De anima*.[27] These reports can represent only a fraction of his teaching activity over more than thirty years. The works he printed in his lifetime were almost all gathered together in the *Tractatus acutissimi, utillimi et mere peripatetici*, published in the year of his death.[28] They include treatises on the interpretation of Aristotelian physics by the fourteenth-century Oxford thinkers so influential in the Italian universities; and one on *Nutrition and Growth*, closely linked to Aristotle's discussions of these themes; along with the *De immortalitate animae* and the treatises – the *Apologia* and the *Defensorium* – which Pomponazzi wrote in response to its critics. These three texts are almost as closely linked with

[25] There is a good account of Pomponazzi's career in Pine, *Pietro Pomponazzi*, pp. 39–52.

[26] See P. F. Grendler, *The Universities of the Italian Renaissance* (Baltimore, Md., 2002), pp. 15–16.

[27] These are listed in Gontier's edition of *De immortalitate*, pp. lxxvii–lxxviii.

[28] P. Pomponazzi, *Tractatus acutissimi, utillimi et mere peripatetici* (Venice, 1525). The works in this collection have been republished, closely based on the text here, but collated with the first editions, with Italian translation, notes and introductions in Raimondi and García, *Pietro Pomponazzi*.

Pomponazzi's teaching as the rest of the volume, since *De immortalitate*, first published in 1516, is based on the lectures he had been giving on *De anima* from the turn of the century. There are, finally, two further important works, which Pomponazzi wrote in his last years and circulated in manuscript but chose not to have printed in his lifetime: *De incantationibus* and *De fato, de libero arbitrio et de praedestinatione*.

The institution to which Pomponazzi belonged so thoroughly was part of a very special sort of medieval university: the arts faculty in its particular, fourteenth- to seventeenth-century Italian variant, as illustrated by its two outstanding examples, Padua and Bologna.[29] Both universities were outstanding centres for medicine and law. Arts were considered part of the preparation for the doctorate in medicine, although it was possible to take a doctorate just in arts, or in arts as well as medicine; and a very few students, including Pomponazzi himself, took a degree in arts and then, some years later, in medicine. However, Pomponazzi never taught medicine: he remained throughout his career an arts professor.

The arts course he and others taught diverged in some important ways from that of the northern universities. Like theirs, it was built around Aristotle's texts, but the arts masters did not usually lecture on either the *Ethics* or the *Metaphysics*, two of the central texts of the arts curriculum in Oxford, Paris and elsewhere. Ethics was given little attention and was usually taught in a limited number of lectures by specialists who carried little prestige. Metaphysics was usually taught, if at all, by the theologians.

It is in regard to the theologians and their position that there is the most striking difference of all between the Italian university model and that found north of the Alps. It was not until the fourteenth and early fifteenth centuries that theology faculties began to be established in the Italian universities: for instance, at Padua in 1363 and Bologna the next year. However, theology (and metaphysics, which was considered to be tied to it) was only very partially integrated into the university's own curriculum. The teaching was generally done in the existing *studia* of the various mendicant and monastic orders, but there were a few university posts. By Pomponazzi's time there were at Padua a professor of Thomist theology and one of Scotist theology; and similarly two professors of metaphysics, one *in via S. Thomae* and one *in via Scoti*. As these job-titles indicate, metaphysics was closely tied to theology and completely apart from the courses followed by medical students. Bologna, however, was among the Italian universities which did little to bring theology and

[29] On Padua, Bologna and other Italian universities, see Grendler, *Universities of the Italian Renaissance*.

metaphysics into its ambit and for most of Pomponazzi's period there was just one post, in metaphysics.[30]

The shape of medieval Latin thinking from the thirteenth century onwards was determined in its outlines by the institutional structure of the universities, especially the division into arts and higher faculties, just as that structure, and that division, were moulded by the thinking of the time. In Paris and Oxford the existence of an arts faculty fostered a form of thinking based on reason and developed through a line-by-line reading of the works of the man who was judged its best exponent, the ancient pagan, Aristotle. However, the prestige of the theology faculties there, and the close ecclesiastical supervision of the universities, placed limits on how far the arts masters were able to develop their own lines of thought when they threatened to go against Christian doctrine. The situation of the arts faculties in Italy might be expected to foster the same form of thinking, but in a version biased towards naturalistic explanation (because of the students' usual intended career and the absence of ethics and metaphysics) and far less restricted by doctrinal scruples (because of the light Church and heavy civic supervision and the absence of influential theologians).

So, indeed, it happened – but with a twist which is of great importance for understanding Pomponazzi's position and the aims behind *De immortalitate.* Arts masters in the thirteenth-century university of Paris did indeed conceive themselves as dedicated expositors of Aristotelian philosophy, which they believed to provide the best understanding of the world based on natural reason. Their wish to work untrammelled within this sphere of rational, Aristotle-based enquiry, expressed most vividly in the work of Siger of Brabant and Boethius of Dacia, had received two rebuffs in the 1270s. Most famously, there were the 1277 Condemnations, in which 219 propositions, some of them linked to the positions of Siger, Boethius or their colleagues, were condemned; and in which, in his preface, Bishop Étienne Tempier criticized those who said that some things 'are true according to philosophy, but not according to faith, as if there were two contrary truths'.[31] Earlier, in 1272, a statute, perhaps written at their request, had forbidden the Paris arts masters from making purely theological questions the subject of their disputations and required them to refute any

[30] Grendler, *Universities of the Italian Renaissance*, p. 382.

[31] Section 5 of the prefatory letter, in *La condemnation Parisienne de 1277. Nouvelle edition du texte Latin*, ed. D. Piché (Paris, 1999), p. 74. A brief account of the condemnations and recent controversy among historians over them is given in J. Marenbon, *Pagans and Philosophers: the Problem of Paganism from Augustine to Leibniz* (Princeton, N.J., 2015), pp. 149–54.

views they discussed which might seem to negate Christian doctrine.[32] This statute formed the basis of the oath for arts masters instituted in Paris in 1279, but the requirement about statements contrary to Christianity was both widened and qualified, since arts masters had to swear that, if they had to determine any question touching on 'faith and philosophy', they would determine it 'on behalf of faith' (*pro fide*) and refute the arguments against the faith 'in so far as it seems to you they should be refuted' (*secundum quod vobis dissolvende videbuntur*).[33]

Although some historians underline the constraining effect of these measures, especially the 1277 Condemnations, on intellectual freedom, it was usually possible for arts masters to follow through their interpretations of Aristotelian texts, even when they went directly against Christian doctrine, simply by declaring that such philosophical doctrines were false and mentioning, however briefly, the teaching of the faith. They adopted, in effect, a type of limited relativism, accepting that the doctrine of the faith was true, but vigorously pursuing their own philosophical discussions and drawing their conclusions, sometimes opposed to Christian doctrine.[34] They were content to keep the two spheres apart in practice and not to press enquiry into their relations. Indeed, the success of this pragmatically relativist approach depended on its not being theorized. The freedom it offered was particularly evident in Italy, for the reasons already mentioned, and in the later fifteenth century the standard interpretation by arts masters there of Aristotle's views on the soul was, as mentioned above, that of Averroes: a clearly anti-Christian position, since it did not allow for individual immortality.

However, such liberty provoked a counter-reaction, which provides the immediate context for *De immortalitate*. First, in 1489, the bishop of Padua banned public disputations on the unity of the intellect, even if the disputants condemned Averroes' wickedness. He did not, however, forbid masters from following Averroes' interpretation of Aristotle's teaching on the intellect in their lectures.[35] Then, in 1513, the Fifth Lateran Council went

[32] *Chartularium universitatis Parisiensis*, ed. H. Denifle and E. Chatelain (4 vols, Paris, 1889–99), i. 499–500 (no. 441); cf. F.-X. Putallaz and R. Imbach, *Profession: Philosophe. Siger de Brabant* (Paris, 1997), pp. 128–34; L. Bianchi, *Censure et liberté intellectuelle a l'université de Paris (XIIIe–XIVe siècles)* (Paris, 1999), pp. 165–201; L. Bianchi, *Pour une histoire de la 'double vérité'* (Paris, 2008), pp. 98–100.

[33] Denifle and Chatelain, *Chartularium*, i. 587 (no. 501); cf. Bianchi, *Histoire de la 'double vérité'*, pp. 101–2.

[34] See Marenbon, *Pagans*, pp. 153–5; and, for an emphasis on the constraining effects of the condemnations, Bianchi, *Histoire de la 'double vérité'*.

[35] See di Napoli, *L'immortalità dell'anima*, pp. 185–6; Grendler, *Universities of the Italian Renaissance*, pp. 283–5.

further.[36] The bull *Apostolici regiminis* ordered all engaged in philosophy, in universities or otherwise teaching publicly, when lecturing on 'the principles or conclusions of the philosophers, where they are known to have deviated from the right faith' to use all their efforts 'to make clear to their hearers the truth of the Christian religion, and teach it by persuading so far as they can, and with the greatest care to rule out and to reject these sorts of the arguments of the philosophers with all their ability, since they all can be refuted'.[37] The view that the soul is mortal, or not individually immortal, is explicitly mentioned as an example of such arguments.[38] The bull's injunction to refute anti-Christian arguments seems to be modelled on the 1279 arts masters' oath, which had been adopted in the later middle ages in, for example, Heidelberg and Vienna, though not, it seems, in Italy.[39] Underlying it is a return to Aquinas, a powerful influence at this time. Aquinas holds that reason and Christian doctrine, both gifts from God, must be in harmony. Since human reason is limited, there may be questions in which neither side can be proven by it and on these neutral questions faith will give the answer; but reason can never prove what is contrary to Christian doctrine. The Lateran Council wished to insist on Aquinas's anti-relativist position to put aside the untheorized, de facto relativism of the arts masters. Since reason is unitary, their philosophical accounts must be mistaken when they contradict Christian doctrine and so, the bull insists, the arts masters themselves should explain how.

Apostolici regiminis posed a direct challenge to the intellectual freedom arts masters had enjoyed until then, especially in Italy. By publishing, just three years later, *De immortalitate*, a work which apparently directly contravenes *Apostolici regiminis*, Pomponazzi launched a counter-challenge on their behalf. Of all those colleagues who shared a similar institutional position, he was best placed to take such a bold step because he had powerful ex-pupils, such as the papal secretary Pietro Bembo, who could, and did, defend him.

[36] The bull is printed in J. D. Mansi, *Sacrorum conciliorum nova et amplissima collectio* (54 vols in 59, Graz 1960–1, repr. of 1902–27 edn), xxxii. 842–3. On its interpretation, see E. Constant, 'A reinterpretation of the Fifth Lateran Council decree *Apostolici regiminis* (1513)', *Sixteenth Century Jour.*, xxxiii (2002), 353–79.

[37] 'mandamus, ut cum philosophorum principia aut conclusiones, in quibus a recta fide deviare noscuntur, auditoribus suis legerint, seu explanaverint, quale hoc de animae mortalitate aut unitate, et mundi aeternitate, ac alia huiusmodi, teneantur eisdem veritatem religionis christianae omni conatu manifestam facere, et persuadendo pro posse docere, ac omni studio huiusmodi philosophorum argumenta, cum omnia solubilia existant, pro viribus excludere atque resolvere' (Mansi, *Collectio*, xxxii. 842DE).

[38] Earlier the bull also inveighs against those who hold that the soul 'is mortal or one for all humans' is true 'at least according to philosophy' (Mansi, *Collectio*, xxxii. 842B).

[39] See Bianchi, *Histoire de la 'double vérité'*, pp. 111–12, 118–20, 125–7.

De immortalitate, then, can be seen – at least in one aspect – as a defence of the traditional intellectual freedom of the arts masters to develop their philosophical ideas, so long as they also acknowledge the truth of Christian doctrine. This reading throws light on the purpose of the passages, such as chapter 15, in which, according to some interpreters, Pomponazzi is dissimulating. Hence far from being sops to orthodoxy, included to avoid censorship or persecution, they are central to Pomponazzi's strategy in opposing the new restrictions imposed by the Lateran Council. The apparatus of contrasting the conclusions of philosophical reasoning with Christian doctrine, which is accepted as the truth, was the essential framework for the arts masters' qualified, pragmatic relativism, which gave them intellectual freedom and was now under threat.

Pomponazzi had to find a very delicate balance in which he simultaneously went against the spirit of *Apostolici regiminis*, so as to reassert the arts masters' traditional independence, but respected the letter of the new regulations sufficiently to avoid having his text condemned. A special difficulty was posed for him by the new requirement to provide refutations of the arguments for the position contrary to Christian doctrine, since the body of the treatise suggests he thought that, within natural reason, it is the view that the soul is mortal which emerges triumphant. Pomponazzi does not provide these refutations. Even when, for the publication of the *Defensorium*, his reply to Nifo's criticisms, the Church authorities insisted on there being refutations of his arguments for mortalism, Pomponazzi satisfied them by having the Dominican theologian Chrysostomus Javelli supply these counter-arguments in his place.[40] Pomponazzi did, however, make a concession to this new demand by declaring that the immortality of the soul is a 'neutral' problem, since the normal implication of this description is that the arguments on both sides are not conclusive and so, in principle, the arguments he makes for mortality could be refuted. Given the way he has argued for mortalism, this remark, at least, may appear to be dissimulation, but a closer look at the whole passage (see the next section) suggests that in fact he may have been able to make it in good faith.

In any case, Pomponazzi seems to have done enough to convince the Church authorities that he was not openly opposing them. He was not punished; and his career flourished even more after 1516 than before, even though in his works replying to the critics of *De immortalitate* he did not

[40] A. Cappiello, 'Le *Solutiones* di Crisostomo Javelli al *Defensorium* di Pietro Pomponazzi. Edizione critica del testo latino', *Noctua*, iii (2016), 74–149; cf. A. Cappiello, 'Una verità senza stonature. Le *Solutiones* di Crisostomo Javelli al *Defensorium* di Pietro Pomponazzi', *Medioevo e Rinascimento*, xxix (n.s. xxvi) (2015), 151–80. Javelli does not, in effect, attempt to refute Pomponazzi's arguments from within the sphere of natural reasoning.

significantly alter his position about mortalism. Historians disagree about the general effects of *Apostolici regiminis* over the coming decades, but it is clear that to a large extent arts masters in Italy continued as before to develop their arguments without stopping to show why they were wrong when they contradicted the faith.[41] They were most probably beneficiaries of Pomponazzi's stand, which helped to qualify or even neutralize the bull from the very start.

Pomponazzi the individual

The picture of Pomponazzi as a figure moulded by his institution and fighting for the values associated with it and his position there, and of *De immortalitate* as countering a threat to these values, captures an important aspect of the truth. However, it is not the whole truth. There are many elements in the treatise not explained by it, just as this description covers only one aspect of Pomponazzi. Pomponazzi was far too powerful, complex and enigmatic a thinker to be a mere product and representative of his institution. Although he was an eminently successful academic insider, Pomponazzi's career had some unusual features: for instance, he chose to lecture, shortly after his arrival at Bologna, on book XII of Aristotle's *Metaphysics,* a text usually left to the theologians (who would be friars or monks); and to add, between 1514 and 1521, to his prestigious, well-paid lectureship there a part-time, very poorly paid post in moral philosophy – he clearly had a strong interest in this subject, side-lined in the universities where he worked.[42]

Arts courses were based on Aristotle, usually studied with the help of the commentator, that is to say Averroes, whose interpretations had statutory authority in the universities where Pomponazzi worked. Although, in fact, arts masters often arrived at novel positions, they rarely did so in explicit contradiction of their authorities. Pomponazzi, by contrast, was willing to reject, often contemptuously, the views of any authority. Even at the start of his career, when he believed that Averroes' theory of one intellect for all humans was the correct interpretation of Aristotle, he rejected it entirely – and, clearly, his opposition had nothing to do with ecclesiastical pressure, given the alternative views he developed.[43] Even in the case of the newly available translations of Greek works, he was quick to turn against their doctrines. Michael of Ephesus's commentary is introduced with

[41] Grendler stresses the arts masters' freedom (*Universities of the Italian Renaissance*, pp. 293–7); Bianchi qualifies this impression (*Histoire de la 'double vérité'*, pp. 134–44).

[42] Grendler, *Universities of the Italian Renaissance*, pp. 398–402.

[43] See A. Poppi, *Saggi sul pensiero inedito di Pietro Pomponazzi* (Rome, 1970), pp. 27–92.

considerable fanfare in the lectures on *De partibus*, but soon Pomponazzi marks his disagreement with it and then stops using it. Even Aristotle was not spared. In lectures on the *Meteora* given late in his life, he remarked: 'I should prefer to be in the state of Socrates, who reached the position which he expressed by saying, "I know one thing: that I know nothing", than that of Aristotle who, I believe, pretended that he knew many things of which he was in fact ignorant'.[44]

Although up to the time of *De immortalitate*, and to an extent in that work too, Pomponazzi's writings were closely linked to his university teaching, in the years from its publication in 1516 to his death in 1525 much of his work was independent of the university curriculum, since he was specially occupied in producing his two long defences against critics of his views on immortality; and two treatises in which he developed his own interests quite independently of the curriculum, *De incantationibus*, on miracles, and his work on fate and predestination. This treatise, the longest of all Pomponazzi's writings, is a most unusual work to have been produced by an arts master. It was the very *raison d'être* of arts masters' profession, in Italy as everywhere, that they were *not* theologians: their questions and their authorities were philosophical, not theological. Nonetheless, in books 3–5 of *De fato* (200 pages in the modern edition) he devotes himself completely to discussing human freedom and predestination from the point of view of Christian doctrine.

These details about Pomponazzi's interests and other writings cast aspects of *De immortalitate* in a new light. The lengthy discussion on ethics is clearly not there just to reinforce a point about the freedom of arts masters, but to contribute to an area of thought Pomponazzi considered centrally important.[45] Perhaps, too, as both his interest in theology and his scepticism about the certainty of Aristotelian science indicate, his methodological stance embraced, but went beyond, the traditional independence of the arts masters.

To follow up this suggestion, the central paragraph in chapter 15 on the immortality of the soul as a neutral problem needs to be examined carefully. After saying that, in the light of what he has said, the immortality of the soul seems to be a neutral problem (*neutrum problema*), Pomponazzi goes on:

[44] Quoted in *Pietro Pomponazzi. Expositio super primo et secundo De partibus animalium*, ed. S. Perfetto (Istituto nazionale di studi sul rinascimento. Studi e testi, xliii, Florence, 2004), p. xlii, n. 74.

[45] See J. Marenbon, 'Pomponazzi's ethics and the philosophical tradition', in *Regards sur les traditions philosophiques (XIIe – XVIe siècles)*, ed. Z. Kaluza and D. Calma (Ancient and Medieval Philosophy, series 1, lvi, Leuven, 2017), pp. 309–22.

> Mihi namque videtur quod nullae rationes naturales adduci possunt cogentes animam esse immortalem, minusque probantes animam esse mortalem, sicut quam plures doctors tenentes eam immortalem declarant. Quare nolui ponere responsiones ad alteram partem, cum alii ponant, et praecipue divus Thomas luculenter, copiose et graviter. Quapropter dicemus, sicut Plato in primo *De legibus,* certificare de aliquo cum multi ambigunt solius est dei. Cum itaque tam illustres viri inter se ambigant, nisi per deum hoc certificari posse existimo.[46]

According to the widely used and only complete English translation, this means:

> For it seems to me that no natural reasons can be brought forth proving that the soul is immortal, and still less any proving that the soul is mortal, as very many scholars who hold it immortal declare. Wherefore I do not want to make answer to the other side, since others do so, St. Thomas in particular, clearly, fully, and weightily. Wherefore we shall say, as Plato said in the *Laws* I, that to be certain of anything, when many are in doubt, is for God alone. Since therefore such famous men disagree with each other, I think that this can be made certain only through God.[47]

The line of thought, as expressed in the translation, is puzzling. The first statement does, indeed, fit with the idea of immortality of the soul as a neutral problem by declaring that there are no proofs based on natural reason on either side, although the remark that none can be found for the soul's mortality directly contradicts pages of argument in the preceding chapters. If the remark which follows is attached to what immediately precedes it, as would be expected, then it seems rather pointless, since it says that many scholars who hold that the soul is immortal believe there are no proofs that it is mortal. The next sentence deepens the puzzle. What is 'the other side', since the previous sentence has mentioned both sides (that the soul is immortal; that it is mortal)? Since the sentence begins with 'Wherefore' (*Quare*), it is supposed to follow on as a consequence, explained by the preceding remark, but it is not clear how it does; and the translator goes on to explain it, rather, by the following remark: that others, such as Aquinas, have given answers. The final two sentences state there is uncertainty over the immortality of the soul, but this was already established by saying it is a neutral problem: it is not clear what argumentative purpose the previous sentences have served or why the disagreement of 'famous men' has been brought into the discussion.

[46] Pomponazzi, *De immortalitate animae*, p. 211 (15.316).

[47] Translation by W. H. Hay II, rev. by J. H. Randall, Jnr, in *The Renaissance Philosophy of Man*, ed. E. Cassirer, P. O. Kristeller and J. H. Randall (Chicago, Ill., 1948), pp. 280–381, at p. 377.

The passage becomes less problematic if the first sentence is translated in the most obvious way for the Latin, although it produces a meaning which is unexpected. The phrase *minusque probantes animam esse mortalem*, as Perrone Compagni, alone among translators, has pointed out, should in the context be rendered 'and showing that it is less arguable that the soul is mortal' or 'showing that there is no proof for the soul's mortality'.[48] Pomponazzi does not, then, give a straightforward gloss on what it means for a problem to be neutral. Rather, completely in line with the preceding chapters, he insists on the mortalist position and says that, within natural reasoning, there are neither good arguments for the immortality of the soul, nor good arguments against its mortality.

Pomponazzi's comment about 'very many scholars who hold it immortal' now becomes far from a bland truism: he is pointing out that many thinkers, such as Scotus, who hold that in truth the soul is immortal, agree with him that natural reason cannot establish its immortality, either positively or negatively, by disproving the arguments for its mortality.[49] Understood in this way, the sentence does indeed offer a reason, as the word *quare* indicates, why Pomponazzi has not given replies to refute the arguments for 'the other side', that is, the view that the soul is mortal: he cannot find any. In the clause which follows, *cum* cannot have the sense of 'because' since the reason Pomponazzi has not chosen to reply to these arguments has already been given; rather, it must mean 'although'. On the one hand, many learned people, Pomponazzi himself among them, cannot find any arguments based on natural reason either for the soul's immortality or against its mortality. On the other hand, others, chiefly Aquinas – whose arguments for immortality had already been presented in chapter 7 – propose many arguments against its mortality; and Aquinas's are lucid, full and weighty (note that Pomponazzi does not say they are cogent). Pomponazzi has, therefore, established that many, including 'famous men' such as Aquinas and Scotus, disagree over whether the soul's immortality can be shown by natural reason; and that, he contends, is a reason for mere humans to suspend judgement. By implication he seems also to give this disagreement as his reason for holding that the problem of

[48] Perrone, *Pomponazzi. Trattato*, p. lxxxviii, n. 174. As well as Hay, and the other translators she mentions, Gontier (*De immortalitate*, p. 210) and Raimondi (*Pomponazzi. Tutti I trattati*, p. 1099) favour the usual version; only di Napoli, *L'Immortalità dell'anima*, p. 256, gives the same, convincing rendering as she does.

[49] See Scotus, *In IV librum Sententiarum*, I, q. 46, a. 2, resp. (as indicated in P. Compagni's translation, *Pomponazzi. Trattato*, p. 114); cf. A. Poppi, 'Consenso e dissenso del Pomponazzi con il 'subtilissimus et religosissimus Ioannes Scotus', in Sgarbi, *Pietro Pomponazzi. Tradizione e dissenso*, pp. 3–39, esp. pp. 11–21.

immortality is neutral, although he himself thinks that there is no rational case for immortality.

In the remaining paragraphs of chapter 15, and at much greater length in his *Apologia*, Pomponazzi defends the view that the immortality of the soul is a position which, although contrary to all the principles used in natural reasoning, can be vindicated by arguing on the basis of the articles of faith, which are not known through natural reason but are believed as a result of revelation.[50] Within the sphere of natural reasoning, arguments for the soul's immortality must be rejected and those for its mortality are cogent. Nonetheless, there is an overall doubt about the reliability of the results of natural reasoning which permits Pomponazzi rationally to juxtapose its mortalist conclusion with the immortalist conclusion reached by the different sort of argument which uses revealed premises; and then to choose to accept as true this conclusion, reached using revelation and endorsed by the Church.

There is every reason, in the light of his work as a whole, to take this as his own genuine, considered position. It is not a concession, made for the sake of appearance so as to avoid censorship and persecution, but a bold stance and an unusual one, shared neither by the Church leaders, under the sway of Thomism, nor his fellow arts masters, whose cause it nevertheless sustained, nor even by his favoured authority, Duns Scotus. As explained above, the arts masters had countered Aquinas's anti-relativism, which the Lateran Council would reaffirm, by ignoring it in practice and not engaging with it theoretically. By contrast, Pomponazzi rejected it explicitly. The best natural reasoning, he holds, can and does come to conclusions contrary to Christian doctrine, such as that the human soul is mortal. Duns Scotus would have agreed that, at least in some cases, even the wisest philosophers cannot but be misled by their reasons.[51] However, these philosophers were, for him, the pagan thinkers of antiquity, such as Aristotle: Scotus himself worked as a theologian, pursuing truth by using, where appropriate, premises from revelation. Except in the last three books of *De fato*, Pomponazzi worked always in the capacity of an arts master, not a theologian. He was content to argue within the sphere of natural reason, which he held to have its own coherence. He defended, as an arts master, what he thought to be the best conclusions of reason, even if they contradicted Christian doctrine, and would not accept that they could, even in principle, be rationally refuted.

[50] Pomponazzi, *Apologia*, pp. 1504–22 (III.iii.8–25).

[51] Scotus thought that the philosophers could not but have been misled about the nature of God, whom they thought to cause necessarily, not contingently (*Ordinatio* I, Prologue, q. unica; cf. Marenbon, *Pagans*, pp. 155–7). With regard to the immortality of the soul, he merely thought that it could not be proved by natural reason.

Yet he also accepted that this whole system of reasoning, considered from the outside, was not beyond question. He could, therefore, happily accept that there is another sphere of argument, sustained by the articles of faith, where certainty is to be found.

Conclusion

The view just suggested about Pomponazzi's underlying aims and beliefs needs much more careful exploration than can be offered here, in the light not only of the methodological statements in the *Apologia,* but also of the comments and procedures in *De incantationibus* and *De fato*. However, it is very clear from the discussion above that explanations based on Pomponazzi's institutional character, as the university insider, go only part of the way towards solving the interpretative puzzle posed by *De immortalitate*. Such a judgement might seem disappointing in relation to the aims of this collection as a whole – a return to the sort of old-fashioned history based on outstanding individuals and great minds, to which the focus on institutional contexts is supposed to provide an alternative. A more careful look, however, at the way the argument about Pomponazzi has unfolded here suggests a different, less negative conclusion.

Reference to institutional norms plays as large a part in the third section of this essay, on Pomponazzi as an individual, as it does in the second, on Pomponazzi as the institutional insider. Pomponazzi's unusual traits and novel views emerge only in the light of institutional practice. However, 'institutional' needs to be taken in a wide sense, for while the tangible institutions of the universities of Padua and Bologna are of some importance, the main explanatory roles are played by the virtual institutions of being-an-arts-master (in early sixteenth-century Italy, but with the weight of a history stretching back to thirteenth-century Paris) and, more widely, of Abrahamic Aristotelianism – the set of texts, aims, assumptions, methods and practices, both shared and disputed by Muslims, Jews and Christians, within which alone the complex argument of *De immortalitate* set out in part 1, and the interpretative choices explored in parts 2 and 3, can be understood. It is above all this and other such chronologically long and geographically broad virtual institutions which must be studied, both to reach a historically plausible, contextualized understanding of individual thinkers and their work; and, more ambitiously, to ensure a social history of philosophy is one day written.

4. Individual and institution in scholastic historiography: Nicholas Trevet

Matthew Kempshall

> Historical narrative narrates things that have been instituted by human beings in the past, but should not, for that reason, itself be counted among human institutions [*humana instituta*]. For what has already gone into the past and cannot be undone [*nec infecta fieri possunt*] must be considered part of the order of time [*ordo temporum*], whose creator and controller is God. There is a difference between narrating what has been done [*facta*] and teaching what should be done [*facienda*]. History narrates past events in a faithful and useful way [*fideliter atque utiliter*], whereas books of haruspices and similar literature set out to teach things to be done, or observed, with the boldness of admonition [*monitoris audacia*] rather than the trustworthiness of a witness [*indicis fide*].[1]

Augustine's epitome of the relationship between the divine institution of history and the human narration of individual historical events presented scholastic readers with as many questions as answers. Understanding the cause of events and setting out the sequence of human actions presupposed different types of knowledge and different purposes in writing. The individual instance of Nicholas Trevet, and the structure and practice of the institutions to which he belonged, indicate the complexity of the relationship between historical causation and historiographical narrative which resulted.

Augustine – the divine and human institution of history

According to Augustine, narrating individual historical events should be closely tied to the divinely instituted *ordo temporum*. This approach was founded on the purpose which such narrative is designed to serve. History, in this sense, should be distinguished from aetiology: 'It is history',

[1] Augustine, *De doctrina Christiana*, ed. and trans. R. P. H. Green (Oxford, 1995), p. 107 (ii.28.109). Translations offered in this essay are from the English editions specified in the footnotes, amended where necessary; otherwise, they are the author's own.

M. Kempshall, 'Individual and institution in scholastic historiography: Nicholas Trevet', in *Individuals and Institutions in Medieval Scholasticism*, ed. A. Fitzpatrick and J. Sabapathy (London, 2020), pp. 107–35.

Augustine writes, 'when deeds done, whether by God or by humans, are commemorated ... it is aetiology when the causes of what is said or done are set out'.[2] This is the conceptual demarcation which underpins his otherwise blunt statement that he will not try to narrate or commemorate the calamities of the second Punic War because, were he to do so, he would become nothing other than a writer of history.[3] Analysing the causes of a particular event, on this reckoning, went beyond the writing of history. If the meaning of past events lay in the reasons *why* something happened, then the task of identifying them belonged, strictly speaking, not to the historian, but to prophets – individuals who proclaim God's will in the future, but also in the past and the present. This did not mean that, for Augustine, narrating history was an otiose act. Writing down an individual's *res gestae*, commemorating their deeds, could still serve a moral-didactic function: the subject-matter of history is useful (*utilis*) because it teaches or nurtures through examples (*exempla*) and hence constitutes the first of seven steps of spiritual understanding.[4] However, this ethical utility clearly needed to stop short of the presumption of augury and divination. The result was an equivocal approach to history, two senses in which its record might be conceived: divine institution in the *ordo temporum*; human institution in the sense familiar from Quintilian and Lactantius (and subsequently Boethius, Cassiodorus, Cassian and Hrabanus Maurus), as a practice which is formative, exemplary and instructive.

One consequence of Augustine's strictures in the middle ages was for writers of history to concentrate on chronography, recording the sequence of events within an overarching order of time. In formal terms, this meant annotating events to Easter tables, but this physical conjunction carried an interpretative significance, too. According to Augustine, humans experience time as a distension of the soul, an expression and consequence of their sin. Past, present and future, by contrast, exist simultaneously in God as a single point of 'now' (*simul nunc*). This differentiation between human and divine perception applies to the temporal succession of individual events, but also to the entirety of world history. As a result, only when the created universe is seen in its totality will the significance of the *ordo temporum* become clear.[5] This is why prophets – humans who share, at least

[2] Augustine, *De Genesi ad litteram imperfectus liber*, ed. J. Zycha (*CSEL*, xxviii.1, Vienna, 1894), p. 461 (ii); *De utilitate credendi*, ed. J. Zycha (*CSEL*, xxv, Vienna, 1891), p. 8 (iii.5).

[3] Augustine, *De civitate Dei*, ed. B. Dombart and A. Kalb (*CCSL*, xlvii–xlviii, Turnhout, 1955), p. 85 (iii.18).

[4] Augustine, *De vera religione*, ed. K.-D. Daur (*CCSL*, xxxii, Turnhout, 1962), p. 218 (xxvi.49).

[5] Augustine, *Epistulae*, ed. A. Goldbacher (*CSEL*, xliv, Vienna, 1904), pp. 129–30

in part, God's atemporal perspective – use the past tense to speak of events in the future. This is also why chroniclers left the providential significance of events open to interpretation by continuators – their historiography was a process, inherited from predecessors and passed on to successors. Such modesty was encapsulated in disclaimers. 'I leave allegorical readings and interpretations appropriate to human conduct to be expanded by the learned', wrote Orderic Vitalis, 'setting myself the task of relating … straightforward history [*simplex historia*]'. Orderic's aim was to record events whose significance might be revealed only in the future, or by those blessed with greater understanding and ability than his own.[6] Likewise, William of Newburgh writes: 'I am only a simple narrator [*simplex narrator*], not a prophetic interpreter [*praesagus interpres*]'.[7]

Such analytical restraint was particularly important for contemporary events. Again, this approach was indebted to Augustine, in this case to a division of the history of the world into six ages. On this reckoning, 'sacred history' was complete at the end of the fifth age, with the death, resurrection and ascension of Jesus Christ. Thereafter, the world had entered into old age (*senectus mundi*) and, as such, was characterized by exterior decay and interior renewal. Events in this sixth age are still governed by God, but they will not necessarily have the significance for the economy of salvation which can be traced for events in ages one through to five. God can, and will, continue to intervene directly in history, but such active providence will be even harder to unveil than in the past: 'God's ways are inscrutable and his judgements past searching out' (Romans XI: 33). More prevalent in the sixth age, if not its defining characteristic, is permissive providence: God will allow events, and nature, to take their course.[8]

Augustine's influence on medieval historiography concentrated attention on the constraints under which it operated: history was distinct from aetiology; chronography from prophecy; permissive providence from active providence. While humans could still learn from individual moral *exempla* and chart a natural order of events which was experienced in time, the providential order of those events might be unknown and, in the sixth age, unknowable. The resulting bifurcation of divine and human institution

(cxxxviii.4–5); *De Civitate Dei*, p. 337 (xi.18). Cf. Bonaventure, *Breviloquium*, in *Opera theologica selecta* (5 vols, Ad Claras Aquas, Florence, 1934–64), v. 1–175, at pp. 8–9 (prol. 2.4).

6 Orderic Vitalis, *Historia ecclesiastica*, ed. and trans. M. Chibnall (6 vols, Oxford, 1969–80), i. 132 (i. prol.); iv. 228 (viii.16).

7 William of Newburgh, *Historia Rerum Anglicarum*, ed. H. C. Hamilton (2 vols, London, 1856), ii. 14 (iv.6).

8 Augustine, *De civitate Dei*, p. 288 (x.14); pp. 865–6 (xxii.30); R. Markus, *Saeculum: History and Society in the Theology of Augustine* (Cambridge, 1970).

clearly raised fundamental methodological questions for historical narration. These came into particularly sharp focus when Augustine's conceptualization was read alongside Aristotle's analysis of knowledge and art.

Aristotle – individual actions and particular experience

Aristotle's account of intellectual induction from particulars carried clear consequences for the individual deeds and events which form the subject matter of human history. The idea that empirical narrative could never, by itself, form the basis for a truly scientific discipline was aired in the *Nicomachean Ethics*, when Aristotle crisply dismissed the claims of sophists to teach political science. The acquisition of political knowledge, he argued, requires systematic reflection on the underlying principles of laws, not just the collection of individual examples. Without an understanding of the goal of the political community or of different forms of government, true knowledge of politics is impossible.[9] In the *Ethics* Aristotle's primary target was law and lawyers, but the criticism was also levelled at history and historians. The *Poetics*, for example, compared history to poetry very much to the former's disadvantage:

> [T]he poet's function is to say, not what was done [*gesta*], but the sort of thing that would happen; as a consequence, poetry is more philosophical and worthwhile than history, for poetry deals more with universal statements, history with particulars [*particularia*]. A universal statement sets out what sort of person would, probably or necessarily, say or do what sort of thing, and this is what poetry aims at, although it attaches proper names; a particular statement tells us what Alcibiades did or what happened to him.[10]

Still more influential was Aristotle's analysis of scientific knowledge in the *Physics*, *Metaphysics* and *Posterior Analytics*.

Since humans know something only when they know its causes and principles, 'science' requires, by definition, a knowledge of causes, and its principles had to be necessary and universal.[11] Both science and art derive from experience, where *experimentum* is the accumulation in the memory of a plurality of individual things. Whereas experience retains knowledge only of those singular particulars, art makes a universal judgement about the

[9] Aristotle, *Ethica Nicomachea*, ed. R.-A. Gauthier (*Aristoteles Latinus*, xxvi.1–3, Leiden and Brussels, 1972–3), pp. 586–7 (x.14).

[10] Aristotle, *De arte poetica*, ed. L. Minio-Paluello (*Aristoteles Latinus*, xxxiii, Brussels, 1968), pp. 12–13 (ix).

[11] Aristotle, *Physica*, ed. F. Bossier and J. Brams (*Aristoteles Latinus*, vii.1.2, Leiden, 1990), p. 7 (i.1); *Analytica Posteriora*, ed. L. Minio-Paluello and B. Dod (*Aristoteles Latinus* iv.1–4, Bruges and Paris, 1968), p. 294 (i.8).

similarities found in the many things memory has stored. Experience may therefore know that something is (*quia*, *quod*), but art knows the cause and the reason why (*causa*, *propter quid*). Moreover, if art expresses a knowledge of causes, then, unlike experience, it can be taught, since teaching, too, requires a knowledge of causes.[12] The object of scientific knowledge is demonstrable and necessary, proceeding sometimes through induction, sometimes through deductive syllogism; art may not be concerned with things which come into being by necessity or in accordance with nature, but it still denotes a capacity to make something in accordance with a true course of reasoning.[13] Singular instances, individual events and empirical particulars all remain, in and of themselves, the subject of experience, not of knowledge. This is not to say Aristotle thought there was no value in those particulars. His approach in the *Historia animalium*, for example, was to accumulate material preparatory to its explanatory study; likewise in the *Politics*, where particular circumstances of individual human communities are analysed to produce more generally applicable 'types' of human association. Nonetheless, the intellectual apprehension of experiential material will depend on the category of knowledge being attempted and addressed. Peter of Abano's exposition of Aristotle's *Problemata* encapsulates the point when explaining why some types of knowledge create a disposition (*habitus*) and others do not. The difference lies in the distinction between the scientific knowledge produced by demonstration and the ordering of cause and effect and the more common application of the term to knowledge drawn from the practically limitless and disordered number of particulars: the latter proceeds from narrative (that is, history), precept (that is, laws) or experience (that is, custom).[14]

For scholastic writers, there were clear implications to reading Aristotle's emphasis on causality as the object of knowledge alongside Augustine's distinction between history and aetiology. Both propositions appeared in close proximity at the start of Aquinas's *Summa theologiae*.[15] Their consequences were spelled out by Vincent of Beauvais. A chronological account of *res gestae* from the beginning of the world to the present day, arranged according to the sequence of time (*series temporum*), will be a source of wonder (*admiratio*), refreshment (*recreatio*) and utility (*utilitas*).

[12] Aristotle, *Metaphysica*, ed. G. Vuillemin-Diem (*Aristoteles Latinus,* xxv.3.2, Leiden/New York/Cologne, 1995), pp. 14–16 (i.2).

[13] Aristotle, *Ethica*, pp. 480–1 (vi.3–4).

[14] [pseudo-]Aristotle, *Problematum Aristotelis cum … expositione Petri Aponi* (Venice, 1505), fo. 248 (xxx.2) (hereafter Peter of Abano, *Expositio Problematum*).

[15] Aquinas, *Summa theologiae*, ed. and trans. T. Gilby et al. (Blackfriars edn., 61 vols, London, 1964–80), Ia, q. 1. a. 2, ad 2, p. 12; Ia, q. 1, a. 10, ad 2, p. 38.

However, such material does not pertain to philosophy, because history narrates only singular deeds and, according to Aristotle, art cannot result from particulars.[16] Its utility is determined by the nature of the audience. Aristotle's *Problemata*, for example, asked why it is that people in general derive more pleasure from *exempla* and fables than from enthymemes and syllogisms. The answer is that the majority of people like to learn quickly, and they always learn more readily, by induction from what is familiar, from particulars accessible to their senses, than by deducing what is universal from demonstrative proofs. For Peter of Abano, this was why reading about the deeds of Trojans and Romans is more likely to keep people awake. It is also why people take greater pleasure from Roman history than *res gestae* which are either very old – his example is (Seneca's) Hercules – or very recent – pope Boniface VIII.[17]

Put Aristotle and Augustine together, in other words, and it becomes clear why the subject of 'history' should have been absent from scholastic classificatory schemata of knowledge.[18] Its material was taught as part of an initial training in grammar and served, at best, as a form of ethical instruction tailored to an audience of young, simple, uneducated or ignorant minds. This is why Giles of Rome opened his mirror for princes with a disclaimer that he would *not* proceed in a narrative manner.[19] Giles never denies the didactic value of an exemplary method – a ruler ought to read about praiseworthy deeds (*laudabilia gesta*) and the history of his kingdom in order to learn how to rule correctly. For philosophers, however, Giles echoes the warning from the *Ethics*: to descend from general principles to particular eventualities is to practise unreflective sophistry.[20]

It has been a longstanding criticism of medieval historiography that it either was not interested in or deliberately ignored the analysis of causes, even though causation had been made central to the definition of history-writing by a range of classical authorities. Tacitus stated his intention to describe 'reasons and causes', not 'occurrences and events'; Virgil declared

[16] Vincent of Beauvais, *Speculum maius* (Douai, 1624), cols. 13 (prol. 16), 3 (prol. 3: *de rebus gestis iuxta seriem temporum suorum ordinate dissererem*), 12 (prol.15), 16 (prol. 20).

[17] Peter of Abano, *Expositio Problematum*, fos. 166v–167 (xviii.3), fo. 169 (xviii.10). Cf. Aristotle, *Rhetorica*, ed. B. Schneider (*Aristoteles Latinus*, xxxi.1–2, Leiden, 1978), pp. 298–9 (iii.10.2).

[18] H.-W. Goetz, 'Die Geschichte im Wissenschaftssystem des Mittelalters', in *Funktion und Formen mittelalterlicher Geschichtsschreibung. Eine Einführung*, ed. F.-J. Schmale (Darmstadt, 1985), pp. 165–213.

[19] Giles of Rome, *De regimine principum* (Venice, 1502), prol.

[20] Giles of Rome, *De regimine principum*, ii.3.20; iii.2.15; G. Bruni, 'The *De Differentia Rhetoricae Ethicae et Politicae* of Aegidius Romanus', *The New Scholasticism*, vi (1932), 1–18, at p. 8.

'happy ... the person who has been able to understand the causes of things'.[21] Concentration on causation had consequences for classification into genre and, in particular, for the distinction between writing history and compiling annals. According to Aulus Gellius (in a text known, in part, to John of Salisbury and, in full, to the Oxford Franciscan *lector* John of Wales), history is an exposition or demonstration of 'deeds done', while annals provide a compilation of these *res gestae*, following the order of each year; history is therefore superior because, whereas annals set out what was done and in what year it was done, history also sets out the reason (*ratio*) and the deliberation or prudential calculation (*consilium*) behind it.[22] It is not the general applicability of this distinction which is at issue here, so much as its affinity to a scholastic historiography which was rooted in Aristotle's analysis of how knowledge and art derive from the experience of particulars. The historical writing of Nicholas Trevet provides a case in point.

Nicholas Trevet – consolation, tragedy and instruction

The outlines of Trevet's career and the chronology of at least some of his writings are reasonably secure. He incepted in theology at Oxford around 1302 and taught there until *c.*1307; a series of quodlibets and *quaestiones* survive, together with commentaries on Genesis and Exodus which were endorsed by the Dominican general chapter at Strasbourg in 1307. From *c.*1308 Trevet was in Paris, at the convent of Saint Jacques, returning to Oxford for a second spell as regent master in 1314 around the time he completed a commentary on the Psalms. From 1324 he was in London as the Dominican *lector*, until his death sometime after 1334.[23] It was during this final period that Trevet wrote, from the early 1320s, his *Annals* and *Chronicles*, the first a record of the deeds of Angevin kings from 1135 to 1307;[24] the second an account of the first five ages of the world from the

[21] Tacitus, *Histories*, i.4, ed. C. D. Fisher (Oxford, 1910); Virgil, *Georgics*, ii.490, ed. F. A. Hirtzel (Oxford, 1900). Cf. Otto of Freising, *Gesta Friderici*, ed. G. Waitz (MGH SRG, xlvi, Hanover, 1884), p. 13 (i.4).

[22] Aulus Gellius, *Noctes Atticae*, ed. P. K. Marshall (2 vols, Oxford, 1968), i. 211–12 (v.18). Cf. J. Swanson, *John of Wales: a Study of the Works and Ideas of a Thirteenth-Century Friar* (Cambridge, 1989), pp. 24–8. For the latter's influence on the Oxford Dominican John of Westerfield, see B. Smalley, 'Oxford University sermons 1290–1293', in *Medieval Learning and Literature: Essays Presented to Richard William Hunt*, ed. J. Alexander and M. Gibson (Oxford, 1976), pp. 307–27, at pp. 322–4.

[23] T. Käppeli, *Scriptores Ordinis Praedicatorum Medii Aevi* (4 vols, Rome, 1970–93), iii. 187–96; iv. 213–15.

[24] Trevet, *Annales sex regum Angliae*, ed. T. Hog (London, 1845). For bk. vi [1272–1307], see F. Mantello, 'A critical edition of the *Gesta Temporum Edwardi Regis Anglorum* of Nicholas Trevet OP' (unpublished University of Toronto PhD thesis, 1977), pp. 230–517.

creation to the birth of Christ,[25] a Latin text from which he subsequently produced an Anglo-Norman adaptation for Edward I's daughter, Mary of Woodstock.[26] What has always intrigued modern scholars is the series of texts Trevet produced alongside these directly exegetical, theological and historical works. In the first instance there was a commentary on Boethius's *Consolation of Philosophy*, written around 1300;[27] followed by a commentary on Seneca's *Declamations* (specifically the *Controversiae*), written perhaps as early as 1306; then commentaries on Seneca's *Tragedies* and the first and third decades of Livy's *Ab urbe condita*,[28] both of which were completed before 1318. At some point between *c.*1300 and *c.*1318 Trevet also produced an exposition of the poetic and historical contents of Augustine's *De civitate Dei*. These were all works which took Trevet beyond the institutional axis of Oxford and Paris, in particular to the Dominican houses of northern Italy (Santa Caterina in Pisa, Santa Maria Novella in Florence) and, after 1308, apparently to the papal court at Avignon, earning him the patronage of the Dominican cardinal Nicholas of Prato (who commissioned the commentary on Seneca's *Tragedies* after reading Trevet on the *Consolation* and *Declamations*)[29] and Pope John XXII (to whom Trevet dedicated a copy

[25] London, British Library, Royal MS. 13 B XVI, fos. 2–334.

[26] A. Rutherford, 'The Anglo-Norman chronicle of Nicholas Trevet' (unpublished University of London PhD thesis, 1932). Cf. R. Dean, 'Nicholas Trevet, historian', in Alexander and Gibson, *Medieval Learning and Literature*, pp. 328–52; H. Pagan, 'Trevet's *Les Cronicles*: manuscripts, owners and readers', in *The Prose Brut and Other Late Medieval Chronicles: Books have their Histories. Essays in Honour of Lester M. Matheson*, ed. J. Rajsic, E. Kooper and D. Hoche (Woodbridge, 2016), pp. 149–64.

[27] R. Dean, 'The dedication of Nicholas Trevet's commentary on Boethius', *Studies in Philology*, lxiii (1966), 593–603; L. Nauta, 'The *Consolation* – the Latin commentary tradition 800–1700', in *The Cambridge Companion to Boethius*, ed. J. Marenbon (Cambridge, 2009), pp. 255–78, at pp. 263–6; L. Nauta, 'The scholastic context of the Boethius commentary by Nicholas Trevet', in *Boethius in the Middle Ages: Latin and Vernacular Traditions of the Consolatio Philosophiae*, ed. J. Hoenen and L. Nauta (Texte zur Geistesgeschichte des Mittelalters, Leiden, 1997), pp. 41–67.

[28] R. Dean, 'The earliest known commentary on Livy is by Nicholas Trevet', *Medievalia et Humanistica*, iii (1945), 86–98; C. Wittlin, *Titus Livius Ab urbe condita I.1–9. Ein mittellateinischer Kommentar und sechs romanische Übersetzungen und Kürzungen aus dem Mittelalter* (Tübingen, 1970); G. Billanovich, *La tradizione del testo di Livio e le origini del'Umanesimo* (Padua, 1981), ch. 2; G. Crevatin, 'Legger Tito Livio – Nicola Trevet, Landolfo Colonna, Francesco Petrarca', *Incontri triestini di filologia classica*, vi (2006–7), 67–79.

[29] Nicholas of Prato, *Epistola*, ed. E. Franceschini, in *Il commento di Nicola Trevet al Tieste di Seneca* (Milan, 1938), pp. 1–2, trans. A. Minnis and A. Scott, in *Medieval Literary Theory and Criticism c.1100–c.1375: the Commentary Tradition*, ed. A. Minnis and A. Scott, with D. Wallace (rev. edn., Oxford, 1991), pp. 340–1.

of his commentary on Genesis).[30] These are also all works which set up an approach to the writing of history which is strikingly at odds with the annals and chronicles Trevet himself went on to compose after 1320.

It is, of course, methodologically problematic to start from an assumption about what sort of text 'should' be produced by a particular writer at a particular time given a particular sort of intertextual background, but Trevet's *Annals* and *Chronicles* offer a prime example. Take the conjunction of Boethius and Seneca which is so central to Trevet's 'literary' output.[31] The *Consolation of Philosophy* emphasized the mutability of fortune and the transitoriness of worldly goods as counterpoints to the immutability of wisdom, virtue and truth. When Trevet expounded Boethius, he accordingly underlined the value of contemplating how temporal power and happiness can be so swiftly overthrown.[32] The writing of history was a natural extension of this principle: '[A]ncient times are full, and the present times are full too, of examples of kings whose happiness changed to misfortune'.[33] This was originally a Stoic insight: for Seneca, 'the greatest solace exists in the thought that what has happened to you has been suffered by everyone before you and will be suffered by everyone who comes after. For that reason … it is the nature of things to have made common what is made hardest to bear so that the equality of fate might be a consolation for its cruelty'.[34] However, it clearly resonated in late antique historiography, from Rufinus of Aquileia's translation of Eusebius's *Ecclesiastical History* to Orosius's generalization from Virgil's *sententia*, 'perhaps it will help one day to remember even these things' – remembrance of the past provided consolation for the sufferings of the present.[35]

[30] R. Dean, 'Cultural relations in the middle ages – Nicholas Trevet and Nicholas of Prato', *Stud. in Philology*, xlv (1948), 541–64. As bishop of Spoleto, Nicholas of Prato was sent by Boniface VIII on a mission to England in 1301; promoted to cardinal-bishop of Ostia in 1303 by Benedict XI (Nicholas of Treviso, Dominican master-general from 1296–99), he was heavily involved in Tuscany and missions to Henry VII, before becoming dean of the College of Cardinals at Avignon from 1312 until his death in 1321. See *Niccolò da Prato e i frati predicatori tra Roma e Avignone*, ed. M. Benedetti and L. Cinelli (Memorie Domenicane, Florence, 2013), esp. pp. 345–71.

[31] B. FitzGerald, *Inspiration and Authority in the Middle Ages: Prophets and their Critics from Scholasticism to Humanism* (Oxford, 2017), ch. 5.

[32] Trevet, *Super Boetio De Consolatione*, ed. E. Silk <http://campuspress.yale.edu/trevet> [accessed 23 Apr. 2019].

[33] Boethius, *The Consolation of Philosophy*, ed. and trans. S. Tester (Cambridge, Mass., 1973), p. 250 (iii.5).

[34] Seneca, *On Consolation*, in *Moral Essays*, ed. and trans. J. Basore (3 vols, Cambridge, Mass., 1928–35), ii. 359 (i.4).

[35] Rufinus of Aquileia, *Historia ecclesiastica* (*PL*, xxi), cols. 461–4 (praef.); Orosius, *Historiae adversus Paganos*, ed. M.-P. Arnaud-Lindet (3 vols, Paris, 1990–1), ii. 8 (iv.praef.1–3);

When Trevet turned to Seneca's *Tragedies* he emphasized their combination of pleasure and utility, defining the latter as the correction of moral conduct through *exempla*. Like a prudent doctor, Seneca coated bitter medicine with honey in order to cloak ethical teaching in pleasing fables, eradicating vice and cultivating virtue.[36] Once again, however, the underlying theme is the impermanence of human power, set alongside the corrupting effects of worldly passion. The result is a narrative of fortune and fate, to which regal families (of Athens, Thebes and Troy) are particularly and destructively susceptible. This process is exemplified by the house of Atreus, in which the consequences of fraternal strife are played out across successive generations.[37] Trevet accordingly introduces the *Tragedies* with a definition of the genre familiar from Isidore's *Etymologies*: its subject matter is *antiqua gesta*, the misfortunes of kings and of great men and the *res publica*.[38]

Between Trevet's exposition of the *Consolation* and the *Tragedies* came his commentary on Seneca's *Declamations*.[39] Schoolroom exercises on legal cases (*causae* or *controversiae*) were not the most obvious text, perhaps, for Trevet to choose, as he put it, to rescue from obscurity, but his justification was that they served a complementary function to Cicero's *De inventione* and the *Rhetorica ad Herennium*. Eloquence, according to Cicero, is acquired in three ways: through art, imitation and exercise. Cicero himself, according to Trevet, provides guidelines for the first, but Seneca for the second and third. The primary value of the *Declamations* therefore lies in their epigrammatic *sententiae* – pithy and striking maxims for which Sallust is held up as a prime exponent. As a result, the text is shot through with reflections on the mutability of fortune, the impermanence of human happiness, on tyranny and tyrants and the degeneration of society through luxury and sloth.[40]

Virgil, *Aeneid*, i. 203; vi. 377.

[36] *Nicolai Treveti Expositio Herculis furentis*, ed. V. Ussani (Rome, 1959), pp. 3–5 (prol.), trans. Minnis and Scott, *Medieval Literary Theory*, pp. 345–6.

[37] Trevet, *Il Commento*.

[38] Trevet, *Il Commento*, pp. 5–8. Cf. Isidore, *Etymologies*, ed. W. M. Lindsay (Oxford, 1911), viii.7, xviii.45.

[39] Trevet, *Expositio super decem libros Declamationum* (Oxford, Bodleian Library, Rawl. MS. G. 186, fos. 1–59). Cf. Seneca the Elder, *Declamations*, ed. and trans. M. Winterbottom (Loeb Classical Library, Cambridge, Mass., 1974); and *Oratorum et Rhetorum Sententiae, Divisiones, Colores*, ed. A. Kiessling (Leipzig, 1872).

[40] Seneca, *Declamations*, p. 230 (ix.1.13). Cf.: 'It is easier for us to learn by example what to imitate and what to avoid' (p. 260, ix.2.27). For subsequent moralization of Seneca's text, see N. Palmer, 'Das "Exempelwerk der englischen Bettelmönche": Ein Gegenstück zu den *Gesta Romanorum*?', in *Exempel und Exempelsammlungen*, ed. W. Haug and B. Wachinger (Tübingen, 1991), pp. 137–72.

When Trevet turned, finally, to Livy's *Ab urbe condita*, he compiled supplementary material and chronology from a range of historical sources: Justin's *Epitome* of Pompeius Trogus; Sallust; Virgil; Valerius Maximus; Eutropius; Augustine and Orosius. Livy's own statement of intent is analysed as a rhetorical *proemium* designed to make its readers benevolent and teachable, especially through setting out its utility. Trevet accordingly reiterates the usefulness of imitating good examples and avoiding the wicked. He also draws out Livy's concern to provide consolation from the decadence of an age 'when neither our vices nor their remedies can be endured'. These evils, Trevet explains, are the avarice, lust and luxury which had been introduced by the passage of time (*processus temporum*) – this is Ovid's age of iron, characterized by greed, lust for wealth and the luxury caused by sloth. Trevet chooses to expand on the consequences – avarice shortens human life and brings physical and material destruction – and gives Livy's consolation from present evils a precise historical context: the pernicious and debilitating effects of the civil wars initiated by Caesar and Pompey. He makes this final point with a reference to Statius's *Thebaid*, but also to Seneca's *Declamations*: in writing about the deeds of the Romans (*de gestis Romanorum sive de rebus Romanis*), Livy was consciously emulating Sallust.[41]

The inference from all these commentaries is clear. Trevet's literal exposition of Boethius, Seneca and Livy suggests an individual who, when it came to writing a history of his own, might reasonably be expected to have constructed a narrative of exemplary moral and political edification, of consolation for the mutability of temporal prosperity, for the vicissitudes of fortune to which rulers are subject from one generation to the next. This was, after all, the approach taken by Albertino Mussato, Trevet's exact contemporary in Padua, another scholar in the orbit of Nicholas of Prato and another close reader of Boethius's *Consolation* and Seneca's *Tragedies* (including Trevet's own commentary on *Hercules furens*). Mussato saw the writing of history explicitly in terms of tragedy (he describes himself as *istoriographus et tragoedus*) and as consolation for the fluctuations of time and fortune. This association made historiography the appropriate vehicle for his narrative of the rise and fall of rulers and led him to write separately on fortune and chance events; Seneca's *Tragedies* provided the model for his *Ecerinis* (1314), in which Ezzelino da Romano serves as exemplary historical commentary on the contemporary threat of Can Grande della

[41] Trevet, *Expositio super Titum Livium* (Lisbon, BN, MSS. Illum. 134–5, fo. 1r–v); Livy, *Ab urbe condita*, ed. and trans. B. Foster et al. (Loeb Classical Library, 14 vols, Cambridge, Mass., 1919–59), i. 2–8 (i.praef.). Cf. Trevet, *Super Boetio*, pp. 252–3 (ii.5); Ovid, *Metamorphoses*, ed. R. J. Tarrant (Oxford, 2004), p. 6 (i. 127–50).

Scala.[42] Mussato, moreover, was himself not just an observer, but an active participant in the political crises he narrated. His missions to Henry VII in 1311 to 1312 prompted a historical account of the emperor's deeds, the *Historia Augusta* (1310–13), while imprisonment in 1314 and exile in 1318 resulted in *De Gestis Italicorum post mortem Henrici VII Caesaris* (1313–21).[43] Here it was Mussato's familiarity with Sallust and Livy (his fellow Paduan historiographer) which left the deepest imprint on his view of history as a means of analysing the corruption and decline of his native city.

Trevet, too, was writing in times of acute crisis – in the aftermath of 1311–12 (the Ordinances); 1314 (the battle of Bannockburn); and the conflict of 1317–18; in the midst of the civil war of 1321 to 1322 (Thomas of Lancaster); and against a backdrop of famine (1315–22), the flight of the Dominicans from London (1326) and the deposition and death of Edward II (1326–7). And yet tragic narrative is not the approach Trevet chooses for his history. Rather than produce an explanatory narrative of events, Trevet compiles a chronographic record of deeds done. In the *Annals*, a digest of events in the Angevin kingdom since 1135 is periodically expanded to include material from Capetian, imperial and papal affairs, as well as from Trevet's own Dominican order, before stopping at Edward I's death in 1307. While epitaphs, character descriptions, natural phenomena, miracles and official documents are included, these are pared down and subordinated to an annalistic format. In the *Chronicles*, Trevet limits himself to what he calls *annotatio annorum* or *annotatio temporum*, for which his explicit model is the comparative and synchronized chronography of Eusebius, Isidore and Bede. Indeed, Trevet makes a point of quoting criticism of both Livy and Sallust for having exceeded the scope of history (*modus historiae*) when they included direct discourse composed in their own style. Trevet's own priority remained the resolution of conflicting chronologies for the events themselves.[44]

[42] A. Moschetti, 'Il *De lite inter Naturam et Fortunam e il Contra casus fortuitos* di Albertino Mussato', in *Miscellanea di studi critici in onore di Vincenzo Crescini* (Turin, 1927), pp. 567–99, at pp. 591–9; *Humanist Tragedies*, ed. and trans. G. R. Grund (I Tatti Renaissance Library, xlv, Cambridge, Mass., 2011), pp. 2–47.

[43] *Rerum Italicarum Scriptores*, ed. L. Muratori (28 vols, Milan 1723–51), x, cols. 9–568, 571–768.

[44] R. Dean, 'The life and works of Nicholas Trevet' (unpublished University of Oxford DPhil thesis, 1938), pp. 446–9, at p. 448; Mantello, 'Critical edition of the *Gesta Temporum Edwardi Regis Anglorum*', appendix I, at p. 523. Cf. Justin, *Epitoma historiarum Philippicarum Pompeii Trogi*, ed. O. Seel (2nd edn, Stuttgart, 1972), p. 258 (xxxviii.3.11).

Nicholas Trevet – the institution of the Dominican order

Why, then, did Trevet's historiography express such literary and analytical restraint? The conventional explanation is that Trevet was in his sixties and simply too busy as Dominican *lector* to do anything more than compile a chronological digest of events.[45] These same institutional duties may also have demanded this sort of approach. Trevet accepted that differences in aptitude and education meant people would come to the truth in different ways – some through logical demonstration, some through authority and some through fables. Such pedagogic flexibility was, in fact, the reason he had originally turned to Seneca. *De disciplina scolarium* (a text attributed to Boethius and widely read among English Dominicans) put Seneca first on its list of recommended authors for elementary instruction in grammar on the basis of his ability to handle and transmit his material (*traditio*).[46] This is a judgement which Trevet repeats: Seneca adapted his teaching and, for simple minds, this meant instruction though plain and unadorned precepts.[47] It was the duty of a Dominican *lector* to accommodate his teaching to the capabilities of his audience; to speak clearly and intelligibly about useful and expedient subjects; to avoid novel opinions; to keep to old and more established ones; and never to talk about what he did not properly understand himself. Leaving aside the multitude of things which could be said about individual passages, the *lector* should only expound the letter of the text.[48] Such institutional practice certainly fits Trevet's approach to his commentaries on Boethius, Seneca and Livy, where his primary concern was always the literal meaning, making sense of the words themselves rather than elucidating their further significance. This was also the case with *De civitate Dei*, where Trevet's exposition of allusions to classical history, mythology and poetry is expressly designed to make books I–X and book XVIII easier to read and comprehend.[49]

Applied specifically to historiography, a *lector*'s pedagogic priorities would certainly be consistent with the production of an updated chronographical

[45] Dean describes Trevet as 'a collector of data rather than a critic or philosopher' ('Earliest known commentary', pp. 97–8).

[46] [pseudo-]Boethius, *De disciplina scolarium*, ed. O. Weijers (Studien und Texte zur Geistesgeschichte des Mittelalters, xii, Leiden, 1976), pp. 95 (i.8), 119–20 (iv.34–35); Trevet, *Super decem libros Declamationum*, fo. 1. Cf. Vincent of Beauvais, *Speculum historiale*, pp. 309–20 (viii.102–36).

[47] Trevet, *Letter to Nicholas of Prato*, ed. Franceschini, *Il Commento*, pp. 2–3; trans. Minnis and Scott, *Medieval Literary Theory*, pp. 341–2.

[48] Humbert of Romans, *Instructiones de officiis ordinis*, in *Opera de vita regulari*, ed. J. J. Berthier (2 vols, Rome, 1888–9), ii. 254 (xi).

[49] Trevet, *In libros Augustini De civitate Dei* (Oxford, Bodleian Library, MS. 292, fos. 119–48), fo. 119r–v (prol.).

handbook. This seems to be the purpose of Trevet's *Computus Hebraeorum*, for example, a 1310 treatise on the Jewish calendar which accompanied his commentaries on the Old Testament.[50] It would also explain why Trevet incorporated so much material from Vincent of Beauvais and Martin of Troppau, viewing his own work as a continuation, adopting the annalistic style and the tabular format of his Dominican predecessors for events after 1277, but ensuring that information about popes and emperors was extended, in his own chronicle, to include deeds of the kings of England and of France.[51] This is an 'encyclopaedic' approach to events of the past, in other words, an instrument and resource for Dominican teaching, following an approach which had its roots in Hugh of St Victor and Peter Comestor. Dominicans received such instruction under the heading *de tadiumon temporum*, a rubric covering the ages of the world, its duration and a chronology which comprised a brief chronicle of biblical history, kings, Christianity and other religions.[52] Collections of moral *exempla* might subsequently draw on such historical material – as Humbert of Romans recommended, 'there are many histories, not only amongst the faithful, but also amongst *infideles*, which work very well in preaching for edification'.[53] Such exemplification, however, was conceived as a separate exercise. Moral instruction may rest on the historical circumstances of person, place and time (and, as Vincent of Beauvais cautioned, *res gestae* which are presented without the certitude of chronology or regnal years are not to be accepted as history),[54] but this always constituted a second level of interpretation.

If chronography and chronicles occupied a significant but circumscribed place within Dominican institutional education, Trevet's approach bears comparison with his contemporary Bernard Gui. In 1304 Gui was commissioned by the general chapter at Toulouse to produce a historical compilation of the deeds and deliberations of the Dominican order, including biographical notices of individual friars and summaries of the proceedings of its chapters. In 1312–13 Gui put together a catalogue of *Reges Francorum* and began to assemble a universal chronicle from the birth of

[50] C. P. E. Nothaft, *Medieval Latin Christian Texts on the Jewish Calendar: a Study with Five Editions and Translations* (Time, Astronomy, and Calendars, iv, Leiden, 2014), ch. 4.

[51] W.-V. Ikas, 'Martinus Polonus' chronicle of the popes and emperors – a medieval bestseller and its neglected influence on medieval English chroniclers', *Eng. Hist. Rev.*, cxvi (2001), 327–41.

[52] M. M. Mulcahey, *'First the Bow is Bent in Study': Dominican Education before 1350* (Toronto, 1998), pp. 204–5, 211.

[53] Humbert of Romans, *De eruditione praedicatorum*, ed. Berthier, ii. 373–484, at pp. 401 (ii.9), 426 (ii.19).

[54] Vincent of Beauvais, *Speculum maius*, col. 4 (prol.5), quoting Hugh of Fleury, *Historia ecclesiastica* (iii.prol.) (*PL*, clxiii), col. 833.

Christ, collecting and excerpting material from earlier chronicles and *gesta*, including Vincent of Beauvais, Gerard of Fracheto and Martin of Troppau. These *Flores chronicarum* were sent, in 1316, to the master-general, Berengar of Landorre, and, in 1319, to Pope John XXII; they were then continuously revised and supplemented until Gui's own death in 1331. Unlike the explicitly exemplary and didactic purpose of Gui's *Speculum sanctorale* (a hagiographical collection undertaken at the request, again, of Berengar and presented, in part, to John XXII in 1324), Gui's chronicles were deliberately focussed on giving greater precision to the date and order of events. They were also explicitly distinguished from the writing of history. Historiography, Gui explains, concentrates on putting singular events together into a full written account of the history and sequence of *gesta*; chronography, on the other hand, is concerned primarily with annotating the times and running succinctly through the deeds to be remembered.[55]

Dominican historiography expressed an institutional practice which also went beyond its foundational role in an educational programme. A definitively chronographical approach served as a marked contrast to other forms of historical writing which were being produced at the same time. Orosius's interpretation of the scourges [*plagae*] of Egypt as the antetype for ten persecutions of the Church – an interpretation whose presumption had been immediately questioned by Augustine – opened the possibility of reading historical events in the Bible as a programmatic template for the period between the New Testament and the Second Coming.[56] Correlating the construction, destruction and restoration of the Temple at Jerusalem, for example, with the planting, scourging and reformation of the Church, or the rise and fall of the kingdoms of Israel and Judah with the rise and fall of Christian kingdoms, provided an attractively clear explanation for the vicissitudes of contemporary ecclesiastical and political events. Twelfth-century writers such as Rupert of Deutz, Honorius Augustodunensis, Gerhoh of Reichersberg and Anselm of Havelberg had all pushed this pattern hard, identifying a *specific* providential order to events in the sixth age and finding it in the seven gifts of the holy spirit from Isaiah or the seven seals and the seven-headed dragon from Revelation. This approach culminated in Joachim of Fiore's elaborate concordance of individual events in the Old Testament with individual events in Christian history since the New Testament – a pairing which revealed the imminence of the opening of the sixth seal in the third *status* of the Holy Spirit and a corresponding

[55] L. Deslisle, *Notices sur les manuscrits de Bernard Gui* (Paris, 1879), pp. 391–4, 421–4. Cf. A.-M. Lamarrigue, *Bernard Gui (1261–1331): un historien et sa méthode* (Paris, 2000).

[56] Orosius, *Historiae*, iii. 70–4 (vii. 27); Augustine, *De civitate Dei*, pp. 650–2 (xviii.52).

age of spiritual renewal.[57] Bonaventure may have tempered Joachim's conclusions, but he retained enough of this historicizing perspective to make his approach influential on subsequent Franciscan historiography.[58] Trevet was not oblivious to the dangers this could pose, since both Nicholas of Prato and Thomas Jorz (provincial prior of the English Dominicans) sat on commissions of inquiry into the work of Peter John Olivi. Apocalyptic frameworks of global history were also not exclusive to spiritual Franciscans: in 1255 Humbert of Romans had issued a joint encyclical with John of Parma which accepted a salvific role for *both* their orders; in 1300 the Dominican John of Paris responded to Arnaud of Villanova's anticipation of Antichrist with a treatise which demonstrated familiarity, if not sympathy, with Joachim of Fiore's historicism; in 1313 Henry of Harclay drew directly on Joachim when discussing whether astrology could be used to calculate the date of the Second Coming.[59] Placed in this context, it remains a striking emphasis of Trevet's dedicatory letter to his *Chronicles* not only that he was completing a work which had broken off after the first three of Augustine's six ages, but also that Trevet himself thought it was finished once he had reached the end of the fifth age – that is, *without* moving on to the sixth. A careful reader of Augustine's *De civitate Dei* knew providence did things differently there, that interpretation of the significance of events since the resurrection risked crossing the line separating history from prophecy.

Trevet's approach to historiography as a Dominican *lector* was shaped, finally, by the insular and provincial context within which he was writing. The immediate sources for his account of the kings of the English in the twelfth century – Robert of Torigni, William of Newburgh and Ralph de Diceto – provided Trevet with clear definitions of, and justifications for, chronicles and chronography (*chronographia, id est temporum descriptio*),[60]

[57] M. Reeves, *The Influence of Prophecy in the Later Middle Ages: a Study in Joachimism* (Oxford, 1969).

[58] B. McGinn, 'The significance of Bonaventure's theology of history', *Jour. Religion*, lviii (1978), 64–81; B. Roest, *Reading the Book of History: Intellectual Contexts and Educational Functions of Franciscan Historiography 1226–c.1350* (Groeningen, 1996).

[59] F. Pelster, 'Die Quaestio Heinrichs von Harclay über die zweite Ankunft Christi und die Erwartung des baldigen Weltendes zu Anfang des XIV. Jahrhunderts', *Archivio Italiano per la Storia della Pietà*, i (1951), 25–82.

[60] Robert of Torigni, *Chronicle*, ed. R. Howlett, *Chronicles of the Reigns of Stephen, Henry II, and Richard I* (Rerum Britannicarum Medii Aevi Scriptores, lxxxii, 4 vols, London, 1884–9), iv. 61 (prol.); Ralph de Diceto, *Abbreviationes chronicorum*, ed. W. Stubbs, *The Historical Works of Master Ralph de Diceto* (Rerum Britannicarum Medii Aevi Scriptores, lxviii, 2 vols, London, 1876), i. 3–263, at p.34, quoting Cassiodorus, *Institutiones divinarum et saecularium litterarum*, ed. R. A. B. Mynors (Oxford, 1937) p. 56 (i.17.2): '*chronica … quae sunt imagines historiarum brevissimaeque commemorationes temporum*'. Cf. Vincent of Beauvais, *Speculum doctrinale*, col. 297 (iii.127).

together with a condemnation of the lies which could be propagated in fabulous and prophetic narratives such as Geoffrey of Monmouth's *Historia regum Britanniae* (a text which Trevet also knew at first hand).[61] When Trevet dealt with the kings of the thirteenth century, he made it clear that a major aim of his own *Annals* was to correct a selective understanding of the previous 120 years. In Trevet's opinion, historical narratives since the beginning of John's reign had been skewed, either by negligence or by a popular hostility to kings. Trevet's appeal to the general utility of his work (*communis utilitas*) was accordingly more than a bland convention – it had correction of Roger of Wendover, Matthew Paris and the *Flores historiarum* firmly in its sights.[62] This approach to Angevin historiography derived additional resonance from the institutional ties which bound the English province to the patronage of both Edward I and Edward II. Trevet's connections here were personal: the body of Piers Gaveston lay in the Oxford convent until its translation to the new Dominican foundation at King's Langley in 1314; John Lenham, dedicatee of Trevet's *Declamations*, was Edward II's confessor until 1315; John of Drokensford (Droxford), dedicatee of Trevet's *De officii Missae*, was master of the wardrobe under Edward I and an important political figure under Edward II.[63] Such proximity may well have heightened Trevet's sensitivity to the abuse of history, therefore, when on 29 December 1314 Henry of Harclay delivered a sermon at Oxford for the feast of Thomas Becket which set out the punishments visited by God upon the second and third generations of those guilty of the archbishop's murder. Starting with King John, whose conduct towards Stephen Langton had clearly imitated the sins of his father, and invoking the prophecies of Merlin (including one from Joachim of Fiore), Harclay suggested that the English defeat at Bannockburn might indicate a continuation of the same retributive justice.[64] In 1317 Nicholas of Wisbech, the Dominican confessor to Margaret of Brabant (sister of Edward II and Mary of Woodstock), appears to have persuaded the king that, were Edward to be anointed with the holy oil of Thomas Becket, his prophesied travails as the fifth ruler after Henry II would come to an end.[65] Viewed from this perspective (Wisbech's

[61] William of Newburgh, *Historia*, pp. 3–10 (proem.).

[62] Trevet, *Annales*, pp. 1–3 (prol.). For the particular hostility of Westminster to Edward II, see A. Gransden, 'The continuation of the *Flores historiarum* from 1265 to 1327', in A. Gransden, *Legends, Traditions and History in Medieval England* (London, 1992), pp. 245–65.

[63] C. F. R. Palmer, 'The king's confessors', *The Antiquary*, xxii (1890), 114–20; Dean, 'Nicholas Trevet, Historian', p. 333.

[64] E. W. Kemp, 'History and action in the sermons of a medieval archbishop', in *The Writing of History in the Middle Ages: Essays presented to Richard William Southern*, ed. R. H. C. Davis and J. M. Wallace-Hadrill (Oxford, 1981), pp. 349–65.

[65] J. Maddicott, 'Poems of social protest in early fourteenth-century England', in *England in the Fourteenth Century: Proceedings of the 1985 Harlaxton Symposium*, ed. W. M. Ormrod

mission to John XXII – for which Edward II wrote a letter to Bernard Gui – was rejected), a historical narrative written by an Oxford Dominican of the deeds of English kings from Henry II to Edward I, let alone a narrative which included prophecies by Merlin, had to negotiate some sensitive political territory.[66] In covering the deeds of Angevin kings towards Becket, Langton and Winchelsea, as well as the events of 1215, 1258 to 1264 and 1297 to 1298, Trevet's *Annals* needed to tread a delicate line. What was said in his historical narrative and, perhaps more significantly, left unsaid, had to be weighed very carefully indeed.[67]

All these institutional considerations, then, may constitute, in themselves, sufficient reason for Trevet to eschew the moralizing approach to history which was invited by his close reading of Boethius, Seneca and Livy and opt, instead, for the annotation of annals and chronography. However, if Trevet's restraint was shaped by an appreciation of Seneca's insistence that subtlety should be concealed behind an apparently straightforward, open text,[68] then it might also serve as an example of a 'scholastic' approach to historiography conditioned by Augustinian and Aristotelian strictures on the distinction between history and aetiology, between what is humanly and divinely instituted. Trevet's self-denial, in other words, also reflected a deliberate, theoretically informed understanding of his subject.

Historiography and causation

Historical causation was an issue Trevet had been compelled to confront by the extended discussion of divine and human causes which he found in the writings of Boethius. In part this derived from a distillation of Cicero's analysis of intrinsic arguments drawn from circumstance – what happened before, during and after a particular event. Such argumentation concentrated on efficient causes and what they bring about. A knowledge of causes produces a knowledge of effects, but also vice versa: just as the cause shows what has been effected, so the effect demonstrates the cause. This extends to secondary causes – what the Stoics termed 'fate' – namely those things (place, time, material, means) which will not, in themselves, produce an effect, but without which that effect cannot be produced. Some

(Woodbridge, 1986), pp. 130–44; J. Phillips, 'Edward II and the prophets', in Ormrod, *England in the Fourteenth Century*, pp. 189–201.

66 For Trevet's handling of Merlin's prophecies, see *Annales*, pp. 197–8, 280, 300.

67 Trevet, *Annales*, pp. 52, 56–7, 67, 70, 78–9, 179–80, 185–6, 192–3, 197, 242, 247–8, 250–66, 333, 353–4, 357–8, 360–2, 366–8, 375–9. Trevet explicitly mentions the confirmation of Magna Carta under Henry III and Edward I; he quotes a Latin text of the *Remonstrances* in full.

68 Seneca, *Declamations*, pp. 20–2 (i.praef.21).

of these secondary causes result from nature, some from human will; some are clear, some lie hidden; causes which are clear pertain to human will; causes which are hidden are subject to 'fortune', a term which serves as shorthand for causes that are unknown: '[S]ince nothing happens without a cause, fortune is simply what is effected by an obscure and hidden cause'.[69]

The exactness which Boethius brought to Cicero's terminology, and the wider debate about the divine ordering of the universe on which he drew, had a profound impact on how the argumentation of cause and effect was subsequently understood. Boethius glossed Cicero's use of the word 'fate', for example, as 'a certain intricate interweaving and chain-like connection of antecedent causes and consequent events'.[70] Like Cicero, Boethius was concerned to reserve freedom for the human will against the necessity of events. He did so by distinguishing between different types of antecedent cause. When discussing Cicero's use of 'fortune', therefore, Boethius proffered a formulation based on Aristotle's definition of chance (*casus*):

> [W]henever something is done for the sake of some given end, and another thing occurs, for some reason or other, different from what was intended, it is called chance ... Now this is indeed believed to have happened by chance but it does not come from nothing; for it has its proper causes, and their unforeseen and unexpected coming together appears to have produced a chance event.[71]

For Boethius, both fortune and chance were terms which denoted the consequence of some other cause. Either as the unintended consequence of a particular action or as the result of a conjunction of separate causes whose combined consequence may have been unforeseen by the individuals who performed the original actions, *casus* should be defined in terms of a chain of causes, not a random force.

Boethius provided scholastic writers with a wide theological and philosophical field in which to place their language of causality. Reference to the 'fluctuations' of fortune and chance might indicate no more than a comparison of the world to the unpredictable character of the sea. However, using the terms fortune and chance could also mark a recognition that unexpected events can arise from the conjunction of antecedent, secondary and efficient causes. In this respect Boethius's *Consolation of Philosophy* dovetailed with Plato's *Timaeus*, where Calcidius offers a comparable discussion of how a divinely ordained universe operates under providence, fate, human power, fortune and chance. Given that some things are necessary,

[69] Cicero, *Topica*, ed. T. Reinhardt (Oxford, 2003), pp. 144–8 (58–64).

[70] Boethius, *In Ciceronis Topica* (*PL*, lxiv), col. 1146 (5).

[71] Boethius, *Consolation of Philosophy*, pp. 387–9 (v.1), quoting Aristotle, *Physica*, ii. 4–6; Trevet, *Super Boetio*, pp. 673–5.

some are possible and some are contingent (*dubium*), there is no intrinsic contradiction in distinguishing between a primary or principal cause and a secondary or incidental cause. Human deliberation over contingent subjects expresses a freedom to perform acts of virtue and vice, but the consequences of these actions may themselves interact and produce results which are beyond human control and at variance with their original intention. Fortune is therefore defined as 'the concurrence of two simultaneously occurring causes that draw their origin from an intention, from which concurrence something happens that occasions surprise independently of what was hoped for'.[72] This view of causation accommodated, rather than rejected, the epistemological uncertainty which might otherwise characterize a particular course of events. Appealing to providence and fortune, in other words, was not an admission of historiographical defeat; instead, it reflected a coherent scheme which acknowledged, not denied, the interweaving of causes and the temporal ordering of what happens in a world that is ultimately governed by God.

When Trevet commented on Boethius, he drew an explicit comparison with Augustine's discussion of fate and fortune, noting his acknowledgment that fortune is shorthand for causes which human understanding cannot grasp.[73] In explaining the operation of divine providence, Trevet also spelled out how the order of things (*ordo rerum*) is executed through the mediation of secondary causes, observing that the sequence or arrangement of these subordinate secondary causes is termed 'fate'. These secondary causes include the actions of free human will, which are entirely consistent with divine foreknowledge. The appearance of disorder in the events of this world, not least the prosperity enjoyed by the wicked, is thus the result of an ignorance of causes (*ignorantia causarum*), but also of a human inability to judge who is good, who is bad and what might be beneficial for either – all that is evident to human eyes is individual human actions (*gesta*). Boethius himself had appealed, in this context, to Lucan's reservations over the providential justice of Caesar's victory over Pompey, given the latter's support from the exemplary wisdom and virtue of Cato. Trevet adds Augustine's similar concerns over the sufferings of the just at the hands of the wicked. The *ordo rerum*, Trevet concludes, has a dual aspect – natural and providential – and, while humans can chart the former, the latter remains inscrutable (Romans XI: 33).[74]

[72] Calcidius, *On Plato's Timaeus*, ed. and trans. J. Magee (Dumbarton Oaks Medieval Library, xli, Cambridge, Mass., 2016), p. 376 (159).

[73] Augustine, *Retractationes* ed. A. Mutzenbecher (*CCSL*, lvii, Turnhout, 1984), p. 7 (i.1.2); Trevet, *Super Boetio*, pp. 605–6, 632 (iv.6).

[74] Trevet, *Super Boetio*, pp. 610–13, 622, 625–6, 632, 637 (iv.6). Cf. Lucan, *Pharsalia*, ed. A. E. Housman (Oxford, 1926), pp. 3, 5–6 (i.67, i.126-8)

If Trevet's reading of Boethius made him familiar with a distinction between primary and secondary causes within the *ordo rerum*, this was given a still sharper historiographical edge by the discussion of God's knowledge of future contingents which had been prompted by the propositions condemned at Paris in 1277.[75] The question of the contingency of future events also had its roots in Boethius's *Consolation*, but it extended to consideration of events in the past.[76] In Augustine's view, events which have happened in the past cannot be undone (*nec infecta fieri possunt*). However, if an event is contingent before it occurs, will it become necessary as soon as it has happened or does it retain its original contingency? At Oxford Trevet used his quodlibetic and disputed questions to discuss the precise nature of the causal relationship between providential foreknowledge and human agency. God's knowledge may be a necessary cause of all things, he concluded, but this efficient cause can co-exist with the secondary and immediate causes of contingent events.[77] In February 1315 Trevet was signatory to Henry of Harclay's condemnation of some of the more extreme propositions which had been drawn from the notion of God's absolute power.[78] Viewed from this perspective, Trevet's explicit distinction between a natural order of events, which takes place in time and can be known by humans, and a providential ordering of those same events, which may be unknown or unknowable, provides an important point of departure for his subsequent historiographical restraint in simply annotating the *series temporum* with a compilation of human *gesta*.[79]

Trevet's apprehension of the divine institution of events in the *ordo temporum*, finally, was matched by an appreciation of the human institution

[75] R. Hissette, *Enquête sur les 219 Articles Condamnés à Paris le 7 Mars 1277* (Louvain, 1977), pp. 39–43. Cf. C. Schabel, R. Friedman and I. Balcoyiannopoulou, 'Peter of Palude and the Parisian reaction to Durand of St. Pourçain on future contingents', *Archivum Fratrum Praedicatorum*, lxxi (2001), 183–300.

[76] Boethius, *Consolation of Philosophy*, pp. 426–35 (v.6); Aristotle, *Ethica*, p. 480 (vi.2); Aristotle, *De Interpretatione*, ed. L. Minio-Paluello and G. Verbeke (*Aristoteles Latinus*, ii.1–2, Bruges, 1965), pp. 13–18, 47–50 (ix). Cf. Aquinas, *Summa theologiae*, Ia, q. 25, a. 4, pp. 166–8.

[77] Basel University, MS. B. IV, fos. 47a–52a; M. Schmaus, 'Nicolai Trivet Quaestiones de causalitate scientiae Dei et concursu divino', *Divus Thomas*, ix (1932), 185–96. Cf. H. Gelber, *It Could Have Been Otherwise: Contingency and Necessity in Dominican Theology at Oxford 1300–1350* (Studien und Texte zur Geistesgeschichte des Mittelalters, lxxxi, Leiden and Boston, 2014).

[78] A. E. Larsen, *The School of Heretics: Academic Condemnation at the University of Oxford 1277–1409* (Education and Society in the Middle Ages and Renaissance, xl, Leiden, 2011), ch. 4.

[79] Cf. Seneca, *Declamations*, p. 456 (iv.6): 'I do not know and therefore do not state'.

of its narration. This point emerges from his commentary on the Psalms.[80] Bonaventure's fourfold distinction between writer, compiler, commentator and author provided an influential framework within which both the form and the content of the Psalter could be discussed. A *scriptor* does not add or change anything which is written by others; a *compilator* adds to what is written by others but nothing of his own; a *commentator* adds his own material to that of others, but only for clarification; an *auctor*, finally, writes his own material, adding that of others only for support.[81] The particular role of Ezra in the Psalms, compiling historical material whose primary and secondary efficient causes were God and David respectively, naturally invited discussion of the distinction which should be drawn between deeds or events (*res gestae*) and their subsequent collection and organization. Ezra's compilation, Trevet observed, replaced the historical order of the Psalms with an artificial order so as to elicit their praise of God.[82] The act of compilation, in other words, was not a neutral activity; it was itself an interpretative act. Maintaining the temporal sequence of historical deeds (*ordo rerum gestarum*) reflected a different level of meaning and interpretation from their literary re-presentation or artificial re-ordering. In his own historical writing Trevet was, by this measure, a writer and compiler of human deeds and events, not a commentator or author using them to support an opinion of his own; and, if he was a compiler, then this should not involve rearranging his material from the chronological order instituted by God.

Boethius's discussion of causes which human understanding may or may not grasp, combined with Augustine's distinction between the divine and human institution of history, gave Trevet a particular perspective on historiography. Reluctance to claim insight into the divine meaning of events was balanced by a well-developed language of causation and by an awareness of the causes which *were* more clearly discernible, namely individual human actions (*res gestae*). When Trevet presents the order of these events and deeds in his *Annals* and *Chronicles*, therefore, this was a deliberate acknowledgment of the limits on his own human understanding. This is of a piece with Aristotle's classification of science, art and the experience of particulars, but also with Augustine's distinction between history and aetiology. None of this amounted to a lack of interest in causation, be it the primary cause of God's providence or the secondary cause of human *gesta*.

[80] A. Kleinhaus, 'Nicholas Trevet O.P., Psalmorum Interpres', *Angelicum*, xx (1943), 219–36; A. Minnis, *Medieval Theory of Authorship: Scholastic Literary Attitudes in the Later Middle Ages* (Aldershot, 1988), pp. 85–6, 90–1, 151–2.

[81] Bonaventure, *Commentaria in IV libros Sententiarum* (*Opera theologica selecta*, i–iv), i. 12 (proemium q. 4).; Minnis, *Medieval Theory of Authorship*, pp. 94–5.

[82] FitzGerald, *Inspiration and Authority*, pp. 69–72.

Far from it. What it represented was a recognition that analysis of efficient and, above all, final causes would take a narrative of events beyond a strict definition of the *series temporum*, either towards moral instruction or to prophecy. Setting out and compiling the *ordo rerum* within the divinely instituted sequence of time, the divine institution of history, was one task; commenting on and understanding the providential order of those same events was quite another; using those individual human *gesta* as particular *exempla* to instruct a less learned audience in more general truths of ethical conduct, the human institution of history, was different again. In each case, the choice of literary format for the narrative of what was done – chronography, prophecy, poetry, tragedy, maxim, or homily – presupposed a particular explanatory purpose and a particular level of comprehension in an audience. Trevet's chronography, therefore, indicates a choice, not a failure of historical imagination or a lack of conceptual and methodological sophistication. Reading Augustine, Aristotle and Boethius made Trevet aware of the line he had to tread; reading Geoffrey of Monmouth, Roger of Wendover, Matthew Paris and the *Flores historiarum* – and listening to Henry of Harclay – made him acutely aware of the dangers of getting it wrong.

Historical knowledge as a scholastic discipline

Aristotle's epistemology presented scholastic historiography with a particular conceptual challenge. Given that the individual, by definition, constituted a unique collection of proper features not to be found elsewhere,[83] historical narrative needed to find a means of universalizing or generalizing the accidents of time, place and position so that this experience (*experimentum*) could become the subject both of knowledge and teaching. Either individual things (*res*) could be ordered in terms of their causes, or their common features could be identified and abstracted so that an inductive comparison of these particulars produced general principles. Writers of historical deeds (*res gestae*) accordingly elicited an intellectual order either through chronology or through ethical typology. In the case of moral philosophy, this process yielded truths 'for the most part' (*ut frequentius*),[84] exemplary paradigms of human conduct, or maxims of political counsel and deliberation. In the case of ordered causation in time, apprehension of the meaning of these individual *res* depended either on a simultaneous vision of the entirety of history or on prophetic insight;

[83] Porphyry, *Isagoge*, ed. L. Minio-Paluello (*Aristoteles Latinus*, i.6–7, Bruges and Paris, 1966), pp. 13–14 (vii.22–24).

[84] Aristotle, *Ethica*, p. 376 (i.3).

otherwise, knowledge of the co-efficiency of their primary cause (divine providence) and secondary cause (nature, human will) will necessarily be tempered by ignorance. The *series temporum*, however, was a divinely instituted order which remained accessible to human understanding, even if it needed to be left as an open-ended record of events to be continued by successive generations and even if the sixth age imposed its own limitations on whether its events belonged to an overarching pattern of sacred history. The result, in short, was a bifurcation of historiographical approaches – on the one hand, universalized or exemplified individual human *gesta*, and, on the other, a sequence of events recorded within a universal chronography – each of which rested on, and expressed, a different understanding of the human experience of time.[85]

Trevet's formal choice of annals and chronicles marked a deliberate restatement of Augustinian restraint at a time when the same historical material was clearly being deployed by other writers for very different theological and political ends. Trevet was an individual with his own contingent circumstances of time, place and position, moreover, and he intersected with a number of overlapping institutional structures and practices (the Dominican convents at Pisa, Florence, Paris and London; the university at Paris; the papal court at Avignon; the Angevin court in England). These reveal much about his 'scholastic' historiography, first and foremost the particular way in which, as a Dominican *lector*, he read and responded to a range of authoritative scriptural, patristic and classical texts by recovering and expounding the literal meaning which had been intended by their authors. Nor did Trevet have to move outside his Dominican order to become interested in the conjunction of Aristotelian philosophy and classical historiography. If he was sent to northern Italy in the late 1290s as part of the expansion of Dominican *studia* in the province, the friars with whom he is likely to have come into contact formed, in themselves, a classically learned group. Trevet himself states that he expounded Boethius in response to the entreaties of fellow Dominicans, sending a copy of his commentary to his former teacher and now colleague 'Paulus' (possibly Paulo dei Pilastri, prior of Santa Caterina in 1297 to 1298 and Santa Maria Novella in 1298 to 1299).[86] Tolomeo of Lucca, whose interests extended to Livy, Sallust and Valerius Maximus, was prior of Santa Maria Novella from 1300 to 1302, while Bartolomeo of San Concordio, who commented on Virgil

[85] H.-W. Goetz, 'The concept of time in the historiography of the eleventh and twelfth centuries', in *Medieval Concepts of the Past: Ritual, Memory, Historiography*, ed. G. Althoff, J. Fried and P. J. Geary (Cambridge, 2002), pp. 139–65.

[86] E. Panella, 'Priori di Santa Maria Novella di Firenze 1221–1325', *Memorie Domenicane*, xvii (1986), 253–84, at pp. 259–63.

and Seneca's *Tragedies* and translated Sallust into Tuscan, was in Florence between 1297 and 1304.[87] It was not access to, or interest in, classical texts themselves, however, which defined Trevet's approach to historiography, but the particular Augustinian and Aristotelian perspective from which he did so. Trevet's institutional practice, in this respect, remained the product of the provincial Dominican *studium* at Oxford and, in particular, of the pedagogic tradition initiated by Robert Kilwardby.

In expounding *De civitate Dei*, Trevet reveals that he followed the chapter divisions created by Kilwardby in order to facilitate the teaching and studying of Augustine's text.[88] Kilwardby's influence extended to *De ortu scientiarum*, a work which Trevet describes as 'fascinating and useful' (*curiosus utilisque*).[89] Following his commentary on the *Posterior Analytics*, Kilwardby had analysed how Aristotle's 'scientific' methodology should be applied to both speculative philosophy and the active philosophy of ethics and mechanics, 'linguistic disciplines' (*scientiae sermocinales*) which deal with human actions. It was possible to attain knowledge of the latter, he argued, but only in so far as their singular subject matter is abstracted into the sort of universal that forms the basis of science. Knowledge of universals, he explains, is produced by intellectual reflection on what is common to the multitude of particular sense experiences and to the exclusion of the circumstances of time and place in which they occurred. The 'sciences' of ethics and mechanics, in other words, deal with the contingencies of human conduct, but these singulars have to contain a form of the universal in order to become known and be taught. For this last requirement, Kilwardby developed a concept of the 'vague' or indefinite singular (*singulare vagum vel incertum*) which he found in Avicenna: whereas the singular individual is specific to place and time, the vague individual is abstracted from the circumstances which properly individuate it.[90]

[87] C. Davis, 'Ptolemy of Lucca and the Roman Republic', in C. Davis, *Dante's Italy* (Philadelphia, Pa., 1984), pp. 254–89, at p. 267; R. Witt, '*In the Footsteps of the Ancients*': *the Origins of Humanism from Lovato to Bruni* (Studies in Medieval and Reformation Traditions, lxxiv, Leiden, 2000), pp. 187–8.

[88] Trevet, *In Libros Augustini*, fo. 119. Cf. D. A. Callus, 'The *Tabulae Super Originalia Patrum* of Robert Kilwardby O.P.', in *Studia mediaevalia in honorem admodum Reverendi Patris Raymundi Josephi Martin*, ed. B. L. van Helmond (Bruges, 1948), pp. 243–70. For Kilwardby's influence on literal exegesis and pedagogic aids at Oxford, see J. I. Catto, 'Theology and theologians 1220–1320', in *The History of the University of Oxford*, i. *The Early Oxford Schools*, ed. J. I. Catto and R. Evans (Oxford, 1984), pp. 471–517.

[89] Trevet, *Annales*, p. 278.

[90] R. Kilwardby, *De Ortu scientiarum*, ed. A. G. Judy (Turnhout, 1976), pp. 134–5, 151 (xli.381, xlvii.437–438). Cf. Avicenna Latinus, *Liber primus naturalium*, ed. S. van Riet (Louvain and Leiden, 1992), pp. 12–14 (i).

For scholastic writers of history, the danger posed by ethical exemplification was that it would become more and more detached from its contingent and individuating historical circumstances until historiography was modelled simply on the *Facta et dicta memorabilia* of Valerius Maximus.[91] A case in point was John of Salisbury's *Policraticus*, a work which, in Trevet's own summary, persuaded its audience of moral virtue through *exempla* and fables.[92] The risk of such detachment was accentuated if historical narrative was also categorized as a form of ethical instruction best suited for those who are less learned and who are therefore moved to action by *exempla* and enthymemes rather than by demonstrative proofs and syllogisms. Augustine's view of the human institution of history warned against the presumption of divination, but he paired this category with 'similar literature' (*et quaequae similes litterae*) on the basis of a broader distinction between narrating what has been done (*facta*) and teaching what should be done (*facienda*). History may be useful in teaching through examples, in other words, but it becomes something different in the process. Hugh of St Victor picked up on this point when he established clear limits to the scope of historiography. History becomes tropology, he argued, when what has been done (*factum*) is changed into what should be done (*faciendum*), as we turn a narrative of someone else's deeds to our own instruction by conforming to their example of how to live.[93] Trevet's writing of history embodied the same concern. History remained, in essence, the *annotatio temporum* rather than the *institutio morum*. It should therefore limit itself to a chronographical ordering of events in which the deeds of individuals express the co-efficiency of the primary cause of divine providence with the secondary cause of human agency. When it came to considering the relationship of these two efficient causes to the final cause, for a writer or compiler of history to accept restrictions on his human understanding might constitute more prudent counsel than his presumption of a prophetic proclamation of God's will.

This did not mean Trevet was unable to conceive of an alternative approach to the writing of history: his close reading of Boethius, Seneca and Livy gave him a different model for historiography and Albertino Mussato demonstrated the type of narrative which could result. Mussato knew Aristotle's *Metaphysics*, including the commentaries by Albertus

[91] B. Smalley, *English Friars and Antiquity in the Early Fourteenth Century* (Oxford, 1960).

[92] Trevet, *Annales*, p. 95. Cf. P. von Moos, *Geschichte als Topik. Das rhetorische Exemplum von der Antike zur Neuzeit und die historiae im 'Policraticus' Johanns von Salisbury* (Hildesheim, 1988).

[93] W. M. Green, 'Hugo of St Victor: *De Tribus Maximis Circumstantiis Gestorum*', *Speculum*, xviii (1943), 484–93, at p. 491.

Magnus and Thomas Aquinas, and his contact with Dominicans extended to a debate over the nature of poetic theology with the *lector* at Padua, Giovannino of Mantua (1315–16).[94] Not enough is known about Trevet's sojourn in northern Italy to say how much he may have been familiar with the Paduan 'humanism' initiated by Lovato dei Lovati, and there is no evidence that Trevet visited Padua in person (although the Dominican general chapter did meet there in 1308). Nonetheless, the comparison of Trevet with Mussato reveals one final institutional practice which may, in itself, account for the contrast in their approach to historiography.

If Aristotle was at his most 'historical' when setting out the contingent circumstances of individual communities in the *Politics*, he did so from the perspective of a specific medical diagnosis, namely the avoidance of stasis or *mutatio*. The efficient cause of political instability was an imbalance in the constituent elements of the body politic. This was a lesson, and an approach, which was taken to heart by Mussato: his understanding of historical causation may have been conditioned by the relationship of human agency to fortune, fate and the divine will, but it extended to considerations of nature, astrology and geography. In particular, Mussato recast his Sallustian and Livian emphasis on the corruption caused by avarice and luxury as a *natural* process of 'constitutional' development, from health to decay. Like Marsilius of Padua, who explicitly distinguished between primary and secondary efficient causation, sought the cause of tranquillity in the healthy disposition of the constituent parts of the political community and identified the hidden cause of illness as the historical *gesta* behind papal plenitude of power,[95] Mussato's approach to historical explanation drew on the epistemological model of medicine. Mussato's friendship with Marsilius is well attested (Marsilius was the dedicatee of his dialogue on Seneca's *Tragedies* in *c.*1315), but their shared institutional context in the *studium* at Padua is more suggestive still. Mussato had actively encouraged Marsilius to study medicine; and it is the relationship of both writers to the teaching of Peter of Abano which led them to concentrate on the secondary material and efficient causes of nature – including the history of human *gesta*.[96]

Viewed from the perspective of the divine and human institution of history, the primary and secondary efficient causation of *gesta* across time, the difference in emphasis between Trevet and Mussato is marked. In this respect Lorenzo Valla can serve as an illuminating codicil, not so

94 FitzGerald, *Inspiration and Authority*, ch. 6.

95 Marsilius of Padua, *Defensor pacis*, ed. C. W. Previté-Orton (Cambridge, 1928), pp. 3 (i.1.3), 68 (i.15.4), 447 (ii.28.17).

96 N. G. Siraisi, *Arts and Sciences at Padua: the Studium of Padua before 1350* (Toronto, 1973), pp. 48–9.

much for his virtuoso deployment of judicial rhetoric on the Donation of Constantine as for his commemoration of the deeds of Ferdinand of Naples. Valla's prologue to these *Gesta* emphasizes the utility of history by turning Aristotle's hierarchy of disciplines on its head. Some philosophers, he writes, not just any but the greatest and most ancient among them, have placed history beneath poetry on the grounds that poetry is closer to philosophy because it deals with what is general and sets down universal precepts on the basis of made-up *exempla*. Homer actually teaches people to become good and wise, whereas Thucydides merely narrates what Pericles did next. Aristotle, Valla responds, was simply wrong to claim that history does not deal with universal propositions. The second half of Valla's prologue is then devoted to the task of demonstrating just how difficult history is to write. It requires care, insight and judgement to find out about something when it is the subject of so much disagreement; it is very rare, he points out, for the same action or event to be narrated in the same way by several people, because different individuals have different reasons for demonstrating either ignorance or credulity; it is also hardly possible for one person to perceive with their five senses all the individual circumstances which attend a particular deed. A historian's investigation of the truth is, in this regard, an activity which requires no less accuracy and wisdom than are shown by a judge or a doctor (*aut iudici … aut medico*).[97] Valla's choice of comparison here is revealing.

For the writing of history to emphasize the particular contingencies of time and place which moral exemplification needed to transcend, and to do so without remaining at the level of experience or incurring the charge of unreflective sophistry, required association with the judicial rhetoric for which appreciation of these individual circumstances was essential to its forensic practice. For the writing of history to concentrate on natural causation rather than voluntary causation, on efficient causes which go beyond the human agency of *gesta*, required familiarity with an intellectual tradition – medicine and, by extension, astrology – that was more comfortable with drawing reliable causal inferences from individual experience and external effects. This is the aetiology embodied by Galen: establishing causes from external effects and signs, thereby securing the 'scientific' nature of medical knowledge against the inductive experience of the empiricists. In neither case was such an approach necessarily or fundamentally incompatible with Augustine's view of the human institution of history. The phrase

[97] L. Valla, *Gesta Ferdinandi regis Aragonum*, ed. O. Besomi (Padua, 1973), pp. 3–8 (proem.). Cf. A. Momigliano, 'History between medicine and rhetoric', in A. Momigliano, *Ottavo contributo alla storia degli studi classici e del mondo antico* (Rome, 1987), pp. 13–25.

fides indicis (trustworthiness of a witness) literally points its finger to one aspect of this equation: the circumstances of time and place which are central to the rhetoric of judicial inquiry. The subsequent history of the term 'aetiology', however, indicates the other. As exemplified by Nicholas Trevet and Albertino Mussato, if a 'scholastic' approach to the divine and human institution of history was to move away from the chronographical historiography which had been adumbrated by Augustine and reinforced by Aristotle, then such a development would be precipitated, not by the reading or recovery of exemplary historical texts from antiquity, but by the study of law and medicine.

II. Institutions and individuals: organizations and social practices

a. Individuals and organizations

5. The charismatic leader and the *vita religiosa*: some observations about an apparent contradiction between individual and institution

Gert Melville

The *Decretum Gratiani* includes a canon (C. 19 q. 2 c. 2) whose content, according to the legal historian Peter Landau, 'was able to lead directly to a relativisation of any ecclesiastical legislation'. 'There are two laws: one is public, the other private' (*Duae sunt … leges: una publica, altera private*), the paragraph begins and then explains. *Lex publica* was to be understood as the canon law which had been written down from the time of the Church Fathers; *lex privata*, by contrast, had to be seen as what was inscribed in the heart by an 'impulse of the Holy Spirit' (*instinctu Sancti Spiritus*; the term *afflatus* will be used for this). Subsequently, a relevant case is presented: a secular clergyman was permitted to join a monastery even if this conflicted with his bishop's wishes, provided that – under inspiration from the holy spirit – he wanted to seek his salvation there. This is justified by the observation that the *lex privata* was worthier than the *lex publica* since the former was the law of the spirit of God and those who acted in the spirit of God were guided by the law of God. Who, then, as is asked in that paragraph, could defy the Holy Spirit? 'Where the Spirit of the Lord is, there is freedom [*ubi Spiritus Dei, ibi libertas*]'; and thus a person guided by the spirit of God was exempt from any ecclesiastical law.[1]

Landau rightly deems the aforementioned *lex privata* to be the 'right of freedom in relation to the prohibitions of the *lex publica*, the *ius comune* of the Church'. He continues that 'the *lex privata* is valid independently of any written form … and can lead directly to a relativisation of the ecclesiastical legal order. It can be directly employed to break with positive legislation by means of the idea of a superordinate subjective law (*überpositiven subjektiven Rechts*)'.[2] This interpretation refers to a legal norm which was equipped not

[1] 2 Corinthians III: 17. See below.

[2] P. Landau, '*Officium* und *Libertas christiana*' (Sitzungsberichte der Bayerischen

G. Melville, 'The charismatic leader and the *vita religiosa*: some observations about an apparent contradiction between individual and institution', in *Individuals and Institutions in Medieval Scholasticism*, ed. A. Fitzpatrick and J. Sabapathy (London, 2020), pp. 139–55.

with a casuistic but with a general claim to validity and in fact represents a juridical legitimization liberating the individual from institutional constraints by way of a transcendental appeal to a higher authority – that of God.

According to this norm, any individuals who were convinced of their ability to invoke an *afflatus* of God could disregard all ecclesiastical institutions; in fact, the individual required no regulation of his life through the channels of the official Church. The personal discovery of a norm rooted by God in the heart – something which could only spring from the individual conscience and had to be claimed before that conscience[3] – stood against the positive law of an institution which on principle defined itself as the mediator of salvation interposed between God and individual. Here, the institution was instead confronted with a statement of a person's immediate access to God, from which, indeed, a basic right to individual freedom could be inferred. This chapter therefore explores how medieval Christian thinkers and leaders – specifically 'charismatic' ones – tried to articulate a freedom of movement which was not arbitrary but structured by the theological and canonical precepts of the tradition. These latter stand for 'scholasticism' as an approach here; and although this chapter does not particularly comment on scholasticism systematically *per se*, the norms of theology and law permeate an exploration of the *Problematik* of how charismatic individuals could articulate themselves and whether they could do so institutionally.

***

The ecclesiology of the period incrementally developed an understanding of the Church which was both the bride of Christ or the mystical body of Christ as well as the institution – as a community (*universitas*) – of redemptive power.[44] The two were not mutually exclusive. From its roots

Akademie der Wissenschaften, philosophisch-historische Klasse 1991, i, Munich, 1991), pp. 55–96, at p. 60.

[3] M. Breitenstein, 'Das "Haus des Gewissens". Zur Konstruktion und Bedeutung innerer Räume im Religiosentum des hohen Mittelalters', in *Geist und Gestalt. Monastische Raumkonzepte als Ausdrucksformen religiöser Leitideen im Mittelalter*, ed. J. Sonntag (Vita regularis, lxix, Berlin, 2016), pp. 19–55.

[4] S. A. Chodorow, *Christian Political Theory and Church Politics in the Mid-Twelfth Century: the Ecclesiology of Gratian's Decretum* (Berkeley, Calif., 1972); P. von Moos, 'Krise und Kritik der Institutionalität. Die mittelalterliche Kirche als "Anstalt" und "Himmelreich auf Erden"', in *Institutionalität und Symbolisierung. Verstetigung kultureller Ordnungsmuster in Vergangenheit und Gegenwart*, ed. G. Melville (Cologne and Vienna, 2001), pp. 293–340.

in the apostles' charismatic community and resting on its gospel base, the Church institutionalized itself over the centuries as a spiritual system and, at the same time, a firmly established organization. It was increasingly furnished, on the one hand, with a gradually solidifying body of sacraments in terms of perceptible, grace-conferring signs, as well as with the sacrality of ordinations, etc.; and, on the other hand, with precisely defined offices in pre-set hierarchies with both codified norms and normative practices together with juridical and administrative proceedings with rituals and symbols. This institutionalizing process generated normative traditions which were understood as divine revelations and thus linked with the Gospel. Their accessibility and connection to the truth of Church teachings, and thereby also to the latter's redemptive power, were consequently based on two principles (sacraments and offices), the proper understanding of which was handed over to the judgement of the ecclesiastical *magisterium*. At the latest from the late eleventh-century Gregorian reforms onwards a proposition was in force, one set in stone: 'S/he is not held a Catholic who does not agree with the Church of Rome' (*Quod catholicus non habeatur, qui non concordat Romane ecclesie*),[5] a phrase which gained its normative depth in connection with the *dictum* already formulated in patristic writings: 'outside the church, no salvation' (*extra ecclesiam nulla salus*).[6]

The Church was thus an institution conceived as God's foundation, armed with a well-functioning organization with the ability to assert itself legally and through a symbolic world anchored in spiritual transcendence. Confrontation with just such a power was necessary for all those who believed that by appealing to the call of the Holy Spirit it was possible to derive a right to individual freedom from ecclesiastical regulation. If the formula *ubi Spiritus Dei, ibi libertas* is already found in Paul's second Letter to the Corinthians (2 Corinthians III: 17) and delineated the Church's basic 'pneumatic' principle, it nevertheless finds itself similarly faced with the Gregorian proposition stressing the rights of the Church.[7] It was no coincidence that the fundamental tension between the official Church and individual freedom in the Spirit of God was extremely explosive during just

[5] H. Fuhrmann, '"Quod catholicus non habeatur, qui non concordat Romanae ecclesiae". Randnotizen zum *Dictatus Papae*', in *Festschrift für Helmut Beumann zum 65. Geburtstag*, ed. K. U. Jäschke and R. Wenskus (Sigmaringen, 1977), pp. 263–87.

[6] J. Johrendt, '"Nulla salus extra ecclesiam". Innocenzo III e la chiesa come istanza mediatrice di salvezza', in *Il lateranense IV: le ragioni di un concilio. Atti del LIII convegno storico internazionale: Todi, 9–12 ottobre 2016* (Spoleto, 2017), pp. 245–60.

[7] In the sense of *pneuma* as spiritual rather than earthly wind. On the medieval reception of 2 Corinthians III: 17 cf. von Moos, 'Krise', pp. 326–36; briefly also G. Melville, '"Dove c'è lo Spirito del Signore, lì è la libertà". Aspetti del trascendimento istituzionale medievale', in *Libertas (secoli X–XIII). VI Settimana della Mendola*, ed. N. d'Acunto (Milan, forthcoming).

this period, that is, from the late eleventh century onwards. In principle, this was about the confrontation between the official Church and those religious movements which – undoubtedly exacerbated by the conflicts of the investiture controversy – propagated a new religiosity stressing conscience and personal responsibility and which spread through Christendom generally, but predominantly in France and Italy.[8] This religiosity was meant to lead to a new religious life by implementing evangelical counsels, imitation of the apostles and relinquishment of all possessions. In the person of charismatically effective holy men – both hermits and itinerant preachers – together with large followings across all social groups, this religiosity had found an extremely diverse, effective embodiment.[9]

Thus, that Pauline statement of free and liberating choice grounded on the *lex privata* did not stand alone. For instance, a letter of Lanfranc of Canterbury (*c.*1010–89) circulated widely and was quoted many times. Lanfranc wrote that he would leave a monastery if he realized he was unable to save his soul there – even if he had sworn never to leave it. This would not be grounds for accusing him of having broken his oath since one did not break away from God if one abandoned the wrong path in order to remain with him.[10] Perhaps the weightiest case of a consequence resulting from such a divinely obliged imperative was the founding of Cîteaux and thus the origins of the Cistercian order at the turn of the twelfth century.[11] Robert, abbot of Molesme (1027–1111), came to think he could not properly fulfil his profession to follow the Rule of Benedict there and that if he remained in the monastery entrusted to him he would persistently transgress against the Rule. As a result he was fearful of the judgement of the heavenly ruler. He thus decided, together with a part of the monastery at Molesme, to travel to Cîteaux, although doing so gravely transgressed the fundamental canonical commitment to stability of place (*stabilitas loci*, that is, remaining at one's monastery) and his abbatial duty of care. He justified his actions

[8] See H. Grundmann, *Religious Movements in the Middle Ages: the Historical Links Between Heresy, the Mendicant Orders, and the Women's Religious Movement in the Twelfth and Thirteenth Century*, trans. S. W. Rowan (Notre Dame, Ind., 1995); G. Melville, *Medieval Monasticism: its History and Forms of Life*, trans. J. Mixson (Collegeville, Minn., 2016), pp. 89–124.

[9] See H. Leyser, *Hermits and the New Monasticism: a Study of Religious Communities in Western Europe 1000–1150* (London, 1984); *Ermites de France et d'Italie, XIe–XVe siècle*, ed. A. Vauchez (Rome, 2003).

[10] *Beati Lanfranci Cantuariensis archiepiscopi epistolarum liber*, Ep. lx, in *PL* 150, col. 549 sq.

[11] Cf. G. Melville, 'Die Zisterzienser und der Umbruch des Mönchtums im 11. und 12. Jahrhundert', in *Norm und Realität. Kontinuität und Wandel der Zisterzienser im Mittelalter*, ed. F. J. Felten and W. Rösener (Vita regularis, xlii, Berlin, 2009), pp. 23–43.

by the fact that he would have committed a sustained breaking of his vows had he remained. A generation later, the greatest of the period's Cistercians, Bernard of Clairvaux (1090–1153), affirmed the propriety of the decision and recommended the same course of action to his contemporaries in times of need: 'If in a given place life cannot be lead in accordance with the Rule, I advise you without reservation to follow the spirit of freedom [*spiritui libertatis* in reference to 2 Corinthians III: 17] and to transfer to another monastery'.[12]

A more pronounced reference to 2 Corinthians III: 17 and the passage from Gratian was employed in order to justify the tenacity of Clare of Assisi (1193/94–1253). The *Legenda versificata Sanctae Clarae* redacted in the mid thirteenth century describes how pope Gregory IX urged Clare to renounce her absolute poverty by accepting provisions in the form of land grants. She refused to accept them, the account continues, as she wanted in no way to be absolved from following Christ (*sequela Christi*). The *Legenda*, however, adds another striking commentary to the account of this occurrence. First, the text acknowledges Clare's opposition as a remarkable risk by underlining Gregory's position as *Summus pontifex*, thereby stating that 'the divine power, the highest authority, granted him the right to loosen and to bind!' (*Pontifici summo, solvendi, sive ligandi | Suppremum cui posse dedit divina potestas!*). The *Legenda* then explains Clare's behaviour, arguing 'that the Holy Spirit led her from within' (*quod agebat eam divinus Spiritus intus*) and that the following principle thus holds true: '[W]here the spirit breathes, there is freedom. Those he moves are not beneath the law: he prejudges every law' (*Est ibi libertas, ubi spirat; quos agit, illi | Non sunt sub lege: legi preiudicat omni*).[13] The author thus bore witness to personal empowerment, granted by God to the individual souls from within and freeing them from institutional compulsion. This empowerment was viewed as greater than the general authorization granted by God to the highest office of the Church for the institutionalized 'power of binding and releasing' (*potestas ligandi et solvendi*).[14] The statement on Clare's position

[12] Bernard of Clairvaux, *De praecepto et dispensatione*, in *Sancti Bernardi opera* (8 vols, Rome, 1957–77), iii. *Tractatus et opuscula*, ed. J. Leclercq and H.-M. Rochais (Rome, 1963), pp. 252–94, at p. 284.

[13] *Legenda versificata Sanctae Clarae*, in *Fontes Franciscani*, ed. E. Menestò and S. Brufani (Assisi, 1995), pp. 2347–99, at p. 2360. Cf. also on the Franciscan context, G. Melville, '"Homo spiritum habens". Francesco fra Chiesa istituzionale e transcendenza individuale', *Collectanea Franciscana*, lxxxviii (2018), 281–300. For the historical background of Clara's afterlife and influence, see M. P. Alberzoni, *Chiara e il papato* (Milan, 1995); *Clara Claris Praeclara: l'esperienza cristiana e la memoria di Chiara d'Assisi in occasione del 750 anniversario della morte, Assisi 20–22 novembre 2003* (Assisi, 2004).

[14] I.e., the commission given by Christ to Peter in Matthew XVI: 29, also XVIII: 18.

greatly exceeded Gratian's postulation and thereby created an extremely broad view regarding the freedom of the holy spirit. With Gratian, it was a matter of 'breaking away from positive legislation', as Landau rightly notes. Here, however, we witness a hierarchical differentiation between two divine norms: a differentiation between a *lex privata* and a *lex publica*, which in this case were *both* divinely inspired law, whereby the *lex* of human freedom licensed the leapfrogging over another, more generally applicable, divine regulation.

Such disregard for existing norms found a justification in a considerably more fundamental and comprehensive framework by means of increased ecclesiastical recourse to 1 Timothy I: 9: '[T]he law is not laid down for the just but for the lawless' (*quia iusto lex non est posita sed iniustis*). Already Augustine had connected this passage to his famous dictum 'Love and do what you will!' (*Dilige et quod uis fac*) because he wanted to express his view that there was no need for laws in the presence of absolute love. He had also connected it to his statement that 'where everything is good, there is no order, for highest equality does not require any order' (*ubi omnia bona sunt, ordo non est. Est enim summa aequalitas quae ordinem nihil desiderat*).[15] This *dictum* similarly enjoyed increased circulation from the late eleventh century onwards. It was in just such a way that Thomas Aquinas interpreted *ubi spiritus Domini, ibi libertas*, namely that 'only that person is free who has ruled over him/herself'. In other words, the Holy Spirit has so perfected the human soul that, saturated with love for God, it is ready to avoid evil on account of its own will, not because a written law forbids it. With that, the soul has reached the summit of religious exertion – and thereby liberated itself from every institutional constraint, including laws, because it no longer needs them.[16]

In all the above remarks, the individual appeared free from the obligation to act according to the rules of institutionalized systems of order. As a result, a trans- or supra-institutional space seemed to open up in which the individual will could develop freely. (This space could even result in an anti-institutional position.) At first glance, this finding appears to be

[15] For Augustine, see *De ordine*, ed. W. M. Green, in *Sancti Avrelii Avgvstini Contra academicos, De beata vita, De ordine, De magistro, De libero arbitrio* (CCSL, xxix, Turnhout, 1970), pp. 87–137, at p. 107. Cf. G. Constable, *'Love and Do What You Will': the Medieval History of an Augustinian Precept* (Kalamazoo, Mich., 1996); G. Melville, '"Liebe und tue, was du willst!" – Eine Herausforderung für den mittelalterlichen Menschen', in *Sorge*, ed G. Melville, G. Vogt-Spira and M. Breitenstein (Europäische Grundbegriffe im Wandel: Verlangen nach Vollkommenheit, ii, Cologne and Vienna, 2015) pp. 79–95.

[16] Thomas Aquinas, *Super II Epistolam b. Pauli ad Corinthios lectura*, cap. 3, lectio 3, n. 112, in *Sancti Thomae Aquinatis, Super Epistolas s. Pauli lectura*, ed. R. Cai (2 vols, Turin/Rome, 1953), i. 463–4.

accurate; yet if looked at more closely it has to be qualified. Severing ties to the rules of earthly institutions was only possible for individuals who knew they were bound to the rules of God and the divine order and acted in compliance with them: that is to say, to act not according to one's own will but according to God's will. Here lay the ethical core of individual autonomy apart from the institutions of this world. At the same time, however, this concrete anthropological articulation was only possible within a framework in which man gained this autonomy as a divine creature which obeyed its creator lovingly, which is why the Spirit of God endowed it with the exceptional ability to recognize the divine will.[17] This brings us to the heart of the matter: the person inspired by the holy spirit was permitted to transcend the earthly institution only insofar as he or she was also bound up in God's transcendence.

***

With that, we have outlined the question and its implications sufficiently to situate the special position of charismatic individuals in their particularly medieval tension between individuals and institutions. What has so far been explained with regard to individuals generally applies equally to medieval charismatic figures. This chapter will deal with several charismatic leaders of religious movements from the eleventh to the thirteenth centuries because the assumption that an individual leader – as a *leader* – must be definitionally opposed to existing institutional norms appears to relate to them most of all. This raises the question of how to define the idea of a *charismatic* leader per se. In the structural sense, a charismatic leader was a highly particular sort of individual who, because of his inherent capabilities, would more readily come into conflict with institutions. Such leaders not only claimed they were legitimately free from institutional norms but, still further, claimed that they themselves were also bearers, enunciators and enforcers of norms.[18]

[17] See for early roots, J. K. Lee, 'The Church and the holy spirit: ecclesiology and pneumatology in Tertullian, Cyprian, and Augustine', *Studia patristica*, xci (2017), 189–206.

[18] Cf. *Charisma und religiöse Gemeinschaften im Mittelalter*, ed. G. Andenna, M. Breitenstein and G. Melville (Vita Regularis, xxvi, Münster, 2005); *Das Charisma. Funktionen und symbolische Repräsentation*, ed. P. Rychterová, S. Seit and R. Veit (Beiträge zu den historischen Kulturwissenschaften, ii, Berlin, 2008); *Charisma and Religious Authority: Jewish, Christian, and Muslim Preaching, 1200–1500*, ed. K. L. Jansen (Europa sacra, iv, Turnhout, 2010); *Faces of Charisma: Image, Text, Object in Byzantium and the Medieval West*, ed. B. M. Bedos-Rezak and M. D. Rust (Explorations in Medieval Culture, ix, Leiden, 2018).

By way of illustration, this chapter focuses on five charismatic religious figures as examples: Stephen of Muret (*c.*1047–1124); Stephen of Obazine (d. 1159); Norbert of Xanten (*c.*1080–1134); Robert of Arbrissel (d. 1117); and Francis of Assisi (1181/2–1226). By reference to these personalities, it is possible to establish proof of norm-creation and anti-institutional behaviour which strikingly match Max Weber's thesis about periods of charismatic intensity. Weber argued that:

> charisma is the great revolutionary power in eras founded on bonds of tradition. However, it operates in contrast to the equally revolutionary power of 'reason' [*ratio*, i.e., instrumental reasoning] which either works directly from the outside in – through changing living conditions and practical problems and hence, indirectly, through the changing attitudes to these which result: or, on the other hand, through intellectualizing them. Charisma can be transformative from the inside out, it signifies a conversion of the fundamental direction of both desire and action – arising from duress or enthusiasm – producing a completely new orientation of all attitudes towards all given ways of life and to the 'world' generally.[19]

Stephen of Muret broke with every tradition of the *vita religiosa* in the most radical way.[20] In 1076 he withdrew to the solitude of the woods near Limoges; took his vows alone there without any ecclesiastical intermediary and thus directly in front of God; and then provided his disciples (who had gathered around him quite quickly) with the following words: 'There is no rule beyond the Gospel of Christ, for this is the rule of rules'.[21] Rules such as those of St Basil, Augustine or Benedict were not the source of piety (*origo religionis*) but merely its outgrowths (*propagines*); not the root

[19] 'Das Charisma ist die große revolutionäre Macht in traditional gebundenen Epochen. Zum Unterschied von der ebenfalls revolutionierenden Macht der "ratio", die entweder geradezu von außen her wirkt: durch Veränderung der Lebensumstände und Lebensprobleme und dadurch mittelbar der Einstellungen zu diesen, oder aber: durch Intellektualisierung, kann Charisma eine Umformung von innen her sein, die aus Not oder Begeisterung geboren, eine Wandlung der zentralen Gesinnungs- und Tatenrichtung unter völliger Neuorientierung aller Einstellungen zu allen einzelnen Lebensformen und zur "Welt" überhaupt bedeutet' (M. Weber, *Wirtschaft und Gesellschaft*, ed. J. Winckelmann, (5th edn, Tübingen, 1972), p. 142) (author's translation).

[20] C. A. Hutchison, *The Hermit Monks of Grandmont* (Kalamazoo, Mich., 1989); J. Becquet, *Etudes grandmontaines* (Ussel, 1998); G. Melville, '*"In solitudine ac paupertate"*. Stephans von Muret *Evangelium* vor Franz von Assisi', in *In proposito paupertatis. Studien zum Armutsverständnis bei den mittelalterlichen Bettelorden*, ed. A. Kehnel and G. Melville (Vita regularis, xiii, Münster, 2001), pp. 7–30.

[21] *Liber de doctrina uel Liber sententiarum sev rationvm beati viri Stephani primi patris religionis Grandimontis*, in *Scriptores ordinis Grandimontensis*, ed. J. Becquet (*CCCM*, viii, Turnhout, 1968), pp. 3–62, at p. 5.

but only the branches; they were merely the work of man. Thus, the gospel alone showed the right way. Francis of Assisi spoke out in a very similar way when he was requested to adopt one of the conventional rules:[22] 'My brethren, God Himself called me to the path of humility and showed me the path of simplicity ... And so I do not want you to name any rule to me, neither that of Holy Benedict nor that of Holy Augustine or that of Holy Bernard, and in general no way or form of life apart from the one that God pitying me has shown and sent'.[23] Norbert of Xanten's followers are said to have asked him to renounce any adoption of an already existing rule since his conduct was entirely sufficient as a guideline of communal life for all:[24] 'The brothers who followed him believed that what they heard from his mouth would suffice for salvation'.[25]

In all these cases there was frank disregard for traditional norms in favour of constituting norms of one's own. These appeared, in principle, as a fundamental, coherent power which, in Max Weber's already quoted words, is indeed to be defined as a 'completely new orientation of all attitudes towards all given ways of life and to the "world" generally'. Those charismatics wanted a form of the *vita religiosa* which represented a complete alternative to the existing monasteries under the Benedictine observance. One pivotal element of this different form was strict poverty. When, on his deathbed, Stephen of Muret's disciples asked him what he would leave them, he said: 'If you adhere to God steadfastly out of love of poverty [*amando paupertatem*] and do not stray from this path of truth, He Himself will give you in abundance in accordance with His providence, through which He rules all things'.[26] This poverty was a frontal assault on the rich monasteries of his time, which collected tithes and had their

[22] Cf. *La regola dei Frati Minori. Atti del XXXVII Convegno internazionale, Assisi, 8–10 ottobre 2009* (Spoleto, 2010); A. Thompson, *Francis of Assisi: a New Biography* (Ithaca, N.Y., 2012); P. Alberzoni, *Santa povertà e beata semplicità: Francesco d'Assisi e la Chiesa romana* (Milan, 2015); F. Accrocca, *Francesco e la Santa Chiesa Romana* (Assisi, 2015); J. Dalarun, *François d'Assise en questions* (Paris, 2016).

[23] *Compilatio Assisiensis*, ed. in Menestò and S. Brufani, *Fontes Franciscani*, pp. 1471–1690, at p. 1498, cap. 18.

[24] Cf. *Norbert von Xanten. Adliger, Ordensstifter, Kirchenfürst*, ed. K. Elm (Cologne, 1984); F. J. Felten, 'Norbert von Xanten, die Gründung von Prémontré und die Entstehung des Prämonstratenserordens', in *Norbert von Xanten und der Orden der Prämonstratenser*, ed. C. Dölken (Magdeburg, 2010), pp. 7–32; S. Weinfurter, 'Norbert von Xanten und sein neuer Lebensentwurf. Gesellschaftsordnung und Wertewandel im frühen 12. Jahrhundert', in Dölken, *Norbert von Xanten*, pp. 151–74.

[25] *Vita Norberti archiepiscopi Magdeburgensis*, ed. R. Wilmans (MGH, SS, xii, Hanover, 1856), p. 683.

[26] *Vita venerabilis viri Stephani Mvretensis a Stephano de Liciaco seu alio coaeuo redacta*, in Becquet, *Scriptores ordinis Grandimontensis*, pp. 101–37, at pp. 123–4.

services in matters of faith remunerated by extensive land grants and other donations, a practice which met with general acceptance in the institutional surroundings.[27] On the part of such charismatics, these monasteries were now reproached for merely satisfying the 'observances of the cloister' (*claustrales observantiae*) with Pharisaic arrogance while neglecting the internalization of the true commandments of the Lord.[28] By contrast, the hermit Stephen of Obazine[29] emphasized that his disciples were 'veterans of the celestial militia' but uneducated in terms of monastic regulations.[30] His *Vita* explained this in the following way: 'And since one had not adopted any statute law of any order, the instructions of the master were valued in lieu of law – instructions that taught nothing but humility, obedience, poverty, discipline and, above all, enduring love. One did not bother about Pharisaic traditions'.[31]

Such an unregulated way of life indeed corresponded to Max Weber's above-quoted definition of charisma's effects as 'a conversion of the fundamental direction of both desire and action'. It could, however, only be achieved by the 'extraordinary virtue' through which – to quote Weber further – the charismatic was believed to be endowed 'with supernatural, superhuman, or at least specifically exceptional powers or qualities, inaccessible to others'.[32] It is precisely on that note that the *Vita* of Stephen of Obazine reads: 'His word is like a burning fire that inflames the souls of his hearers and inebriates them with so much love that … the nature of their life and their ways is changed. And his outer appearance as well as his bearing are a sermon, as it were, and exhibit nothing but an ordered way of life and discipline in customs and action'.[33] Such characterizations have been handed down with reference to all charismatic leaders from any period. The effect of a charismatic is most essentially – albeit not exclusively – linked to the 'performance' of his personal body rather than the grandeur of a transpersonal office. This effect could – as Weber asserts[34] – certainly even assume magical forms of symbolical immediacy. Of Norbert of Xanten, for

[27] G. Constable, *Monastic Tithes from Their Origins to the Twelfth Century* (Cambridge Studies in Medieval Life and Thought, n.s., x, Cambridge, 1964).

[28] G. Morin, 'Rainaud l'ermite et Ives de Chartres: un épisode de la crise du cénobitisme au XIe–XIIe siècle', *Revue Bénédictine*, xl (1928), 99–115, at pp. 109–10.

[29] G. Melville, 'Stephan von Obazine: Begründung und Überwindung charismatischer Führung', in Andenna, Breitenstein and Melville, *Charisma*, pp. 85–102.

[30] *Vie de saint Étienne d'Obazine*, ed. and trans. M. Aubrin (Clermont-Ferrand, 1970), p. 106.

[31] Aubrin, *Vie de saint Étienne*, p. 70.

[32] Weber, *Wirtschaft und Gesellschaft*, p. 140.

[33] Aubrin, *Vie de saint Étienne*, p. 58.

[34] Weber, *Wirtschaft und Gesellschaft*, p. 141.

instance, it was said that when he was absent demons incessantly and cruelly tormented his disciples, yet as soon as he was present again, they vanished at once.[35] Unconventional clothing which symbolically expressed the guiding principles of conduct could be of particular effect, too. Robert of Arbrissel was accused of damaging the reputation of the Church through his ragged appearance; Norbert of Xanten used his torn frock to style himself as John the Baptist. Both saw in their garments the message of the purity of the soul, of poverty and of contempt for the world.[36]

Attacks by the Church were bound to ensue and initially pushed each of those charismatics into the border zone of heresy, even though it was sometimes recognized that these leaders were inspired by God. Probably the most calculated accusation was made by the famous canonist Ivo of Chartres.[37] He accused the charismatically led groups which had removed themselves into solitude of living 'in concealed places according to their own law' (*in privatis locis, proprio iure*) because they evaded all integration into the official Church and behaved like Sarabaites – those groups of monks in late antiquity who lived neither according to a rule nor in keeping with fixed conventions and who had already been condemned by the Benedictine rule. Here an extremely pejorative meaning was attributed to the term *privatum*. As it had, however, been formulated from exactly the point of view of the official Church, this in fact splendidly proves how strongly 'individual freedom' is linked to the *privatum* in the quotation from Gratian with which this chapter began. Therefore, in terms of how they positioned themselves relative to other groups, and how they perceived themselves and others perceived them, charismatically led groups truly seemed to stand in opposition to any form of institutionalism – as appears to be the case with people inspired by the holy spirit, who transcend worldly institutions.

Was this, however, actually the case? So far we have regarded only one part of the charismatic potential: the opposition to traditional authorities (as Weber described them) through the alternative modes of living accompanying the extraordinary virtue of the charismatic. In this one doubtlessly encountered that divergence. Yet if one looks around a little further, one indeed recognizes close points of contact with institutional forms – one can perhaps even discern an institutional structure *in* charisma itself. It depends on what one applies the term 'institution' to and how one defines it.

[35] Wilmans, *Vita Norberti*, p. 685.

[36] Melville, *Medieval Monasticism*, pp. 113, 116.

[37] See G. Melville, '"In privatis locis proprio jure vivere". Zu Diskursen des frühen 12. Jahrhunderts um religiöse Eigenbestimmung oder institutionelle Einbindung', in G. Melville, *Frommer Eifer und methodischer Betrieb. Beiträge zum mittelalterlichen Mönchtum*, ed. C. Andenna and M. Breitenstein (Cologne, 2014), pp. 33–48.

The weakest point of charismatic figures is the fact they are mortal. In order to save their life's work, namely, their guiding principles and values, they have to make them immortal. To this end, however, the charismatic figure needs an institutional form, for only institutional organizations never die (*universitas non moritur* [the group/corporation never dies]).[38] The group around Stephen of Obazine took the most radical measures, as has been handed down with astonishing explicitness: 'Yet since the days of man are short [Job XIV: 5] and human instruction has an effect only as long as the instructor lives and is present, they decided to adopt the creed of one of the orders that are authorized in the Church, so that even after the mentor's end the authority of the written law would remain with them as a never-ending one'.[39] Ultimately, this course of action led to their admission to the Cistercian order while Stephen was still alive. However, the intention that written norms should outlast the transience of the body was of fundamental importance. Other charismatics pursued the same aspiration. With almost the same words, Norbert of Xanten answered his disciples when they suggested there was no need for written norms on account of Norbert's exemplariness; and he introduced the rule of St Augustine to his group because it was the one which most corresponded to his concerns.[40] Robert of Arbrissel authored statutes which were not only to be in force after his death but applicable straightaway whenever he was absent.[41] For many years Francis worked on a rule which was predominantly based on quotations from holy scripture.[42] Above all, he wrote his spiritual will and 'testament' in order to immortalize his message (although Pope Gregory IX abrogated it in his bull *Quo elongati*).[43]

Such written law inevitably articulated organizational institutional structures since an organization was needed, in turn, for the very purpose of guaranteeing the observance of the written law.[44] Thus, a circular reference came into being which could rightly be understood as an institutionalization of the original charismatic guiding principles and values and which – in many cases with support from the official Church – led to the organizational form

[38] E. H. Kantorowicz, *The King's Two Bodies: a Study in Mediaeval Political Theology* (Princeton, N.J., 1981 [1957]), pp. 302–13.

[39] Aubrin, *Vie de saint Étienne*, p. 96.

[40] Wilmans, *Vita Norberti*, p. 683.

[41] J. Dalarun, 'Les plus anciens statuts de Fontevraud', in *Robert d'Arbrissel et la vie religieuse dans l'ouest de la France*, ed. J. Dalarun (Turnhout, 2004), pp. 139–72.

[42] L Pellegrini, 'La tradizione manoscritta della Regula non bullata; la genesi di un testo e la sua vicenda nella storia dell'Ordine minoritico', in *La regola dei Frati minori*, pp. 83–116.

[43] H. Grundmann, 'Die Bulle "Quo elongati" Papst Gregors IX', *Archivum Franciscanum historicum*, liv (1961), 3–25.

[44] On 'institutions' as distinct from 'organizations', see my conclusion below.

of a religious order. One must note, however, that there was a substantial difference on a sliding scale between one who transfers into another, pre-existing organization (Stephan of Obazine), the adaptation of a traditional rule (Norbert of Xanten) and a textualization of norms by the charismatic leader himself (Robert of Arbrissel).

To analyse both ends of this spectrum, Weber offered the model of the 'routinization [*Veralltäglichung*] of charisma'.[45] However, a reference to his threefold typology of authority (*Herrschaft*) – the legal, the traditional and the charismatic[46] – will prove more fruitful here. As has been shown, religious movements under the individual leadership of a charismatic figure opposed the validity of 'traditional authorities'. Ironically, then, with the translation of their guiding principles into written norms, they directly created a form of legal authority which, according to Weber, is characterized by its 'resting on a belief in the legality of enacted rules and the right of those elevated to authority under such rules to issue commands'.[47] The charismatic figure's revolutionary power of liberation from traditionally oriented institutions led to a renewed institutionalization which now constituted the attempt at legal continuation of the charismatic power itself. Provided that such a system of legal authority was actually realized (that is, an order was formally founded), this power of the liberation of the individual could not, however, be transferred immediately to the followers. The latter now became institutionalized members of the order, subject to binding rules and laws. At best, they retained a right of co-determination regarding the writing of laws, something which had never been the case in traditional monastic communities.[48]

What, however, gave charismatic leaders the drive to want their work to continue beyond death? The answer to this question is of particular significance since it also contains the clarification of the afore-mentioned assumption that a particular institutional structure can be discerned *in* charisma itself. Let us remember the observation made at the beginning: although acting *instinctu Sancti Spiritus* signified the desire to obtain autonomy from the rules of earthly institutions, this did not imply pure arbitrariness but signified following the will of God. All charismatic leaders and their followers were convinced they were acting on behalf of God and

[45] Weber, *Wirtschaft und Gesellschaft*, pp. 142–8.

[46] Weber, *Wirtschaft und Gesellschaft*, p. 124.

[47] Weber, *Wirtschaft und Gesellschaft*, p. 124.

[48] G. Melville, 'The abbot of Cluny at the turning point from the charismatic traditional to legal authority: an analysis referring to Max Weber's model', in *Abbots and Abbesses as a Human Resource in the Ninth- to Twelfth-Century West*, ed. S. Vanderputten (Vita regularis, lxxiv, Berlin, 2018), pp. 151–64.

in accordance to his providence. Here, the sociological meaning of the term 'charisma' coincides with the pneumatic one of the apostle Paul to the greatest possible extent.[49] Stephen of Obazine's *Vita* described the point when he was still seeking ecclesiastical instruction, but then decided to live as an autonomous hermit, thus: 'The almighty God did not want him to be subjected to the guidance [*magisterium*] of anyone, so that might be fulfilled which He had intended for this holy man'.[50] Robert of Abrissel once delivered a sermon before Pope Urban II; and the Pope believed that 'the Holy Spirit had personally opened Robert's mouth'.[51] Francis of Assisi had two decisive visions of Christ which showed him the way.[52] When he was writing the last version of his rule, he turned away all who wanted any changes and justified this by stating that the text did not originate from him but from Jesus himself: 'Christ told me this, Christ told me this!' (*Christus mihi dixit, Christus mihi dixit!*). In these examples the blessing of God was bestowed directly and linked with clear mandates. Thus, Francis was able to trust in bibliomancy when he blindly opened the gospel in order to find behavioural norms for himself and his first companions. Later he was able to emphasize in his will and testament that the Most High had instructed him to live according to the form of the gospel; that the Lord had shown him he had to commence a life in atonement; and that he had led him among the lepers in order to practise compassion.

Those charismatic leaders, who perceived themselves as acting on behalf of God, possessed the legitimization of their work through this transcendent reference. They were incarnations, living symbols of divine norms, which they exemplified perfectly and which they tried to enforce: atonement, solitude, poverty, homelessness, love of one's neighbour, compassion. The significance of these norms was, however, that they constituted truths of life which were claimed to be of timeless, eternal validity and neither to need tradition nor be subject to change by traditions – according to the word of Christ, who did not say: 'I am the custom',

[49] For a comparison see K.-S. Rehberg, 'Rationalisierungsschicksal und Charisma-Sehnsucht. Anmerkungen zur "Außeralltäglichkeit" im Rahmen der institutionellen Analyse', in Andenna, Breitenstein and Melville, *Charisma*, pp. 3–23; K. Tanner, 'Die Macht des Unverfügbaren. Charisma als Gnadengabe in der Thematisierung von Institutionalisierungsprozessen im Christentum', in Andenna, Breitenstein and Melville, *Charisma*, pp. 25–44.

[50] Aubrin, *Vie de saint Étienne*, p. 48.

[51] Baudri de Bourgueil, *Historia magistri Roberti*, in *Les deux Vies de Robert d'Arbrissel, fondateur de Fontevraud. Légendes, écrits et témoignages – The Two Lives of Robert of Arbrissel, Founder of Fontevraud: Legends, Writings, and Testimonies*, ed. J. Dalarun (Disciplina monastica, iv, Turnhout, 2006), pp. 130–87, at p. 156.

[52] For the following, see Melville, '"Homo spiritum habens"'.

but 'I am the truth' (John XIV: 6). Thus, for instance, when defending his community against accusations of possessing no rule and no order because a habit alone did not justify identifying them as monks, Stephen of Muret used the following significant logic, which went even further: was there no rule and no order here when he required everyone to live in poverty, seclusion from the world, mutual love and so forth – that is to say – when he maintained the unalterable, basic values which marked out the religious life?[53] Clearly, he wished to remain within the realm of these core values. Fundamentally, the term *ordo* generally signified every religious form of life practised communally and exclusively under the norms of 'divine precepts' (*diuina praecepta*) and the 'gospel of Christ' (*euangelium Christi*). In sum, it was ultimately only those who stood 'outside all order or rule' (*extra omnem ordinem uel regulam*) who deviated from *diuina praecepta*. In Stephen's view, rule and order were manifested primarily by the spirit and not by the letter of the law.

***

Institutions are, in the first place, symbolic systems, regardless of whether they shape organizations around themselves or only substantiate themselves in social practices.[54] All institutional forms ensure perpetuation and reiteration – an achievement which, however, can only be unalterably secured if contextual circumstances can be transcended and produce unchangeable frameworks: that is, if the institutions symbolize deep values and guiding principles through which they create and derive meaning. This criterion also gels effectively with the idea of the Church as an institution, as exemplified by the above-mentioned image of the bride of Christ as a symbol of divine transcendence. That image may itself stand for the virtually inexhaustible set of liturgical rites, daily rituals and sacramental signs and consecration which themselves render the normally unattainable divine symbolically – and in the eucharist even truly – present. These symbolizations were tied to abstract models of behaviour, 'correct' sequences of action, offices and formal norms which were applicable to every believer.[55] They were

[53] For this, see Becquet, *Liber de doctrina uel Liber sententiarum*, pp. 3–62, at pp. 60–2.

[54] G. Melville, 'L'institutionnalité médiévale dans sa pluridimensionnalité', in *Les tendances actuelles de l'histoire du Moyen Âge en France et en Allemagne*, ed. J.-C. Schmitt and O. G. Oexle (Paris, 2002), pp. 243–64; K.-S. Rehberg, *Symbolische Ordnungen. Beiträge zu einer soziologischen Theorie der Institutionen*, ed. H. Vorländer (Baden-Baden, 2014).

[55] For monastic institutions, cf. J. Sonntag, *Klosterleben im Spiegel des Zeichenhaften. Symbolisches Denken und Handeln hochmittelalterlicher Mönche zwischen Dauer und Wandel, Regel und Gewohnheit* (Vita regularis, xxxv, Berlin, 2008).

transpersonal, that is, not restricted to the individuality of a person, and were thus persistent and durable.[56]

Medieval Christian charismatic figures drew on this wider symbolic grammar, notwithstanding their individuality. With it their entirely individual conduct could render the continuous, ubiquitous validity of this transcendent order-system present, visible and tangible here in this world, embedding it in earthly realities in a meaningful way. Since, as individuals, they were symbolic embodiments of divine order, they had an eminently institutional function – without requiring an organization or an office in that regard at all. When a person, as an individual, becomes an institution, that person has to carry and guarantee its continuity just as organizations do. With persistent commitment to a guiding principle and a certain methodical approach this can be achieved for a lifetime, as we have seen in the charismatic figures discussed above. Yet only ever for one lifetime!

This is the case unless one immortalizes – and thereby universalizes – the values of the special, unique and limited life of a given charismatic figure. As shown above, this could be done through institutionalizing a person's exemplary life in the form of a community under a 'legal authority' (in Weber's terms). At this point, what had been a charismatically effective force gradually disappeared into honoured memory, receding behind transpersonally valid norms which became the institution's moving force. This is precisely what happened with Robert of Molesme[57] as the initiator of the Cistercian order, or Dominic[58] as the founder of the Order of Preachers. Yet such an immortalization can also take place by means of a continued existence of the charismatic in a cult of remembrance, granting the dead leader a perceptible and mental presence. For this it also required more 'evangelists' who wrote *vitae*;[59] iconographic programmes; funerary monuments (such as the Basilica San Francesco in Assisi); and redactors of rules who aimed to present retrospectively the dead charismatic figure, such as occurred with Stephen of Muret and others. In this way the individuality of the charismatic became the immortal model or exemplar, the symbolic point of reference for all subsequent generations searching for the 'truth' of

[56] Cf. Kantorowicz, *The King's Two Bodies*, pp. 373–83.

[57] T. Merton, 'Saint Robert of Molesme, 1028 to 1111', *Cistercian Stud. Quart.*, xlvi (2011), 273–6.

[58] A. Wesjohann, 'Flüchtigkeit und Bewahrung des Charisma, oder: War der heilige Dominikus etwa auch ein Charismatiker?', in Andenna, Breitenstein and Melville, *Charisma*, pp. 227–60.

[59] See the important contribution by S. C. Jaeger, 'The saint's life as a charismatic form: Bernard of Clairvaux and Francis of Assisi', in Bedos-Rezak and Rust, *Faces of Charisma*, pp. 181–204.

life. That dead individuality became precisely – in order to penetrate the heart of the matter – the institutionalized form, figure, model and rule of life (*forma*, *figura*, *exemplum* and *regula vitae*) which imparted identity to the religious order.[60]

It is most remarkable how the individual impact of a charismatic leader, *necessarily* opposed to the institutional structures of established authorities to begin with, was then also able to turn into an institutional form which could provide a legitimate counterweight to these authorities.[61] It must be mentioned that this occurred without neutralizing the individuality of the protagonist in the process. On the contrary: religious orders continued to direct believers to their founding figure to the highest degree, even if later generations incessantly quarrelled about precisely how this individuality should be seen as a model.

[60] K. Elm, 'Die Entwicklung des Franziskanerordens zwischen dem ersten und letzten Zeugnis des Jakob von Vitry', in K. Elm, *Vitasfratrum. Beiträge zur Geschichte der Eremiten- und Mendikantenorden des zwölften und dreizehnten Jahrhunderts*, ed. D. Berg (Werl, 1994), pp. 173–93, at p. 192.

[61] For the exemplary case of Francis of Assisi, see Melville, '"Homo spiritum habens"'.

6. An institution made of individuals: Peter John Olivi and Angelo Clareno on the Franciscan experience*

Sylvain Piron

To David Burr

Francis of Assisi had no intention of creating a new institution. His conversion to a life of destitution was, first and foremost, a personal experience. The so-called *Legend of the Three Companions*, which provides the fullest treatment of his gradual severing of social ties, was apparently written by someone who possessed detailed information about his youth in Assisi and his early spiritual practices.[1] It recalls that, after spending some time caring for the lepers, he was drawn to San Damiano to pray. There the crucifix told him: 'Francis, can't you see that my home is falling apart? Go and mend it!' He understood the message as a literal command to repair the derelict building.[2] The only prophetic meaning he gave at the time to these works of restoration was that the premises would one day be devoted to a nunnery.[3] Two years later, when he started to live as a wandering penitent, soon joined by a few companions, he still conceived of his mission as being in support of the Church, not actually as a part of it. The famous statement found in the *Testament* ('After the Lord gave me brothers, no one showed me what I should do, but the Most High revealed to me that I ought to live according to the form of the Holy Gospel') is not an abstract reflection.[4] It strictly corresponds to the scene when Francis, together with his first

* My thanks to John Sabapathy for his help with this article.

[1] Jacques Dalarun believed the author was Rufinus, cousin of Clare of Assisi, which makes considerable sense. For references and the respective roles of the companions, see S. Piron, 'Note sur Léon et Rufin, l'écriture et le corps', *Archivum Franciscanum historicum*, cxi (2018), 365–75.

[2] *Legenda trium sociorum*, in *Francis of Assisi: Early Documents*, ed. R. J. Armstrong et al. (4 vols, New York and London/Manila, 1999–2004), ii. 66–110, at p. 76 (§ 13).

[3] *Legenda trium sociorum*, p. 83, § 2 4.

[4] Francis of Assisi, *Testament* (*Early Documents*, i. 124–7, at p. 125, § 14).

S. Piron, 'An institution made of individuals: Peter John Olivi and Angelo Clareno on the Franciscan experience', in *Individuals and Institutions in Medieval Scholasticism*, ed. A. Fitzpatrick and J. Sabapathy (London, 2020), pp. 157–76.

companions Bernard and Peter, entered the church of San Nicolò in Piazza, opened a liturgical gospel book three times and repeatedly came across the evangelical counsels which would define their way of life: 'If thou wilt be perfect, go and sell that thou hast, and give to the poor'; 'Take nothing for your journey, neither staves, nor pack, neither bread, neither money; neither have two coats apiece'; and 'If any man will come after me, let him deny himself'.[5] Those verses constitute the nucleus of a series of counsels which served as guiding principles to the penitents and were later expanded in different early versions of the rule. This reading through biblical sortilege (*sortes biblicae*) defined not only the contents but also the most distinctive character of the Franciscan experience, as rooted in unmediated obedience to the word of God.

Such bypassing of the ecclesiastical hierarchy in order to establish a direct connection to Christ continued throughout Francis's life, turning at times into a genuine face-to-face dialogue, yet it went together with an intense respect for and submission to the Church. This might be a reason for giving preference to the earlier version of the San Nicolò episode, in which the three young men asked a priest to open the book for them and to translate the passages.[6] The first half of the *Testament* (§§ 4–13) forcefully reiterates what is apparent in many other early documents: a veneration for churches and the priests who minister the holy body of Christ, as well as for the 'theologians' who proclaim his holy word. The argument put forward by Francis does not imply respect for the ecclesiastical institution as such. Instead, it arises from an existential perception of how the divine is concentrated into a limited number of instances of the sacred. Nothing of the Lord is visible on earth apart from his presence in scripture and the eucharist.[7] The Church and her ministers have to be revered as the only vessel through which God is made present and manifest to all. The all-encompassing notion which best describes this attitude towards the clergy is that of a claim to absolute inferiority (*minoritas*). The same notion also

[5] Matthew XIX: 21; Luke IX: 3; Matthew XVI: 24; *Legenda trium sociorum*, pp. 85–6, §§ 28–9. Since they found it on the altar, the book was not a whole Bible but a liturgical codex. Neither was it a full lectionary, since they were specifically looking for 'the word of the Gospel'.

[6] *De inceptione ordinis* (*Early Documents*, ii. 34–59, at p. 38, § 11a). The usual designation of this text as '*The Anonymous of Perugia*' is irrelevant since we know this narrative was written by Brother John, companion of Giles of Assisi.

[7] This notion first appears in the *Epistola ad clericos* (*Early Documents*, i. 52), probably written in 1220. The devotion to the eucharist is also expressed in the first of the *Admonitions* (*Early Documents*, i. 128–37, at pp. 128–9). Even if these texts were produced in the wake of the Fourth Lateran Council, which defined the dogma of the transubstantiation of the bread and wine, it cannot be doubted that these words represent an early concern for Francis.

implies a radical detachment from all sorts of social manners and duties; and an indifference to the frequent mockeries and humiliations the first friars had to endure owing to what was popularly perceived as their outrageous nakedness.[8] This submission would later even be extended to all animals as part of a universal compassion towards all creatures.[9] The *Testament* sums it up in the tersest way: 'we were illiterate and subject to all' (*eramus idiotae et subditi omnibus*). Even as the number of his followers rapidly grew, Francis still conceived of their mission not as taking part in the institution but as dwelling within it as 'pilgrims and foreigners'.[10] Although nobody would have been in a position to express it clearly at the time, a tremendous amount of tension was lodged in this unheard-of situation. Achieving a life based on a strict and literal adherence to the gospel amounted to an implicit challenge to all other forms of Christian life, a theme which became explicit decades later with the notion of 'evangelical perfection'.

The sheer success with which Francis and his first companions met as they toured central Italy made it impossible for them to remain for much longer on the margins of the Church.[11] In the process through which an informal band of penitents evolved into a full-blown institution, the support of the papacy was obviously crucial. The various reports of the first encounter with Innocent III in 1209 are replete with too many interpolations to be taken at face value.[12] The only sure facts may be summarized as follows: besides a general approval of his 'way of living' (*propositum vitae*), Francis was granted permission to preach penance; and only he would be entitled to allow some of his companions to act in a similar fashion. The acquaintance he made on that occasion, and during further stays in Rome, of a number of important people at the curia proved as important as the initial approbation. This trip was soon followed by an unexpected, yet inevitable, outcome which had the potential to undermine the whole project of *minoritas*. Starting with Sylvester, who had supported Francis at an early date, a few priests were admitted into the group as soon as 1210. In a world in which the distinction between lay and clerical status was a fundamental social divide, the presence of clerics among them meant the brotherhood of penitents had now to be

[8] Armstrong et al., *De inceptione*, pp. 42–5, §§ 19–23, based on Giles's memories. See the *Chronica* by Jordan of Giano about the initial missions to Hungary and Germany, J. Schlageter, 'Die *Chronica* des Bruders Jordan von Giano: Einführung und kritische Edition nach den bisher bekannten Handschriften', *Archivum Franciscanum historicum*, civ (2011), 3–63, at p. 35, §§ 5–6.

[9] *A Salutation of the Virtues* (*Early Documents*, i. 164–5, at p. 165, §§ 16–17).

[10] 1 Peter II: 11, quoted in the *Regula bullata* (*Early Documents*, i. 99–106, at p. 103, § 6).

[11] F. Delmas-Goyon, *Saint François d'Assise. Le frère de toute créature* (Paris, 2008), pp. 124–36.

[12] R. Manselli, *François d'Assise*, trans. H. Louette and J. Mignon (Paris, 2001), pp. 237–48.

treated as part of the ecclesiastical institution. This meant Francis had to be ordained a deacon so that a lay person would not be placed over a cleric.

As the number of friars grew, his personal hold over his movement gradually loosened. By 1217 it was described as the 'religion of friar minors', not quite yet an 'order', but a formal way of life characterized by some distinctive habits and practices. The institution was now divided into twelve provinces, placed under the responsibility of ministers who had the capacity to test and themselves admit new friars. The delegation of authority was even more dramatic when Francis travelled to Egypt (1219–20), leaving two vicars in charge. Hearing they had introduced a stricter rule concerning days of fasting, upon his return Francis headed first to Rome to obtain support from the papacy and then had Cardinal Hugolino of Segni appointed as a permanent cardinal protector. Nevertheless, Francis's attempt at regaining control over the evolution of his creation was doomed to failure. What the papacy now conceived of as an *ordo*, in which a year-long noviciate was made compulsory for newcomers, had to be regulated by a specific rule. Responding to Cardinal Hugolino and the 'learned friars' in some dramatic speeches recorded by Brother Leo, Francis at first refused to accept any type of monastic rule, being content only to follow the gospel.[13] The document drawn up in 1221 (the *Regula non bullata*) was still designed as an anthology of evangelical counsels and rejected as such by Pope Honorius III. The shorter version eventually approved in 1223 (the *Regula bullata*) more closely resembled a standard, normative, monastic text, but the personal voice of Francis was still strongly present, warning and urging the friars in the first person. Yet, by that date he had long since resigned as head of the order. Although the hagiographical documents insist his abdication was due to his poor health, the chronology rather suggests that Francis gave up his position as a response to the pressure exerted upon him to normalize his 'religion'. Many episodes narrated by Brother Leo bear witness to his discontent with an institution which did not match his initial inspiration. As Francis dictated his *Testament* to Leo in spring 1226, he spoke in the same voice he had used in the rule in the name of his charismatic authority. When Hugolino as Pope Gregory IX eventually decreed in *Quo elongati* (1230) that this declaration was not binding, the process of normalization had apparently been achieved. However, many seeds of discord had been sown which would bear fruit at different moments. Besides the *Testament* and Leo's record of Francis's intentions, the rule itself provided the friars with an important restriction on standard monastic obedience. It requested them 'to obey their ministers in everything they have promised the Lord to

[13] *Compilatio Assisiensis* (*Early Documents*, ii. 118–230, at pp. 132–3, § 18).

observe and which is not against their soul or our rule'.[14] The possibility of such a reservation implied that individual friars could oppose their personal compliance with the rule to the orders of their superiors.

***

Angelo Clareno died in utmost solitude in June 1337, in a small hermitage in western Lucania. The collection of miracles performed at his grave offers the image of a local saint attracting pilgrims within a radius of less than thirty miles, mostly from the valley of Val d'Agri.[15] This record stands at odds with the vast network of correspondents with whom he had been in touch for decades and his much wider expectations of historical change. In a letter he sent in his final years to the Neapolitan noble on whose land he was hiding, Angelo complained he had suffered many tribulations for almost sixty years while hoping to witness the reformation of Christ's life which had been initiated by Francis.[16] Since he had joined the order sometime around 1274 in the Italian Marches, Angelo and his companions had indeed often been badly treated by their superiors, spending a fair amount of time in prison, on the sole account of their desire 'to adhere to the conscience and teaching of the founder'.[17]

The strife had started at the time of the second Council of Lyons (1274), as a rumour spread through the region that the pope might force the friars minor to accept ownership of possessions. In what appears to have been a public dispute held during a provincial chapter, the zealous (*zelanti*) asserted that it did not fall within the power of the pope or the general council to modify a rule which was evangelical by definition.[18] The debate over various practices which those friars rejected as unfit was merely an extension of this core issue. Essentially, the fight was not about the intensity of poverty practised in the region, but rather touched upon a matter of principle concerning the nature of the Franciscan rule, arguing about

[14] *Regula bullata* (*Early Documents*, i. 99–106, at p. 105, § 10).

[15] F. Accrocca, *Un ribelle tranquillo. Angelo Clareno e gli Spirituali francescani tra Due e Trecento* (Assisi, 2009), pp. 133–9. Identification of places in A. Sancricca, *I 'fratres' di Angelo Clareno* (Macerata, 2015), pp. 67–70.

[16] A. Clareno, *Epistole*, ed. L. von Auw, in *Angeli Clareni opera* (Rome, 1980), i. 204; G. L. Potestà, *Angelo Clareno. Dai poveri eremiti ai fraticelli* (Rome, 1990); D. Burr, *The Spiritual Franciscans: From Protest to Persecution in the Century After Saint Francis* (University Park, Pa., 2000), pp. 279–301.

[17] A. Clareno, *A Chronicle or History of the Seven Tribulations of the Order of the Brothers Minor*, trans. D. Burr and E. R. Daniel (St Bonaventure, N.Y., 2005), p. 150; also Clareno, *Epistole*, pp. 241–4.

[18] Clareno, *Chronicle*, pp. 148–9.

whether its ultimate authority stemmed from divine inspiration or its papal approbation. The two views were ultimately irreconcilable. This explains the fury of those opposed to the *zelanti*, who had the small group jailed without a trial, not even spelling out the nature of their actual misdeed (probably in 1278). The details of their imprisonment are not perfectly clear. In one letter Clareno mentions a transfer of the prisoners to Rome, where they were exposed in public during holy week and then brought back to Ancona. They must have managed to escape, since the same letter adds that they were seized again in southern Sicily two years later (maybe around Easter 1281), exhibited as criminals in every city from Gela to Messina and then expelled to the shores of Calabria.[19]

At any rate, by 1290 they were back in prison in Ancona when the general minister Raymond Geoffroy ordered their release and had them sent to the king of Armenia, Hethum II, who himself took the Franciscan habit soon afterwards. There, they fell into trouble again with friars from Syria and Cyprus. In 1294, upon their return to Italy, Celestine V allowed them to form a separate order as 'Poor Hermits', changing their name in order to let them fulfil their vocation.[20] Boniface VIII swiftly cancelled that decision when he took power, prompting the group to set sail anew towards the east. In his long quest to obtain the reformation of the 'Poor Hermits' during the following decades, Angelo was again submitted to a certain amount of rough treatment until John XXII freed him from obedience to his superiors by transferring him to the branch of the Benedictine order founded by Celestine himself. As Angelo settled, not with the Celestines but at the Benedictine monastery of Subiaco, he retained the observance of Francis's commands and probably never took off his habit. Although he had by then given up all hope of re-establishing the 'Poor Hermits' as an institution, the major works he composed at Subiaco in the 1320s were a *Chronicle* of the Franciscan order and a commentary on its rule (*Expositio Regulae*), quite telling signs that he was not in the least alienated from the Franciscan project.

Written at the request of a friar named Tommaso, the *Expositio* displays a very neat sense of a hierarchy of norms. As the opening sentence shows, the main purpose of this work is not to elucidate the text alone, but rather to explain 'the pure, simple and ultimate intention of the seraphic man Francis in the rule that was divinely inspired to him by Christ'.[21] Thus,

[19] Clareno, *Epistole*, p. 80. The letter continues with a reference to a journey overseas to Cyprus and Romania which took place in the following decade.

[20] Clareno, *Epistole*, p. 241; Potestà, *Angelo Clareno*, pp. 126–7.

[21] *Early Commentaries on the Rule of Friars Minors*, iii: *Angelo Clareno*, ed. and trans. D. Burr (St Bonaventure, N.Y., 2014), p. 1.

throughout the commentary the rule has to be understood in the light of other documents in which Francis explained the nature of his project, namely, '[i]n his *Testament*, *Admonitions*, *Letters*, and other words, and especially in the replies which that holy man, Brother Leo, writes that he [Francis] gave to his companions when, toward the end, they asked him about such matters'.[22] The reference to Leo is crucial here. Clareno builds on various extracts from the collection currently known as the 'Assisi Compilation' in order to explain in what frame of mind and in the midst of what tensions the rule was written: 'In order to understand it ... it is extremely helpful to know accurately the story of its beginnings and the circumstances surrounding its creation'.[23] The prologue and the first chapter of the *Expositio* include a summary of Francis's life, while other parts explain the wording of the rule in the light of Francis's reluctance to write it and of his prophetical warnings of the dangers awaiting the friars in the future.

Throughout his work Clareno makes numerous references to the *Regula non bullata*, presented as the document approved by Innocent III. Despite their differences, both rules are seen as complementing each other since all evangelical quotations present in the longer text are considered as implicitly referred to in the officially published version.[24] The concordance of all Franciscan documents demonstrates that the founder's first and final intention was simply to follow the Gospel. Therefore, professing the rule amounts to following a 'law of grace, truth and charity' which immediately connects the individual friar to Christ. The sense of belonging to a community comes second: common life, compliance to the uniformity of habit and practices and strict obedience to the superiors are requested as ways to foster the evangelical virtues. Nonetheless, Clareno also emphasizes the necessity of disobedience in certain situations in which the strict observance of Christ's life would otherwise be in danger. In the rule Francis had promised obedience to Honorius and all his 'canonically elected' successors, having in mind the many anti-popes of the twelfth century. In turn, this very phrase fuelled the prophetic expectation that one day a usurper would be falsely elected whom the true professors of evangelical perfection would have to resist.[25] In Clareno's eyes this moment had not yet come. Despite his sharp criticism of John XXII and the corrupt Church hierarchy, he consistently maintained the duty of obedience to a legitimate papacy as a crucial part of the vow. Distancing himself from the centre of power by 'fleeing to the

[22] Burr, *Angelo Clareno*, p. 1.
[23] Burr, *Angelo Clareno*, p. 9.
[24] Burr, *Angelo Clareno*, p. 28.
[25] Burr, *Angelo Clareno*, p. 39.

mountains' (in the evangelical phrase he used) was the surest way to avoid having his submissiveness put to the test.[26]

An original feature of Clareno's approach lies in his abundant use of patristic references and especially of numerous Greek Fathers, many of whom he translated specifically for these works. Among them Basil of Caesarea and his rule hold a central place. Clareno sometimes translates him speaking in a typically Franciscan vocabulary, describing his community as a 'fraternity' devoted to the fulfilment of evangelical perfection and renouncing any landed property.[27] Besides his two stays in the east, during which he certainly made contact with Greek speaking monks, Angelo had a good motive to rely so heavily on the Cappadocian Father. This move was justified by one of Francis's stronger statements, in which he vociferously refused to follow any monastic rule, naming those of Benedict, Augustine and Bernard. Having the first two in mind, Clareno lists the ways in which the Franciscan rule 'differs from the two rules that hold primacy in the Roman church, and how arduous it is compared to them'.[28] By contrast, the Greeks provided an undisputed authority, located much closer to the source of the evangelical tradition than any Latin Father. Clareno's precise historical awareness shows, for example, in the way he refers to Jerome as a disciple of Gregory of Nazianzus.[29] Since Jerome not only translated the Bible into Latin, but also transmitted to the west many testimonies of eastern asceticism, this detail somehow manages to subordinate one whole tradition to the other. The result of the operation is remarkable. Hosted in the very premises in Lazio where Benedict of Nursia had his first eremitic experiences before founding the monastery of Monte Cassino, for which he composed his famous rule, Clareno bypasses the father of western monasticism in order to present the Franciscan project as a true renewal of the evangelical life. Yet, such a conjunction was not totally unheard of, since the sacred cave (*sacro speco*) of Subiaco also preserves the oldest known representation of Francis, drawn during his lifetime.

However, the most pervasive source of inspiration for the *Expositio* is certainly Peter John Olivi. His name shows up only three times in the final pages, accompanied by some extraordinary praise.[30] However, as Gian Luca

[26] Burr, *Spiritual Franciscans*, pp. 293–5. The allusion is to Matthew XXIV: 16.

[27] Burr, *Angelo Clareno*, p. 15.

[28] Burr, *Angelo Clareno*, p. 16.

[29] Burr, *Angelo Clareno*, p. 151.

[30] He is 'that man of great sanctity and virtue as well as outstanding wisdom' (Burr, *Angelo Clareno*, p. 169), 'the holy man of God' (p. 224), 'this man who, above all others in his time, was a lover and extoller of his order … a man Christ loved and singularly illumined with his wisdom' (p. 231).

Potestà noted, Olivi's own commentary on the rule is the real backbone of Clareno's work.[31] Their relationship is even stronger than historians have supposed. In his letter to Roberto of Mileto (quoted above), Angelo started by remembering that, 'about forty years ago, taught by Christ, [he] recognized that the Father of mercy and light had decided to place the spirit of the founder in the man of God, Peter', whom he then decided to follow and obey as the herald of Francis's foundation.[32] Following Livier Oliger, Potestà understands this reference as recording the decision to accept Olivi's advice, given in September 1295 in a letter to Conrad of Offida, to admit the legitimacy of Celestine's resignation and Boniface's election. However, the wording of Clareno's remembrance is so strong that it rather seems to imply a continuous commitment to Olivi as a spiritual model. To be valid, such an interpretation would require some degree of personal acquaintance.

Although the hypothesis has never been tested, there are grounds for thinking that such an encounter did actually take place and on the exact date indicated in the letter. One important clue has surfaced recently. In his treatise on the mass (*De missa*) (before 1298), Olivi quotes an extract from 'Climacus' which he could only have come across in Clareno's translation of the *Ladder of Paradise* (*Scala paradisi*).[33] This implies that the translation was produced not in Greece after 1295, as is usually thought, but during the stay in Cilicia before 1294. A confirmation that some contact was made between the Languedoc friar and the exiled *Marchegiani* comes from a letter in which Angelo recalls the chicanery of Jerome of Catalonia, later bishop of Caffa, who approached his group in Greece, around 1300, claiming he was carrying some books Olivi was sending them.[34] Without providing a full reconstruction here, it is only possible to stress the plausibility of some otherwise undocumented events. Between Celestine's election in July and his resignation in December 1294, either during his stay at L'Aquila or while he was taken to Naples by King Charles II, Olivi could have taken a trip from Narbonne to meet the new pope and the Italian Spirituals who were still present at the court. This is when a personal meeting could have occurred, one which produced a deep impression on the Italian friar.

[31] Potestà, *Angelo Clareno*, p. 155.

[32] 'Christo docente, cognovi, iam fere sunt anni XL elapsi quod Pater misericordiarum et luminum decreverat in homine Dei P. ponere spiritum fundatoris, ideo subesse, sequi et conformare me ei tanquam nunctio signato primi lapidis angularis Francisci, integre et cordialiter amo' (Clareno, *Epistole*, p. 203).

[33] S. Piron, 'La bibliothèque portative des fraticelles, 1. Le manuscrit de Pesaro', *Oliviana*, v (2016), at §§ 21–7 <http://journals.openedition.org/oliviana/804> [accessed 7 July 2019].

[34] 'portans secum libros … nobis missos a sancte memorie Petro Iohanne' (Clareno, *Epistole*, p. 248).

This timing may fit in well with the dates Clareno recalls in his 'testament'. Scholars tend to agree the letter should be dated to sometime soon after the summer of 1334, when he arrived alone in Lucania after having had to leave Subiaco in haste in order to escape the inquisitor sent to catch him.[35] A period of 'almost sixty years' of tribulations points precisely to the controversies which started in the Marches soon after the end of the second Council of Lyons in 1274, while 'almost forty years' would match perfectly a meeting with Olivi at the court of Celestine. Establishing such a personal connection has more than merely anecdotal value. On the contrary, it helps to understand the importance of the individual relationships which constitute the core of a 'Franciscan' life outside the regular institution. There is some debate as to whether Angelo conceived of himself as a 'general minister' of the Fraticelli who admitted his leadership.[36] The extant documentation rather suggests he only exerted his authority by acting as a spiritual master towards a number of individuals or small groups of friars by way of epistolary contacts or personal guidance. Some among his disciples, such as the Augustinian friar Simone Fidati da Cascia, would behave in turn as spiritual masters along slightly different lines.[37] After the condemnation of the Languedoc Spirituals in 1317 and his own exit into the Benedictines, Angelo's re-enactment of the Franciscan project had faded to the point of becoming a personal network of devotees committed to the imitation of Francis's way of life and the expectation of its imminent return. His continuing references to the Franciscan rule and the order suggest he perceived these loose groups as embodying the true institution, ready to fulfil its historical mission in the apocalyptic future – hence his highly selective approach and account of the reception of new friars, illustrated with many examples from Greek monasticism. This issue was crucial, 'for faulty and indiscrete reception into this religion will be one of the ways in which the demons attack it'.[38] When reflecting on an ideal order – which he kept on calling by its early name of 'religion' – what Angelo had in mind was a charismatic institution, consisting of just a handful of heroic individuals, connected by their sense of continuing a historical mission started by Francis.

***

[35] Potestà, *Angelo Clareno*, pp. 279–95.

[36] Potestà, *Angelo Clareno*, pp. 283–6.

[37] X. Biron-Ouellet, 'Simone Fidati da Cascia's spiritual direction in fourteenth-century Italy', in *Agostino, Agostiniani e Agostinismi ne Trecento italiano*, ed. J. Bartuschat, E. Brilli and D. Carron (Ravenna, 2018), pp. 67–86.

[38] Burr, *Angelo Clareno*, p. 45.

Peter John Olivi was certainly a charismatic figure. At the very least, the amount of hatred and hostility concentrated on him during his lifetime and after his death bears testimony to the passions he was able to arouse. His grave in Narbonne was the site of a pilgrimage for two decades until it was destroyed by order of the pope in 1318, when four of his supporters were burnt at the stake in Marseilles. Although the doctrinal trial against his commentary on the Apocalypse (*Lectura super Apocalypsim*) had not yet reached a conclusion, he was treated *post mortem* as a heretic and his ashes were scattered in the Rhône in Avignon at night.[39] During this period of twenty years some celebrated him as a saint and miracles took place at his tomb, of which we know next to nothing save for a few echoes which survive in inquisitorial depositions. The only hagiographical document to cast some light on his person is actually the section of the *Chronicle* which Angelo Clareno devotes to him.[40] It should be noted that, besides Francis, only John of Parma receives similarly extensive treatment. Apparently, Clareno obtained information from witnesses who had first-hand knowledge and fused it with a number of legends he could gather while himself attending the celebration of Olivi's feast in Narbonne in March 1313.

Charisma is a very general notion. It may be useful to try to discern the aspects under which it applies to this remarkable friar. Had his sainthood been recognized by the papacy, he would have been classified as a saintly scholar, alongside Thomas Aquinas, who was indeed canonized in the very years of Olivi's condemnation. The quantity and depth of his writings made a strong impression among his followers, in his lifetime and for generations after his death. References to his writings (*scriptura*) abound in inquisitorial documents from lay people who could only access them on the occasion of collective readings of vernacular translations, performed in small circles in which members of the Franciscan third order usually described as 'beguins' would gather weekly.[41] Clareno records different episodes which illustrate his considerable scholastic ability to produce arguments and counter-arguments. Judging by the number and complexity of the disputed questions he held before obtaining any university degree, his versatility and subtlety must have distinguished him very early on. This professorial charisma may have extended to his actions as a preacher, but this side of his activity is less well documented since only a handful of sermons have been preserved, all belonging to the scholarly genre of the inaugural lecture

[39] S. Piron, 'Censures et condamnation de Pierre de Jean Olivi: enquête dans les marges du Vatican', *Mélanges de l'École française de Rome. Moyen Age*, cxviii (2006), 313–73, at p. 353.

[40] Clareno, *Chronicle*, pp. 129–44.

[41] L. A. Burnham, *So Great a Light, So Great a Smoke: the Beguin Heretics of Languedoc* (Conjunctions of Religion and Power in the Medieval Past, Ithaca, N.Y., 2007).

(*principia*). Besides this facet of his life as a public teacher, a few clues show that Olivi also acted towards some persons as more of a private instructor. Ubertino da Casale describes him acting as a spiritual master in the period they both spent in Florence at Santa Croce (1287–89).[42] Even more secretly, Olivi admitted on his deathbed to having received some knowledge through divine inspiration. The record of his last moments which circulated among his followers extends this inspiration as the source of 'all his learning', which is obviously an exaggeration. The content of this revelation, which is said to have happened in Paris and therefore at the beginning of his teaching career, is beyond the scope of critical enquiry, although one may surmise it had to do with the historical meaning of Francis's revival of evangelical perfection.[43] Nevertheless, the very fact of such a revelation has to be taken into account and helps to make sense of the astonishing self-assurance Olivi demonstrated throughout his own tribulations. As for the personal qualities of the 'holy man' presented in Clareno's account of his life and in the few personal letters he sent to his friends, qualities such as humility, compassion and patience, one has to decide for oneself. However, since the coherence between teaching and action is one of his major ethical claims, there may be reason not to dismiss totally such testimonies or declarations.

What makes Olivi such an interesting character owes even more to the historical circumstances into which he was thrown. He entered the order in Béziers in 1260 at the age of twelve, just as hundreds of friars were gathering at a general chapter at the nearby city of Narbonne and most probably under the effect of their example. The only record of his initial education in lower Languedoc shows him sharing the memories of the early generations of friars minor. As a novice he was taught by the elderly Raymond Barrau, who had become a friar sometime around 1233, having previously spent at least two decades as a canon in Carcassonne cathedral, being in that quality a personal acquaintance of St Dominic and a witness of the arrival of the first Franciscans in the region.[44] Besides this connection to the heroic period of the founding fathers, Olivi also enjoys the peculiarity of being one of the first major intellectuals exclusively taught within the order, whereas

[42] A. Montefusco, 'Autoritratto del dissidente da giovane. Gli anni della formazione di Ubertino nel primo Prologo dell'*Arbor vitae*', in *Ubertino da Casale: atti del XLI Convegno internazionale: Assisi, 18–20 ottobre 2013* (Spoleto, 2014), pp. 27–82.

[43] According to Pierre Tort's deposition, this happened while Olivi washed his hands, preparing himself to celebrate a mass in Paris (Burr, *Spiritual Franciscans*, p. 226). This implies he must have been at least 25 and probably not much more since his presence in Paris is recorded only up to 1273, when he was precisely that age.

[44] É. Griffe, 'Un chanoine de Carcassonne, ami de Saint Dominique', *Bulletin de littérature ecclésiastique*, lxxviii (1977), 54–7.

theologians from earlier generations, up to Bonaventure or John Peckham, all joined when they were already university students.

His intellectual achievement was, therefore, entirely shaped by his Franciscan identity. To a lesser degree, a similar claim could be made concerning Bonaventure, whom Olivi presents as the greatest master he encountered during his studies in Paris (*c.*1266–73) and the only one worth mentioning. It is, therefore, telling to observe the core issues on which they differ.[45] One key idea for Bonaventure is the participation of all creatures in the divine nature, humans having, in addition, the privilege of a 'special resemblance' by way of the three powers of the soul which bear a similarity to the Trinity. In this theology God is forcefully present within the world. In a sharp contrast, Olivi insists on the abyssal divide which separates God's inconceivable perfection from the limits and imperfection of all creatures. The crucial factor for this reversal of perspective comes from the stress he places on the freedom of the will, both human and divine, which radically sets apart all intellectual and spiritual beings. This move may be perceived as a result of the ongoing philosophical disputes of the 1270s and, in particular, of his confrontation with the Parisian 'Averroists' in an effort to counter a perception of the world as consisting of emanations flowing from the first principle.[46] However, under another angle, this metaphysical approach can also be understood as being part and parcel of his reflection on the Franciscan vocation.

David Burr is the first scholar to have reached a global view of Olivi, both as a sophisticated thinker active in many different fields and as an intriguing personality. When discussing his contribution to the debate on poverty, Burr correctly emphasized that the main issue at stake was not so much the degree of asceticism as the definition of the Franciscan vow.[47] In the summer of 1279 Olivi wrote an impressive series of 'Questions on evangelical perfection' (QPE), while a commission of prelates, including many Franciscans, were working on a new explanation of the rule, which Pope Nicholas III published on 14 August as *Exiit qui seminat*. The questions on obedience, which focused mainly on obedience to papal power, were certainly written while the commission was at work. Olivi, like other friars, seems to have been extremely worried about the outcome. The very title of this series also indicates a sense of continuity with similar works produced a decade or two

[45] S. Piron, 'Olivi and Bonaventure: paradoxes of faithfulness', *Franciscan Stud.*, lxxiv (2016), 1–14.

[46] S. Piron, 'Olivi et les averroïstes', *Freiburger Zeitschrift für Philosophie und Theologie*, liii (2006), 251–309.

[47] D. Burr, *Olivi and Franciscan Poverty: the Origins of the Usus Pauper Controversy* (Philadelphia, Pa., 1989).

earlier by Bonaventure and Peckham on 'evangelical perfection'. In many respects the Languedoc friar was correct in thinking he was following in his elders' footsteps. The major development Olivi introduces lies in his shifting of the debate from the rule to developing instead a theology of the vow. A brief but fundamental question (QPE 5) enquires whether it is better to achieve a good action through a vow or a one-time decision (*simplex propositum*).[48] The former is certainly preferable. Whereas the goodness of an act is limited both in time and scope, a vow implies that all the freedom and power to accomplish such acts are offered to God. Since this power potentially contains an infinity of acts, its dedication is, therefore, infinitely superior to the achievement of a single action. One crucial argument is set out along the way. Since this freedom is constitutive of human nature, once assumed it can never be abdicated: 'This grant that is made to God by a vow does not remove the property [*proprietas*] we have, in that we are naturally the proprietors [*domini*] of our acts and of everything that depends on our faculty of free will'.[49] Thus, a perpetual vow cannot be pronounced once and for all. Instead, it has to be repeated at every instant and is correctly defined as a 'continual vow' (*votum continuatum*). The retention of freedom in the very act of self-abnegation is the most original philosophical feature in Olivi's approach. It should be stressed that such a definition constitutes a complete reversal of the Benedictine rule, in which the monk is requested to give up his free will in total submission to his abbot.

There are good reasons for describing Olivi as the most radical thinker on the freedom of the will in the western philosophical tradition. The intensity of his involvement on that issue would not be comprehensible were it not for the central purpose to which he wished to apply it. First, total freedom is a necessary condition for engaging oneself in the pursuit of evangelical perfection, since here no vow could tolerate even the slightest form of constraint. The evangelical vow then opens up a whole field of action in which freedom is constantly required. This is particularly true of achieving the highest poverty. Renouncing all rights over any material goods (*abnegatio juris*) implies that all legal relationships are voluntary, a notion which in turn became central to Olivi's acute economics.[50] Evangelical poverty implies a

[48] The 'Questions on evangelical perfection' are edited in A. Emmen, 'La dottrina dell'Olivi sul valore religioso dei voti', *Studi Francescani*, lxiii (1966), 88–108.

[49] 'donatio facta Deo per votum non aufert proprietatem illam quam habemus per hoc quod naturaliter sumus domini actuum nostrorum et omnium eorum quae subiacent facultati liberi arbitrii.' It continues, 'Donatio etiam ipsa, qua datum fuit a principio quod erat iuris proprii, in eo cui votum placet, semper manet et semper replicatur' (Emmen, La dottrina dell'Olivi', p. 104). The translation is mine.

[50] P. J. Olivi, *A Treatise on Contracts*, ed. S. Piron and trans. R. Thornton (St Bonaventure, N.Y., 2016); original Latin text and French translation in P. J. Olivi, *Traité de contrats*, ed.

constant will not to possess or attach oneself to any thing. The crucial test is not to claim any goods in court, even if they were unjustly seized by a third party. However, the severing of all legal bonds (*abdicatio omnis iuris*) is not sufficient in itself to define a positive relationship to the material world. Such poverty would be 'formless and confused, unstable, elusive and empty or vain and sterile' without a moral limitation described as 'poor use'.[51] *Usus pauper* is the Olivian concept which provoked the sharpest discussion. As David Burr demonstrated, the core of the matter was not the harshness of the practices it involved. On the contrary, the notion was meant to encompass as valid different levels of ascetic achievement according to the capacities of each individual. *Usus pauper* was conceived as a virtue in an Aristotelian way, admitting variations within a certain breadth (*latitudo*). The conflictual issue was its inclusion in a vow which Olivi conceived of as 'indeterminate'. Precisely because it consists in the exercise of freedom, the vow cannot be reduced to the observance of a series of fixed precepts. The proper behaviour may have to be adjusted according to the circumstances. His opponents objected by pointing to the dangers of obliging oneself to duties whose contents are not known in advance at the risk of falling into mortal sin unknowingly. Olivi's answer was simply that one should put one's trust in the gospel. He who professes to follow the life of Christ shall always find the proper measure of all actions in his conscience. It would be hard to be closer to what Francis meant when he said he did not care about a rule. Equally, and in turn, the Franciscan order as an institution was not ready to accept such a high degree of risk and indeterminacy.

The keystone of evangelical perfection was, therefore, located within the conscience of the individual. In expressing such views, Olivi was drawing the ultimate consequences of a strict identification of the Franciscan rule with the gospel.[52] All his discussion constantly refers to 'evangelical vows', taken immediately to Christ. In the face of such a commitment, the duty of all religious and ecclesiastical superiors is to support its fulfilment and never to impede it. Ultimately, the evangelical vow implies a potential limitation of the power of the pope. This was the most problematic corollary of Olivi's indeterminate conception of the Franciscan vow. According to Olivi, the sovereign pontiff does not have the authority to modify the contents of the vow, since that would amount to ruling against the gospel. A pope

and trans. S. Piron (Paris, 2012).

[51] P. J. Olivi, *Quaestio de usu paupere. The Quaestio and the Tractatus*, ed. D. Burr (Florence and Perth, 1992), p. 35: 'Unde sicut materia sine forma est informis et confusa, instabilis, fluxibilis et vacua seu vana et infructuosa, sic abdicatio omnis iuris sine paupere usu se habet'. The translation is mine.

[52] R. Lambertini, '*Idem quod evangelium Christi*: interpretazioni dell'identità tra regola francescana e Vangelo da Olivi a Clareno', *Cristianesimo nella storia*, xxxvi (2015) 299–327.

who would attempt to diminish the Franciscan rule would fall into heresy by doing so.[53] What Olivi discussed as a working hypothesis in 1279 had gained much more reality by the time of John XXII's election to the papacy. The 'Spiritual' friars from Languedoc resisted their superiors on the basis of the same texts and then repeated their opposition to the Franciscan inquisitor Michael Monachus (Monge). The general sermon he delivered in Marseilles in May 1318, returning four rebels to the secular arm, contains the sharpest expression of the conflicting visions of the two sides: 'This rule is not identical to the Gospel, but some sort of laudable way of life approved and confirmed by the Roman pontiffs and simply and absolutely subjected to their declarations, modification and decisions'.[54] As a response to the Spirituals' evangelical understanding of the rule, the normalization of the Franciscan order as simply one part of the Roman Church had never been expressed so strongly.

Often, what matters more is not what one does, but the reasons for which one does it. For Olivi and his followers the stress put on the freedom of the will was not a simple scholastic device, but a vital choice which characterized their conception of the Franciscan project and for which they were ready to sacrifice their lives. In their perception, the fabric of the 'institution' consisted in a set of free individuals bound together and united by the goal they were pursuing in common. This does not mean they had no sense of the institution as such, nor that they despised the need to maintain some degree of uniformity within it so as to preserve its unity. On the contrary, the Spirituals also attributed a powerful meaning to the Franciscan order as an institution which was achieving a specific historical function. Moreover, Olivi developed a remarkable and unusual reflection on what constitutes an 'institution'. These are the final pieces we need to put together briefly in order to obtain a full vision of the puzzle.

***

[53] P. J. Olivi, *Quaestiones de Romano pontifice*, ed. M. Bartoli (Grottaferrata, 2002).

[54] 'Regule vero predicte et quorumcunque religiosorum omnis tenor et vigor sic a romane sedis potestate manat ut nulla sit eius auctoritas que ab indulgencia seu confirmacione sedis apostolice non decurrat. Non faceret igitur romanus pontifex contra evangelium et fidem Christi, etiamsi statueret contra, mutaret vel tolleret ipsam regulam. Nec est ipsa regula idem quod evangelium, sed est quedam vite laudabilis forma a romanis pontificibus approbata et confirmata, ipsorum declarationi, mutationi et omnimode dispositioni simpliciter et absolute subiecta' (M. Monachus, '*Inquisitoris sententia contra combustos in Massilia*', *Oliviana*, ii (2006), § 8 <http://journals.openedition.org/oliviana/36> [accessed 7 July 2019]).

As an opening to his discussion of the sacraments Olivi raises an unexpected question: what sort of reality is posited by civil right or political power (*Quid ponat ius*)?[55] This intriguing text is often referred to, but its implications are rarely explained in full. A significant part of its importance is what it reveals about both the power – and therefore the risk – which Olivi associated with the reification of spiritual impetus within regularized forms which then took priority over the impulses. It takes as its starting point an expression used by Bonaventure while discussing Peter Lombard's definition of the sacrament as 'the sign of something sacred' (*sacrae rei signum*). If the sacrament belongs to the category of signs, it cannot be of the type which signifies according to its nature (as a scream naturally connotes pain or fear). Owing to the fact that it has been instituted by God in order to convey some specific meaning, the sacrament has to be qualified as a 'voluntary sign'.[56] Accepting this term, Olivi opens a much wider discussion, bringing together other types of 'voluntary signs', such as rights, power and language. The question he raises is concerned with the metaphysical qualification of such signs and of the obligations they create. Do they posit any reality which adds to the subjects in which they are grounded? It would not be inappropriate to translate the question in modern terms as: what does an institution consist of?

Olivi's answer is not immediately eloquent. Those signs do produce some real effects, as an impressive series of examples makes clear, but they do not add any new essence to their subjects. They only consist in being the object of the divine will. To grasp fully the meaning of such a phrase, it is necessary to recall a central feature of Olivi's metaphysics. Breaking with all forms of 'participation' of the creatures in the Creator, he also rejects the notion that the first cause would be operating in each operation of the secondary causes, to paraphrase Aquinas.[57] For Olivi the transcendence of divine will is such that it can only translate into immediately creative acts. Therefore, God does not act within or through his creatures. Instead, he provides them with autonomous agency while preserving them in existence at every instant (since he could as well annihilate them instantly).

The reflection on 'voluntary signs' takes on a clearer meaning in such a perspective. Humans are not solely defined by their free will. Their rational nature also requires them to demonstrate towards each other the virtues of justice, concord and friendship and to exert their domination over irrational

[55] P. J. Olivi, '*Quid ponat ius vel dominium*', ed. F. Delorme and S. Piron, *Oliviana*, v (2016) <https://journals.openedition.org/oliviana/882> [accessed 7 July 2019].

[56] Bonaventure, *Commentaria in quattuor libros Sententiarum Magistri Petri Lombardi*, in *Opera omnia* (10 vols, Ad Claras Aquas, 1882–1902), iv. 14.

[57] Thomas Aquinas, *Summa theologiae*, I, q. 105, a. 5.

beings.[58] Such requirements imply they possess some normative capacity through which they may organize their communication and coexistence by setting out political, juridical and linguistic rules. In order to make such rules binding, God wants them to stand as if they were taking his place. Those institutions can, therefore, be said to be the object of God's will, while being strictly human institutions. Unusual in its formulation, the question draws the consequences of the full autonomy granted to secondary causes into the realm of human sociability. The same metaphysical principles also underlie Olivi's approach to economics, in which he stresses likewise the voluntary nature of contractual relationships.

Olivi's brief *Quid ponat ius?* does not discuss the metaphysical consistency of the Franciscan order or of the Roman Church as a whole, yet the way in which he refers to those institutions in his commentary on Revelation or his questions on evangelical perfection leaves no doubt they should be understood along the same lines. It is worth also observing the polysemy of the notion of *ordo* in Revelation. The word does not only refer to some ranks within the Church, as in Pseudo-Dionysius's vocabulary (priestly, pontifical order; *ordo sacerdotalis*, *pontificalis*, etc.), or to forms of Christian life appropriate to the different stages of history, as in Joachim (order of martyrs, doctors (*ordo martyrum doctorum*), etc.). Instead, when discussing the latest stages of history, it applies to specific modern institutions. Among them, the evangelical order (*ordo evangelicus*), which is meant to play a major role in the confrontation with the soon-to-come Antichrist, clearly stands for the order of friars minor.[59]

The reference to Francis as possessing a distinctive historical signification was common in the central decades of the thirteenth century, including his depiction as an other Christ (*alter Christus*), or as the angel of the seventh seal. Such typological identifications would point to him as a person, or might sometimes extend to the group of his companions. Even so, it is striking that the tendency to attribute a strong historical meaning to the Franciscan institution itself would develop especially among a minority group; and that this use would grow stronger the more they were marginalized and 'de-institutionalized'.

In order to understand the rise of the 'order' as a historical agent, we must again turn to Brother Leo. For years Leo had been Francis's closest associate, acting as his confessor and secretary, writing under his dictation many of the Latin texts which are currently known as Francis's writings. Understandably,

[58] 'Natura rationalis ... est etiam debitrix virtutis iustitie et unanimis ac fidelis concordie et amicitie ad omnes personas rationales' (Olivi, '*Quid ponat ius*', § 30).

[59] P. J. Olivi, *Lectura super Apocalipsim*, ed. W. Lewis (St Bonaventure, N.Y., 2015).

this relationship continued after Francis's death, in the form of visions and apparitions in which the saint would sometimes explain the meaning of his earlier prophetical announcements.[60] When Leo first wrote his account, twenty years after Francis's death, he made few references to such visions. However, Leo lived on much longer and added more testimonies in which he (and the saint's speech to him) grew increasingly bitter towards what the institution was becoming, especially in the collection known as *Verba sancti Francisci*, and stronger still in what Leo told Conrad of Offida in the late 1260s.[61]

In those texts, one prophecy attributed to Francis deserves particular attention. It claims that the order will never cease but will be reduced to a very few friars during the sharpest tribulations; they will resist the Antichrist and regenerate the Church in the new Age of the Spirit after his downfall. In a way which is not without examples in modern political movements, the minority asserts a claim to represent the whole, claiming to be its most legitimate incarnation. In his lifetime Olivi could still feel that the number of true practitioners of the rule within the order was sufficient to defend it as a whole. When the confrontation really started the leaders claimed to represent the 'community' of the order while the 'Spirituals' asserted their identity as 'true' friars minor.[62] Although he had been often rejected and even expelled, Clareno still imagined himself and his band as representing the true order. At an even later date, in the mid fourteenth century, the prophet, visionary and alchemist John of Rupescissa kept on defending a vision of the order as non-dependent on the institution. After all, he admitted the pope could change or suppress the order in the eventuality that no one was following the rule any longer.[63] As a prophet, he knew this would never be the case and that the order could live on, reduced to one person only. This is a striking – logical – conclusion to the trajectory described here across several generations of Franciscans. It was already implicit in Celestine's permission to Angelo and his group to practise their Franciscan vocation outside the Franciscans and within the 'Poor Hermits'. All were wrestling with the problem set by Francis, namely how to reconcile or even articulate

[60] E.g., Thomas de Celano, *The Remembrance of the Desire of a Soul*, bk ii, ch. 23 (*Early Documents*, ii. 239–393, at pp. 281–3), also reflected in *Actus beati Francisci et sociorum ejus*, ed. P. Sabatier (Collection d'études et documents, iv, Paris, 1902), p. 38.

[61] *Verba fratris Conradi. Extrait du Ms. 1/25 de S. Isidore*, ed. P. Sabatier, in *Opuscules de critique historique* (Paris, 1903), pp. 370–92.

[62] M. Cusato, 'Whence "the community"?', *Franciscan Stud.*, lx (2002), 39–92; S. Piron, 'Le mouvement clandestin des dissidents franciscains au milieu du XIVe siècle', *Oliviana*, iii (2009) <http://journals.openedition.org/oliviana/337> [accessed 7 July 2019].

[63] S. Piron, 'L'ecclésiologie franciscaine de Jean de Roquetaillade. À propos d'une édition récente', *Franciscan Stud.*, lxv (2007), 281–94, at p. 292.

the inbuilt tensions of a spiritual impulse which was never supposed to be an institution, let alone a formal religious order. Within it, as Olivi and some others argued, the vow took precedence over any set of rules, most fundamentally because such an evangelical vow was always larger and more all-encompassing than any particular set of institutionalized prescriptions, Franciscan or otherwise.

***

As a conclusion to the third book he devoted to Olivi, David Burr brilliantly summarized his understanding of him: '[H]e could be the patron saint of those who refuse to put their trust in institutions'.[64] This is a comment which has served me as a compass while trying to navigate the immensity of Olivi's works. A coda may now be added: Olivi's distrust is even more understandable, since he knew all too well the power of institutions.

[64] D. Burr, *Olivi's Peaceable Kingdom: a Reading of the Apocalypse Commentary* (Philadelphia, Pa., 1993), p. 263.

7. Rolando of Cremona and the earliest inquisition depositions of Languedoc*

Peter Biller

In this chapter we speculate about the possible contribution of a scholastic theologian, Rolando of Cremona, to a procedure and a document which came to be at the heart of inquisition into heresy: an interrogation recorded in a deposition. The inclusion of inquisition in a collection of essays discussing scholastic institutions might raise some eyebrows, for its 'institutional' character was one of the targets in the late twentieth-century dismantling of the medieval version of 'The Inquisition'. We begin, then, with brief comment on this question. The 'scholastic' implications will emerge in due course.

An institution?

Because most of it was so obvious, the demolition job was easy. All that was needed was a crowbar. First, there was a new historiographical classic in Edward Peters's general history of inquisition. Its later chapters were on early modern inquisition and the modern black legend of inquisition – riffed on in Monty Python's sketch 'Nobody expects the Spanish Inquisition!'[1] These were salutary reminders of the humble and decentralized character of the medieval precedent. Second, a historian of medieval law, Henry Kelly, provided another salutary reminder that inquisition was just one example among various inquisitions, enquiries into various things, conducted by variously denominated *enquêteurs* and inquisitors. Inquisition and inquisitors needed to be brought down to size and set among the others.[2]

* My largest debt is to Lucy Sackville, for sharing ideas and materials about two Dominicans of Cremona, Rolando and Moneta and for comment on this chapter. Editorial suggestions for improvement have been of unusual care, penetration and helpfulness.

1 E. Peters, *Inquisition* (Berkeley, Calif., 1988). The Python sketch can be found at <https://www.youtube.com/watch?v=HqF_nPbX_Ow>.

2 H. A. Kelly, 'Inquisition and the prosecution of heresy: misconceptions and abuses', *Studies in Church History*, lviii (1989), 439–51.

P. Biller, 'Rolando of Cremona and the earliest inquisition depositions of Languedoc', in *Individuals and Institutions in Medieval Scholasticism*, ed. A. Fitzpatrick and J. Sabapathy (London, 2020), pp. 177–95.

Finally, Richard Kieckhefer produced a comprehensive criticism of the assumption, present in most work on medieval inquisition, that it and its officials constituted an 'institution'. Rather, we needed to set these aside and think instead of a task, job or office carried out by an individual equipped with one-off authorization. Medieval inquisition did not tick the boxes of a list of institutional attributes derived from Max Weber.[3]

This 'institutional turn' made the older, insouciant language intellectually incorrect. There were semantic and typographical consequences. Medieval historians of 'The Inquisition' and the 'Office of the Inquisition' lowered the initial capital letters of the key nouns and dropped the definite article. There came to be preference among some scholars for the word 'inquest' and the plural 'inquisitions' over plain 'inquisition'. The multiplicity of types of inquisition gave the historian a duty to remind the reader of specificity, inquisition 'into heresy'.

This was not a total victory. Even Kieckhefer did not claim it. He conceded that inquisition must have become an institution by the later middle ages, for how, otherwise, could we have arrived at the early modern upper-case Inquisition? Some of the troops were disgruntled and murmured, especially those belonging to two special units. One of these units comprises the scholars who burrow patiently in the archives in their reconstruction of local inquisitions in the middle ages. Their documents show them a local inquisition equipped with a special building ('house of inquisition'), financial organization, a household of servants and officials, local continuity and symbolic representation in a seal. This is how things appear in a new general study of inquisition in Italy, which argues that it was clearly an 'institution' by around 1250.[4] Another unit comprises those who study the manuscripts of inquisitors' how-to-do-it manuals, compendia of law relating to inquisition and procedural formulae: Vasil Bivolarov, Riccardo Parmeggiani and Lucy J. Sackville.[5] In his 327-page study with editions

[3] R. Kieckhefer, 'The office of inquisition and medieval heresy: the transition from personal to institutional jurisdiction', *Jour. Eccles. Hist.*, xlvi (1995), 36–61. For more recent discussions of inquisitions, see *L'enquête au moyen âge*, ed. C. Gauvard (Rome, 2008); and J. Sabapathy, 'Some difficulties in forming persecuting societies before Lateran IV Canon 8: Robert of Courson thinks about communities and inquisitions', in *The Fourth Lateran Council: Institutional Reform and Spiritual Renewal*, ed. G. Melville and J. Helmrath (Affalterbach, 2017), pp. 175–200.

[4] J. Moore, *Inquisition and its Organisation in Italy, 1260–1350* (Heresy and Inquisition in the Middle Ages, viii, Woodbridge, 2019).

[5] V. Bivolarov, *Inquisitoren-Handbücher. Papsturkunden und juristische Gutachten aus dem 13 Jahrhundert mit Edition des Concilium von Guido Fulcodii* (MGH, Studien und Texte, lvi, Wiesbaden, 2014); R. Parmeggiani, 'Introduzione', in R. Parmeggiani, *I consilia procedurali per l'inquisizione medievale (1235–1330)* (Bologna, 2011), pp. ix–xxxv; and *Explicatio super*

Bivolarov consigned the topic of 'institution?' to a footnote startling in its brevity and disdain. Its thirty words provide: an approving quotation from a great historian of an older generation, Yves Dossat, on the foundation of 'The Inquisition' as immediately 'a special permanent tribunal'; the citation of Kelly's and Kieckhefer's articles; and their condemnation as 'utter rubbish' (*völlig irrig*).[6] Weber is not mentioned.

We can imagine that this verdict arises from Bivolarov's prolonged exposure to several things: first, the interchanges and conversations between the inquisitors and inquisition of France and Italy; second, the extraordinary growth in the thirteenth century of specialized law and procedures for inquisition into heresy; and, especially, third, the new genre of inquisitors' professional literature. In this context it would be useful to hear a systematic exposition of the case *contra* demolition.

The emergence of the inquisition deposition

There is one document which was at the centre of inquisition into heresy. Though it was preceded and succeeded in the process by various forms – summonses; lists of set questions; abjurations; and executive summaries of items of guilt called *culpae* and sentences – the deposition was *the* key document in the proceedings. Its form was new. Very quickly in the 1240s we find specification of many of its elements in the legislation of Church councils and the procedural formulae of inquisitors' manuals, themselves shared between different regions – a story of dissemination which continues throughout the middle ages. There were shifts in emphasis and varying degrees of elaboration and ponderousness. However, its fundamental form is still recognizable centuries later, for example, in inquisitions in Szczecin between 1392 and 1394 or Piedmont in the 1480s, by which date no one doubts 'The Inquisition'.[7] The character and history of this unique artefact of the inquisition might well play a role in the discussion of inquisition as institution; here our concern is with its genesis.

Let us go back in time and look at one deposition which originated in Languedoc late in 1237.[8] The text is in Latin. After specifying the date, 5

officio inquisitionis. Origini e sviluppi della manualistica inquisitoriale tra due e trecento, ed. R. Parmeggiani (Rome, 2012), pp. vii–lxvi; L. J. Sackville, 'The inquisitor's manual at work', *Viator*, xliv (2013), 201–16; and 'The earliest inquisitor's manual: the *Ordo processus Narbonensis*' (forthcoming).

[6] Bivolarov, *Inquisitoren-Handbücher*, p. 259, n. 17.

[7] P. Biller, 'Inquisitors' interrogations of Waldensians', in *A Companion to the Medieval Waldenses*, ed. M. Benedetti and E. Cameron (Brill Companions to the Christian Tradition, Leiden, forthcoming), provides a general survey for one sect from the early 13th century to 1500.

[8] Paris, BNF, MS. Collection Doat 24, fos. 108v–116v.

October 1237, it names a deponent, Bartac, alias William Matfred, knight of Puylaurens, and records his taking the oath to tell the truth. Replies to questions follow. The first is his initial sighting of a heretic: who the heretic was; where he saw him; who else was there; and how many years ago this was. All Bartac's later responses also have these follow-up questions: who, where, who else and when. A neat pattern is discernible. The follow-up questions to the first heretic to be seen, Bernard Engelbert, are related to the first time (six years before), then the second time (five years before), the third time (three years before) and the fourth time (two years and a bit). The pattern is repeated with the second heretic to be seen, Raymond of Carlipa, with his sightings in chronological order, each with follow-up questions. At the end the text of the deposition states that Bartac appeared in front of the friars Ferrier and Peter of Alès; these inquisitors had been deputed to work in the dioceses of Carcassonne, Narbonne and Albi.[9] The five men who witnessed the proceedings are then listed and then the scribe: 'And Bertrandus de Farico who wrote this (*Et Bertrandus de Farico, qui hæc scripsit*)'.[10] Bartac appeared again two days later. He added (*addidit*) to his previous confession. There is again, within the framework of the document, the same pattern of sightings and dealings with heretics. The deposition again concludes with the statement of Bartac's appearance before the two friars, the listing of witnesses (now seven of them) and the same scribe's declaration that he had written these things.

The only questions Bartac was asked – insofar as his answers imply them – concerned actions. These were things such as seeing heretics; speaking with them; escorting them; adoring them; and seeing them administer their ritual *consolamentum*; and in what contexts: where; who else was there; who else did the same things; and when? Questions included listening to what heretics said, but not its substance, nor what Bartac believed. In later and virtually identikit depositions (1245–6) there are a few modifications to this. One was a concluding question about belief in the heretics or their errors, or whether they were good men. Another was a super-rapid, summary question on a quintet of errors: God not making visible things; the host

[9] Y. Dossat, *Les crises de l'inquisition toulousaine au xiiie siècle (1233–1273)* (Bordeaux, 1959), p. 140, n. 241.

[10] It has not proved possible to identify Bertrand's place of origin. He witnessed three depositions for the Carcassonne inquisition in 1250 (*Documents pour servir à l'histoire de l'inquisition dans le Languedoc*, ed. C. Douais (Paris, 1900), pp. 254, 270, 275). When witnessing a charter for the abbey of La Grasse in 1268, he was given as 'Bertrandi de Faricon, monachi Caunensis', that is, monk of the Benedictine abbey of Caunes in the Minervois (*Recueil des chartes de l'abbaye de La Grasse*, ed. E. Magnou-Nortier, A.-M. Magnou and C. Pailhès (2 vols, Paris, 1996–2000), ii. 372). Here and elsewhere the English translations are the author's.

not being the body of Christ; baptism and marriage not helping salvation; there being no resurrection of the flesh.[11] One minor formal change was the switch from third to first person in the scribe's or notary's conclusion, which became 'and I Bertrandus who wrote this' (*et Bertrandus qui hæc scripsi*).

Bartac's deposition already has the fingerprints of the full models prescribed in the legislation and inquisitors' manuals of the 1240s (e.g., the *formula interrogatorii*), but it comes from the previous decade. What can we see bearing upon its emergence? The reconstructions of the 1230s in general histories of inquisition and the evidence of the bulls with which Gregory IX mandated early Dominican inquisitors in Languedoc make the decade seem very familiar to us – we know it rather well, we think.[12] However, they are a smoke-screen, for there is not much with which to work. We need a quick reminder of the little we do have, beginning with its chronological boundaries. At one end there is evidence relating to 1229–30, when the provisions of a provincial Church council and description in a chronicle provide a view of procedure and the records these years may have produced in Toulouse. The papal legate Romano, Cardinal of Sant' Angelo, held a council in Toulouse in November 1229.[13] In the existing system for the repression of heresy, a bishop visited a parish and took sworn evidence from a few trustworthy laymen. The council's first provision tweaked this, stipulating the addition of a priest to the oath-taking laymen in each parish and turning them from passive-reactive into active: they were to hunt out heretics and report them to ecclesiastical or secular authorities. In a chronicle written forty-five years later we have a description of what the papal legate then did, in the wake of the 1229 council. He ran an *inquisitio*, which William of Puylaurens (born *c.*1200) described. William was a man of senior administrative experience and a sometime inquisition witness and temporary inquisitor. Although in his seventies when writing, he still

[11] P. Biller, 'Cathars and the material world', in *God's Bounty? The Churches and the Natural World*, ed. P. Clarke and T. Claydon, *Studies in Church History*, xlvi (2010), 89–110, at pp. 98–106.

[12] Dossat, *Crises*, pp. 108–45; H. Maisonneuve, *Études sur les origines de l'inquisition* (2nd edn, L'Église et l'État au Moyen Age, vii, Paris, 1960 [1942]), pp. 237–42, 270–5; W. L. Wakefield, *Heresy, Crusade and Inquisition in Southern France, 1100–1250* (London, 1974), ch. 8; L. Kolmer, *Ad capienda vulpes. Die Ketzerbekämpfung in Südfrankreich in der ersten Hälfte des 13. Jahrhunderts und die Ausbildung des Inquisitionsverfahrens* (Bonn, 1982).

[13] On Romano, see W. Maleczek, *Papst und Kardinalskollege von 1191 bis 1216. Die Kardinäle unter Coelestin III. und Innocenz III* (Vienna, 1984), pp. 189–95. The council's canons were printed in G. D. Mansi, *Sacrorum conciliorum nova et amplissima collectio* (54 vols in 59, Graz, 1960–1; repr. of edition published in 1902–27), xxiii. 191–204. They are translated in *Heresy and Inquisition in France, 1200–1300*, ed. and trans. J. H. Arnold and P. Biller (Manchester Medieval Sources, Manchester, 2016), pp. 190–7.

displayed a very crisp, clear mind.[14] 'It was organized like this' (*Fuit sic ordinata*), wrote William.[15] The bishop of Toulouse, Fulk, produced the witnesses. To expedite matters the jobs were shared. Each bishop examined some of the witnesses and each bishop returned the statements recording in writing (*dicta in scriptis redacta*) to Bishop Fulk. Summoned first were those people who were regarded as faithful and Catholic; and they were presumably questioned about the *fama* (public reputation) of suspects. Summoned second were the suspects. The suspects who did appear carefully avoided saying anything against each other. If only we could see the records of the *dicta in scriptis redacta* of this second category, the suspects! Unfortunately, when the papal legate returned to Rome he took the whole lot away with him: *secum totam inquisitionem exportavit*. However much we can appreciate the wit and hint of the bureaucrat's regret in these words, the main thing is that we are up against a brick wall. William is all we have.

At the other end we have Bartac's deposition. It is the earliest to survive. The space between 1229/30 and October 1237 is almost entirely devoid of texts directly emanating from the examination of heretics. Almost: apart from two texts, which are not straightforwardly helpful. One of these is a set of earlier written testimonies about heresy from, almost certainly, early 1234. They are legally and procedurally traditional: sworn testimonies, made by reputable ecclesiastics and laymen, about the *fama* of involvement in heresy of members of a powerful aristocratic family, the Niorts.[16] The other is nearer our concerns. Bartac's deposition has a twin, which is the only other extant deposition from hearings before the inquisitors Ferrier and Peter of Alès when acting together. It is from a few months later, dated 18 February 1238, and appears to be a, possibly compressed, 1238 copy of a confession made to William Arnold (discussed below) in 1235. There is nothing else. If

[14] The best modern discussion of William is in M. Meschini, 'Il "negotium pacis et fidei" in Linguadoca tra XII e XIII secolo secondo Guglielmo di Puylaurens', in *Mediterraneo medievale. Cristiani, musulmani ed eretici tra Europea e Oltremare (secoli IX–XIII)*, ed. M. Meschini (Milan, 2001), pp. 131–68. Additional evidence is noted in *Inquisitors and Heretics in Thirteenth Century Languedoc: Edition and Translation of Toulouse Inquisition Depositions, 1273–1282*, ed. P. Biller, C. Bruschi and S. Sneddon (Studies in the History of Christian Traditions, cxlvii, Leiden, 2011), pp. 56, 108–9, 510–13.

[15] The current paragraph summarizes William's account: Guillaume de Puylaurens, *Chronique*, ed. J. Duvernoy (Paris, 1976), pp. 138–41 (§ xxxviii, parallel Latin and modern French translation); *The Chronicle of William of Puylaurens: the Albigensian Crusade and Its Aftermath*, ed. and trans. W. A. Sibly and M. D. Sibly (Woodbridge, 2003), pp. 83–5.

[16] BNF, MS. Collection Doat 21, fos. 34–50v. On this, see W. L. Wakefield, 'The Family of Niort in the Albigensian crusade and before the inquisition. Part 1', *Names*, xviii (1970), 97–117, at pp. 111–13; Y. Dossat, 'La repression de l'hérésie par les évêques', in *Le credo, la morale et l'inquisition* (Cahiers de Fanjeaux, vi, Toulouse, 1971), pp. 217–51, at pp. 241–7; Kolmer, *Ad capienda Vulpes*, pp. 82–107.

we cannot trace the evolution of the deposition as a practical tool through a neat chronological set of textual examples, what is left for us to do?

A cluster of people

One of the most distinctive voices in modern writing about the Church in the decades around 1200 is that of the American scholar Jessalynn Bird. In a way that is reminiscent of John Baldwin, she uses everything, from theological and legal commentaries to *exempla*, sermons and chronicles. She interweaves many themes, new religious orders, reform, preaching, crusade and dealing with heresy. The canvas she paints is that of the *pointilliste* period in French impressionism. There are many coloured dots: writers, legates, reformers, bishops, cardinals and preachers. She includes as many of them as she can in her picture; and shows them working, preaching, travelling, meeting and exchanging knowledge and ideas.[17] Bird's remarkable success in grasping and presenting a substantial fraction of how that world actually worked is a very useful reminder. We may not have a parchment trail, but we do have a picture crowded with the people who were around in Toulouse during the years in question. It was painted by the Dominican William Pelhisson in his chronicle of the Toulouse convent.[18]

Pelhisson came from a (probably) middling Toulouse family and entered the order (probably) by 1230. He acted both as inquisitor and as a witness to hearings, was for some years master of works (*operarius*) of the Toulouse convent and died in 1268.[19] A later Dominican historian, Bernard Gui,

[17] A representative as well as very important work is J. Bird, 'The wheat and the tares: Peter the Chanter and the *fama*-based inquest against heresy and criminal sins, *c.*1198–*c.*1235', *Proceedings of the Twelfth International Congress of Medieval Canon Law*, ed. U.-R. Blumenthal, K. Pennington and A. A. Larson (Monumenta iuris canonici, series C, Subsidia, xiii, Vatican City, 2008), pp. 763–856.

[18] *Guillaume Pelhisson, Chronique (1229–1244)*, ed. J. Duvernoy (Paris, 1994); particularly useful is the annotation to the English translation in Wakefield, *Heresy*, pp. 207–36. Bernard Gui copied Pelhisson's treatise on Toulouse convent properties into his *De fundatione et prioribus conventuum provinciarum Tolosanae et Provinciae Ordinis Praedicatorum*, ed. P. A. Amargier (Rome, 1961), pp. 32–42.

[19] *Scriptores Ordinis Praedicatorum*, ed. T. Kaeppeli and E. Panella (4 vols, Rome, 1970–93), ii. 132–3, iv. 105; Dossat, *Crises*, pp. 123–4, 128, 130–2, 134–5, 138, 221, 241; Y. Dossat, 'Patriotisme méridionale du clergé au XIIIe siècle', in *Les évêques, les clercs et le roi (1250–1300)* (Cahiers de Fanjeaux, vii, Toulouse, 1972), pp. 419–52, at pp. 428–30; J. Feuchter, *Ketzer, Konsuln und Büßer. Die städtischen Eliten von Montauban vor dem Inquisitor Petrus Cellani (1236/1241)* (Spätmittelalter, Humanismus, Reformation, xl, Tübingen, 2007), pp. 278–80; C. C. Ames, *Righteous Persecution: Inquisition, Dominicans and Christianity in the Middle Ages* (Philadelphia, Pa., 2009), pp. 114–18. A master Arnold Pelhisson was canon and precentor of St Stephen's in Toulouse (from 1236), witnessed interrogations and sentences (1237, 1245–7) and at some stage received heresy confessions (Pelhisson, *Chronique*, pp. 8–9).

confined his comments to Pelhisson's role as *operarius*. Gui's careful words about his conscientiousness, hard work and more than medium usefulness carry a hint of faintness of praise: 'diligent, hard-working and not moderately productive' (*sollicitus, laboriosus et non mediocriter fructuosus*).[20] Pelhisson had an eye for mundane things. Notable in his treatise on the Toulouse convent's acquisition of properties is its detailing of the locations and entrances of the lavatories.

Though Pelhisson does have a stab at spelling out the purpose of preserving history and providing the theme of the early friars' great deeds and travails, most of the time what his chronicle provides are the streets and buildings of the city, crowds and people talking and doing things. The stories about dealing with heretics convey both drama and a jumbled, improvised and 'let's all muck in' impression of these years. While historians of inquisition despair as they try to extract a precise chronology from Pelhisson, here we are trying to see the procedural disorder, experiment and creativity of this period through the frosted glass of Pelhisson's mind. However, Pelhisson does paint people – and many of them. At one point he says there were about forty friars in the convent and he proceeds to name many of them: Dominic of Baretge; John of St Michel; Geoffrey, an Englishman and great cleric – and so on.[21] Many more strut across his pages, including others from England and Italy.

Pelhisson was a Douanier Rousseau, a Sunday painter, not a sophisticated *pointilliste*. Nevertheless, let us try to use him in an exercise inspired by Bird. From Pelhisson's Toulouse gallery we shall pick out four: Peter Seila; William Arnold; Rolando of Cremona; and Peter of Alès. We shall set them and their training and outlook alongside the inquisition deposition which was emerging in these same years and its characteristics. Salient in particular are the following: the form of a legally authenticated document; the near total confinement of topics in the *formula interrogatorii* to actions rather than beliefs; the compression of the latter to a 'yes' or 'no' question about belief in the heretics or their errors; and the modification of this by the intrusion – sometimes – of a quintet of beliefs. If we take these four characteristics and Pelhisson's four persons we shall, with patience, be able to suggest something about the institutional nature of inquisition during this period and some intellectual and scholastic trends within it. The reader should be warned that scholastic theology only enters with the third figure, Rolando of Cremona.

A Durand Pelisson was one of 1028 Toulouse men taking an oath in 1243 to maintain the Peace of Meaux-Paris (J. H. Mundy, *Society and Government at Toulouse in the Age of the Cathars* (Toronto, 1997), pp. 371, § 14). See p. 155 on these not including the poor.

[20] Gui, *De fundatione et prioribus*, p. 42.

[21] Pelhisson, *Chronique*, p. 48; Wakefield, *Heresy*, p. 211.

A gallery: Peter Seila, William Arnold, Rolando of Cremona and Peter of Alès

Peter Seila

Our figures begin with Peter Seila, the first man to join Dominic and at that point already an old man.[22] Belonging to what Feuchter calls the 'capitalist elite' of Toulouse, he had come from a family which combined wealth with a tradition of high administrative service. The earliest extant act witnessed by one of the family was written and authenticated in the house of William Seila in 1168.[23] Peter himself had served in the courts of three successive counts of Toulouse, Raymonds V–VII. He had survived tough treatment by Richard the Lionheart after his capture.[24] Peter gave the friars their first building in Toulouse, which came to function as the house of inquisition (*domus inquisitionis*). Alongside William Arnold and Pons of Saint-Gilles he was one of the three earliest inquisitors in the Toulouse region; and as a very old man he was still one of the most vigorous of all inquisitors and clearly a towering figure. Bernard Gui may have been reserved in his words about Pelhisson, but he let rip with Peter: he 'grew old upon the earth, like one of the prophets of old'.[25]

The texts surviving from Seila's inquisitions are not his depositions but his *culpae*, meaning extracts of the bad things, confessed in depositions, which would be useful for the inquisitor's calculation of an appropriate penance. Given the commonplace that inquisitors' interrogations were shaped by both formulaic questions and an individual inquisitor's outlook, it is worth looking at what can be inferred about Seila from these *culpae*. On the one hand, there is much in them which reflected what was becoming standard in these years. Old he may have been and educated long before 'Dominican scholasticism', but the bright and very experienced Seila will have learnt quickly. However, there is one thing in his *culpae* which is very striking: they are densely packed with references to writing – from written prayers and vernacular gospels to the drawing up of wills. Among inquisitorial minds, Seila's was the one most alert to texts, their drawing up, possession and use.[26] There is nothing quite like it elsewhere, in the approximately 1.8

[22] The fundamental account of Peter is Feuchter, *Ketzer, Konsuln und Büßer*, ch. 5; and of the Seila family Mundy, *Society and Government at Toulouse*, pp. 341–5. On their comital service see also L. Macé, *Les comtes de Toulouse et leur entourage. Rivalités, alliances et jeux de pouvoir, xxe–xiiie siècles* (Toulouse, 2000), pp. 131, 338, 391, n. 75.

[23] L. Macé, *Catalogue raimondins. Actes des comtes de Toulouse, ducs de Narbonne et marquis de Provence (1112–1229)* (Toulouse, 2008), pp. 129–30, #117; see also pp. 170–1, #186.

[24] *Chronica Magistri Rogeri de Houedene*, ed. W. Stubbs (4 vols, London, 1868–71), ii. 339.

[25] Gui, *De fundatione et prioribus*, p. 59.

[26] *L'inquisition en Quercy. Le registre des pénitences de Pierre Cellan 1241–1242*, ed. J.

million words of the extant inquisition records of Languedoc between the 1230s and 1320s.[27]

Though the point is obvious and could be urged using other figures, it still needs stating. The convent was situated in a city noted for the precocious development of the notarial profession from around 1100 and for its massive production of authenticated acts.[28] In the early 1230s the friars embraced, on the one hand, the humble Pelhisson ferreting around in the convent's charters and authenticated documents, 'in charters and instruments' (*in cartis et instrumentis*) when writing his history of convent properties; and, on the other hand, one of the most distinguished bureaucrats of the previous fifty years. As the classic inquisition deposition was emerging, it was bound to acquire the formal clothing of the authenticated instruments of this time and place. It would be surprising if Seila's immense authority and administrative experience did not affect it: even if in no longer precisely discernible ways.

William Arnold

The second figure is the inquisitor William Arnold, famous for his murder at Avignonet along with all the members of his household in 1242.[29] Why might he figure in our gallery? There has already been mention of one of the main characteristics of the deposition: that questions concentrated on actions rather than beliefs. This had a legal and a theological facet; and it is

Duvernoy (Castelnaud La Chapelle, 2001), pp. 34 (gospel in Occitan; letters; legacy), 40 (heretics' book in peace ritual), 56 (carrying heretics' book), 60 (legacies), 66 (keeping heretics' book), 72 (writing a will for heretics), 80 (reading in heretics' book), 82 (heretic reading), 84 (keeping heretics' book, read by anyone who wanted to read it), 94 (heretics' letters), 102 (receiving book from a heretic), and *passim*.

[27] This figure is based on counting a few sample pages and leaves of the principal sets of printed and manuscript records and multiplying by the page or leaf numbers. While digitization will ultimately correct this elementary calculation, it does provide an order of magnitude.

[28] J. H. Mundy, *Liberty and Political Power in Toulouse, 1100–1250* (New York, 1954), pp. 35–7, 115–21; and J. H. Mundy, *Men and Women at Toulouse in the Age of the Cathars* (Toronto, 1990), pp. 10–12.

[29] William Arnold's name is on many inquisition documents and therefore appears on many pages of histories of early inquisition; and there are several eye-witness accounts of his murder. Hardly anything else is known. According to Pelhisson he was from Montpellier and a legal expert. The earliest known date of his authorization as inquisitor seems to be January or February 1234 (Dossat, *Crises*, p. 122). Although in his list of Toulouse priors Bernard Gui put William Arnold between Peter Seila (1235–7) and Colombe of Provence (from 1242), he was also clear that little was known. He was 'prior for some time, but I have not found in what year or for how long' (Gui, *De fundatione et prioribus*, p. 50). He was murdered during the night of 28 May 1242.

the legal story which is our concern in this section. Its recapitulation is most usefully done in reverse chronological order. In the early to mid 1240s the texts of a wide range of southern French and Spanish Church councils are awash with definitions of various categories of supporters of heretics, chief among them that of the *credentes*, the believers. They were mainly defined by actions; and behind that lay a decade or more of experience, thought, and debate. The substantial contribution of lawyers is very clear in two texts. One is a *consilium* from the lawyer and former royal official Guy Foulcques (later Pope Clement IV, 1265–8). The consultation's date of composition has recently been revised: it may come from as early as 1238.[30] There is first a brief statement of the tautology, that admitting to believing in what heretics say amounts to believing in the errors of heretics. There then follows a long, brilliant discussion of the inaccessibility of the secrets of the human heart and consideration of proof of someone's inner disposition in Roman law.[31] This meant actions. Earlier, in 1235, Dominicans had asked a group of legal experts in Avignon to consider and define what constituted a 'believer' in Waldensian heretics. Following the tautology is the core of the formal, detailed answer they received, which was, of course, a list of actions.[32]

As we ponder what precedes this, we have in our mind three solid things about 1235. What constituted a believer was a live issue at that date. Dominican inquisitors were obtaining formal legal advice on it. The law schools at this time were to the east, in the cities of Provence, especially Avignon and Montpellier. A lawyer's view of a 'believer' may have come earlier than this, from the other 'first' inquisitor, William Arnold. Legal reflection clarified inquisitorial categories, for when William Arnold is first depicted in his chronicle, Pelhisson tells us only two things about him: that he was learned in law, a jurist (*iurisperitus*); and that he came from Montpellier.[33]

30 Bivolarov, *Inquisitoren-Handbücher*, pp. 239–41; date: pp. 215–17.

31 P. Biller, '"Deep is the heart of man, and inscrutable": signs of heresy in medieval Languedoc', in *Text and Controversy: Essays in Honour of Anne Hudson*, ed. H. Barr and A. M. Hutchison (Turnhout, 2005), pp. 267–80.

32 *Quellen zur Geschichte der Waldenser*, ed. A. Patschovsky and K.-V. Selge (Texte zur Kirchen- und Theologiegeschichte, xviii, Gütersloh, 1973), pp. 50–4; Parmeggiani, *I consilia procedurali*, pp. 10–13, with further bibliography at p. 11; translated in Arnold and Biller, *Heresy and Inquisition*, pp. 215–17.

33 Pelhisson, *Chronique*, p. 44. Since William Arnold was a common name, there is no surprise in finding another William Arnold who was a jurist, still active 10 years after the inquisitor William Arnold's death (Y. Dossat, 'L'université de Toulouse, Raymond VII, les capitouls et le roi', in *Les universités du Languedoc au xiiie siècle* (Cahiers de Fanjeaux, v, Toulouse, 1970), pp. 58–91, at pp. 77–8.

Rolando of Cremona

Pelhisson's gallery contains only a few learned men who could be candidates for inclusion in a discussion of scholasticism. Near the beginning of his chronicle he states many Paris masters and scholars had been sent to Toulouse so that there might be a mendicant university (*studium generale*) and the faith might be taught there, as also the liberal arts (*scientia liberales*).[34] He does not date this and names no names, confining himself to a scathing comment on their ineffectiveness. They did not manage to uproot heresy. Rather, when hearing 'unfamiliar things' (*insolita*) from them, heretical sympathizers mocked them. These 'unfamiliar things' were presumably the technical vocabulary as well as the topics of the Paris schools, not adapted to a Toulouse audience.

Shortly after this Pelhisson moves nearer to his own times. He begins to include dates, though in an insouciant manner relying heavily on 'in those days' (*in illis diebus*) and 'at that time' (*tunc temporis*). He interweaves into the story a chronological sequence of three masters who came from Paris to lecture on theology: Rolando of Cremona, John of St Giles and Lawrence, the arrival of the latter dated 5 or 6 November 1235. While John and Lawrence have small spaces in Pelhisson and no words or actions are attributed to them, Rolando, as we shall see, cuts a large figure.

He was born around 1178. By the second decade of the thirteenth century Rolando had become a famous figure at Bologna, where he taught medicine and philosophy. His writings indicate a mind well-stocked and familiar with Greco-Latin and Arabo-Latin translations of a remarkable range of philosophical and medical writings, with a penchant for moving fast into medical and bodily vocabulary and analogies. He was one of the early coups in recruitment for the high university by the young Dominican order, entering it perhaps in July 1218. He was sent to Paris in 1219 to teach the friars at Saint Jacques, did this briefly and then probably returned to Lombardy. He was in Paris again in the late 1220s and was awarded the chair in theology in 1229: the first Dominican in this new position. He held this for perhaps a year and then went to Toulouse.[35]

His main writings are a *Summa* of theology in four books and a *Postilla in Job*, whose references to the *Summa* (but not vice versa) indicate that

[34] Pelhisson, *Chronique*, p. 38.

[35] R. Parmeggiani, 'Rolando da Cremona († 1259) e gli eretici. Il ruolo dei frati predicatori tra scatologismo e profezia', *Archivum Fratrum Praedicatorum*, lxxix (2009), 23–84, at pp. 24–5. Still fundamental is E. Filthaut, *Roland von Cremona O.P. und die Anfänge der Scholastik im Predigerorden. Ein Beitrag zur Geistesgeschichte der älteren Dominikaner* (Vechta-im-Oldenburg, 1936).

they were produced in that order.[36] The most frequent evocations of the contemporary world in the *Summa* suggest that the geographical poles of Rolando's mind were northern France (*Francia*) and Lombardy. (Wine is more expensive in northern France than in Lombardy, Rolando observed.[37]) Paris moulded the two texts in important ways. First, one Paris master often named in the *Summa* was William of Auxerre.[38] Rolando's own *Summa* acquired its shape and core through its copying and incorporation of the questions of William's *Summa aurea*. Second, Rolando's commentary on Job was produced in compliance with the duty of the regent master in theology in Paris: to lecture and comment on a particular book of the Bible.

Rolando turned this duty into the opportunity to write in his *Postilla* a virulent attack on heresy, in particular the Cathars (*Cathari*, his usage) and another group of heretics who were in his eyes less dangerous, the Lyonists (*Leoniste* – meaning Waldensians). While his *Summa* naturally does not have this narrowness of focus, since it is a general theological treatise, a comparison between Rolando's *Summa* and William's *Summa* always shows a contrast, one which betrays Rolando's preoccupation. Where William does deal with heresy or heretics, Rolando picks up the ball and runs with it. What is a short passage in William on heretics' willingness and ability to endure the pain of being burnt to death is tripled in length in Rolando and dealt with from several more angles; and Rolando keeps returning to the topic.[39] In various questions which the authors share, Rolando inserts heresy and repression where William is silent.

The knowledge, memories and rumours likely to be found in both of Rolando's milieux – Bologna and Paris – are suggested in passing allusions, which also help to locate Rolando chronologically. In his *Verbum adbreviatum* (1191–2) Peter the Chanter had advocated imprisonment rather than execution

[36] The most accessible work is *Summae Magistri Rolandi Cremonensis O.P. Liber Tercius*, ed. L. Cortesi (Bergamo, 1962), a transcription with hardly any apparatus of a work about 550,000 words long; Luigi Cortesi's first name was rendered as Aloysius in Latin, hence the A. Cortesi of some catalogues. There are references in the 3rd book to the 1st and 2nd books, but not to the 4th (*Summa*, pp. 266, 294, 548, 994). Around 1960 Cortesi made incomplete transcriptions of books 1, 3 and 4 of the *Summa* and the *Postilla in Job*; these have now been published by U. Midali (Bergamo, 2015–17). In this chapter we rely on the 3rd book of the *Summa* in Cortesi's edition and on the *Postilla* through the extensive quotation of it in A. Dondaine, 'Un commentaire scripturaire de Roland de Crémone: "Le livre de Job"', *Archivum Fratrum Praedicatorum*, xi (1941), 109–37; and in Parmeggiani, 'Rolando da Cremona'. We follow Parmeggiani's approach to the works' dates and their Paris context.

[37] Rolando, *Summa*, p. 1068.

[38] Rolando, *Summa*, pp. 672, 734, 995, 1105, 1107, 1108, 1133, 1224, 1340; Filthaut, *Roland von Cremona*, p. 83.

[39] William of Auxerre, *Summa aurea*, ed. J. Ribailler (Spicilegium Bonaventurianum, xvi–xx, 5 vols in 7, 1980–7), iii, pt. 2. 825 (bk. iii, § 43.2); Rolando, *Summa*, pp. 1132–3.

for Cathars who confessed and were convicted of heresy.[40] The airing of these ideas in Paris and among the Chanter's followers may be the background to Rolando's restatement and rejection of the proposition put forward by some: that heretics should not be killed.[41] Elsewhere Rolando asks who was responsible for a heretic's death: the capturer who handed the heretic on; or the secular authority which ordered the execution? Discussion of the responsibility of secular authorities led on to the topic of authorities which killed heretics regardless of the latter's willingness to return to the faith. Perhaps there was a 'Blackadder' element in Rolando's humour, for he illustrates this with a rumour about a well-known uncontrollably bad man: 'King John, who had heretics in prison, is said to have acted like this. He said to them, "Whether you want to return or not, I'm going to kill you!"'. [42] This probably goes back to 1206 and John's successful siege of Montauban, followed by the capture of many of its inhabitants.[43] The likelihood of these containing adherents of heretics is very high, for in the 1230s Peter Seila interrogated and sentenced 256 of them.[44]

Peter the Chanter's argument and (probably) King John's capture of Montauban put forward the dates 1191–2 and 1206; and other dates – some only probable, some surer – begin to supply the outlines of a chronology. Rolando's discussions of summary executions of heretics by secular authorities could be put alongside various examples from the Albigensian crusade, for example, the execution of 140 heretics after the capture of Minerve in 1210. The last session of the Fourth Lateran Council in November 1215 was evoked in a reference to the count of Toulouse losing his lands through support for heresy.[45] The allusions to those with the role of *podestà* acting against heretics may refer to events in Lombard cities between 1228 and 1229.[46] Finally, there is the most significant chronological point in Rolando's discussions of heresy. He assumes it is bishops who proceed against heretics.[47] At the same time there

[40] J. W. Baldwin, *Masters, Princes and Merchants: the Social Views of Peter the Chanter and His Circle* (2 vols, Princeton, N.J., 1970), i. 322; Peter the Chanter, *Verbum adbreviatum. Textus conflatus*, ed. M. Boutry (*CCCM*, cxcvi, Turnhout, 2004), p. 508 (§ i.76).

[41] Rolando, *Summa*, p. 1365; Parmeggiani discusses later debate on the topic ('Rolando da Cremona', pp. 75–6).

[42] Rolando, *Summa*, p. 1364: 'Sic enim dicitur fecisse rex Iohannes qui habebat hereticos in carcere. Dixit enim eis, "Sive velitis, sive non, ego interficiam vos"'.

[43] Roger of Wendover, *Flores Historiarum*, ed. H. G. Hewlett (3 vols, London, 1886–9), ii. 13–14.

[44] Feuchter, *Ketzer, Konsuln und Büßer*, p. 241. One of them had sold wine to King John in 1205 (Feuchter, *Ketzer, Konsuln und Büßer*, pp. 153–4).

[45] Dondaine, 'Un commentaire scripturaire', p. 117.

[46] Parmeggiani, 'Rolando da Cremona', p. 65.

[47] Rolando, *Summa*, pp. 1362, 1366.

is a total absence of any reference to mendicant friars possessing authorization and exclusive competence in this area.[48] Leaving aside occasional references to early Church heresies, we see a precise chronology in Rolando's mind: from the 1190s to around 1230, in other words, shortly before the institution of mendicant inquisition.

Rolando himself had already been at work directly with heretics. In one reminiscence he talks about questioning heretics and overpowering them in argument; and in another he claims to have captured eighteen in a day.[49] Nothing helps us to contextualize these anecdotes. However, they do not argue for a later date, for there is nothing surprising in Dominicans helping in repression in the years before the formal institution of mendicant inquisition. The Dominican Ferrier was already active against heretics in 1229, authorized by the archbishop of Narbonne.

These then are the outlines of the life and writings of Rolando, before his move from Paris to Toulouse and into a leading role in Pelhisson's chronicle. 'Master Rolando lectured in theology' in Toulouse, Pelhisson tells us, and then he recounts three stories. In the first, the people of Toulouse reacted strongly against a Dominican sermon stating that there were heretics in the city, holding assemblies there and spreading heresies. 'Very agitated and worked up', they summoned the prior of the Dominicans to the house of the commune and ordered him to tell the friars to stop preaching such stuff. They uttered threats. When master Rolando heard this from the prior he declared, 'Certainly now what we should do is press on even more and more with preaching against the heretics and their believers'. Rolando did this manfully and powerfully; and the others did likewise. Pelhisson goes on to the second story. A *donat* (lay brother)[50] of St Sernin had become a canon on his deathbed and was buried in the cloister wearing the surplice. The canons had not known that he had also been hereticated (that is, received the *consolamentum*). When Master Rolando came to hear this, he went off with friars and some clergy and they dug up the body, dragged it to a fire and burnt it. The third story is about a great leader of Waldensians called Galvan, who had died. This did not escape Master Rolando's notice and he stated it publicly in a sermon. Friars, clergy and people went off to Galvan's house, destroying it and converting it into a sewer. They dug up Galvan's body from the cemetery in the new town, processed through the town with it and burnt it on common ground outside the town.[51]

[48] Parmeggiani, 'Rolando da Cremona', p. 69.

[49] Rolando, *Summa*, pp. 1364, 1376.

[50] On *donats*, see C. de Miramon, *Les donnés au moyen âge: une forme de vie religieuse laïque (vers 1100–vers 1500)* (Paris, 1999).

[51] Pelhisson, *Chronique*, pp. 40–5.

In each story Rolando heard something and this led to action. This pattern acquires more force through repetition. Pelhisson's text constructs the polar opposite of the ineffective Paris masters and scholars who had come earlier to Toulouse: Rolando was a figure of dynamism and energy. However, he is a figure in three strip cartoons, for Pelhisson did not have the outlook or range to assess and depict Rolando's presence in any other way.

Let us recapitulate. Rolando came from Paris to Toulouse around 1230 and left Toulouse for Lombardy three years later in 1233. Roland will narrowly have missed the clear-up work undertaken in the aftermath of the Council of Toulouse by southern bishops. In November 1229 they had been at work examining successively Catholic witnesses and heresy suspects and delivering written records of these proceedings to Fulk, the bishop of Toulouse. At the other end of Rolando's years in Toulouse there is the earliest date we know Rolando was back in Italy, October 1233. He may still have been in Toulouse in April, when the letters started arriving from Gregory IX which mandated southern French Dominicans to carry out inquisitions. During this period one of the cleverest, most learned men in Latin Christendom, and one who was almost obsessed with the fight against heresy, was lending his support to the prior and friars of the Dominican convent and lecturing in theology. Rolando's northern French, German (probably) and Lombard knowledge and experience of proceedings against heretics will have contributed much *savoir-faire*. Further ransacking of his writings would add to our view of what Rolando brought to the table. However, here we shall concentrate on the significance of Rolando's importation into Toulouse of a commonplace of Parisian theology about simple believers.

In Rolando's *Postilla in Job* heresiarchs and their believers form part of the devil's body; prelates and Catholic believers the body of Christ or the Church.[52] The heresiarchs and prelates in the Church, for example, are the bones. Rolando concentrates mostly on heretics (that is, the leaders), particularly their believers. 'In these believers lies the strength of heretics', wrote Rolando. 'They join themselves to the heretics', he continued, 'by defending them and lodging them' (*in quibus credentibus herreticorum fortitudo est. Illi enim hereticos defendant, et hospitando sibi conjungunt*). He deliberately uses the words denoting categories of support for heresy which had been deployed in Church legislation since the decretal *Ad abolendam* in 1184. The intimacy and strength of the link are strengthened by Rolando

[52] The following is based on Parmeggiani, '"Rolando" da Cremona', pp. 45–9. At the time of writing, *Expositio libri beati Job Magistri Rolandi Cremonensis*, ed. L. Cortesi and U. Midali (Bergamo, 2017), was not available to me.

the medic, relishing the opportunity to deploy the corporeal language of Job XL: 12. If the heresiarchs are hardened fistulae or bones, their believers are the surrounding cartilage. If the heresiarchs are testicles, their believers are nerves within these testicles. In the consumption of error, heresiarchs provide the molar teeth which grind the doctrine, while believers' anterior teeth continue the job.

Let us keep in mind the startling physicality of this, the focus on believers and the formal parallels between the parallel pairing of heresiarchs-prelates and believers-simple faithful in the bodies of both heretical sect and Church, as we turn to Rolando's discussion of faith in book 3 of the *Summa*. At one point he investigates a theme which had been given important earlier formulations by Hugh of St Victor, Peter Lombard and William of Auxerre: the faith of the simple faithful (*fideles simplices*).[53] The question was this: what degree of precise comprehension and ability to articulate and distinguish between specific articles of faith was required of a simple believer? This believer was specified by some commentators as stupid or uneducated and also came eventually to be represented by the stock figure of a *vetula*, a little old woman. William of Auxerre had introduced or secured the currency of the phases and notions of 'implicit' and 'explicit faith'.[54] 'Implicit faith' meant a 'simple believer' believing what the clergy set above them believed. Discussions had also introduced the idea of a handful of doctrines, just four or five, which were the irreducible minimum of explicit belief. Rolando of Cremona uses the same heading, 'On implicit and explicit faith'; he repeats the language and all the points; and the main difference is that he triples the length of William's discussion. Novelty in Rolando's usage of these distinctions and contrasts is not the issue: their inclusion in his luggage when he arrived in Toulouse is.[55]

A recapitulation and a conjunction: Peter of Alès

Let us recapitulate the suggestion that two areas of higher learning, Roman law and scholastic theology, shaped inquisitors' questions. Consulted on who should be adjudged a *credens*, Avignonese lawyers provided – alongside the simple fact of saying that one believed in the heretics or their faith – a list of actions. Foulques's later consultation spelled out the reasoning: Roman law on the problem of proof of inner disposition. Hence we see

[53] There is a short general account by P. Biller, 'Intellectuals and the masses: oxen and she-asses in the medieval Church', in *The Oxford Handbook of Medieval Christianity*, ed. J. H. Arnold (Oxford, 2014), pp. 323–42, at pp. 324, 328–9.

[54] William of Auxerre, *Summa aurea*, iii, pt 1, pp. 212–13 (bk. iii, § 12.5).

[55] Rolando, *Summa*, pp. 312–16; Rolando's minimum was God's creation of visible and invisible things, the trinity, passion and resurrection (p. 316).

the typical early deposition, in which a *credens* is asked numerous questions about seeing heretics, lodging them, giving them things and so on; and finally one brief 'yes' or 'no' question on belief in heretics. Converging with Roman law was scholastic theology. Against the background of the parallel taxonomies of Church and sect – clergy and lay people in one, heretics and *credentes* in the other – there was a powerful line of thought about the 'explicit' faith required of the clergy and the 'implicit' faith required of the simple lay person. The minimum – a lay person believing what his parish priest believed – was the equivalent of a *credens* believing what his heretic believed. The scholastic theological concept of the implicit faith of the simple faithful drove in the same direction as Roman law: reduction in what one expected of *subditi*, those subordinate either to clergy or to heretics. There was a small modification for both groups. Scholastic discussions of explicit faith produced four or five doctrines in which the simple faithful had to have explicit faith. By the mid 1240s some inquisitors were concluding their action-questions put to *credentes* with a follow-up on four or five heretical doctrines.[56]

While these consultations demonstrate the influence of law, the case for the input of scholastic theology is conjectural: it rests upon modern scholarship putting together what Rolando wrote, the way a local historian saw him and chronology. After teaching in Paris, Rolando lived in Toulouse for these three years, lecturing in theology and visibly leading the fight against heresy. While Pelhisson was contemptuous of the 'remote and ineffectual' earlier immigrant dons, Rolando was his powerful hero. There is one eerie coincidence: the earliest deposition, that of Bartac in 1237, records an interrogation by two inquisitors, one of them the former prior of Toulouse, Peter of Alès.[57] Pelhisson records one conversation between Rolando and a friar in the Toulouse convent. It is Peter of Alès. Peter asks Rolando what to do. Rolando tells him what to do.

[56] If this was through the influence of discussions of implicit faith, we would investigate the later development of theological learning in Toulouse after Rolando's departure from the city.

[57] Pelhisson, *Chronique*, pp. 40–5. Gui found documents naming him as the prior of Prouille in 1226, 1227 and 1231 (Gui, *De fundatione et prioribus*, pp. 14, 24). Pelhisson's treatise on Toulouse properties refers to him as prior of Toulouse in 1232; and Gui says he was prior from this year; he lists the next one as prior from the year 1233 (Gui, *De fundatione et prioribus*, pp. 33 and 49). Though sometimes referred to as 'of Alais' or 'of Alet', Peter's place of origin (Alestum) is Alès, a diocese in the Gard *département* (*Pouillés des provinces d'Auch, de Narbonne et de Toulouse*, ed. M. François, C.-E. Perrin and J. de Font-Réaulx (2 vols, Paris, 1972), ii. 859).

Institution

Let us return to the institutional question through Bernard Gui's treatise on inquisition (1319–23). Gui referred to it in its prologue as a *Tractatus de practica inquisitionis*: a discursive treatise about the practice of inquisition rather than a 'how-to-do-it' pocket book.[58] Gui was a man of few words but he made this text as long as he could. In the wake of the Council of Vienne (1311–12) Gui was protesting against its attempt to reform inquisition, providing in the *Tractatus* a general apologia for inquisition, its power and the necessity of its unfettered operation.[59] He did this in part by a demonstration of the procedural orderliness of the customary working of inquisition in the Toulousain. This is the theme of the treatise's first three parts. One hundred and thirty-one forms for 131 distinct inquisition actions provide its massive demonstration. On one of these forms, which is for appointing a new prison guard, the inquisitor refers to both himself and his successors; another form warns against anyone other than the seneschal staying in the house of inquisition (*domus inquisitionis*) while the inquisitor is away and dwells on its importance for the safe-keeping of inquisition records.[60] The permanence and complexity of this organization are palpable.

If this is an institution, can we say when it became one? Should we look at the earliest years? There is architectural continuity in Toulouse, where Peter Seila had given the Dominicans the building used for inquisition, it seems, from 1233;[61] and the inquisition's key-document, the deposition, had emerged by 1237. While these beginnings make us pause, the instantaneous materialization of an 'institution' in the early 1230s is an unrealistic idea. This author is reluctant to pick a point between the 1230s and Bernard Gui, preferring just to fall back on the words of Topsy in *Uncle Tom's Cabin*: inquisition just 'growed'.

[58] Bernard Gui, *Practica inquisitionis heretice pravitatis*, ed. C. Douais (Paris, 1885), p. 1.

[59] Together with the inquisitor of Carcassonne, he also wrote a letter of complaint to John XXII; its wording suggests Gui was the principal author (BNF, MS. Collection Doat 30, fos. 90–132v).

[60] Gui, *Practica*, pp. 61–2, 66–7.

[61] Feuchter, *Ketzer, Konsuln und Büßer*, p. 56.

II. Institutions and individuals: organizations and social practices

b. Individuals and practices

8. Robert of Courson's systematic thinking about early thirteenth-century institutions*

John Sabapathy

What went through the diseased mind of Robert of Courson on 6 February 1219, 'dying in the sands of Damietta before the river was crossed',[1] during the siege of the city by the epidemic-ridden crusading army? Englishman, master of theology at the university of Paris, canon of Noyon, cardinal priest of San Stefano in Monte Celio, sometime papal legate to northern France, ecclesiastical legislator, university reformer and, lastly and terminally, preacher to the fifth crusade, did Courson think of the enormous crush of the great council at the Lateran church and palace four years earlier; the stench of burning flesh and towns during the Albigensian crusade; the noise of his preaching campaigns; the haggling at the reforming councils he had co-ordinated in northern France; the days teaching and writing in Paris; his university reform of his shape-shifting *alma mater*; the tense diplomacy with hard men like King John and Philip Augustus; the friendships with the other bright young theologians in the circle of Peter the Chanter; his strained relations with Pope Honorius III; or his youth in England about which we know nothing?[2]

* I am very grateful to the conference participants for comments on my original paper and – for numerous suggestions and corrections to the written version – especially to Emily Corran, David d'Avray and Antonia Fitzpatrick.

[1] For Courson at Damietta see Oliver of Paderborn, *Historia damiatina*, in *Die Schriften des Kölner Domscholasters, späteren Bischofs von Paderborn und Kardinal-Bischofs von S. Sabina, Oliverus*, ed. H. Hoogeweg (Tübingen, 1894), pp. 161–280, at p. 187 (quote); also Oliver's *Historia regum Terre Sancte*, pp. 83–158 at p. 158; *Register*, at p. 287; and pp. xviii, xix, xxiv, lxxvii, clxv, clxxi, clxxxi; *Lettres de Jacques de Vitry (1160/1170–1240), évêque de Saint-Jean-d'Acre*, ed. R. B. C. Huygens (Leiden, 1960), p. 116 (#5); M. Dickson and C. Dickson, 'Le cardinal Robert de Courson, sa vie', *Archives d'histoire doctrinale et littéraire du Moyen Âge*, ix (1934), 53–142, at pp. 132–4. All translations are the author's own unless otherwise stated.

[2] For Courson's biography, see Dickson and Dickson; J. W. Baldwin, *Masters, Princes, and Merchants: the Social Views of Peter the Chanter and his Circle* (2 vols, Princeton, N.J., 1970), i. 19–25 and s.v. 'Robert de Courson'; J. E. Sayers, 'Courson, Robert de (d. 1219)',

J. Sabapathy, 'Robert of Courson's systematic thinking about early thirteenth-century institutions', in *Individuals and Institutions in Medieval Scholasticism*, ed. A. Fitzpatrick and J. Sabapathy (London, 2020), pp. 199–216.

Courson's life intersected with some of the major religious movements and contemporary concerns of his day. Many were 'institutional', taking that term to cover macro-organizational forms (the Church, the university of Paris); meso-level religious practices (ecclesiastical councils, anti-heresy campaigns, the fifth crusade); and micro-level ones (diet, sacraments). It is, therefore, particularly interesting to investigate the tenor of Courson's attitude to institutions. His breadth of engagement was shared more widely with the 'biblical-moral tendency' of Peter the Chanter which so struck John Baldwin, although Baldwin was more interested with respect to their particular 'social policy' positions (ordeals, usury, tithes, etc.).[3] Commenting on their 'social theory' as a whole, Baldwin's compliments were somewhat backhanded:

> The Parisian theologians discussed each occupation as a separate entity, making little effort to unify their ideas in coherent social theory. Since their chief task was to evaluate the concrete moral act, not to speculate about the nature of society, they produced little social theory which resembled the hierarchical systems ... of the mid-thirteenth century under the influence of Aristotelian notions of justice. What their theories lacked in consistency and unity, was compensated by richness of detail. Although their particular views of society were fragmentary and unconnected, their writings provide a brilliant mosaic for the social life of their times.[4]

ODNB <https://doi.org/10.1093/ref:odnb/6956> [accessed 27 June 2018]. Courson figures importantly in J. L. Bird, 'The construction of orthodoxy and the (de)construction of heretical attacks on the eucharist in *pastoralia* from Peter the Chanter's circle in Paris', in *Trials and Treatises: Texts and the Repression of Medieval Heresy*, ed. C. Bruschi and P. Biller (Woodbridge, 2003), pp. 45–61; J. L. Bird, 'Paris masters and the justification of the Albigensian crusade', *Crusades*, vi (2007) 117–55; J. L. Bird, 'The wheat and the tares: Peter the Chanter's circle and the *fama*-based inquest against heresy and criminal sins, *c.*1198–*c.*1235', in *Proceedings of the Twelfth International Congress of Medieval Canon Law: Washington, D.C. 1–7 August 2004*, ed. U.-R. Blumenthal, K. Pennington and A. A. Larson (Monumenta iuris canonici, series C, Subsidia xiii, Vatican City, 2008), pp. 763–856; and E. Corran, *Lying and Perjury in Medieval Practical Thought: a Study in the History of Casuistry* (Oxford, 2018), *passim* with appendix. Courson's thought on inquisitions and communities has been analysed in Sabapathy, 'Some difficulties', pp. 175–200.

[3] This chapter cannot explore the precise relationship between the Chanter and Courson: their approach is very similar and Courson cites 'the Chanter' repeatedly. The phrase 'biblical-moral tendency' was coined by M. Grabmann, *Die Geschichte der scholastischen Methode* (2 vols, Freiburg, 1909–11), ii. 476–501; for a critique, see M. J. Clark, *The Making of the Historia scholastica, 1150 1200* (Toronto, 2015), pp. 16–22, 257–9. Clark's account of Langton's reception and refinement of his teacher Peter Comestor's writings seems to parallel Courson's relationship with the Chanter. See also M. J. Clark, 'The biblical *Gloss*, the search for Peter Lombard's glossed Bible, and the school of Paris', *Mediaeval Stud.*, lxxvi (2014), 57–113; M. J. Clark, 'Peter Lombard, Stephen Langton, and the school of Paris: the making of the twelfth-century scholastic biblical tradition', *Traditio*, lxxii (2017), 171–274.

[4] Baldwin, *Masters, Princes*, i. 58–9.

The criteria are arguably somewhat unfair ones with which to twit these thinkers. That consistency and unity are, first, required and, second, achieved through a particular route requires demonstration. Nor is coherence the same as consistency: indeed we can show for one of the Chanter's circle – Innocent III – that it was not.[5] There should be ways of judging the quality of this thought other than indexing it against texts it had not received. This chapter explores that quality through Courson's 'thought style', to use Mary Douglas's term: the thought beneath the thought which shapes the group.[6] It suggests that what seems striking about Courson's thought is the way he approaches particular problems as products of social relations and the degree to which he responds to them as such, whatever the topic (diet, sex, abusive lords). The main source is Courson's *Summa* (by mid 1212), which draws important inspiration from his master Peter the Chanter's posthumously arranged *questio* collection, the *Summa de sacramentis et animae consiliis*.[7] Courson's *Summa* first addresses fields which attract penitential concern (for example, excommunication, usury, rapine); then moves to a range of social bonds, effects and procedures (vows, scandal, due process); then discusses the sacraments and (in one manuscript) ends by considering the afterlife.[8] It is these practices as social institutions on which this chapter focuses. Courson was 'systematic' but in a style distinct from that of later thinkers such as Aquinas. The systematization here lies less in the exhaustive order of topics in the *Summa* than in the fact that Courson treated given issues as widely *connected* to others, not narrowly compartmentalized from them – as, indeed, they might be experienced by parishioner or priest.[9]

[5] J. Sabapathy, 'Thinking politically with Innocent III: prudence and providence', *Thirteenth Century England*, xv (2015), 115–36, at pp. 133–6.

[6] M. Douglas, *Thought Styles: Critical Essays on Good Taste* (Thousand Oaks, Calif., 1996). For a discussion of this style's wider context, see Emily Corran's article in this volume.

[7] Specifically, Paris, BNF, MS. lat. 3477. Baldwin argues that Courson's work was 'a final product of the school of Peter the Chanter' (*Masters, Princes*, i. 23, 24–5, esp. nn. 66, 76). The question of distinct approaches by associated thinkers cannot be properly addressed here but see n. 42 below.

[8] For dating, see Sabapathy, 'Some difficulties', p. 181, n. 27. For the contents of the *Summa,* see V. L. Kennedy, 'The contents of Courson's *Summa*', *Mediaeval Stud.*, ix (1947), 81–107. BNF, MS. lat. 14524 and MS. lat. 3259 have been used. For editions and long quotations from Courson's *Summa* see the works cited in n. 2 above; and G. Lefèvre, *Le traité 'De usura' de Robert de Courçon* (Travaux et Mémoires de l'Université de Lille, x. 30, Lille, 1902); V. L. Kennedy, 'Robert Courson on penance', *Mediaeval Stud.*, vii (1945), 291–336, J. W. Baldwin, *The Language of Sex: Five Voices from Northern France around 1200* (Chicago, Ill., 1994), appendix 1, pp. 239–45; J. M. M. H. Thijssen, 'Master Amalric and the Amalricians: inquisitorial procedure and the suppression of heresy at the University of Paris', *Speculum*, lxxi (1996) 43–65, at pp. 61–5; Corran, *Lying and Perjury*, appendix.

[9] This chapter draws very loosely on N. Luhmann, *Social Systems*, trans. J. Bednarz Jr. with D. Baecker (Stanford, Calif., 1995).

There are different forms of 'systematic' scholastic thinking and this one emerged at an interesting moment: Courson was as much a member of an intellectual generation as of a school.[10] This chapter, first, shows Courson's recognition of the systemic way these institutions hung together socially. It demonstrates, second, how the constructions of groups could prove problematic; and looks at important considerations underlying Courson's reasoning when evaluating such institutions. Finally, it contextualizes this by reflecting on Courson's conciliar activity and ends by reconsidering the way in which Courson's thought is systematic.

Systems, rules, traditions

The complexity of the social systems with which Courson engaged and their entangled nature can be illustrated by Courson's sympathy for the perplexed (*perplexi*):

> A most difficult question follows, also about those things necessary in the penitential field, arising from perplexity in relation to equal, greater and lesser crimes. Such perplexity can often be overwhelming, as Gregory shows in the *Moralia* [32.20.39 to Job XL: 12, 'He setteth up his tail like a cedar, the sinews of his testicles are wrapped together [*perplexi*]'] that where a mind is caught between greater and lesser sins, the lesser should always be chosen, so that someone who is hemmed in on all sides by the ramparts of the walls should flee to where the wall seems shorter. By such perplexities do modern heretics [*moderni heretici*] say that they are confused – and they can be perplexed to such a degree that they cannot be saved, so that if they profess the perfection of their sect [*perfectionem secte sue*] and afterwards eat meat or contravene [the sect] in any way, or in their moment of death when they cannot take counsel with their consolers [*consolidatoribus*] they say that they cannot be saved, as happens in many cases when they say that they cannot avoid many established rules without incurring the damnation of death, but an infinity of authorities cry out against each other [*in contrarium*].[11]

Even a heretic's worldview is a woven whole which hangs together. It is the interconnection of things which indeed produces confusion and why unpicking them is complex (and, here, doomed).

[10] Though Baldwin was more interested in their social commentary, *Masters, Princes* necessarily treats them as a generation. For their successors, see S. M. Young, *Scholarly Community at the Early University of Paris: Theologians, Education and Society, 1215–1248* (Cambridge Studies in Medieval Life and Thought, Cambridge, 2014); and N. Gorochov, *Naissance de l'université: les Écoles de Paris d'Innocent III à Thomas d'Aquin (v. 1200–v. 1245)* (Paris, 2012). For complementary analyses of Courson as casuist on these themes, see Corran, *Lying and Perjury*, pp. 85–9, 97–8.

[11] BNF, MS. lat. 14524, fo. 90rab (§ 26.2), corrected against BNF, MS. lat. 3259 fo. 113vab. The Latin is not quite right here. My thanks to Antonia Fitzpatrick for discussion.

The underlying question of how rules should form coherent wholes for society and the need to disaggregate the good and bad also receive sustained attention in Peter the Chanter's compendium of ethical problems, the *Verbum adbreviatum*. The Chanter took a strong position in relation to positive law within the *Verbum*: 'Positive justice has nothing solid about it' is one heading. This was the case because so much controversy followed the feeling and will of judges, producing additions to God's 'clear laws' (*certae leges*).[12] In his chapter 'Against the burdensome multitude of human traditions [*tradicionum humanarum*]' the Chanter set out three types of problematic tradition:

> There are three types of tradition [*tradicionum*]: those which are illicit and the invention of the Devil rather than man and are completely contrary to God's law; those which are licit and useful but seem to go contrary to divine precepts, as some monastic traditions and so are dubious; others do in fact go contrary to God's law and harm by their sheer number and so should be rather avoided, for they make transgressors out of the disobedient.

The problem is in the right arrangement of a hierarchy of divine to human demands and the proper privileging of evangelical precepts. The Chanter's general position seems a minimalist one legislatively: '[Traditions] should only be established sparingly and minimally for manifest reasons and utility, since they are an impediment to divine precepts and seem to set up barriers to them'.[13]

The problem of untangling this hierarchy of commitments can be illustrated by Courson's handling of Jepthath's vow (Judges XI: 29–40). The spirit of the Lord comes over Jepthath, who bargains with God, promising that if God will give the Ammonites over to him 'then whoever comes out of the doors of my house to meet me, when I return victorious from the Ammonities, shall be the Lord's, to be offered up by me as a burnt-offering'. It is Jepthath's daughter who greets him on return, of course, and, after two month's grace to bewail her lost life, she returns home willingly and is burnt.

[12] Petrus Cantor, *Petri cantoris parisiensis verbum adbreviatum, textus conflatus*, ed. M. Boutry (*CCCM*, cxcvi, Turnhout, 2004), p. 337 on marriage laws (§ 1.51) (henceforth, Chanter, *Verbum)*. For the theologians' complex position on law, see further P. Buc, *L'ambiguïté du livre: prince, pouvoir, et peuple dans les commentaires de la Bible au Moyen Âge* (Paris, 1994), pp. 239–70; K. Chambers, '"When we do nothing wrong, we are peers": Peter the Chanter and twelfth-century political thought', *Speculum*, lxxxviii (2013), 405–26, at p. 424.

[13] For this and the previous quotation, see Chanter, *Verbum*, p. 514 (§ 1.77). Thomas of Chobham uses 'institutum' for practical human solutions to problems (e.g. covering the wine cup and altar and celebration of the eucharist indoors to avoid spiders and bird droppings in the wine (Thomas of Chobham, *Summa confessorum*, ed. F. Broomfield (Analecta mediaevalia namurcensia, xxv, Louvain, 1968), pp. 138–9 (A. 4 d. 2 q. 6.4)).

Courson discusses this in the context of evaluating a given vow's 'necessity'. Does a public vow to kill whatever comes through the door first trump an earlier or more necessary Christian vow to follow the Decalogue and gospels (Do not kill; love your neighbour)?[14] Courson asks various questions. Was it Jepthath's punishment because he had actually hoped his detested wife would come through the door? What if a dog had come out of the door first?

> Solution: We say that Jepthath's vow was made indiscretely and against God. No vow expressed like this is binding, but in such cases a wrongful oath should be repented; the spirit of the Lord did not come into Jepthath to make the vow, because in this matter he simply was not led by the familiar counsel of the Holy Spirit, as with Samson and Abraham. If the Spirit came into him it was before he took the oath, namely to attack the enemy.[15]

A means of differentiating the good from bad comes from the Chanter. This is the so-called 'triple truth' of life, doctrine and justice.[16] The Chanter takes truth of life to be 'not only that without which eternal life cannot be had, but also that which it cannot easily be had without'. Doctrinal truth is clear enough: I should create a scandal rather than obeying a bishop who has forbidden me from declaring that he has been covertly preaching heresy. Defending the truth of justice entails not only that the law's precepts and judgements should be preserved per se, but also that one should ensure they are not despised since this will undermine them in the long run. Hence a prelate who has 'noble horses and precious trappings from the Crucified's patrimony' may scandalize those who see him. Nevertheless, he should not discard them since 'if I had vile clothing and appeared as one cast down and contemptible, and not like those who punish the delinquent, at once my

[14] Courson discusses the Chanter's threefold structuring of the vow according to (1) what is fundamental to a Christian, e.g. baptism; (2) voluntary vows obligatory once taken, e.g. vows of continence, but some types of which may be dispensed with; (3) lesser third vows of necessity which can be dispensed with (BNF, MS. lat. 14524, fos. 79vb–80ra (§ 21.4)). See also Petrus Cantor, *Summa de sacramentis et animae consiliis*, ed. J.-A. Dugauquier (Analecta mediaevalia Namurcensia, iv, vii, xi, xvi, xxi, 3 vols in 5, Louvain, 1954–67), iii, pt 2a, pp. 200–6 (§ 224) (henceforth, Chanter, *Summa*).

[15] BNF, MS. lat. 14524, fo. 80rb–80va (§ 21.7).

[16] BNF, MS. lat. 14524, fo. 87ra–b (§ 25.4) and Chanter, *Summa*, iii, pt. 2a, pp. 375–7 (§ 319). Courson attributes the formulation to Jerome but this cannot be corroborated with the *Patrologia latina* database. For further discussion, see C. Nemo-Pekelman, 'Scandale et vérité dans la doctrine canonique médiévale (XIIe– XIIIe siècles)', *Revue historique de droit français et étranger*, lxxxv (2007), 491–504. Cf. its use by a subsequent generation of theologians in William of Auxerre, *Summa aurea Magistri Guillelmi Altissiodorensis*, ed. J. Ribaillier (Spicilegium Bonaventurianum, xvi–xx, 5 vols in 7, Paris, 1980–7), iii, pt 2, pp. 1020, 1026, 1029, 1030, 1033 (§ 3.52 on scandal). See pp. 221, 232 below.

subjects would become disobedient and do evil and thus I would be unable to exercise justice, and thus my subjects' truth of life would be endangered since they would have the grounds to sin [because I was not enforcing the law]'.[17] Such formulations both show the wide latitude created to safeguard Christian *doxa* but also the socially canny pragmatism applied by these activists to the systems in which they envisaged intervening.

Institutions and the problem of shared meaning

For Courson, then, the problem of institutional life is a holistic one, complicated by the fact that communities may construct institutional practices of which theologians disapprove – be they local customs, legal procedures or dietary rules. He acknowledges quite plainly the socially constructed meanings and practices, but in his chapter on perplexity argues that real perplexities arise only from incompatibilities of *experience* (de facto), not from incompatibilities of law (*de iuris*): 'Perplexity of law is said to be where superficially authorities and canons contradict one another, but which can be resolved into concord through the rule of the Old and New [Testament], and thus nothing legal can be perplexing because no one can be in such a state that the law cannot come to his aid, and that he cannot obtain the grace to repel all perplexity'.[18] Reality, not law, produces perplexities. Those realities are secured by human convention and Courson recognizes that particular practices are the product of collective agreement and that one has to engage with this, whether one is opposed to or supportive of that agreement.[19]

These social systems are strong and tricky to intervene in. They may have their own logic; and distinct versions of apparently shared practices can facilitate misapprehension across groups.[20] Suppose you visit a monastery where the custom is to eat meat on the sabbath. There is a risk, if you decline, that you will be called a 'Cathar or Papelard' (that is, a heretic or an unorthodox extremist).[21] Courson determines ultimately that the risk

[17] Chanter, *Summa*, iii, pt. 2a, pp. 377 (§ 319). There is a striking contrast with contemporary mendicant attitudes here. See Emily Corran's chapter in this volume for a parallel discussion of the triple truth at p. 221..

[18] BNF, MS. lat. 14524, fo. 90rb (§ 26.3). Cf. the more technical approach to perplexity in the very slightly later William of Auxerre, *Summa aurea* (between 1215 and 1229, probably by 1218), v. 16 (dating discussion), iii, pt. 2, pp. 1044–54 (§ lv, 'de perplexitate'). For William see Young, *Scholarly Community*, ch. 3 and appendix.

[19] On institutions as human conventions, see the discussion of John Searle in the introduction at p. 428.

[20] BNF, MS. lat. 14524, fos. 88va–90ra (§ 25.15–21).

[21] BNF, MS. lat. 14524, fo. 88vb (§ 25.16).

of being thought a Cathar does not outweigh the risk of scandal if you eat the meat (this example is analysed further below). The relevant point here is that being taken (incorrectly) for a heretic would again be a product of the *social* (mis-)construal of what such eating *means*. A similar case is that of a priest enjoined by the 'king of the land, his bishop and the custom of the land' to 'bless the white-hot iron and water used in judgement' when this was theologically problematic since it tempted God to intervene inappropriately (*temptatur Deus*). Here Courson answers, as he does in other cases, that one should follow the custom of the realm even when the practices are diabolical (*diabolice inuentiones*).[22]

Another set of potential misunderstandings arises when there is disagreement about a shared conceptual definition: for instance, the idea of 'notoriety', which Courson discusses in the context of fraternal correction.[23] He criticizes those 'moderns' (*quidam modernorum*) who think that something is not notorious unless 'it has been made manifest by conviction or confession in law'.[24] Courson's preference is for a more 'common-sensical' approach, in which legal conviction or confession is not always necessary. Those are two of three ways someone can be condemned as notorious, but notoriety should also be sufficiently clear when 'evidence of crime is so great that nothing can be hidden by subterfuge, as with the Corinthians' [sexual] crime and the crime [in the Gospels] of selling doves in the church'.[25] Nor is the problem simply definitional, since such disagreement leads (at least here) to argument about the structure of the social practice with which it is connected (fraternal correction).

The socially joined-up nature of these institutional practices is both a fact and a potential problem when groups have different versions of them. A number of external aspects seem important when Courson determines how such institutions should work. First, publicity may considerably alter how far an institution should be observed. Second, the status of given groups within a community may likewise inflect how practices should play out because of how the community will react subjectively, given that status. Third, this is at the same time an admission that the institutions with which one has to live are imperfect and sub-optimal. Let us look at some instances.

First, publicity can be determinative. Against the idea that the strong internalization of a vow is key to its efficacy, it is the publicly affirmed vow which can be compelled because it has been externally affirmed:

[22] BNF, MS. lat. 14524, fos. 91vb–92ra (§ 26.8–9).

[23] BNF, MS. lat. 14524, fo. 78ra (§ 20.9).

[24] BNF, MS. lat. 14524, fo. 78ra (§ 20.9) and fo. 79ra (§ 20.11) for the reference to moderns, also fo. 78rb–78va.

[25] BNF, MS. lat. 14524, fo. 78va (§ 20.10).

'Thus if someone publicly avows continence orally, or that he will enter a cloister, the Church can compel him to fulfil such a vow, even if he had not firmly formed this in his mind, but rather the opposite'.[26] The social solemnities of vows can enhance and strengthen their tightness because of the dependence of the solemnity of such vows on its wider reception: 'We concede to this, saying that the solemnities in vows oblige those vowing to the vows' fulfilment more since the solemnities intensify the effect of the vow and its nature more than a greater intention and make a vow-breaker more guilty'.[27] This solemnity is inextricably connected to publicity and the establishment of the vow as a collective institution. Thus, vows to go on pilgrimage or crusade are taken 'in the face of the Church before the altar or between the hands of a priest or abbot and such vows oblige more than private ones, as is proven by the contrary, that the transgression of such [vows] offends both God and the Church more than the transgression of a private vow. Therefore, we accept that a solemn vow obliges more than a private one'.[28] The effect is a somewhat relativistic, or variable, position with respect to the institution (here vow-taking) in which publicity affects the standing of the vow.

Courson develops this by saying, second, that the standing of different groups affects institutions differentially: these are *ad status* institutions, so to speak. It is not quite that there are rules particular to specific status groups (though there are). It is rather that Courson thinks the way in which an institution should be expressed shifts in light of context-sensitive concerns about the status of the actors involved. The majority of these are clerical status groups, but there are other criteria or groups, especially those differentiated by intellect and power. These are nicely brought out when discussing liabilities to undertake fraternal correction:

> Just as a man need not render his marital debt to his wife at all times nor conversely (because of many impediments which we might discuss elsewhere), so many reasonable factors may intervene because of which it is not necessary for a private person to be obligated to correct someone greater. Suppose someone is an imbecile, or a simple cloister monk, or a private person with no ability to approach a prince; if their life is infamous such that no one would receive them, if they are excommunicate, if they are held in prison, or prevented by innumerable other invincible reasons [then they could not]. However, if a learned person is in a cloister, and the subversion of the faith or Church threatens, then he is bound to break his obedience to the abbot because of his

[26] BNF, MS. lat. 14524, fo. 79va (§ 21.3).

[27] BNF, MS. lat. 14524, fo. 80vb (§ 21.9).

[28] BNF, MS. lat. 14524, fo. 80vb (§ 21.9). The emphases are quite different to those analysed by Sylvain Piron in his chapter in this volume.

> obedience to a greater, namely God, and set himself to the wall against heresy and for the house of God.[29]

There is a strong interest here in the socially determined *effectiveness* of how correction works. A private person lacks the authority to gain access to a prince. A learned person can correct by virtue of greater apparent insight. Both licences are ultimately granted by their audiences. The practicalities of applying a collective practice – fraternal correction – cannot be understood or implemented outside that shared system.

The institution or organization to which one belongs also has a role in determining what one should do – principally if that institution is the Church and, as a priest or prelate, one acts as a synecdoche for it. The exemplariness of one's social status provides a feedback loop to affect how one should respond to a problem or apply a given rule in a specific situation. Suppose:

> there is a custom in many churches that clerics and monks eat meat on the sabbath. You are learned and deemed a person of great authority among them. The whole city is scandalized to see so great a convent of clerics and monks eating meat on such a day when the common laity never eat meat on such a day. If you eat meat on such a day with the others great will be the scandal because of you, because you are of so high a standing among them that your eating really will increase the scandal. If you do not eat you will offend the abbot or your bishop and the whole convent of clerics and monks who will call you a Cathar or Papelard. What are you to do in such a case? [Further cases follow before Courson's resolution.] … We say that the abbot with his convent and the prelate with his clerics sin gravely by scandalizing the neighbourhood by eating meat on the sabbath and thus are bound to abstain from such eating in order to avoid so grave a scandal. And if you are learned and a person of great standing among them you should not consent to your prelate in eating flesh with him on such a day to the people's scandal, following the example of the apostle Paul, who said, 'If my food scandalize my brother I will never eat meat' [1 Corinthians VIII: 13].[30]

The thought experiment is nicely tailored.[31] The protagonist has social standing but no official role (or, if it is assumed he is a priest, an inferior one). On this ecclesiastical axis his status is inferior to that of his host,

[29] BNF, MS. lat. 14524, fo. 76va (§ 20.3), corrected with BNF, MS. lat. 3259, fo. 95rb–va.

[30] BNF, MS. lat. 14524, fos. 88vb and 89va (§ 25.16 and 21), corrected with BNF, MS. lat. 3259 fos. 111rb–112v.

[31] Such thought experiments seem distinct from modern ones. Modern thought experiments aim to reduce the question to essentials (e.g. Rawls's veil of ignorance); these medieval ones aim to achieve a more textured set of plural complexities.

who is, furthermore, literally at home in the customary setting he has established. His learned status nevertheless gives him a different axis along which to offer resistance to the dominant rules of the game in this particular community.

Scandal is an obviously interesting area within which to think about how wrongdoing is constructed. By its nature it is perhaps an extreme case: scandal is an 'ex post facto' institution. Like a joke, only your audience can tell you whether scandal is present: 'So it is accidental whether the actual sin is scandalous, since if it is done before many people who are consequently led to consent to sin then it is a scandal. But if it is done in secret with no one else knowing then it will not be a scandal'.[32] Publicity again matters, but so, too, does perception. At one level this can seem arbitrary; at another it is simply pragmatic. There is, of course, a risk, however, that perceived scandal, treated as an absolute bad, enables communities to resist behaviour or regulation which they may disingenuously claim undermines their faith. It is in such circumstances that the triangulations of the 'triple truth' would prove useful.

Such an attitude asserts absolute (if ambiguous) lines beyond which social practices must submit to external rules. At the same time the rules concede the imperfection of the world in which – as a priest, prelate, confessor – one intervenes and which is irredeemably social. This seems a third sub-text of Courson's diagnostic operating assumptions. On the question of fraternal correction there may be an ideal rule, but in practice it should be applied discriminately: 'It seems to us as we learnt it from the Chanter of Paris. That irrespective of whether someone is greater or lesser, free or servant, they are bound to correct their brother so that he is corrected with the zeal of justice, but not at all times or places, since there is a time for being quiet and a time for speaking, as Solomon says [Ecclesiastes III: 7]'.[33] General rules can be very heavily qualified (as with the simple cloister monk above).

The degree, then, to which actual institutions have to accommodate themselves to the undesirable social dynamics of actual groups is a powerful feature of Courson's analysis. An example which shows the messy literal intermixture of multiple concerns is the 'very difficult question which we have often seen in practice' of what to do when a prince or pseudo-prelate takes money to market as a melted mass which has been obtained from usurers through *tailles* and exactions and which is there re-coined and put back into circulation as legal tender:[34] 'It is asked, therefore, whether it is

[32] BNF, MS. lat. 14524, fo. 87ra (§ 25.3).

[33] BNF, MS. lat. 14524, fo. 76rb (§ 20.2).

[34] For the quotations, see BNF, MS. lat. 14524, fos. 55va– 56ra (§ 12.1). See also Baldwin, *Masters, Princes*, i. 242–3.

permissible for you or others to enter into market agreements involving this money'. Here Courson's answer hinges on the actors' knowledge or ignorance of these facts. An example illustrating the deformities arising from inappropriate intra-*ecclesiastical* group relations concerns 'what a parish priest should do wanting to accuse a subject according to the prescribed form before a bishop who does not want to hear his accusation'.[35] The 'prescribed form' is the admonition in Matthew XVIII: 15–17: first privately; second with witnesses; and – for the incorrigible – third before the Church. The problem here is:

> if the bishop does not want to hear the proof but inclines to the accused's side, stroking his vice or dissembling, either out of flattery or fear of the prince, or because of some temporal good which he hopes from him. It is asked here what that priest ought to do about the subject whose care he has, when he can see that he is a putrid member scandalizing his whole parish and making the whole neighbourhood return to the vomit of sin. If he gives up on him the whole parish will be corrupted by him. But if he excommunicates him on his own authority at once the other will appeal to the court of the bishop who connived in his sin, and if the priest goes against the bishop's mandate in this or otherwise he will be excommunicated and thrown out of his position, yet if he goes with the opposing side of the bishop and the excommunicate all of his remaining flock will be scattered, meanwhile he has no recourse to the metropolitan or cardinal or pope, since they will better believe a bishop than a shabby priest [*sacerdoti pannoso*].

The admission of institutional fallibility is frank. Courson comes close, though, to acknowledging that his solution remains locked within the original problem. All he can suggest is, again, the threefold admonition of the bishop and then recourse to the metropolitan, legate or pope, notwithstanding his earlier scepticism: 'for we are not investigating here what happens, but what ought to happen'.[36]

The sub-optimal world of which socio-religious institutions are a product is simply part of life. Sub-optimal, too, is the degree to which they can be tailored to that world. The art of such tailoring lies less, however, in the flat application of a rule and more in fitting it contextually and shaping it flexibly.[37] Here internal disposition can matter. Thus, in general with

[35] BNF, MS. lat. 3259, fo. 96vb (§ 20.7).

[36] This and the previous quotation can be found at BNF, MS. lat. 14524, fo. 77va (§ 20.7), corrected with BNF, MS. lat. 3259, fo. 96vab. See also the case of the lord so powerful no one dare act against him and whose purgation would be popularly deemed a sham (Sabapathy, 'Some difficulties', pp. 185–7 (on § 25.22)).

[37] E.g. in the context of the poor foreigner seeking judgement from an individual (BNF, MS. lat. 14524, fo. 87va (§ 25.7)). See Sabapathy, 'Some difficulties', p. 195.

genuine cases of perplexity, 'when someone runs into such perplexities in fact [de facto] he should do whatever he can in a way that is always full of saving love and always choose the less undesirable of alternatives'.[38] Take a church threatened with arson when you are inside and risk death. Here the question, in relation to your potential resistance, is whether you are perfect or imperfect, given that a summary execution for the criminal will follow if you cry fire. However, 'if in fact you are imperfect it is licit for you to repel force with force and to call the neighbourhood in defence of the *ecclesia* and *res publica*. And then you have to strive in every way you can so that the person is not corporally punished, through your demonstration that you do nothing out of spiteful vindictiveness but only zeal for justice'.[39]

One could say this is a sort of medieval rational-choice theory in which achieving an acceptable but not optimal outcome is the order of the day, given the impossibility of the latter in a fallen world. However, understanding the correct relative value which should be placed on different goods was the underlying judgement, one it was crucial to make correctly, a process complicated by their interaction with one another.[40] The Chanter concluded his chapter in the *Verbum adbreviatum* against those who 'out of learning or crass ignorance' soften the rigour of scripture by invoking Jerome on the unfruitful vineyard in Isaiah V and those who call the evil good and the good evil:

> As Jerome says, it is no small error to rank the lesser good before the greater and more useful good. For a change [*mutatio*] in the order of merits changes the substance [*forma*]. Similarly, woe to those who call the greater evil the less evil, or the less evil the greater evil. I do not say this absolutely [*simpliciter*] but comparatively [*comparacione*] and with respect to the greater evil.[41]

Calibrating action in an imperfect world so as to choose the lesser over the greater sin is a non-trivial and continuously necessary matter.[42]

[38] BNF, MS. lat. 14524, fo. 90va (§ 26.4).

[39] BNF, MS. lat. 14524, fo. 106ra (§ 30.5). See also the case of the psychopath in the woods: should an individual defend himself and kill him/her; or love, and not murder, this 'neighbour' (BNF, MS. lat. 14524, fo. 88va (§ 25.14))?

[40] Cf. F. Morenzoni, *Des écoles aux paroisses: Thomas de Chobham et la promotion de la prédication au début du XIIIe siècle* (Paris, 1995), p. 97.

[41] Chanter, *Verbum*, pp. 548–9 (§ 1.78).

[42] The Chanter and Courson seem neighbouring points on a spectrum which can only be sampled here. Robert of Flamborough's *Liber poenitentialis* (between 1208 and 1215) acknowledges the importance of established custom (e.g. § 178), the role of publicity (§ 67) and the need for credibility to audiences (§ 108) but questions are treated more individualistically (e.g. on sexual relations with sisters § 65) (Robert of Flamborough, *Liber poenitentialis: a Critical Edition*, ed. J. J. F. Firth (Toronto, 1971)). Peter of Poitiers's post-

Counsel and councils

In the light of the complexity and social sensitivity underlying Courson's penitential thinking it is instructive to set it alongside another major area of activity, his acts as a legate and legislator. It is harder to find a more apparent contrast than with his actions at Morlhon (between Cahors and Rodez) during the Albigensian crusade against Occitan heresy in April and May 1214. As the eyewitness historian Pierre des Vaux de Cernay wrote:

> There was in our army Master Robert of Courson, legate of the apostolic see … who had very recently come from French lands. Soon after his arrival our men advanced towards Morlhon and began to attack their enemies violently. The men of the citadel, seeing that they could not resist any more, handed themselves over to the legate to follow his every wish. Our men, at the legate's behest, completely destroyed the castle. Nor should it go unmentioned that here we found seven heretics of that sect which are called Waldensians, who, at once being led to the legate, confessed to their disbelief [*incredulitatem*] fully and plainly. Seizing them, our pilgrims [*peregrini*, i.e., crusaders] burnt them with great rejoicing.[43]

Weeks later, on 25 June, Courson held a council at Bordeaux, where one of the canons revived the third Lateran Council's 1179 legislation against heresy (cap. 27).[44] Here Courson reiterated the penalty of excommunication against *routiers*, heretics and murderers as well as their receivers, supporters, teachers and defenders, in addition to sixty days of indulgence for those opposing them.[45] As Baldwin noted, the tension between the nuanced

---

1215 *Compilatio praesens* tends to be more definitional than exploratory, but addresses a wider social nexus at points (e.g. § xxviii on confessors who fear to absolve knights who retain tithes; also esp. § li) (Peter of Poitiers, *Compilatio praesens*, ed. J. Longère (*CCCM*, li, Turnhout, 1981). In his *Liber poenitentialis* (pre-1191–1203), the older Alain of Lille (b. *c.*1120/1130?) stresses a moderating, medicinal approach, arguably bridging older approaches and newer ones (Alain of Lille, *Liber poenitentialis*, ed. J. Longère (Analecta mediaevalia Namurcensia, xvii–xviii, 2 vols, Louvain, 1965)). See also Corran, *Lying and Perjury*, pp. 88–90.

[43] *Petri Vallium Sarnaii Monachi Hystoria Albigensis*, ed P. Guébin and E. Lyon (3 vols, Paris, 1926–39), ii. 207–8 (§ 513).

[44] *Conciliorum oecumenicorum generaliumque decreta. Editio critica*, ii.i: *The General Councils of Latin Christendom: From Constantinople IV to Pavia-Siena (869–1424)*, ed. A. García y García et al. (Turnhout, 2013), pp. 145–7. For such re-transmission as an active process by recipients, see D. Summerlin, 'The reception and authority of conciliar canons in the later-twelfth century: Alexander III's 1179 Lateran canons and their manuscript tradition', *Zeitschrift der Savigny-Stiftung für Rechtsgeschichte, Kanonistische Abteilung*, c (2014), 112–31.

[45] *Foedera, conventiones, litteræ, et cujuscunque generis acta publica*, ed. T. Rymer (4 vols in 7, 1816–69), i, pt. 1, p. 122.

discrimination of Courson's counsel and the simple sharpness of conciliar precept could be striking.[46]

More interesting implications lie behind the basic explanation (different *fora* with different purposes produce different guidance). The Chanter and his collaborators' generation began to think concertedly about the sorts of practical problems produced by the theological agenda emerging at the end of the twelfth century.[47] The 1179 and 1215 Lateran statutes wanted to regulate all Christendom (and the difference between the statutes shows the growing ambition). Their resurgent ambition to scale up such attention did not, however, entirely converge with their ability to do so. Courson's *mise-en-scène* often concedes this: a marginalized, isolated priest, lacking reinforcements, deep in enemy territory, having to make complicated cost-benefit decisions, sometimes at risk to his life. This was typical of the period in many places before the coming of the friars and their mass preaching, as far as that went. It was two years after Courson's death before there were Dominicans in his home country, five before there were any Franciscans.[48] If Courson's *Summa* illustrates the hair-fine attention theologians would have liked to give perplexed parishioners, his legislation indicates the broad brush needed when working at scale. At Bordeaux Courson regulated across a fragmented France, indeed, in English-held Guyenne.[49] There was a gulf between the vistas of such statutes and the smaller-scale counselling of concrete communities and individuals which Courson's *Summa* takes as its horizon. Courson sat at the crux of an interesting imbalance between ecclesiastical ambition and ability. The sheer monumentality of 1215 encourages a temptation to suppose it marks the full winding-up of ecclesiastical mechanisms which could then run themselves

[46] On judgements of blood at Lateran IV, see Baldwin, *Masters, Princes*, i. 190–1.

[47] In terms of broad pastoral responsibility there is a longer continuity: see S. Hamilton, 'Penance in the age of Gregorian reform', *Studies in Church History*, xl (2004), 47–73; W. H. Campbell, 'Reconciliation in thirteenth-century England', *Studies in Church History*, xl (2004), 84–94; W. H. Campbell, *The Landscape of Pastoral Care in 13th-Century England* (Cambridge, 2017); R. Springer, 'Prelacy, pastoral care, and the instruction of subordinates in late twelfth-century England', *Studies in Church History*, lv (2019), 114–28. In terms of theological concern with heresy, orthodoxy and thresholds of Christian literacy, the late 12th century does seem to mark an ambitious turn: N. Bériou, *L'avènement des maîtres de la Parole: La prédication à Paris au XIIIe siècle* (2 vols, Paris, 1998), i. 15–21.

[48] J. R. H. Moorman, *Church Life in England in the Thirteenth Century* (Cambridge, 1955), pp. 368–70. For their novelty, see *The Historia Occidentalis of Jacques de Vitry*, ed. J. F. Hinnebusch (Fribourg, 1972), pp. 158–63 (§ 32).

[49] O. Guyotjeannin, 'L'intégration des grandes acquisitions territoriales de la royauté capétienne (XIIIe – début XIVe siècle)', in *Fragen der politischen Integration im mittelalterlichen Europa*, ed. W. Maleczek (Vorträge und Forschungen, lxiii, Ostfildern, 2005), pp. 211–39.

(out?).[50] However, if Lateran IV set parameters, there are no grounds for thinking it magically flicked the ecclesiastical lights on across Europe, in France any more than elsewhere. It has been powerfully argued that *c.*1200 marks the end of a long incremental process establishing the Church as the necessary physical space for European sacramental reification and religious orientation.[51] Be this as it may, there remained much long, slow, repetitive work needed to bridge local practices and desires on the one hand and ecclesiastical expectations and aspirations on the other, none of which had foregone conclusions.[52] The period may be better thought of not as a settlement terminating the Gregorian reforms but as a hinge, a time when many political actors were buttressing multiple and potentially conflicting modes of power with not-yet-clear consequences.[53]

Is there, then, a real contrast between the absolutes of Morlhon and the more nuanced approach of Courson's *Summa*? Three points may be made. First, power or coercion mattered in the operation of medieval pastoral care, just as in more obvious coercive forms of legislation or military action. There are plenty of absolutes in the *Summa*. These were different means to similar ends. Nevertheless, the pastoral mode required a more empathetic engagement with local concerns and norms, even when theologians like Courson might disagree with them. Thus, second, while there is a tension between the Morlhon-Courson and the *Summa*-Courson, there is not a paradox. (In Courson's view the heretics of Morlhon clearly broke the truth of life and doctrine after all.) What makes this tension interesting was that Courson stressed the *difficulty* of generally elaborating rules as a means of resolving the particular, bizarre and 'de facto' problems of human life. It may appear ironic that someone who drafted reforming statutes for provincial

[50] E.g. R. I. Moore, *The First European Revolution c.900–c.1215* (Oxford, 2000), pp. 180–1, but cf. p. 174. For different models for thinking about the Church institutionally, see I. Forrest, 'Continuity and change in the institutional Church', in *The Oxford Handbook of Medieval Christianity*, ed. J. H. Arnold (Oxford, 2014), pp. 185–200; and Forrest's 'social church' model as developed in I. Forrest, *Trustworthy Men: how Inequality and Faith Made the Medieval Church* (Princeton, N.J., 2018), outlined at pp. 4–6.

[51] D. Iogna-Prat, *La Maison Dieu: un histoire monumentale de l'église au Moyen Âge* (rev. edn, Paris, 2012), pp. 23, 401–2, 613–17.

[52] For an explanation of how this worked in England, see Forrest, *Trustworthy Men*. His basic argument is that the practical gulf between the episcopal Church and its localities post–1200 was bridged by a series of accommodations and liaisons between ecclesiastical authorities and local parish elites, but that it was these elites, which the Church could deem trustworthy, which were fundamental. For a complementary argument published as this chapter was completed, see J. M. Wayno, 'Rethinking the Fourth Lateran Council of 1215', *Speculum*, xciii (2018), 611–37.

[53] These issues are discussed in my forthcoming analysis of 13th-century Europe, *The Cultivation of Christendom*.

Churches, which in turn influenced ecumenical councils, took the more general position that greater elaboration of rules did not automatically equal greater elucidation of the problems they were supposed to address. However, finally, in the particular circumstances of this transitional period there may well be grounds for thinking that in his later legislative *acta* Courson was merely taking his pragmatic satisficing of moral dilemmas onto a new level. If, in due course, counselling such as the *Summa* envisaged was needed generally, at least now, *faute de mieux*, Bordeaux-type legislation would do.[54]

Systematic and social thinking

Had Sir Richard Southern finished his great *summa* on scholastic humanism and the unification of Europe it seems likely he would have cast his thirteenth-century narrative as one of 'increasing difficulties encountered, especially from the middle of the thirteenth century onwards, by those who aimed to make the system complete in substance and operation'.[55] In Southern's account, central to these difficulties was scholars' compulsion for both completeness and order, since 'systematization requires selection, selection requires omission, and omission impairs completeness'.[56] Historians of scholasticism need not agree with Southern's chronology, nor with his suggestion that from 1200 (or even 1160) onwards developments in learning had only increasingly 'marginal and often conspicuously deleterious effects on the conduct of government' (though this certainly places Courson's generation at an interesting juncture).[57]

It is, nevertheless, very interesting to think about Southern's stress on completion and system in light of the 'Biblical-moral' group. He said little specifically about them, grouping the Chanter with Hugh of St Victor, Peter Lombard and other 'representatives of a scene of intellectual development over a century, diversified in their contributions, but consistently developing towards a final statement of systematic truth. They were the heralds of the

[54] For Innocent III's attitude, cf. H. Grundmann, *Religious Movements in the Middle Ages: the Historical Links Between Heresy, the Mendicant Orders, and the Women's Religious Movement in the Twelfth and Thirteenth Century, with the Historical Foundations of German Mysticism*, trans. S. Rowan (Notre Dame, Ind., 1995 [1961 edn.]), p. 50.

[55] As described on the hardback cover of R. W. Southern, *Scholastic Humanism and the Unification of Europe* (2 vols, Oxford, 1995–2001), ii.

[56] Southern, *Scholastic Humanism*, ii. 54.

[57] Southern, *Scholastic Humanism*, ii. 5. His argument was that the ambitions of government became too great, its literate elite's pretensions unsustainable. Cf. R.W. Southern, *Robert Grosseteste: the Growth of an English Mind in Medieval Europe* (2nd edn, Oxford, 1992), pp. 270–81, 285–91. Southern seemed to indicate inconsistent chronologies of decline. See also Emily Corran's comments about this style's longevity in this volume.

final consummation of all knowledge within the reach of human enquiry'.[58] *Did* Courson's *Summa* seek completion in terms of giving a 'final statement of systematic truth'? At one level that position can be defended: Courson did work systematically through a range of penitential problems, dynamics and sacraments.[59] However, the systematic nature of Courson's thought is different. The 'completion' he sought was not so much in exhaustiveness of treatment or resolution as in a holistic acknowledgment that pastoral care and reform needed to mesh with the actual social systems which themselves constructed how communities understood those penitential and sacramental phenomena. Beryl Smalley characterized this biblical-moral group as being focused on the 'art of the possible' and systematic pragmatists would be a good way of describing them.[60]

The thinking of this particular generation and group is, therefore, better evaluated for its attempt to engage with its particular milieux and less as an unfulfilled anticipation of later trends. The rich detail Baldwin implied was compensation for the lack of structure in this style of thought arguably becomes central to its diagnostic method. God was in the detailed – and interminable – *puta, esto, item* through which Courson explored his precepts and problems. One of the striking, and engaging, things about the so-called biblical-moral scholars of Paris is neither their biblicalism nor their moralism, but rather their engagement with experience – the de facto. That engagement arises from the mediation they sought between actual individuals and social practices, reflecting on and wrestling with the systemic complexity of what they thought being a Christian should mean in early thirteenth-century France.

58 Southern, *Scholastic Humanism*, i. 190.

59 Kennedy, 'Contents of Courson's *Summa*'.

60 B. Smalley, *The Gospels in the Schools c.1100–c.1280* (London, 1985), p. 115.

9. 'Better to let scandal arise than to relinquish the truth': the cases of conscience of the masters of Paris in the thirteenth century

Emily Corran

This volume addresses the ways in which institutions 'did or did not constrain, enable and inflect the substantive thinking of individuals' (see the introduction to this volume, p. 25). A number of the chapters explore this theme by identifying ways in which scholastic authors developed their own position within the boundaries imposed by institutional loyalties. Fitzpatrick's and Linde's chapters in this volume, for example, show how, at the turn of the thirteenth and fourteenth centuries, scholastic debate simultaneously pushed forward intellectual arguments and defined the parameters of disputes between Dominicans, Franciscans and the secular clergy. In contrast, quodlibets dealing with cases of conscience, the subject of this chapter, are something of an exceptional case in scholastic thought: moral quodlibets usually did not correspond directly to the syllabus organized around commentaries on the *Sentences* and they addressed questions which were not in the strictest sense theological, but which related to pastoral care. This chapter argues that responses to moral quodlibets should be understood neither as personal responses to a controversy, nor as attempts to carve out a position in a debate between rival 'schools'. Rather, they are best explained as interventions within a separate genre of penitential thought and have a close relationship with manuals for confessors. In penitential manuals, the imperative on the author was less to devise appropriate responses to open questions and more to offer practical advice on how one should act. This was no less true of the moral quodlibets answered by theology masters. When masters gave responses within this genre, they found themselves constrained and enabled by institutions, but in a rather different way from when they answered questions in other kinds of theology.

The practice of quodlibets first appeared in the 1230s and came to be a biannual event which took place in Advent and Lent and in which the audience, made up of students, masters and the general public, were invited

E. Corran, '"Better to let scandal arise than to relinquish the truth": the cases of conscience of the masters of Paris in the thirteenth century', in *Individuals and Institutions in Medieval Scholasticism*, ed. A. Fitzpatrick and J. Sabapathy (London, 2020), pp. 217–34.

to pose any question they liked for debate. On the first day arguments were proposed for and against; and on the second occasion the regent master gave a resolution.[1] Almost from the beginning practical moral problems were among the questions addressed in quodlibets;[2] and especially from the 1250s onwards moral dilemmas ('cases of conscience') became a frequent feature. These questions have been a fertile source for intellectual historians. Palémon Glorieux pointed out the importance of quodlibets for accurately tracking the progression of arguments over time: quodlibets tend not to represent a theologian's most detailed treatment of a subject, but they are repetitive (we often have records of several quodlibets given by a master over several years) and can be precisely dated, thus allowing the historian to demonstrate the chronology of an argument.[3] More specifically on moral questions, Elsa Marmursztejn and Ian Wei have argued that these quodlibets mark a transformation in the university masters' authority.[4] From the 1260s onwards theology masters answered questions on the ethical duties of a theology master, including questions on the morality of choosing university disputation over active pastoral care, the formation of future prelates and the proper lifestyle of a master. Their responses to these questions set out a vision of university masters as sources of moral authority and advice for the rest of the clergy, as well as possessors of what Alain Boureau has called 'a vocation for judging all things'.[5] Many moral quodlibets deliver penitential verdicts on commercial transactions, questions of Church and state, oaths, vows and war, to name but a few examples. On this basis, Marmursztejn goes so far as to speak of the theology masters in Paris as a new form of normative

[1] P. Glorieux, *La Littérature quodlibétique de 1260 à 1320* (2 vols, Kain and Paris, 1925–35), i. 18–20; J. F. Wippel 'Quodlibetal questions, chiefly in theology faculties', in *Les Questions disputées et les questions quodlibétiques dans les facultés de théologie, de droit et de médecine*, ed. B. C. Bazàn et al. (Typologie des sources du Moyen Âge occidental, xliv–xlv, Turnhout, 1985), pp. 153–222; a passage on procedure and format is at pp. 158–62; J. Hamesse, 'Theological *quaestiones quodlibetales*', in *Theological Quodlibeta in the Middle Ages: the Thirteenth Century*, ed. C. Schabel (Brill's Companions to the Christian Tradition, Leiden, 2006), pp. 17–48.

[2] Guerric of Saint-Quentin answered a few questions on moral dilemma in his 5th and 6th quodlibets, which took place between 1233 and 1242 (Glorieux, *La Littérature quodlibétique*, ii. 109–11).

[3] Glorieux, *La Littérature quodlibétique*, i. 66, 70–5.

[4] I. P. Wei, *Intellectual Culture in Medieval Paris: Theologians and the University, c.1100–1330* (Cambridge, 2012), pp. 174–9; E. Marmursztejn, *L'autorité des maîtres: Scolastique, normes et société au XIIIe siècle* (Paris, 2007), pp. 21–82.

[5] A. Boureau, 'Intellectuals in the middle ages, 1957–95', in *The Work of Jacques le Goff and the Challenges of Medieval History*, ed. M. Rubin (Woodbridge, 1997), pp. 145–55, at p. 155.

power alongside the secular clergy and lay authorities.[6] A larger argument about the masters of Paris during the turn of the thirteenth and fourteenth centuries notes the increasing frequency with which the French monarchy and the papacy relied on Paris masters to deliver judgements on contested questions of doctrine and jurisdiction. One could cite William of Mâcon's and Simon of Beaulieu's use of arguments developed in the university of Paris during the secular-mendicant controversy in the 1280s, or Philip the Fair's appeal to the university during the trial of the Templars. The rise in 'normative' quodlibets coincided, then, with a wider acknowledgement of the Paris masters' intellectual authority.[7]

This chapter describes the influence of penitential thought on the masters' moral quodlibets, with particular reference to questions involving the sin of scandal (of which more below). The debt to penitential writings in these university debates adds important nuance to our understanding of the masters' authority, since the significant innovation in moral thought was going on in the pastoral writings of this period, rather than in the theology faculty. When Paris masters were asked moral questions, as often as not the same question had already been addressed in a confessors' manual and the master would rarely answer a question in a different way from the penitential text. Even when the question posed was entirely specific to the university, the Paris masters would answer along lines similar to questions already treated in penitential literature.

This has implications for understanding Parisian intellectual culture, but also for one branch of scholastic thought. In these quodlibets we can see part of a larger intellectual development, namely the creation of a discipline of scholarly moral advice which would eventually beget the casuistry of the seventeenth century. Casuistry – an academic discipline of moral questions for confessors – did not exist by that name or as a recognized genre in the thirteenth century. However, in quodlibets like these and in similar genres, including canon law and confessors' manuals, we can see that there were common conventions for addressing moral problems which had the qualities of a distinct genre by this time. Hence moral quodlibets are important in the development of an institution, in the sense of a lasting common practice. Theology masters did not explicitly acknowledge they were participating in an institution of this kind when they responded to casuistical quodlibets, but they participated in a style of reasoning held in common among themselves and the authors of penitential thought more generally.

6 Marmursztejn, *L'autorité des maîtres*, p. 265.

7 R. W. Southern, 'The changing role of universities in medieval Europe', *Hist. Research*, lx (1987), 133–46; A. Destemberg, *L'honneur des universitaires au Moyen Âge. Étude d'imaginaire social* (Paris, 2015).

Scandal

The medieval concept of scandal does not map directly onto the modern meaning. The word itself comes from the Greek for a 'trap' or 'snare' and its moral-theological meaning derived primarily from Gregory the Great's sixth-century homily on Ezekiel which said that a person in authority should not lead others into sin, even if his words or actions are not inherently sinful.[8] Scandal, as it came to be understood, was the fault of leading other people to sin through one's own words or actions, or bringing disrepute to the Church.[9] A famous medieval case of scandal taken from Gratian's *Decretum* involved a priest who openly kept a concubine. As well as the sin of clerical marriage, he was guilty of scandal, because his actions would cause his parish to lose faith in the holiness of the clergy.[10] The term scandal appears quite often in judicial judgements in ecclesiastical courts of the late middle ages.[11] It was a way of determining whether a crime should be dealt with in a public court or was a private matter of conscience.[12] If, for example, a priest has had an affair about which nobody knows, the canon-law court would say that it would cause scandal if the crime became known: it would damage the souls of the people in the community, therefore the priest should do penance in private. On the other hand, if there is a notorious crime – for example, someone has punched a priest in public with many witnesses – then this has to be dealt with in a public procedure, because it will cause scandal to the many if it appeared that the crime had gone unpunished.[13]

As well as this legal definition, the concept of scandal was the subject of a theological and penitential debate about the relative importance of public harm and personal integrity in moral dilemmas. Gratian discussed

[8] Thomas Aquinas, *Summa theologia*, in *Opera omnia iussu Leonis XIII*, iv–xii (Rome 1886–1906), IIa–IIae, q. 43, a. 1; Hostiensis [Henry of Susa], *Summa Aurea* (5 vols, Venice, 1574), i. col. 165 (Tit. *De renunciatione*, no. 9). On scandal see R. H. Helmholz, '*Scandalum* in the medieval canon law and in the English ecclesiastical courts', *Zeitschrift der Savigny-Stiftung für Rechtsgeschichte, Kanonistische Abteilung*, xcvi (2010), 258–74; A. Fossier, '"Propter vitandum scandalum": histoire d'une catégorie juridique (XIIe–XVe siècle)', *Mélanges de l'École française de Rome. Moyen Âge*, cxxi (2009), 317–48; C. Nemo-Pekelman, 'Scandale et vérité dans la doctrine canonique médiévale (xiie–xiiie siècles)', *Revue historique de droit français et étranger*, lxxxv (2007), 491–504.

[9] Nemo-Pekelman, 'Scandale et vérité', p. 492.

[10] *Decretum Gratiani*, dist. 33, c. 5. in E. Friedberg (ed.), *Corpus Iuris Canonici* (2 vols, Leipzig, 1879–81; repr. 1959), i. cols. 123–4; cf. Nemo-Pekelman, 'Scandale et vérité', p. 495.

[11] Helmholz, '*Scandalum*', pp. 263–8.

[12] A. Fossier, *Le bureau des âmes. Écritures et pratiques administratives de la Pénitencerie apostolique (XIIIe–XIVe siècle)* (Rome, 2018), ch. 8.

[13] Helmholz, '*Scandalum*', pp. 264–7.

these matters to a certain extent, but it was Peter the Chanter, a master of the Paris schools at the end of the twelfth century, who made the subject interesting. It is not surprising that Peter the Chanter was the first to deepen the discussion about scandal in his *Summa de sacramentis et animae consiliis*, since the point of this treatise, unlike his more popular preaching manual, the *Verbum adbreviatum*, was to move quickly through the obvious and well-known teaching on penitential matters in order to dwell on the more difficult problems. In the case of scandal, Peter the Chanter talks briefly about the canon law cases in which a priest commits crimes, such as simony and fornication, and causes scandal in the community, but moves quickly on to a subtler set of problems.[14] These concern actions which are not inherently sinful but nevertheless cause suspicions among the general public which could lead them into scandal and sin. The formula he offers to solve these problems are the three truths: one should always avoid scandal, unless it endangers a truth of life, justice or doctrine.[15]

One such case is a woman who forms the pious intention not to marry, to avoid the company of men and to observe a fast. These actions are good in themselves, but if they cause her neighbours to think she is a Cathar, then that might lead to scandal. A woman who causes scandal in this way, says the Chanter, should either enter a convent or agree to marry (an action which is not in itself sinful). Marrying would not ruin a 'truth of life', which is to say, it would not be sinful; and so the woman should choose this course of action so that scandal can be avoided.[16] In a second dilemma, the Chanter quotes the case of a prelate who keeps fine horses, wears precious ornaments and employs a number of lawyers and jurists in order to regulate his diocese. This causes scandal among his subjects because they see him spending money on this instead of helping the poor. However, in this case it is better to allow the people to be scandalized because if the prelate wore cheap clothes, or appeared lowly and contemptible, or had no one to punish wrongdoers in his diocese, this would prevent the truth of justice, by which the Chanter means he would be unable to exercise justice in his diocese.[17]

Peter the Chanter's teaching was influential on his immediate circle of students. For example, Robert of Courson also had cases on scandal in his *Summa*: should a preacher declare truths which will offend the audience and cause scandal? Should a judge give a verdict on a foreign poor man's case

[14] Petrus Cantor, *Summa de sacramentis et animae consiliis*, ed. J.-A. Dugauquier (Analecta mediaevalia Namurcensia, iv, vii, xi, xvi, xxi, 3 vols in 5, Louvain, 1954–67), iii, pt. 2a, pp. 372–81 (§ 318–21) (hereafter Chanter, *Summa*).

[15] Chanter, *Summa*, iii. pt. 2a. pp. 376–7 (§ 319). See also pp. 204–5 above.

[16] Chanter, *Summa*, iii. pt. 2a. p. 376 (§ 319).

[17] Chanter, *Summa*, iii. pt. 2a. pp. 376–7 (§ 319). See also pp. 204–5 above.

if he risks angering the local rich men, or should he instead find an excuse to delay the case to avoid scandal? If two men have been promised the same benefice, should the benefactor worry about causing one of the men scandal when he is inevitably disappointed?[18] Peter the Chanter's teaching was significant for its content – he was the first to introduce the idea of the three truths, as far as we know – but it was no less important because of its innovative methodology. His thought was unremittingly ordered towards practical courses of action, rather than theoretical completeness. These cases are as much about how to apply the rules in particular cases as they are about establishing ethical principles.[19] This kind of reasoning about what a person should do is very unusual for a scholastic enquiry. Riccardo Quinto gave a definition of scholasticism as a specialized way of reading texts which strives to resolve logical contradictions in order to find the truth.[20] This works in most cases but it was not Peter the Chanter's method: when he answered these problems, he did not refer to an apparent contradiction between texts, but instead an apparent contradiction between moral imperatives in a practical situation. The Chanter's methodology was, therefore, an exceptionally empirical pocket of scholastic thought.

Scandal in penitential literature

Peter the Chanter's and Robert of Courson's distinctively practical approach had a fairly limited influence among the next generation of theologians; and within the university the case-of-conscience method appeared to be in danger of falling into disuse in the second quarter of the thirteenth century. The big names of the following generation – Stephen Langton, Geoffrey of Poitiers, William of Auvergne – focused their teaching on the more theoretical aspects of theology rather than the practical issues involved in moral dilemmas.[21] Nevertheless, the Chanter's legal-theological approach, the distinctively practical way of addressing problems, did also appear in confessors' manuals and pastoral literature during these years. Significantly, penitential writing had a wider diffusion outside the university, such that it could claim to be a more influential kind of normative writing. This meant that when theology masters later answered questions on scandal in quodlibets, they were conscious of a popular precedent in the pastoral tradition, particularly confessors' manuals such as Raymond of Peñafort's

[18] Robert of Courson, *Summa* (Paris, BNF, MS. lat. 14524, fos. 87rb–88rb (§ 25.4, 7, 12)).

[19] Cf. John Sabapathy's chapter in this volume, which draws a distinction between coherent and consistent thinking.

[20] R. Quinto, *'Scholastica': storia di un concetto* (Padua, 2001), p. 416.

[21] E. Corran, *Lying and Perjury in Medieval Practical Thought: a Study in the History of Casuistry* (Oxford, 2018), pp. 88–90.

Summa de casibus (1225/1227, revised 1235–6) or John of Freiburg's *Summa confessorum* (1297–8).

Like the late twelfth-century theology masters, confessors' manuals continued to use many aspects of case-based practical ethics. Raymond of Peñafort included a series of practical dilemmas in each chapter of his *Summa de casibus* with the intention they should demonstrate to a confessor how to deal with ambiguous sins. Raymond had a pragmatic, case-by-case approach: he quotes the rule about avoiding scandal except in cases of a truth of life, doctrine and justice. If a religious man finds himself the subject of suspicion, even though he has a clean conscience he is morally obliged to try to explain his intentions in order to prevent any chance of scandal. He should try to convince people of his good intentions; and only if they are determined to find fault with his behaviour should he stop trying to explain himself to them.[22] If a multitude are in a state of sin – for example, a crowd persistently refusing to pay tithes or taking part in duels and tournaments – should the bishop excommunicate them all if they refuse to be corrected?[23] Raymond suggests that if the crowd know they are in the wrong but refuse to stop, the bishop should pass over the matter in silence in order to avoid a schism. Instead, he should send written threats and try to win back the wiser, more powerful sinners and so break down the resistance gently. If, on the other hand, they refuse to acknowledge they are sinning, then the bishop should treat them more severely.[24] As in Peter the Chanter's cases, the question is what to do in extraordinary circumstances and how to weigh principle against pragmatic effect.

The inclusion of cases on scandal in the *Summa de casibus* meant that these ideas became widespread and accessible. Raymond of Peñafort's manual was dispersed across Christendom and remained in use throughout the middle ages, which ensured that the subject remained in the clerical vocabulary. There was the beginning of a consensus about what scandal is and how a cleric in a position of responsibility should either avoid it or allow it to happen, something which would not have been the case if Peter the Chanter alone had been interested in the theological implications of scandal. All this is significant. There was a type of thought which was quite specialized and dedicated to solving a certain kind of moral problem. It appeared in areas of intellectual writing which were particularly concerned with confession and clerical duties and had influence beyond the university.

[22] Raymond of Peñafort, *Summa de poenitentia et matrimonio cum glossis Ioannis de Friburgo* (Rome, 1603; repr. Farnborough, 1967), p. 355 (iii.30.3).

[23] Raymond of Peñafort, *Summa de poenitentia et matrimonio*, pp. 355–6 (iii.30.4), with details from William of Rennes's *Apparatus*.

[24] Raymond of Peñafort, *Summa de poenitentia et matrimonio*, pp. 355–6 (iii.30.4).

The university of Paris and pastoral care

With this background in mind, we can turn to questions of scandal in quodlibets in Paris.[25] We can see that the quodlibets approach moral problems in the same way as these earlier pastoral writings and writings in the circle of Peter the Chanter. They answer practical, moral dilemmas which are particularly relevant to responsible churchmen; and, like the confessors' manuals, there was a preference for difficult circumstances. The debt to the earlier pastoral writings was so important that the theology master often simply restated or paraphrased teachings which had already been developed in confessors' manuals.

The answers elicited by such questions appear problematic for an intellectual historian in that they often say very little which is really new. Quodlibets are often described in the secondary literature as sparring grounds: occasions when masters could work out their positions on controversial matters and position themselves against other schools of thought.[26] This does not apply to moral problems. Many of the questions on practical, moral decisions in fact seem remarkably safe and do nothing to improve on the pastoral manuals they quote. For example, there is a collection of practical quodlibets containing the determinations by a number of different masters which was donated to the Sorbonne by Bishop Nicholas of Bar. One master determined on a question which appears in both Raymond's *Summa* and Hostiensis's chapter on penitence in the *Summa aurea*: a wife has a child in adultery and brings it up as her husband's first son. Is she obliged to admit the deception to her husband? The quodlibet simply restates Raymond of Peñafort's solution.[27] The same collection includes standard questions on the duty to reveal the truth under oath and the morality of saving a life by lying, again with no real originality in the responses.

It is not in itself surprising that some quodlibets were not innovative: the masters could not control the choice of questions and could not have provided a new answer on every possible topic. Yet, these moral quodlibets also had a function which was rather distinct from that of their more controversial metaphysical or ecclesiological counterparts. These were real-life problems: what was required was simply good advice rather than novelty. A philosophical opinion ceases to be relevant once everyone has conceded it to be true; not so a moral opinion, since people can be repeatedly or

[25] The following section draws on arguments in Corran, *Lying and Perjury*, pp. 119–23.

[26] Glorieux, *La littérature quodlibétique*, i. 63–6.

[27] Iohannes de Murro, Quodlibet 1.4: 'Queritur si constante matrimonio mulier ex adulterio suscipiat filium, vir suus credat esse suum et mulier in confessione dicat sacerdoti sic esse, utrum sacerdos debeat ei dicere quod filium illum repellat a se et quod dicat talis non debet esse heres?' (BNF, MS. lat. 15850, fo. 23va).

continuously troubled by essentially the same dilemmas. Masters were being asked to provide reassurance as much as a contribution to a debate. This can be seen in a quodlibet by Berthaud of Saint Denis, who was asked whether it was sinful to dissimulate instead of carrying out fraternal correction because of scandal.[28] The situation he had in mind was the following: a responsible superior knows he ought to correct a subordinate but is worried what the man's reaction to correction will be. Berthaud gave advice similar to that of William of Rennes in his *Apparatus*: if a prelate and those below him fail to correct their brothers for reasons of negligence, they are culpable; but if they omit or hide the correction for justified prudential reasons, their actions are praiseworthy.[29] However, with a well-chosen quotation from Augustine, Berthaud fleshes out the recommendation. He warns that a prelate might be afraid his reproaches will be met with anger; he may fear that the subject he corrects will either abuse him to his face or complain behind his back.[30] The prelate should dismiss all such fears: as Augustine says, it often happens that the person being corrected is initially upset and disputes the criticism but, when he considers the matter again quietly, realizes his own error and changes his actions.[31]

The answer is conventional in that it restates well-worn pastoral teaching. No one was going to disagree. It seems fair to conclude that Berthaud simply meant to strengthen the resolve of his audience, which certainly included people who would be called upon to make such decisions. The response is best seen in the context of the culture discussed above of consulting theologians, especially in the university of Paris, as experts in matters of spiritual jurisdiction and pastoral care.[32] It is Berthaud's wisdom and authority, rather than his dialectic prowess, which were sought. He took the question to refer not to hypothetical principles but to a concrete decision involving personalities and predictable reactions. This was the

[28] Berthaud of Saint Denis, Quodlibet i.8 (BNF, MS. lat. 14726, fo. 174rb, edited in Corran, *Lying and Perjury*): 'Utrum aliquis propter scandalum dissimulans a correptione fraterna peccet dissimulando?' (pp. 172–7).

[29] 'Credo autem quod peccant Episcopi, et inferiores praelati, ad quos pertinet huiusmodi admonitionem facere: (inferiores enim eam possunt facere, etiam si sint simpices sacerdotes, curati tamen; cum constitutio illa non specificet, quod ab episcopo sit facienda) si per negligentiam, aut alias corrupta intentione omittant eam facere; si autem ex iusta causa omittant, quia forte vident ibi multorum stragem iacere, vel aliud simile, non peccant' (cf. William of Rennes's *Apparatus* to Raymond of Peñafort, *Summa de poenitentia et matrimonio*, p. 360 (iii.30.9), at v. 'Suspenditur').

[30] Berthaud of Saint Denis, Quodlibet i.8, in Corran, *Lying and Perjury*, p. 174 [§ 5].

[31] Berthaud of Saint Denis, Quodlibet i.8, in Corran, *Lying and Perjury*, p. 174 [§ 6].

[32] This was a culture the masters of Paris actively fostered themselves (Wei, *Intellectual Culture in Medieval Paris*, pp. 174–9; Marmursztejn, *L'autorité des maîtres*, pp. 21–82).

way in which masters habitually dealt with pastoral quodlibets: here they participated in a discipline devoted to procedure in practical decision-making. The intellectual work involved was somewhat distinct from the theologian's usual bread and butter. By the late thirteenth century, when these quodlibets took place, the answer to the various categories of dilemma, including scandal, had become fairly conventional and established.

A theology master's duty to avoid scandal

The rest of this chapter concerns the quodlibets on scandal which touched particularly on a master's duty to teach in the light of official bans on certain subjects. A number of moral quodlibets asked questions about whether a master should run the risk of causing scandal to his audience by teaching on doctrine which had been forbidden by a local bishop. By virtue of coming very close to the bone for the masters who answered these questions and of being bound up with some specific events, these are the questions on scandal which most closely affected the masters who commented on these problems. As such, they are a revealing final example of the form of moral teaching which masters offered in quodlibets.

During the final quarter of the thirteenth century there was a growing fear among responsible ecclesiastics that disputation might not always lead smoothly to a clear solution. It had become apparent that contentious papal privileges had generated fruitless argument. A council of masters in Paris in December 1286 forbade masters from answering any 'provocative question' (*quaestio litigiosa*) and Godfrey of Fontaines ascribed the decision to a desire to stem the tide of argument about mendicant confession.[33] Fear of theological error consequent on irresponsible use of philosophical texts motivated a number of condemnations of doctrine. Most notably, the bishop of Paris, Étienne Tempier, banned a series of philosophical propositions in 1271 and more extensively in 1277, with automatic excommunication for those who taught them.[34] There were condemnations in Oxford in 1277, 1280 and 1282 to 1283; London in 1286; and Paris in 1314 and 1316–17.[35]

These events had various practical and moral implications for the theology masters, depending on which side they found themselves in institutional and doctrinal disputes. Some masters were stung because they chose to continue discussing a matter they had been warned off: Jean de Pouilly's teachings

[33] Godfrey of Fontaines, Quodlibet 4, q. 13, in Godfrey of Fontaines, *Les quatre premiers quodlibets de Godefroid de Fontaines*, ed. M. de Wulf and A. Pelzer (Louvain, 1904), p. 276. This quodlibet is the only source for this council.

[34] There is an extensive bibliography on this subject, the seminal study being R. Hissette, *Enquête sur les 219 articles condamnés à Paris le 7 mars 1277* (Louvain, 1977).

[35] Southern, 'Changing role of universities', p. 139.

on the mendicant privilege were condemned at Avignon in 1321; theology masters had been told to stop discussing the privilege in 1290 by the then papal legate Benedict Gaetani.[36] Others, like John Peckham and Peter John Olivi, accused their rivals of deliberately using superfluous and misleading arguments in the face of authoritative pronouncements to the contrary. Still others were asked questions on condemned articles or forbidden legislation and so had to choose whether to perpetuate stale quarrels and to defy a prohibition.[37] Henry of Ghent recounts a situation in which the papal legate positively told him to teach a contentious doctrine – the plurality of forms – without publicly condemning the opposing view (Henry was himself unsure about this doctrine).[38] Luca Bianchi has described the hostile atmosphere of censure and self-censure which followed the 1277 condemnations and in which many masters refused to answer sensitive questions.[39] Given this range of experience and agendas, one might expect a number of different perspectives on the ethics of teaching a contentious doctrine and the question of disguising one's true views. Quodlibets asked whether a master should respond to litigious questions, whether he was morally obliged to teach the whole truth, or whether he could refuse to teach a truth he knew to be beneficial.[40] However, a detailed look at the cases shows that the masters were not tempted to advocate either widespread concealment or defiantly 'free speech'. They universally applied the same moderate set of teachings taken from the casuistical tradition on scandal.

The consensus about the ethical duties of a theology master turned on weighing the possible benefit of a lesson against any likely harm it could

[36] On both of these cases, Southern, 'Changing role of universities', pp. 135–7.

[37] See Henry of Ghent's comments to questions on angels in P. Porro, 'Doing theology (and philosophy) in the first person: Henry of Ghent's *Quodlibeta*', in Schabel, *Theological Quodlibeta*, pp. 171–231, at p. 194.

[38] L. Hödl, 'Neue Nachrichten über die Pariser Verurteilungen der tomasischen Formlehre', *Scholastik*, xxxix (1964), 178–96, at pp. 183–5.

[39] L. Bianchi, *Il vescovo e i filosofi: La condanna parigina del 1277 e l'evoluzione dell'aristotelismo scolastico* (Bergamo, 1990), pp. 31–5.

[40] Quodlibets on this subject not discussed here include: Gerard of Abbeville, Quodlibet 10, q. 3, 'Utrum arguenda non arguere sit peccatum?' (BNF, MS. lat. 16405, fo. 80ra–rb); Henry of Ghent, *Opera omnia*, ed. R. Macken et al. (multiple vols, Leuven, 1979–), xvi. 91–3 (Quodlibet 12, q. 16, xvi: 'Utrum scholastice docens falsum ex sinistra affectione motus peccet mortaliter?'); Servais of Mont Saint Éloi, Quodlibet 1, q. 55, 'Queritur de peccato magistri in theologia disputantis de quolibet, qui renuit accipere questionem sibi propositam quia tangit aliquos quos timet offendere, peccet in hoc mortaliter?' (BNF, MS. lat. 15350, fo. 281rb); Hervaeus Natalis, Quodlibet 2, q. 16, 'Utrum magister in theologia tractans questiones curiosas et dimittens utiles non peccat mortaliter?' (Hervaeus Natalis, *Quodlibeta* (Venice, 1513; repr. Ridgewood, N.J., 1966), fo. 65v).

cause. Richard of Mediavilla's 1296 quodlibet was typical.[41] He was asked whether a master must accept a question which will bring ill will on him, given that the question is a useful one to know. In his response Richard was studiously bland. A master was guilty of mortal sin if he refused to answer a question with a bearing on true faith and morals, especially if he thought he could avert scandal by answering the question. He only sinned venially if he refused a question which could be beneficial to his audience, but which had no bearing on faith. He acted well if he refused to answer a question which would cause no benefit to faith if he answered it, but probably would cause argument, scandal and bad judgements. Such a solution could offend no one. It affirmed the theology masters' vocation for explaining unclear questions of faith yet conceded that it might be permissible to refuse a question on occasion. It admitted the social nature of the judgement: if teaching on a matter would only lead people into further sin, then it was permissible to suppress the truth. The answer thus allowed pragmatic obedience to condemnations and prohibitions on given articles. Which questions exactly should be refused was left diplomatically undetermined; it was up to the individual to judge which topics were more harmful than beneficial.

This opinion was echoed on all sides of various disputes. Henry of Ghent, for example, had been vocally in favour of the theology masters' right to dispute the mendicant privilege. He was one of the theologians who formulated the 219 condemned articles in 1277.[42] When he was asked in 1286 whether a master sins mortally if in public he does not answer a question to which he knows the answer, he follows the same casuistical precedents.[43] He prefaces his response with a restatement of the law of scandal: scandal should always be avoided unless a truth of life, justice or doctrine is endangered. He describes the moral character of a master in terms of a duty towards teaching the truth.[44] A teacher must only assume his office in order to help the ignorant (*propter imperitos*).[45] He describes in detail the sin which is involved in teaching falsehood, or in failing to

[41] Richard de Mediavilla, *Quodlibet III*, ed. and trans. A. Boureau (Paris, 2017) pp. 298–303 (q. 23), commentary at p. lxxv. Glorieux gives the date 1286 (*La littérature quodlibétique*, i. 270–1).

[42] Henry of Ghent, *Opera omnia*, vi. 67 (Quodlibet 2, q. 9).

[43] Henry of Ghent, *Opera omnia*, xiv. 304–7 (Quodlibet 10, q. 16: 'Utrum doctor sive magister determinans quaestiones vel exponens scripturas publice peccet mortaliter non explicando veritatem quam novit?'); discussion in Marmursztejn, *L'Autorité des maîtres*, p. 60.

[44] Henry of Ghent, *Opera omnia*, xiv. 306 (Quodlibet 10, q. 16, ll. 44–5).

[45] Henry of Ghent, *Opera omnia*, xiv. 306 (Quodlibet 10, q. 16, ll. 42–4).

explain difficult matters of faith to the people.[46] This would be equivalent to failing to point out a hidden precipice to an unsuspecting traveller who is in danger of falling to his death. However, when he came to the decision on whether to teach a truth which might harm those listening, he was no less pragmatic than Mediavilla: one must be willing to hide the truth in order to save a soul.[47]

When Henry was later asked, either in Advent 1291 or Lent 1292, 'whether the power of prelates should be disputed by masters', the question was even more topical.[48] The year before, Cardinal Benedict Gaetani had rebuked the Parisian masters for doing just this when the university masters had criticized Martin IV's privilege allowing Franciscans to hear confession without seeking the permission of the local bishop. Gaetani responded astringently that masters had no right to criticize the privilege and denied them any role in deciding matters of doctrine or Church government.[49] Henry of Ghent himself had been prominent among the masters who had wished to amend the legislation; it was his feathers which were ruffled by Gaetani's rudeness. He is reported to have complained about the contradiction that masters who disputed the word of God should not be permitted to discuss the pope. Gaetani reportedly suspended Henry from teaching (although, clearly, he was teaching again the following year).[50] This is the background to his quodlibetical question in 1291/2. It is a work of rhetoric meant as self-justification against his opponents. However, what is controversial in his answer lies in its implications, not what it overtly concludes about the moral dilemma. Once again he argues for a prudent, subtle approach to disputing difficult questions and concealing harmful truths.

Henry starts by establishing his own *bona fides*. Those who dispute the power of prelates with a view to diminishing their jurisdiction are completely in the wrong: they are like those philosophers who tried to reduce the power of God and Christ with their Averroistic arguments.[51] The comparison is self-interested: Henry of Ghent had himself been among the group of theologians under Étienne Tempier who had drawn up the list of condemned Averroist doctrines in 1277. Henry is, therefore, reminding

[46] Henry of Ghent, *Opera omnia*, xiv. 306 (Quodlibet 10, q. 16, ll. 49–60).

[47] Henry of Ghent, *Opera omnia*, xiv. 306 (Quodlibet 10, q. 16, ll. 61–9).

[48] Henry of Ghent, *Opera omnia*, xx. 147–54 (Quodlibet 15, q. 15: 'Utrum licitum sit magistris disputare de potestate praelatorum?'; cf. Marmursztejn, *L'autorité des maîtres*, pp. 71–3; Wei, *Intellectual Culture in Medieval Paris*, pp. 181–2).

[49] Southern, 'Changing role of universities', p. 136.

[50] H. Finke, *Aus den Tagen Bonifaz VIII: Funde und Forschungen* (Münster, 1902), Quellen, pp. iii–vii.

[51] Henry of Ghent, *Opera omnia*, xx. 148–9 (Quodlibet 15, q. 15, ll. 26–53).

those present that he has in the past been a defender of the bishop's power over errant philosophers. No one could accuse him of arguing doctrine merely for the sake of pride or secular curiosity.

Disputing prelates' power in order simply to know better what those powers are and in order to judge when it is right to obey them is, on the other hand, entirely licit and beneficial, according to Henry.[52] He does not mean that matters agreed by universal councils should be dragged back into doubt. Rather, prelates should be happy for those matters to be disputed which need it, since they will then know exactly which powers they can exercise and which they should not. Subjects will know when they should obey their prelates and when they should, rather, disobey.[53] Henry quotes Bernard of Clairvaux and St Matthew to show that subjects must judge when to obey their superiors.[54] He concludes that if a prelate is seen to discourage disputation of any of his powers, the validity of that power will be held suspect: he compares such a prelate to Mohammed, who, aware of the shakiness of his own doctrine, banned his followers from disputing his law.[55] All this contrives to make a prelate who denies masters' right to dispute Church legislation (as Benedict Gaetani had seemed to do) look petty and insecure.

Henry certainly criticizes prelates who try to control discussion of the truth; the response was an apology for the free intellectual activity of university masters. However, what Henry concretely says about the moral dilemma of whether always to reveal the truth does not venture into any unexpected territory. Boiled down, his argument is that a master should not dispute powers if his intentions are evil, but should do so if he means to serve the Church and foresees that his comments will be useful. Henry makes the conventional provisos: if a question has reached the point at which further disputation is unhelpful, masters should withhold their comments. This is the case for Nicholas III's constitution on the Franciscan rule.[56] There is no advantage to be gained from disputing a truth which no one doubts. The Talmud, for example, was only produced when Jewish law was placed in doubt through the influence of Christianity and philosophy.[57] It is not the moral teaching itself but its application in a particular case which is the source of controversy. Henry objected to Benedict Gaetani telling the masters what they should and should not dispute, but his view

[52] Henry of Ghent, *Opera omnia*, xx. 150 (Quodlibet 15, q. 15, ll. 87–90).
[53] Henry of Ghent, *Opera omnia*, xx. 150–1 (Quodlibet 15, q. 15, ll. 91–109).
[54] Henry of Ghent, *Opera omnia*, xx. 151–2 (Quodlibet 15, q. 15, ll. 110–23).
[55] Henry of Ghent, *Opera omnia*, xx. 152–3 (Quodlibet 15, q. 15, ll. 139–42).
[56] Henry of Ghent, *Opera omnia*, xx. 153 (Quodlibet 15, q. 15, ll. 144–51).
[57] Henry of Ghent, *Opera omnia*, xx. 153–4 (Quodlibet 15, q. 15, ll. 151–66).

on dissimulation was nuanced: he neither argued for bringing out the truth at all costs, nor denied that dissimulation, even a prelate's ban on disputing forbidden articles, could sometimes be advisable.

By contrast, Godfrey of Fontaines' allegiances were different. He appears largely to have supported masters who gave opinions on the mendicant privilege. He praises those who chose to give an opinion in spite of the ruling by Paris masters against further disputation; those who refused to answer on the question, he says, 'may be excused to some extent'.[58] More significantly, he disapproved of the bishop of Paris's condemnations of 1277. Later in life he would criticize them as an impediment to students' progress, a cause of scandal among those studying and an obstruction of good doctrine.[59] In his seventh quodlibet, in 1290, Godfrey answers a question on whether a theology master should teach an article of doctrine which he believes to be true if the same article has been condemned by the local bishop.[60] More than Henry of Ghent or Richard of Mediavilla, Godfrey's personal circumstances led him to consider defying authority more concretely and we can detect a current of disapproval against bishops.

It is clear from the outset that Godfrey was talking exclusively about Étienne's condemnations. He concedes initially that a master should avoid publicly affirming the condemned articles, but should remain silent about both the false doctrine approved by the bishop and the condemned true doctrine.[61] However, when Godfrey went on to criticize the bishop who passed such legislation, his audience knew to whom he was referring. If a bishop publicly excommunicates anyone who professes a condemned opinion which is actually true, or which can be asserted as true by a probable opinion, his condemnation would be mistaken.[62] It is not for an individual to disobey the condemnation – that would break the bond of obedience – but he must urge the prelate to revoke his decision.[63] If the question is one necessary to salvation, on the other hand, and the master knows he is right

[58] 'aliquo modo possunt excusari' (Godfrey of Fontaines, Quodlibet 4, q. 13, in de Wulf and Pelzer, *Quatre premiers quodlibets*, p. 276).

[59] Godfrey of Fontaines, Quodlibet 12, q. 5, in *Les quodlibets onze-quatorze*, ed. J. Hoffmans (Louvain, 1932), pp. 100–5.

[60] Godfrey of Fontaines, Quodlibet 7, q. 18, in *Les quodlibet cinq, six et sept*, ed. M. de Wulf and J. Hoffmans (Louvain, 1914), pp. 402–5; cf. Marmursztejn, *L'autorité des maîtres*, pp. 69–71; Wei, *Intellectual Culture in Medieval Paris*, pp. 179–81.

[61] Godfrey of Fontaines, Quodlibet 7, q. 18, in de Wulf and Hoffmans, *Quodlibet cinq, six et sept*, p. 403.

[62] Godfrey of Fontaines, Quodlibet 7, q. 18, in de Wulf and Hoffmans, *Quodlibet cinq, six et sept*, pp. 403–4.

[63] Godfrey of Fontaines, Quodlibet 7, q. 18, in de Wulf and Hoffmans, *Quodlibet cinq, six et sept*, p. 404.

and the condemnation wrong, he must disobey the bishop openly. The sting in the tail is when Godfrey finally asserts that even if the master only believes himself to be right, but is actually mistaken, he must still teach what he thinks despite the excommunication.[64] It is more important to follow one's own conscience (even an erroneous one) than to hold back for fear of punishment.

Despite the belligerent asides, however, the casuistical judgements remain the same. Godfrey concludes, like the others, that it is a question of balancing ultimate harm to those listening against the advantage of teaching. An inconsequent truth should not be endorsed at the expense of the order of the Church and a teaching necessary to salvation should be included whatever the consequences. These masters disagreed bitterly over theological doctrines to which the moral dilemma referred; they took up intransigent opposing stances on the mendicants' privileges, the Franciscan vow and Thomistic propositions. Yet they were in accord when it came to the parameters of the moral dilemmas: they agreed it was a pragmatic decision and concurred on which circumstances were pertinent. They never deviated from the principles of scandal established in pastoral literature. In short, their use of casuistry was straightforward, even on occasions when the comments surrounding the practical advice were rather barbed.

Moral arguments about scandal were a feature of several of the major controversies which would affect the Paris theology faculty in the late thirteenth century. Masters did not advocate dissimulation as a response to censures on philosophical positions, nor did they argue for telling the truth at all costs. On the contrary, these responses say remarkably little because of their emphasis on the necessity of making a personal judgement in the circumstances. The casuistry of scandal itself was not affected by the prohibitions or mutual blame. Some masters did defend their choice to conceal articles of philosophy, or to remain silent about legislation with which they did not agree, but they did not develop the casuistry for the purpose: they remained faithful to the principal of avoiding scandal except in cases of a truth of life, doctrine or justice. The moral reasoning was already well-established in its own right: it advised masters on how to make their decisions as individuals in remarkably neutral terms while the larger intellectual quarrels and institutional conflicts played out.

Conclusion

All this points to some conclusions about the conventions and expectations surrounding moral quodlibets in the thirteenth century. In the responses

[64] Godfrey of Fontaines, Quodlibet 7, q. 18, in de Wulf and Hoffmans, *Quodlibet cinq, six et sept*, pp. 404–5.

discussed here, there is a clear distinction between the masters' theological positions and their ethical reasoning. The former are, in each case, a personal set of judgements about doctrine: each theologian mentioned here had his own view on the big, controversial questions. At the same time they all took an interest in the procedure for deciding how a master should teach responsibly and agreed on all the important aspects: which considerations were pertinent to questions of scandal; to whom the teacher's responsibilities were owed; when and on what subjects he should hold disputations. The masters who answered these questions were aware, in short, that a special kind of answer was required in questions of moral conscience. They were asked to engage with casuistical conventions in these cases, which foregrounded circumstantial deliberation and personal judgement.

The term casuistry was not coined until the seventeenth century as a term of disparagement for Catholic – and particularly Jesuit – rules of confession. Nevertheless, the 'thought style' which came to be known as casuistry was fully in existence by the end of the thirteenth century. Thought about cases of conscience spread from one genre of scholarly discussion to another during the period: from theology masters and canon lawyers to penitential authors and back to theology masters. In terms of methodology, the late thirteenth-century masters' approach to questions of scandal had more in common with penitential manuals than it did with their answers to the more abstract branches of theology. Considerable original thought about the resolution of moral thought had appeared in the work of authors such as Peter the Chanter and Raymond of Peñafort; when the theology masters came to address the same problems, they were more interested in applying this thought helpfully to their own problems than in developing new arguments.

These conclusions nuance our understanding of the university masters' authority. Marmursztejn talked about theology masters claiming an extra basis of authority and 'intellectual jurisdiction'. The findings here suggest this was a more specific kind of jurisdiction than previously acknowledged. Masters engaged in an institution of counsel of conscience (*consilium animae*) when answering these questions. These were problems which constantly reappeared in life, but for which there was a standard means for arriving at an answer – and the masters simply restated this means and pointed out the possibilities for circumstantial variation.

This discovery has implications for scholasticism as a discipline. Traditional definitions of scholasticism, particularly Riccardo Quinto's, have emphasized factors such as scientific interest in knowledge for its own sake, the use of reason and in particular the analysis of texts for contradictions. Casuistry has some features of traditional scholastic method: it focuses on contradictions; it is in a question-and-answer form. Yet, practical situations, not texts, are at its centre. Theology masters do cite relevant texts in their casuistic problems but their answers often lie in reconciling the circumstances of the case rather than the words of an authority. Cases of conscience permit us, therefore, to broaden the definition of scholasticism to include practical pastoral enquiry and to acknowledge that scholastic method could accommodate a degree of empirical thought.

A final comment should be made about casuistry as an institution. In the late twelfth century, school masters like Peter the Chanter perceived the need for practical solutions to conflicts of duty involving the danger of scandal. He forged procedures on how to make moral decisions which, by the late thirteenth century, were second nature, thanks to a widely-diffused penitential literature. University masters answering quodlibets on scandal dispensed their advice not primarily as great speculators but in their additional role as pastoral counsellors. It was characteristic of this style of reasoning that it was stable and explicit in stating a method for moral choice, but left it entirely to the individual to decide in a particular case, allowing room for personal adjustment. Because of this agreement in method across the genres, thirteenth-century casuistry, including the moral quodlibets of the theology masters, deserves recognition as an institution in its own right, in the sense of a lasting common practice.

10. Of parish priests and hermaphrodites: Robert Holcot's discussion of *Omnis utriusque sexus*

Cornelia Linde

The Dominican Robert Holcot (d. 1349) was one of the foremost theologians of his time. Witty, razor-sharp and challenging, his writings provide insight not just into the medieval lecture halls but also into modes of influence and interaction between individual and institutional thought. Holcot's discussion of suitable confessors in his *Super quattuor libros Sententiarum questiones*, the focus of this chapter, provides an eloquent example of how an individual thinker introduced institutional thought, in this case that of the Dominican order, into a different institutional context, that is, the university's, and thereby spread one institution's ideas beyond its borders by propagating it through another institution.[1]

Robert Holcot spent his entire life in England. After joining the Dominican order, probably at Northampton, Holcot was sent to Oxford as a student around 1326, where he lectured on Peter Lombard's *Sentences* in 1331 to 1333.[2] He was appointed regent master of theology at the university between 1336 and 1338.[3] Between 1338 and 1340 Holcot, who was one of the 'classicizing friars' studied by Beryl Smalley, established a close connection to the household of Richard Bury, bishop of Durham, through which he gained more access to classical literature.[4] Holcot then lectured on the Book

[1] See also the introduction to this volume.

[2] For Holcot's life and works, see J. T. Slotemaker and J. C. Witt, *Robert Holcot* (Great Medieval Thinkers, Oxford, 2016), pp. 1–12. Slotemaker and Witt offer improved biographical information compared to that provided in the ground-breaking article by B. Smalley, 'Robert Holcot O.P.', *Archivum Fratrum Praedicatorum*, xxvi (1956), 5–97, at pp. 7–8.

[3] Slotemaker and Witt, *Robert Holcot*, p. 2; F. Hoffmann, *Die theologische Methode des Oxforder Dominikanerlehrers Robert Holcot* (Beiträge zur Geschichte der Philosophie und Theologie des Mittelalters. Neue Folge, v, Münster, 1971), p. 1; and Smalley, 'Robert Holcot', p. 8, date his *inceptio* to 1334 and 1332, respectively.

[4] Slotemaker and Witt, *Robert Holcot*, pp. 2–3. On Holcot's use of the classics, see B. Smalley, *English Friars and Antiquity in the Early Fourteenth Century* (Oxford, 1960), pp. 133–202.

C. Linde, 'Of parish priests and hermaphrodites: Robert Holcot's discussion of *Omnis utriusque sexus*', in *Individuals and Institutions in Medieval Scholasticism*, ed. A. Fitzpatrick and J. Sabapathy (London, 2020), pp. 235–52.

of Wisdom for two years, possibly as regent master at Cambridge, between 1340 and 1343. His commentary on Wisdom made Holcot hugely famous and survives in over 100 manuscripts and several early printed editions.[5] In 1343 he returned to Northampton and over the next five years was regularly granted licences to hear confessions. He is said to have died of the Black Death while caring for the sick in 1349.[6]

His commentary on the *Sentences* was Holcot's earliest work, composed in the years 1331 to 1333 and re-worked a few years later during his regency.[7] In keeping with the fashion at Oxford at the time, Holcot commented not on the entire text of the *Sentences* but instead tackled select issues derived from the text by formulating and answering specific questions (*quaestiones*).[8] Question 5 in book 4 addressed a problem close to the heart of the Dominican order: 'Whether a penitent who has confessed his sins to a priest who has a general licence to hear confessions but who is not his own priest has to confess the same sins again to his own priest [*proprio sacerdoti*]'.[9] The issue raised by Holcot had its origins in two interconnected developments dating back more than 100 years to the early thirteenth century: the Fourth Lateran Council's call for annual confession and the rise of the mendicant orders. Holcot's discussion in his *quaestio* revolves entirely around the interpretation of canon 21 issued by the Fourth Lateran Council in 1215, better known under its incipit, *Omnis utriusque sexus*: 'Every one of the faithful of both sexes [*Omnis utriusque sexus fidelis*] after reaching the age of discretion should at least once a year faithfully confess alone all their sins to their own priest [*proprio sacerdoti*]'.[10] The crucial words

[5] Slotemaker and Witt noted that the evidence for Holcot's regency at Cambridge stands on shaky ground (*Robert Holcot*, pp. 3–4); cf. Smalley, 'Robert Holcot', pp. 20–1. For the immediate success of Holcot's Wisdom commentary, see J. C. Wey, 'The *Sermo finalis* of Robert Holcot', *Mediaeval Stud.*, xi (1949), 219–24, at p. 219. Wey observed correctly that rather than lacking seriousness, the *Sermo finalis* is a sign of 'the lighter side of university life which is both traditional and natural to students of all ages who are sane enough to possess a sense of humour' (p. 219). See Slotemaker and Witt for the large number of manuscripts and incunabula (*Robert Holcot*, p. 10).

[6] Smalley concluded her article on Holcot with the remark that upon Holcot's death, 'the future of theology in England lay with grimmer, narrower men' (Smalley, 'Robert Holcot', p. 97).

[7] Slotemaker and Witt, *Robert Holcot*, p. 3. Smalley dated the reworking to 1336 ('Robert Holcot', p. 7).

[8] For this format, see Slotemaker and Witt, *Robert Holcot*, pp. 5–6.

[9] R. Holcot, *Super quattuor libros Sententiarum questiones* (Lyons, 1497; used: London, British Library, IB.41933), sig. a i^{r}–o v^{r}, at sig. n iii^{vb}. For a very brief discussion of this *quaestio*, and an outline of Holcot's views on confession in general, see Slotemaker and Witt, *Robert Holcot*, pp. 111–18.

[10] *Decrees of the Ecumenical Councils*, ed. N. P. Tanner S.J. (2 vols, Washington, 1990), i.

in the Latin text are the final two, *proprio sacerdoti*, as it is on these two words and their interpretation that most debates about *Omnis utriusque sexus* hinge. A common – but by no means unchallenged – interpretation, both in the middle ages and also in modern scholarly literature, is that one's own (*proprius*) priest is one's parish priest. Such a definition would imply that each believer had to confess to his or her parish priest once a year. Since a parish priest can never be a mendicant, this interpretation of *proprius sacerdos* threatened to deprive the mendicants of substantial income and influence as well as sense of purpose. Up until Holcot's time, however, the definition of what role mendicants were allowed to play in the framework of pastoral care, which the Dominicans in particular regarded as part of their order's *raison d'être*, changed with almost every pope and was debated ever more hotly by seculars and mendicants.[11] Unsurprisingly, then, Holcot's discussion revolved around the correct interpretation of the phrase 'proprius sacerdos'.

The phrasing itself of the *quaestio* promises a powerful contribution to the continuing debate over the status of licensed mendicants as confessors, for it alludes to the key question of whether licensed mendicants can be truly suitable and acceptable confessors, or whether confession is only fully valid when made to one's parish priest. For Holcot, the fact that there was even a discussion about whether or not one has to confess to one's parish priest once a year rested upon a misguided interpretation of the canon.[12]

Nicaea I to Lateran V, pp. 245–245*. Translation slightly adapted from M. C. Mansfield, *The Humiliation of Sinners: Public Penance in Thirteenth-Century France* (Ithaca, N.Y., 1995), p. 66. The text of *Omnis utriusque sexus*, only the beginning of which is quoted here, spread widely and rapidly after its publication. It was integrated into synodal statutes and was commented on and discussed by canonists and theologians alike (N. Bériou, 'Autour de Latran IV (1215): la naissance de la confession moderne et sa diffusion', in *Pratiques de la confession. Des Pères du désert à Vatican II. Quinze études d'histoire* (Paris, 1983), pp. 73–93, at p. 80).

[11] See Bériou, 'Autour de Latran IV'. Bériou particularly stressed the role of Odo of Sully and Stephen Langton in implementing regular confession and promoting greater attention to the sacraments (p. 75). Peter Biller pointed out 'that this great text, *Omnis utriusque sexus*, was not legislating in a vacuum. Rather, it was making something uniform out of the norms and practices of various regions, and universalising this for the Church as a whole' (P. Biller, 'Confession in the middle ages: introduction', in *Handling Sin: Confession in the Middle Ages*, ed. P. Biller and A. J. Minnis (York Studies in Medieval Theology, ii, Woodbridge, 1998), pp. 1–33, at p. 8). For the non-innovative character of *Omnis utriusque sexus*, see also Bériou, 'Autour de Latran IV', p. 80. For a broad study of the history of penance, see T. N. Tentler, *Sin and Confession on the Eve of the Reformation* (Princeton, N. J., 1977).

[12] Holcot, *Super quattuor libros Sententiarum questiones*, sig. n iv[ra]: 'In ista questione oritur tota difficultas pro maiori parte de illo capitulo de penitentia et remissionibus *Omnis utriusque sexus*'.

Holcot, predictably, rejected the interpretation of *proprius sacerdos* in *Omnis utriusque sexus* as referring to one's parish priest. Instead, by arguing for a more nuanced interpretation of *proprius sacerdos*, he defended the legitimacy of licensed mendicants as fully acceptable confessors.

At the beginning of his *quaestio* Holcot acknowledges that, according to *Omnis utriusque sexus*, once a year each member of the Church has to confess to his or her priest. Since it could be argued that a friar preacher or a friar minor is not one's own priest, *proprius sacerdos*, one would technically have to confess the same sins again to one's parish priest even if one had previously confessed to a licensed mendicant.[13] However, this, in Holcot's view, would be interpreting the relevant passage too narrowly; and he provides six reasons to show why *Omnis utriusque sexus* was never intended in this way. These six reasons refer directly to the trial against the secular cleric John of Pouilly, which took place only a decade before Holcot composed his commentary on the *Sentences*.

The trial against John of Pouilly, a master of theology at Paris, had its roots in the ever-changing papal legislation on hearing confession. Already in 1254 Innocent IV had drastically curtailed the friars' right to hear confession in the bull *Etsi animarum*. Innocent died later the same year and was succeeded by Alexander IV, the former cardinal protector of the Franciscan order. Not entirely impartial in his attitude, Alexander rescinded *Etsi animarum* the following year. A major milestone was the bull *Ad fructus uberes* issued by Pope Martin IV on 13 December 1281. In it he granted the mendicants the right to hear confessions independent of the wishes or consent of local priests or bishops. As this had harsh consequences for parish priests, the secular clergy soon demanded that those who confessed their sins to mendicants should then have to confess once more to their parish priest, thus calling for double confession. The seculars also argued that *Ad fructus uberes*, like other pro-mendicant bulls concerning this topic, disrupted the order of the Church.[14]

The mendicant privilege of hearing confession was again restricted in 1300, when Boniface VIII published *Super cathedram*, which revised the

[13] Holcot, *Super quattuor libros Sententiarum questiones*, sig. n iii^{vb}: 'Sed talis audiens ex commissione, sicut sunt predicatores et minores ab antiquo, non est proprius sacerdos, ergo non obstante confessione facta tali tenetur eadem peccata numero iterum confiteri proprio sacerdoti'.

[14] J. Dunbabin, *A Hound of God: Pierre de la Palud and the Fourteenth-Century Church* (Oxford, 1991), p. 57. The bulls have been published in H. Denzinger, *Enchiridion Symbolorum definitionum et declarationum de rebus fidei et morum. Kompendium der Glaubensbekenntnisse und kirchlichen Lehrentscheidungen. Lateinisch – Deutsch*, ed. P. Hünermann (44th edn, Freiburg, 2014).

existing legislation in favour of the seculars. While the seculars applauded this bull, it aroused the ire of the mendicants, as it restricted their earlier rights to preach in parish churches and hear confession. Now only friars who had been granted a special licence by the local bishop were allowed to hear confession and only in the narrowly defined region for which they had obtained the licence. In addition, they had to share their income from, for instance, performing funerals with the local parish priests.[15] The mendicants were thus put on a tight leash by Boniface.

Boniface, however, died in 1303 and was succeeded in office by Niccolò Boccasini, the former master general of the Dominican order, who took the papal name of Benedict XI. In 1304 Benedict XI revoked *Super cathedram* and issued the bull *Inter cunctas*, in which he gave even greater rights to the mendicants than they had held before. In addition to legitimizing confessions made to any mendicant without the need of consent from the local bishop or parish priest, the bull also addressed the question of double confession and explicitly spelt out that re-confessing to one's parish priest was not necessary after previous confession to a mendicant. Nevertheless, despite denying the necessity of double confession, Benedict still recommended a repeat confession to the parish priest.[16]

Unsurprisingly, the seculars were now outraged and alarmed. Yet Benedict's papacy was short-lived, lasting not even ten months. His successor was Clement V, who convened the Council of Vienne where, under pressure from prelates, he called for the revocation of *Inter cunctas* and the reinstatement of *Super cathedram*, a demand he articulated in the decree *Dudum* on 6 May 1312.[17] Clement's death in April 1314, before *Dudum* had been debated by the council, proved to be a cruel twist of fate as this meant that its legal status remained debatable. It was not until late in 1317 that Clement's successor, John XXII, who was elected after more than two years of *sede vacante*, officially promulgated the council's decrees.[18]

It was probably unavoidable that in these three years, from 1314 to 1317, seculars would draw on *Dudum* in an attempt to assert their position. Most

[15] J. Koch, 'Der Prozeß gegen den Magister Johannes de Polliaco und seine Vorgeschichte (1312–1321)', in J. Koch, *Kleine Schriften* (2 vols, Rome, 1973), ii. 387–422, at p. 388; Dunbabin, *Hound of God*, pp. 57–8.

[16] A. Migliavacca, *La 'Confessione frequente di devozione'. Studio teologico-giuridico sul periodo fra i Codici del 1917 e del 1983* (Rome, 1997), p. 231; Dunbabin, *Hound of God*, p. 58.

[17] Dunbabin, *Hound of God*, p. 58; Koch, 'Prozeß gegen den Magister Johannes de Polliaco', pp. 388–9; S. Menache, *Clement V* (Cambridge, 1998), p. 291. For an edition of *Dudum*, see Tanner, *Decrees of the Ecumenical Councils*, i. 365–9.

[18] Dunbabin, *Hound of God*, p. 58. For the question of the validity of *Dudum* before its promulgation by John XXII, see also Koch, 'Prozeß gegen den Magister Johannes de Polliaco', p. 389.

prominent among them was John of Pouilly, who in his quodlibetal questions actively propagated the validity of *Dudum* and thus the reinstatement of *Super cathedram*. Furthermore, John did not limit his activities to the university world, but even managed to convince a local synod to return officially to the rules laid out in *Super cathedram*. Unsurprisingly, John's activities stirred both Franciscans and Dominicans into action: they fiercely attacked the secular party, and especially John of Pouilly, for several years to come.[19]

The criticism levelled by John against the mendicants became so extreme that in 1318 he was finally summoned to appear at the papal court in Avignon before Pope John XXII. The trial lasted for three years and ended with his condemnation on 24 June 1321, when three of his propositions regarding confession were condemned in the bull *Vas electionis*.[20] The condemned propositions were: first, that those who have confessed to friars with a licence to hear confession have to re-confess their sins to their own priest; second, that while *Omnis utriusque sexus* is in force, neither the pope nor, for that matter, God can decide that parishioners do not have to confess to their own priests, that is their parish priests, once a year; third, neither the pope nor God can assign power to hear confession, so that somebody who has confessed to someone with a licence to hear confession has to re-confess to their parish priest.[21] After his condemnation in 1321, a remorseful John

[19] Dunbabin, *Hound of God*, pp. 58–9; Koch, 'Prozeß gegen den Magister Johannes de Polliaco', p. 389. The main protagonist on the Dominican side and John of Pouilly's main opponent was the Paris master Peter de Palude (Dunbabin, *Hound of God*, p. 59). For a study of the controversy between John of Pouilly and the Dominican Peter de Palude on the topic, see J. G. Sikes, 'John de Pouilli and Peter de la Palu', *Eng. Hist. Rev.*, xlix (1934), 219–40.

[20] R. Zeyen, *Die theologische Disputation des Johannes de Polliaco zur kirchlichen Verfassung* (Frankfurt am Main, 1976), p. 33.

[21] The text of the bull is published in *Chartularium universitatis Parisiensis*, ed. H. Denifle and E. Chatelain (4 vols, Paris, 1889–99), ii. 243–4 (#798): 'Primo: Confessi fratribus habentibus licentiam generalem audiendi confessiones tenentur eadem peccata que confessi fuerant iterum confiteri proprio sacerdoti. Secundo, quod stante statuto Omnis utriusque sexus, edito in Concilio generali Romano, pontifex non potest facere quod parrochiani non teneantur confiteri omnia peccata sua semel in anno proprio sacerdoti quem dicit esse parrochialem curatum, immo nec Deus posset hoc facere, quia, ut dicebat, implicat contradictionem. Tertio, quod papa non potest dare generalem potestatem audiendi confessiones, immo nec Deus quin confessus habenti generalem licentiam teneatur eadem iterum confiteri suo proprio sacerdoti, quem dicit esse, ut premittitur, parrochialem curatum'. Koch pointed out that the three condemned propositions were taken from John of Pouilly's *Responsiones* (Koch, 'Prozeß gegen den Magister Johannes de Polliaco', p. 409). For the uncertainty about the legal situation after the issuing of *Vas electionis*, see K. Walsh, 'Archbishop Fitzralph and the friars at the papal court in Avignon, 1357–60', *Traditio*, xxxi (1975), 223–45, at p. 236.

of Pouilly recanted his views in a lecture hall before 300 people.[22] Andrew Larsen has argued that despite this public revocation, John's ideas remained popular among those who opposed the mendicants.[23] Yet the memory of his condemnation was also kept alive by the mendicants themselves: even the title of Holcot's *quaestio* echoes in large part the first proposition condemned in *Vas electionis*.

Ten years after the condemnation, Holcot drew on John of Pouilly's defeat to support his order's institutional standpoint. As a Dominican, Holcot gloated over the secular cleric's failure to curtail the role of the friars in hearing confession.[24] In his account of the proceedings against John, Holcot claims that the secular master had presented his teachings before the pope and cardinals with the explicit request that they be judged.[25] According to Holcot, John, who had strongly opposed any encroachment upon what he saw as the parish priests' prerogatives with regard to hearing confession, had thus had the audacity to approach the pope himself, but had rightly been put in his place by the papal court. John of Pouilly's alleged request to be judged, however, seems to have been an invention by Holcot, as there is no evidence for this boldness in *Vas electionis*.[26] In all likelihood, then, Holcot embellished the story to make his case even more strongly, by ridiculing what he perceived to be the absurdity of John's position.

Holcot summarizes the papal decision propagated in *Vas electionis*: the pope, he writes, had decreed that the very opposite of John's condemned propositions was true; namely first, that nobody had to confess to his parish priest if they had confessed to a friar who held a licence to hear confession; second, that even with *Omnis utriusque sexus* in force, the pope can decree that annual confession to one's priest is not obligatory; and, third, that the pope can assign general licences to hear confessions and that those who

[22] Zeyen, *Theologische Disputation*, p. 33.

[23] A. E. Larsen, *The School of Heretics: Academic Condemnation at the University of Oxford, 1277–1409* (Education and Society in the Middle Ages and Renaissance, xl, Leiden, 2011), p. 95.

[24] Holcot quotes the condemned propositions from *Vas electionis*: 'Unum sciendum est quod anno domini MCCCXXVI [*sic*] magister quidam Parisiensis dictus Johannes de Poliaco sacre theologie professor errores tres qui subscribuntur et docuit et tenuit in scolis sicut in sacra institutione domini Johannis XXII que sic incipit "Vas electionis et cetera" etiam plenius continetur' (Holcot, *Super quattuor libros Sententiarum questiones*, sig. n iiii[r]).

[25] 'Hic tamen magister licet predictos articulos defendisset et publice docuisset et sic posse defendere diceret, quando apparuit coram papa et cardinalibus, asseruit se velle in premissis quod sedes apostolica diffiniret. Unde multis sibi disputationibus assignatis tam in consistorio quam seorsum illos articulos publice reuocauit dicens rationibus factis in contrarium se respondere non scire' (Holcot, *Super quattuor libros Sententiarum questiones*, sig. n iv[r]).

[26] Nor is it mentioned by scholars who have written about the trial, such as Koch.

have confessed to someone with such a licence do not need to re-confess to their parish priest.[27] All these decisions by John XXII were, of course, very much in favour of the mendicants, strengthening their role within the Church. By referring to the case of John of Pouilly and the resulting papal decision, Holcot makes it clear that the view that licensed mendicants could be fully acceptable confessors was not just correct, but had also only recently been confirmed by the (current) pope, hence putting this position beyond question.[28] He rebuts John of Pouilly's standpoint that the parish priests' right to hear confessions comes directly from God rather than from the papacy. A prerogative, Holcot notes, can only be taken away if it existed in the first place. In this instance, however, parish priests had held no prerogative. Also, higher-ranking prelates can commission others to provide the cure of souls for the believers under their jurisdiction. For instance, if the pope sends a legate who represents him to England, this legate should rank above parish priests as he is sent by the pope himself – who, after all, is the *proprius sacerdos* of all Christianity. Consequently, certain *proprii sacerdotes*, for instance the pope and bishops, can rightfully pass this status on to others.[29] The argument that not exclusively parish priests, but also priests further up in the hierarchy were *proprii sacerdotes* is crucial and goes back to a time before Holcot. It denies ultimate power and control to the parish priests and reassigns it to persons such as bishops, who hold the authority to delegate the right to hear confessions to other

[27] 'Nam in constitutione papa determinauit quod iste tres propositiones sunt vere. Primo quod nullus confessus fratribus habentibus generalem licentiam audiendi confessionem tenetur iterum eadem pecccata confiteri proprio sacerdoti plus quam si alias fuisset sacerdoti proprio eadem peccata confessus teneretur iterum. Secundo quod stante constitutione Omnis Utriusque Sexus et cetera Romanus pontifex potest facere quod parochianus non tenetur omnia sua peccata semel in anno confiteri proprio sacerdoti. Tertio quod papa potest dare generalem licentiam audiendi confessionem et quod confessus habenti huiusmodi licentiam non tenetur eadem peccata confiteri proprio sacerdoti' (Holcot, *Super quattuor libros Sententiarum questiones*, sig. n iv^{r}).

[28] John XXII died in Dec. 1334, so after Holcot had finished his lectures on the *Sentences*. References to John XXII in this section of his commentary give no indication that he is deceased, so Holcot may well not have updated this part of the text during his regency a few years later.

[29] 'Dicunt doctores quod sibi non sit preiudicium quia nunquam sit preiudicium alicui nisi ei substrahantur quod sibi est in favore, indultum sed potestas iurisdictionis non est curato indulta in favore persone sed in utilitatem plebis et honorem Dei. Et ideo si superioribus prelatis videtur expedire ad salutem plebis et honorem Dei possunt post modum committere aliis a prelatis inferioribus iurisdictionem in subditos eorum et sine preiudicio eorundem, ut si papa faceret unum simplicem sacerdotem legatum in Anglia in nullo preiudicaret episcopis nec inferioribus prelatis' (Holcot, *Super quattuor libros Sententiarum questiones*, sig. n v^{r}). For more on the status of *proprius sacerdos*, see below.

priests and thus to mendicants. This notion, and especially the aspect that the pope as head of the Catholic hierarchy is by office *proprius sacerdos* to all Catholics and can therefore rightfully distribute the power of absolution, came to be repeated again and again by mendicant interpreters of *Omnis utriusque sexus*.[30]

Holcot's six arguments against the narrow interpretation of the *proprius sacerdos* of *Omnis utriusque sexus* as parish priest are as follows.[31] First, such an interpretation implies that even someone who had confessed to the pope or his confessor would then still have to confess again to his parish priest, which as far as Holcot is concerned is plain silly (*fatuum*) and wrong. Second, contrary to what is claimed by John of Pouilly, there is no way the pope could possibly lose his jurisdiction over and ability to absolve others as he is the representative of Christ on earth. Third, if one wanted to confess to a priest who is not one's own priest, one's own priest, according to a later passage in *Omnis utriusque sexus*, has to give his consent. That the consent has to be granted by the parish priest, however, is not specified and thus the *proprii sacerdotes* could also be priests other than parish priests. If, however, the term *proprius sacerdos* in this passage was supposed to refer exclusively to parish priests, this would entail that only they, and thus not even the pope, could commission other priests to hear confession, which would be absurd.[32]

Fourth, Holcot insists, it is possible wantonly to misinterpret the text, which is precisely what happens if the meaning of *proprius sacerdos* is limited to 'parish priest'. If one interpreted the first three words of the canon, *Omnis utriusque sexus*, similarly narrowly, it could be argued that this decree refers exclusively to hermaphrodites,[33] which, while conceivable, would be a frivolous interpretation. Taking the literal understanding to the other extreme, the canon's opening words could be understood as referring to absolutely everybody. In this case, each and every human being, including the pope, bishops, as well as their legates, would have to confess to a lowly parish priest, which, once again, would

30 The idea goes back to the time of the Fourth Lateran Council (Sikes, 'John de Pouilli and Peter de la Palu', p. 219).

31 Holcot, *Super quattuor libros Sententiarum questiones*, sig. n iv^{rb-vb}.

32 On this point, see Slotemaker and Witt, *Robert Holcot*, p. 117.

33 W. A. Pantin noted the incident of the Dominican Richard Helmslay, who when preaching at Newcastle in 1379/1380 put forward the same over-interpretation of '*omnis utriusque sexus*' as referring to hermaphrodites as part of an attack on the secular clergy. The incident was reported to the papacy and Helmslay, who became known as *Frater Ricardus utriusque sexus*, recanted. It stands to reason that Helmslay had derived this interpretation from Holcot (W. A. Pantin, *The English Church in the Fourteenth Century* (Cambridge, 1955), pp. 164–5).

be absurd. Hence, the canon must not be interpreted literally but has to be approached with flexibility.

The fifth argument against an exclusive understanding of *proprius sacerdos* as parish priest is based on the ever-potent argument of *consuetudo* (custom). Holcot points out that it is a long-established practice that people other than parish priests hear confession: bishops appoint confessors who can absolve everyone in their diocese. Similarly, the pope appoints the head of the apostolic penitentiary for the absolution of sins. These well-established alternative confessors would, however, be irreconcilable with John of Pouilly's misguided views. The importance of *consuetudo* also crops up elsewhere in the *quaestio*. It is customary, Holcot notes, that in all kingdoms both clerics and lay people confess to those who have been commissioned with the power to absolve – that is, not just parish priests – without then confessing the same sins again. Kings, bishops and noblemen are in the habit of confessing their sins to friars minor and friars preacher who have received licence from the pope or bishops and, therefore, surely their right to hear confessions must not be questioned. Finally, Holcot concludes, it is noteworthy that the wording of *Omnis utriusque sexus* explicitly speaks of the *proprius sacerdos* and not the *presbyter parochialis* (parish priest). Had the intention been to codify the necessity of confession to one's parish priest, that could have easily been achieved by simply specifying it in the canon. The fact that this was not done means there was never an intention to refer only to parish priests.

Having thus dismissed John of Pouilly's interpretation of *Omnis utriusque sexus*, Holcot then expounds what he regards as the correct interpretation of *proprius sacerdos*. To start with, the pope is by default the *proprius sacerdos* of every Catholic, just as a bishop is the *proprius sacerdos* of everybody in his diocese.[34] Consequently, annual confession to the pope or one's bishop fulfils the demand of *Omnis utriusque sexus* and does not require additional confession to a parish priest. In addition, those who receive permission to hear confession either from the pope or from a bishop, as is the case for licensed friars preacher and friars minor, also count as *proprii sacerdotes*: their commission automatically removes any status of their being *alieni* [aliens] and instead they become *communes* [common to the local community], so part of the local community, and thus *proprii sacerdotes*.[35] With this broader

[34] 'Primo modo papa est proprius sacerdos cuiuslibet catholici, et episcopus cuiuslibet catholici existentis in eius episcopatu' (Holcot, *Super quattuor libros Sententiarum questiones*, sig. n iv^{vb}).

[35] 'Illi vero qui habent commissionem a papa immediate vel ab episcopis localibus sicut modo est de fratribus predicatoribus et minoribus sunt proprii sacerdotes primo modo quia non alieni sed communes' (Holcot, *Super quattuor libros Sententiarum questiones*, sig. n iv^{vb}).

definition of *proprius sacerdos*, Holcot removes any doubt that confessing to a licensed mendicant might not satisfy canon 21 of Lateran IV.

The history of the Dominican interpretation of *Omnis utriusque sexus* remains to be written, for Robert Holcot was by no means the first Dominican to dwell at length on the question of what confessing to one's *proprius sacerdos* means. A century earlier Albert the Great, who is quoted by Holcot,[36] had addressed the same problem. In his early *De sacramentis*, probably composed before he was sent to Paris, Albert remarks that there are different routes towards becoming a *proprius sacerdos*, including by means of being granted the privilege of hearing confession.[37] Albert addressed the same problem again in his *Super Sententias*, composed at Paris between 1241 and 1245. There he discussed whether a believer has to confess to his or her own priest, or whether confession to any priest – and thus also to a priest who is not one's parish priest – is valid. In his discussion, Albert stressed the concept, later repeated by Holcot, that the pope is at the top of the Catholic hierarchy and can therefore grant the power of absolution.[38]

Changes in the Dominican approaches to and interpretations of *Omnis utriusque sexus* can already be found in these two works by Albert the Great: his later commentary on the *Sentences* is far more polemical, outspoken and detailed than his earlier *De sacramentis*. This is quite probably due to the radical change in intellectual sphere which came with his move from Germany to Paris. In his later work he attacks the alleged failings of secular clergymen, pointing out that many parish priests know nothing or next to nothing about the cure of souls, while others are so rotten that they

[36] See, e.g., Holcot, *Super quattuor libros Sententiarum questiones*, sig. n v^{va}: 'Albertus distinguit de proprio sacerdote id est presbytero parochiali quia vel est pastor sicut rector perpetuus vel vicarius vel est tantum sacerdos conductus'.

[37] Albertus Magnus, *De sacramentis*, ed. A. Ohlmeyer, in Albertus Magnus, *Opera omnia* (31 vols to date, Münster, 1951–), xxvi. 1–170, at pp. 106–7 (Tract. VI, *De paenitentia*, pars 2, q. 2, a. 15). For Albert's departure to Paris around 1240, see I. M. Resnick, 'Albert the Great: biographical introduction', in *A Companion to Albert the Great: Theology, Philosophy, and the Sciences*, ed. I. M. Resnick (Brill's Companions to the Christian Tradition, Leiden, 2013), pp. 1–11, at p. 6. For a summary of Albert's view on the sacrament of penance, see H. Lauer, *Die Moraltheologie Alberts des Großen mit besonderer Berücksichtigung ihrer Beziehungen zur Lehre des hl. Thomas* (Freiburg i. Br., 1911), pp. 308–31. C. Rigo argues that *De sacramentis* was composed between the late 1130s and 1141, while Albert was still in Germany (C. Rigo, 'Zur Redaktionsfrage der Frühschriften des Albertus Magnus', in *Albertus Magnus und die Anfänge der Aristoteles-Rezeption im lateinischen Mittelalter/Albertus Magnus and the Beginnings of the Medieval Reception of Aristotle in the Latin West*, ed. L. Honnefelder et al. (Münster, 2005), pp. 325–74, at p. 360).

[38] Albert the Great, *Commentarii in quartum librum Sententiarum (Dist. I–XXII)*, in Albertus Magnus, *Opera omnia*, ed. E. C. A. Borgnet (38 vols, Paris, 1890–9), xxix. 724 (IV.17.40). For Holcot see above.

themselves pose a threat to their flock. Others again simply cannot be bothered to hear confession or are constantly absent from their parishes. While a believer would, in these cases, still have the option of confessing to his bishop or even the pope as his own priest, these options, Albert notes, were simply not accessible to most people. Things were thus not looking bright for the average sinner's soul. Luckily, however, as Albert points out, the negligence of pastors was counterbalanced by specially appointed preachers and confessors. The populace could thus, after all, not merely confess, but confess to a worthy priest. Albert here brings into the discussion a point raised in *Omnis utriusque sexus*, namely that the sacrament of penance can be administered by another priest if the *proprius sacerdos* has given his permission.[39] These specially appointed preachers and confessors were obviously understood to be mendicants, although this is not spelt out by Albert.

Still, Albert insists that confessing to one's *proprius sacerdos* is preferable to confessing to a specially appointed priest; and that one's own priest should be the person to turn to even when a legitimate alternative would be available. Should a penitent nevertheless turn to an alternative confessor, this confessor may administer the sacrament, yet should still encourage that confession to the parish priest follow as quickly as possible. In fact, the licensed confessors should exhort the faithful to confess to their parish priests in the first place. Thus, despite all his criticism of the secular clergy, Albert regards confession to one's own priest – be it one's parish priest, one's bishop, or the pope – as preferable to confessing to a licensed mendicant. This insistence might seem odd for a mendicant, yet Albert explains his stance with the comment that this approach is necessary to uphold the order of the Church.[40] For him, confession to one's own priest constitutes the proper implementation of *Omnis utriusque sexus*. Confession to someone else, and hence to a commissioned mendicant, is only legitimate in very special circumstances and by no means to be encouraged.

This, of course, is contrary to Holcot's later standpoint, yet Holcot finds a neat solution to this apparent Dominican dilemma in John XXII's *Extravagantes*: in Holcot's opinion, the pope had advanced the view that licensed confessors should encourage the faithful to re-confess to their

[39] For this paragraph, cf. Lauer, *Die Moraltheologie Alberts des Großen*, pp. 325–6; Albertus Magnus, *Opera omnia*, ed. Borgnet, xxix. 724 (*Commentarii in quartum librum Sententiarum*, IV.17.40, 42, 44). The relevant passage from *Omnis utriusque sexus* reads: 'Si quis autem alieno sacerdoti voluerit iusta de causa sua confiteri peccata, licentiam prius postulet et obtineat a proprio sacerdote, cum aliter ille ipsum non possit absolvere vel ligare' (Tanner, *Decrees of the Ecumenical Councils*, i. 245).

[40] For this paragraph cf. Lauer, *Die Moraltheologie Alberts des Großen*, pp. 326–8.

priest, not for the sake of the validity of the sacrament but for the sake of obligation, because the sinner had confessed to somebody to whom he was not bound.[41] Re-confession to one's parish priest was thus not a matter of salvation, but more a question of appropriate behaviour.

The other Dominican quoted by Holcot is, unsurprisingly, Thomas Aquinas. Thomas, whose writings became official Dominican teaching not long after his death in 1274, started his lectures on the *Sentences* at Paris in September 1252.[42] In his commentary on the Lombard's work, Aquinas concludes that for the sacrament of penance it is essential that the priest serving as confessor hold jurisdiction over the believer. Whether one's own priest is a suitable confessor is not up to the believer to decide. Instead, this decision lies with the superior prelate.[43] By definition, every parishioner has more than one *proprius sacerdos*: his parish priest, his bishop and the pope, all of whom may rightfully commission additional confessors for the faithful under their jurisdiction. Those commissioned by the bishop or the pope rank higher in the hierarchy than the parish priest. While it is sufficient to confess to someone who has been commissioned as a confessor, Aquinas, like Albert and unlike Holcot, nevertheless advises that the penitent should re-confess to his own priest and that his confessor should urge him to do so. Still, even if the penitent refuses to do so, he should be absolved from his sins.[44] Thus, while Aquinas regards commissioned confessors, who included commissioned mendicants, as suitable, he nevertheless insists on the importance of confession to one's *proprius sacerdos* – be it the parish priest, the local bishop or the pope – even though re-confession was not necessary for salvation.

Holcot repeats Aquinas's conclusion that any commissioned priest, by power of his rank, can absolve from sin.[45] Aquinas had also raised another

[41] 'Sed contra predicta videntur esse quedam que ponit Iohannes monachus [i.e., John XXII] … Movet dubitationem an confessus fratri teneatur confiteri iterum proprio sacerdoti, et respondet innuitive quod sic. Hoc tamen "non est ex necessitate sacramenti sed ex obligatione" tantummodo. Loquitur in secunda persona ad confirmationem, "qui voluntarie ad fratrem accessisti", et vult dicere quod licet talis parochianus confessus fuerit fratri, tamen non liberatur a dicta constitutione *Omnis utriusque sexus*, quia "relicto patre spirituali cui fuit astrictus" voluntarie ivit ad illum cui non fuit astrictus. Et ad hanc conclusionem quod scilicet confessus fratri remitti debeat ad curatum et similiter iterato confiteri arguit multipliciter' (Holcot, *Super quattuor libros Sententiarum questiones*, sig. n v^{va}).

[42] J.-P. Torrell, *Saint Thomas Aquinas*, trans. R. Royal, i. *The Person and His Work* (rev. edn, Washington, D.C., 2005), p. 37.

[43] Thomas Aquinas, *Scriptum super Sententiis*, IV.17.3.3.4 <http://www.corpusthomisticum.org/snp4016.html> [accessed 20 July 2018].

[44] Aquinas, *Scriptum super Sententiis*, IV.17.3.3.5.

[45] 'Hic dicit [*sc.* Thomas] duas conclusiones. Prima est quod quilibet sacerdos potestate

point adopted by Holcot: namely, that certain people, such as bishops, do not have a *proprius sacerdos* to whom to confess. In this matter Holcot gives an even broader definition than Aquinas by arguing that the meaning of *proprius sacerdos* must be expanded to include other legitimate confessors, such as licensed mendicants, penitentiaries and legates.[46]

Judging from the three examples of Albertus Magnus, Thomas Aquinas and Robert Holcot, the Dominican interpretation of *proprius sacerdos* in *Omnis utriusque sexus* underwent considerable change in the course of one century. It shifted to an increasingly wide understanding of the phrase, comprising a range of possible confessors; and re-confession to one's parish priest, while initially encouraged, was no longer regarded as necessary by Holcot. Similarly, the references to friars, both implicit and explicit, increase significantly. Initially, Albert does not mention friars explicitly in this context and even covert references are rare, even though he must, of course, have had the position of mendicants in mind in his discussion. This lack of explicit comment may well be due to the fact that Albert first commented on the *Sentences* in Germany around 1240, before the well-known secular-mendicant clashes and before the friars were widely regarded as serious competition by parish priests. Holcot, on the other hand, refers to mendicants explicitly and repeatedly.

Certainly, by the time Holcot was writing circumstances had changed considerably from the situation faced by Albert when he composed *De sacramentis*, when there was apparently neither strong competition nor serious conflict regarding the hearing of confession; and even from the more inflamed situation Aquinas encountered at Paris when he gave his lectures on the *Sentences*. Yet neither Albert nor Aquinas was as polemical and outspoken about the role of licensed mendicants as confessors as Holcot was to be less than a century later.

The reception and interpretation of *Omnis utriusque sexus* and the subsequent history of confession are still in need of further exploration. It is, of course, not possible to make valid pronouncements about intellectual developments and traditions on the basis of just three Dominican

ordinis regulariter potest a quolibet peccato absolvere. Secunda est quod licet omnis sacerdos habeat potestatem ordinis non tamen habet potestatem iurisdictionis exercitii nisi in subditos' (Holcot, *Super quattuor libros Sententiarum questiones*, sig. n v^vb^).

46 'Sic ergo videtur dicendum quod quicunque subditus presbytero parochiali potest licite confiteri istis subscriptis: Domino pape in quo est plenitudo iurisdictionis in omnes catholicos; eius penitentiario generali; item eius penitentiariis generalibus; item episcopo dyocesano; item cuilibet habenti commissionem a sedem apostolicam vel a dyocesano vel a presbytero quia quilibet istorum potest dare licentiam super subditos parochialis presbyteri, videlicet papa, episcopus, et curatus' (Holcot, *Super quattuor libros Sententiarum questiones*, sig. n v^ra^).

commentators on the *Sentences*. Whether the view of any of the three authors can be regarded as representative for their order as a whole in their respective eras can, for now, only be speculated. It is worth noting, however, that the Franciscans seemed considerably less preoccupied with the interpretational intricacies of *Omnis utriusque sexus*. Bonaventure discusses the question of whether believers may confess to somebody more discreet than their own priest and whether they then still have to confess to their own priest. William of Ockham, however, whose works Holcot knew, did not devote a *quaestio* to this matter in his commentary on the *Sentences*.[47] Similarly, the subject is not raised in the commentary on the *Sentences* by the Franciscan Walter Chatton, written sometime between 1321 and 1323 (that is, just at the time of John of Pouilly's condemnation in *Vas electionis*).[48] This, too, is a tiny sample, so it might turn out that Franciscans devoted just as much attention to the question as Dominicans. However, on first inspection it would seem that the topic of confession, in particular with regard to the role of mendicants and the question of the correct interpretation of *Omnis utriusque sexus*, was more of a concern to Dominicans than to Franciscans.

When Holcot was writing in the early 1330s, the question of the legitimacy of mendicant confessors had seemingly been put to rest over a decade earlier. Yet if it had been resolved by the papacy and was at that time no longer a hot topic, why did he lecture his students on this subject for so long and with so much verve and detail? Holcot's account, at times polemical and even melodramatic, may have been influenced by, or even had its origin in, particular sets of circumstances. The most likely cause for his involvement with the issue is that papal legislation on the topic had been constantly changing since the mid thirteenth century, almost from one pope to the next. The Dominicans must thus have been well aware that the situation as it was under John XXII would not necessarily remain unchanged. In fact, the numerous bulls issued and controversies conducted on the topic in the course of the previous decades strongly suggested the matter was not permanently settled. By issuing a strong argument for the legitimacy of licensed mendicant confessors, Holcot defends his order's necessity and legitimacy. Additionally, Holcot's interest in the question may be hinting at a problem or dispute specific to England, or even more locally to the

[47] Bonaventure, *Opera omnia* (10 vols, Ad Claras Aquas, 1882–1902), iv. 452–55 (*Commentaria in quatuor libros Sententiarum*, IV.17.3.1.2: 'Utrum contra voluntatem proprii sacerdotis liceat poenitenti confiteri alii discretiori, an teneatur confiteri proprio sacerdoti'); William of Ockham, *Quaestiones et decisiones in IV libros Sententiarum, cum centilogio theologico* (Lyons, 1495).

[48] W. Chatton, *Reportatio super Sententias*, ed. J. C. Wey and G. J. Etzkorn (4 vols, Toronto, 2002–5).

Lincoln diocese or Oxford, concerning the validity of licensed mendicants as confessors. Slotemaker and Witt have shown that the question of who makes an acceptable confessor in England was relevant well past the middle of the fourteenth century; the registers of John Grandisson (bishop of Exeter, d. 1369) record numerous clashes with unlicensed mendicant confessors.[49] It has, however, not proved possible to find any traces of debate or controversy with regard to licensed mendicant confessors.[50]

What promised to be another potential explanation similarly turned out to be a dead-end. At the same time as Holcot was lecturing on the *Sentences*, another important theologian-in-the-making was teaching at Oxford: Richard FitzRalph, famous for his hostile attacks on the mendicants in the 1350s, was regent master in theology in 1331/32,[51] exactly the same period as Holcot's lectures on the *Sentences*. Yet while his later clashes with the mendicants are well known, his anti-mendicant streak cannot be traced back to the 1330s. In fact, FitzRalph was rather well-disposed towards the mendicants earlier in his life.[52]

It appears we must conclude, then, that the discussion, or rather the fierce defence, of the legitimacy of licensed mendicants as confessors within the Church was an intra-institutional topic especially close to the heart of the Dominican order, the urgency of which was driven by the fear and suspicion that, through pressure by seculars, papal legislation could change

[49] Slotemaker and Witt, *Robert Holcot*, p. 115. While these clashes were not about mendicants with a licence to hear confession, which according to Holcot would make them *proprii sacerdotes*, but about unlicensed mendicants, they nevertheless illustrate the ongoing concerns surrounding the topic of confession. Slotemaker and Witt pointed out that in the next question debated in his *Sentences* commentary, Holcot insisted on the necessity of commission for mendicants. In his view, unlicensed mendicants did not count as *proprii sacerdotes* (*Robert Holcot*, p. 116).

[50] Several Dominicans received licence to hear confession in the Lincoln diocese in the decade preceding the composition of Holcot's commentary on the *Sentences*: on 10 July 1321 Simon de London was granted licence to hear confession; on 27 Feb. 1332 Richard de Farle was licensed to hear confession in the archdeaconry of Oxford; in 1332 Holcot himself received licence to hear confession in the diocese of Lincoln. A few years later, on 5 March 1337, Philip Lavenham was licensed to hear confession in Bedford and Buckingham.

[51] K. Walsh, *A Fourteenth-Century Scholar and Primate: Richard FitzRalph in Oxford, Avignon and Armagh* (Oxford, 1981), p. 36. For a brief summary of FitzRalph's engagement with mendicants in the 1350s, see Larsen, *School of Heretics*, pp. 96–8.

[52] Walsh has pointed out that Holcot engages intensively with FitzRalph's commentary on the *Sentences* (*A Fourteenth-Century Scholar*, p. 37). Yet, in all likelihood it did not contribute to Holcot's discussion of *Omnis utriusque sexus*: FitzRalph devoted only one or perhaps two questions to bk. IV; the surviving question deals with the eucharist (M. W. Dunne, 'Accidents without a subject: Richard FitzRalph's question on the eucharist from his Lectura on the Sentences', in *Richard FitzRalph. His Life, Times and Thought*, ed. M. W. Dunne and S. Nolan (Dublin, 2013), pp. 11–29, at p. 11).

once again to the detriment of the mendicants. It may have been for this reason that Holcot expounded on the subject in detail in his lectures on the *Sentences*.[53]

Joseph Goering has argued that the most important development for the history of penitential thought in the later middle ages was the creation of schools and universities.[54] Goering also insists that 'it would be a mistake … to think of these scholastic jurists and theologians as being primarily concerned with settling arguments about dogma or with determining fine points of doctrine'. Instead, he emphasizes their role as teachers who introduced their students to the tradition of theology they represented.[55] From a twenty-first century perspective, it is easy to lose sight of this original function of many medieval commentaries. Holcot's text originated in the classroom and was primarily intended to teach the next generation of theologians, not just Dominicans but other mendicants and seculars, too. Like many medieval theologians, he frequently wove references and discussions of contemporary events into his commentaries.[56] In the case discussed in this chapter he took the opportunity not just to provide mendicant students with concrete arguments which defended the role of licensed mendicants as valid confessors, but also to expose secular students to the Dominican reasoning concerning this topic.

While Holcot's commentary on the *Sentences* may have been of far less importance than his biblical commentaries,[57] it nevertheless contains strong, well-argued views which he sought to impart to his students as well as his readers.[58] The vast problems arising from *Omnis utriusque sexus* in

[53] This is confirmed by Holcot himself: 'Sacrosancta romana ecclesia ius et auctoritatem canonibus impartitur sed non eis alligatur' (*Super quattuor libros Sententiarum questiones*, sig. n vi[ra]).

[54] J. Goering, 'The scholastic turn (1100–1500): penitential theology and law in the schools', in *A New History of Penance*, ed. A. Firey (Brill's Companions to the Christian Tradition, xiv, Leiden, 2008), pp. 219–37, at p. 219.

[55] Goering, 'The scholastic turn', p. 219.

[56] E.g., in his commentary on Wisdom, Holcot comments on the controversy on the Beatific Vision under John XXII; and in his commentary on Amos he ridicules the Carmelites and Austin Friars (Smalley, 'Robert Holcot', pp. 19–20 and 85–7).

[57] See Walsh, *A Fourteenth-Century Scholar*, p. 35; for a critical view of Holcot's commentary on the *Sentences*, see A. Maier, 'Diskussionen über das aktuell Unendliche in der ersten Hälfte des 14. Jahrhunderts', in A. Maier, *Ausgehendes Mittelalter. Gesammelte Aufsätze zur Geistesgeschichte des 14. Jahrhunderts* (3 vols, Rome, 1964–77), i. 41–86, at pp. 81–2.

[58] In addition, Holcot refers frequently to aspects of canon law rather than questions concerning strictly theology, which reflect the more practical bent to his work. This tendency supports Goering's view that there was a close co-operation between the two faculties of law and theology throughout the middle ages (Goering, 'The scholastic turn', pp. 228–9).

intellectual circles were due to a phrase, *proprio sacerdoti*, which proved to be open to numerous interpretations.[59] To defend the friars' position, and to influence his audience, Holcot used the institutional and intellectual framework provided by the Dominican order and its connection to the university of Oxford. He exploited his lectures on the *Sentences*, which were compulsory for anyone pursuing a degree in theology, to disseminate distinctly Dominican ideas to a wider audience, composed not just of friars preacher or mendicants.[60] In the schools, he thus disseminated his order's viewpoints on an issue which was relevant to the entire Church and of great importance to the friars preacher. Holcot did so with a decidedly pro-mendicant bent, thereby spreading his order's position beyond its institutional borders. As an individual thinker and theologian, he thus instrumentalized his affiliation with one institution – namely the university – to uphold and propagate the privileges of another institution – that is, the Dominican order.

[59] See also Dunbabin, *Hound of God*, p. 57.

[60] For the popularity of the mendicant schools, see I. W. Frank, *Hausstudium und Universitätsstudium der Wiener Dominikaner bis 1500* (Archiv für österreichische Geschichte, cxxvii, Vienna, 1968), p. 57, where he quotes Roger Bacon, *Compendium studii philosophie*, in Roger Bacon, *Opera quaedam hactenus inedita*, i, ed. J. S. Brewer (London, 1859), p. 428.

11. The cult of the marriage of Joseph and Mary: the shaping of doctrinal novelty in Jean Gerson's *Josephina* (1414–17)

Isabel Iribarren

On 8 September 1416 Jean Gerson, then chancellor of Paris university, preached a sermon at the Council of Constance for the feast of the nativity of Mary, with the main objective of promoting the cult of her marriage with Joseph. Gerson was well aware of the undesirability of multiplying feast days – a subject of debate during the council – but insisted on the relevance of his proposition on ecclesiological grounds: 'Why promote another feast? So that, through the merits of Mary and the intercession of the great and commanding influence of Joseph on his spouse, from whom Jesus the Christ is born, the Church be brought back to her unique and truthful spouse, the Supreme Pontiff, vicar of Christ'.[1] However, the novelty was not only liturgical: it was also doctrinal. Intent as he was on inciting popular devotion to St Joseph, Gerson advanced a series of doctrinal statements which would not earn a favourable reaction from the conciliar assembly. Indeed, the latter represented the very 'institution' the chancellor's statements could seem to threaten: an established doctrinal tradition, as well as a set of existing liturgical practices which the Church promoted as normative and considered necessary for social order. Seeking to optimize the acceptability

[1] 'apud ecclesiasticos et de ecclesiasticis talia loquimur dum de celebritate virginalis conjugii Joseph cum Maria vel de ipsius felici transitu fieri solemnitatem exoptamus. Ad quid ita? Sane quatenus meritis, et intercessione tanti tamque potentis et imperiosi quodammodo patroni apud sponsam suam, de qua natus est Jesus qui vocatur Christus, reddatur Ecclesia unico viro vero et certo, Summo Pontifici sponso suo vice Christi' (J. Gerson, 'Jacob autem genuit', in *Oeuvres complètes de Jean Gerson*, ed. P. Glorieux (10 vols, Paris, 1960–73), v. 344–62, at pp. 362, 365). The sermon is articulated around four subjects: 'Collegamus tamen ex his principiis laudes utriusque, Joseph scilicet et Mariae … et hoc sub quadruplici consideratione fiat. Agetur in prima de nobilitatis origine Mariae et Joseph; agetur in altera de sanctificatione utriusque; agetur in tertia de fomitis repressione in utroque; agetur in quarta de multiplici nativitate Christi respectu Joseph et Mariae' (v. 345). All translations are the author's own unless otherwise stated.

I. Iribarren, 'The cult of the marriage of Joseph and Mary: the shaping of doctrinal novelty in Jean Gerson's *Josephina* (1414–17)', in *Individuals and Institutions in Medieval Scholasticism*, ed. A. Fitzpatrick and J. Sabapathy (London, 2020), pp. 253–68.

of his position, in the sermon Gerson adopts a threefold strategy, which is examined in what follows: he claims affinities with established doctrinal tradition; grafts the new cult onto existing liturgical practices; and argues for the possibility of a historical development of doctrinal truths which allows for the introduction of probabilistic arguments. All three approaches are finely intertwined in the *Josephina*, an epic poem of some 3,000 Latin hexameters composed by the chancellor between 1414 and 1417 during the Council of Constance.[2] This poem constitutes a prime example of how an individual's intellectual project sought to earn acceptability through the instrumentalization of an established tradition and its doctrinal patrimony.

Before examining the relevant passages of the *Josephina*, let us dwell a little longer on the Constance sermon cited above, since it brings out the institutional setting in which the poem was composed. Deliberating on the privileges of Joseph and Mary, the chancellor raises the question of their royal lineage as descendants of the house of David. The question itself was not surprising. The evangelical text presents such genealogical records (Matthew I: 1–16; Luke III: 23–38) as a way to establish Jesus' noble descent.[3] Citing the opinion of Richard FitzRalph, however, Gerson raises the specific issue of royal succession through the female line in a way which seems to justify English claims to the French crown:

> A rather recent doctor, the archbishop of Armagh [Richard FitzRalph], had inquired [in *De pauperitate Salvatoris* (1350–8)] on the nobility of Joseph and Mary, asking whether it came from David by rightful genealogical law, such that Mary and Joseph themselves should be exalted as lawfully belonging by hereditary line to the temporal kingdom of David. And [he also asked] whether Jesus, the blessed fruit of Mary's womb, should rightfully occupy David's royal seat and throne as a temporal king and particularly of the Jews. Whereby he consequently asked whether a female, considered as unsuitable, as regard to males, for the rightful inheritance of royal succession, should be regarded as befitting kingship according to divine law, invariably and imprescriptibly. This

[2] For a critical edition of the poem with a French translation, see *Josephina. L'épopée de saint Joseph*, ed. G. Matteo Roccati, trans. with introduction, notes and comments by I. Iribarren (2 vols, Paris, 2019). This chapter will refer to this edition.

[3] See also the commentaries on these verses by Bernard of Clairvaux, *Homiliae super 'Missus est' (In laudibus Virginis Matris)*, hom. 2, 16, in *Sancti Bernardi opera* (8 vols, Rome, 1957–77), iv. ed. J. Leclercq and H.-M. Rochais (Rome, 1966), p. 33, col. 70B; Thomas Aquinas, *Summa theologiae Tertia pars*, ed. P. Caramello (Turin, 1962), iii, q. 28, a. 1, ad 2; q. 31, a. 2, ad 1; Matthew of Acquasparta, *De Annuntiat. B.V.M.*, in *Matthaei ab Aquasparta, Sermones de B.M. Virgine*, ed. C. Piana (Quaracchi, 1962), p. 52 (sermon 1); Peter John Olivi, *Lectura super Mattheum*, MS. Vat. lat. 1001, fo. 8c–d (ch. 1, quaestio praeliminaris), cited by A. Emmen, 'Pierre de Jean Olivi, sa doctrine et son influence', *Cahiers de Joséphologie*, xiv (1966), 209–70, at p. 251.

caused a rather significant dispute between the two most renowned Christian kingdoms, France and England, creating and fostering controversy.[4]

In September 1416, as he was preaching his sermon, Gerson seemed to underestimate the impact such statements would have at a politically delicate time: French defeat at Agincourt was still fresh in people's minds and civil war raged in the royal capital. The question of St Joseph's promotion was thereby precipitated into the centre of the Anglo-French conflict. Pre-empting probable critics, Gerson hastened to add that the royalty in question was not a temporal, but a spiritual one. Indeed, Joseph and Mary's nobility lay in their moral qualities and religious piety.[5] By preaching the magnanimity of the holy couple, the chancellor was hoping to encourage its imitation by the Parisian aristocracy at a time of internecine war. From this perspective he had, a few years earlier in November 1413, addressed a letter to Jean de Berry, uncle of Charles VI, seeking the duke's support for the instauration of a solemn feast in honour of the marriage of Joseph

[4] 'Et an Jesus benedictus fructus ventris Mariae fuerit jure ponendus super sedem David et thronum ejus tamquam rex temporalis et specialis Judaeorum. Unde consequenter inquiritur ab aliquis si mulieri sexui, deficiente masculino apud reges jus successionis ad regnum debeat etiam jure divino et invariabili vel imprescriptibili competere. Quae disceptatio non parvam inter duo regna christianorum clarissima, Franciae et Anglia, vel fecit vel fovit controversiam, sicut ex opusculis hinc inde confectis sciri potest; quorum sententias omittere decrevimus pro praesenti' (Gerson, *Jacob autem genuit*, v. 347). The chancellor was only repeating here what he had already stated in a previous treatise, *Considérations sur saint Joseph*, written in middle French around 1414 (*Oeuvres complètes*, vii, pt. 1, pp. 69–72, at p. 70). In his translation, with commentary, of Aristotle's *Politics*, Nicole Oresme advanced the same argument, according to which it is illegitimate to invoke the genealogy of Jesus to justify the transmission of royalty through the female line, since His kingdom is not of this world (N. Oresme, *Le livre de Politiques d'Aristote. Published from the Text of the Avranches Manuscript 223. With a Critical Introduction and Notes by Albert Douglas Menut* (Philadelphia, Pa., 1970), p. 156. I wish to thank Serge Lusignan for bringing this source to my attention.

[5] Gerson, *Considérations sur saint Joseph*, pp. 70–7; also *Oeuvres complètes*, ix. 479, § 12 (*De nobilitate*): 'Nobilitas humana respiciens principaliter animam vel hominem ut homo est, magis attenditur a philosophis juxta illud: nobilitas sola est animum quae moribus ornat'. Cf. Ludolph of Saxony: 'nihil de nostris vilitatibus erubescens; per ita proculdubio docens ut nos quoque nunquam de vitiis erubescamus parentum, sed unum illud queramus semper nobilitari propriarum honore virtutum. Non est omnino, non est nec de virtute nec de vitio parentum, aut laudandus aliquis aut culpandus; nemo inde vere aut obscurus, aut clarus est. Immo ut considerantius aliquid dicamus nescio quo magis ille respondet, qui ex parentibus a virtute prorsus alienus existens, ipse tamen fuerit de virtute mirabilis; nullus igitur in superbiam de gloria elevetur parentum, sed considerans progenitores Domini omnem evacuet et comprimat mentis tumorem et de solis virtutibus glorietur' (Ludolphe Le Chartreux, *Vita Jesu Christi ex Evangelio et approbatis ab ecclesia* ..., ed. L.-M. Rigollot (4 vols, Paris, 1870), i. 69).

and Mary. Of Orleanist allegiance like Gerson, the duke of Berry had also endured Burgundian violence during the Cabochien revolt in the aftermath of Louis of Orléans's murder in 1407 by agents of John the Fearless. In his letter the chancellor claims that the fall of the Cabochiens was due to a miracle worked by St Joseph, whom he had promoted to the status of protector of the city of Paris alongside St Geneviève and St Denis in an earlier speech addressed to the king.[6] A symbol of the union of God and his Church, the cult of the virginal marriage of Joseph and Mary was also intended to promote peace and unity within the kingdom.[7]

Gerson's letter to Jean de Berry is not an isolated example. From a series of other letters written around the same period we know he committed himself thereafter to the double task of instituting a solemn feast in honour of the marriage of Joseph and Mary and of employing – in vain – his oratorial talents to condemn Jean Petit's justification of tyrannicide and reopen the case against the duke of Burgundy.[8] Not surprisingly, the Burgundian faction present at Constance looked for an opportunity to discredit the chancellor. Retaliations came without delay. A record (*schedula*) based on notes taken during Gerson's sermon on behalf of Martin Porée, bishop of Arras and principal ambassador to John the Fearless, accused the chancellor of justifying royal succession through the female line in order to attract English favour.[9] Other doctrinal blunders incriminating Gerson included the claim that Joseph, like John the Baptist, had been sanctified *in utero*. The chancellor was well aware of the unprecedented nature of such statements, as the sermon's initial *caveat* testifies:

[6] See Gerson, *Rex in sempiternum vive!* (4 Sept. 1413), in *Oeuvres complètes*, vii, pt. 2. pp. 1005–30.

[7] Gerson, letter to the duke of Berry, 23 Nov. 1413, in *Oeuvres complètes*, ii. 155–7. See M. Lieberman, 'La lettre de Gerson au duc de Berry', *Cahiers de Joséphologie*, ix (1961), 199–265. For Joseph as protector of the city, see *Rex in sempiternum vive!*, p. 1030. For other documents testifying to Gerson's efforts to promote the new cult, see the letter to the universal Church ('Office pour la fête de saint Joseph') of Aug. 1413, in *Oeuvres complètes*, vii, pt. 1, pp. 55–60; and *Bonne exhortation generale pour la feste de la Desponsacion de Nostre Dame* (26 Sept. 1413), in *Oeuvres complètes*, vii, pt.1, pp. 11–15.

[8] E.g., *Veniat pax* (1408), in *Oeuvres complètes*, vii, pt. 2, pp. 1100–23. In his *Tractatus de nuptiis Christi et Ecclesiae (Nuptiae factae sunt)*, of 17–27 Jan. 1417 Gerson establishes a significant parallel between the errors of Jan Hus, harmful to clerics, and those of Jean Petit, harmful to secular princes (*Oeuvres complètes*, vi. 190–210, at pp. 208–10).

[9] Martin Porée's *schedula* is published in *Ioannis Gersonii opera omnia, novo ordine digesta, et in V. tomos distribute*, ed. E. du Pin (Anvers, 1706), v. 663B–D. Note, however, that in Oct. 1416, at Calais, John the Fearless recognized Henry V as legitimate heir to the crown of France. It was only in April 1417 that the incriminating *schedula* against Gerson was made public!

> In what follows, I shall imitate the method of the holy doctors who have said many things about the saints and the holy persons in order to incite devotion among the good souls. We are led to believe these things on the grounds of probable or conjectural reasoning, without thereby being obliged to accept them as necessary by faith. That is how I would like my statements to be understood: not that things happened *de facto* the way I pretend they did, but as we can piously believe that they could have happened, without temerity or prejudice towards other opinions.[10]

The choice of terms used in this programmatic passage will be commented on later. Other arguments advanced by Gerson to mitigate the effects of his doctrinal statements appeal to their ancestry: the idea that Joseph had been sanctified *in utero* appears already in an *officio Jerosolymitano*, a liturgical office probably in use among Carmelites in the thirteenth century.[11] He adds that such a belief is desirable on devotional grounds, for it encourages hope and devotion among parents of unborn children – even if 'it has not been confirmed by any revelation' and cannot be directly deduced from the scriptures. More revealingly, Gerson makes a doctrinal link between Mary's privileges through her immaculate conception and the spiritual promotion of her husband.[12] Indeed, the cult of their virginal marriage, which he was so

[10] 'Erit autem deductio nostra imitatrix sanctorum ac devotissimorum patrum qui ad commovendam piarum mentium devotionem dixerunt multa de sanctis et divinis quae et qualia, *magis ex conjecturali quadam probabilitate* quam ex fidei necessitate, tenenda sciebant. Sic eorum quae dicentur plurima volo posterius intelligi ita ut non tam quae facta sunt quam quae fieri potuisse pia quadam religiositate credi possunt, absque ulla assertionis temeritate et sine praejudicio sententiae sanioris referantur' (Gerson, *Jacob autem genuit*, pp. 345–6) (my emphasis).

[11] On this subject, see M. Lieberman, 'Les sources jóséphologiques de Gerson et l' "Office des Carmes"', *Cahiers de Joséphologie*, x (1962), 17–57, 189–249 (with an edition of the office from the Tours MS. at pp. 198–220); 'Pierre d'Ailly, Jean Gerson et le culte de saint Joseph I–III', *Cahiers de Joséphologie*, xiii (1965), 227–72; xiv (1966), 273–314; xv (1967), 5–113; 'Chronologie Gersonienne. IV: Gerson poète', *Romania*, lxxvi (1955), 289–333; 'La lettre de Gerson au duc de Berry', *Cahiers de Joséphologie*, ix (1961), 199–265. See also I. N. Maegawa, 'La doctrine de Jean Gerson sur saint Joseph', *Cahiers de Joséphologie*, vii (1959), 181–94. For the *officio Jerosolymitano* mentioned by Gerson, see *Oeuvres complètes*, v. 349 (*Jacob autem genuit*, secunda consideratio); and the letter addressed to Dominique Petit, chanter of Chartres, on 7 Sept. 1416, in *Oeuvres complètes*, ii. 169. See also J. Dusserre, 'Les origines de la dévotion à saint Joseph', *Cahiers de Joséphologie*, i (1953), 1–60 and i.2 (1954), 61–86; B. P. McGuire, 'When Jesus did the dishes: the transformation of late medieval spirituality', in *The Making of Christian Communities in Late Antiquity and the Middle Ages*, ed. M. F. Williams (London, 2005), pp. 131–52.

[12] 'Maria de qua natus est Jesus sicut fuit in utero sanctificata priusquam nasceretur, ita de Joseph virginali viro suo pia probabilitate credi potest quamvis forte non omnino similiter. Potest forsan haec dissimilitudo notari in hoc quod Joseph post originale contractum sanctificatus est in utero baptismo flaminis sicut Joannes Baptista et aliorum plurimi. Sic

keen to encourage, depended on the doctrinal rehabilitation of the much-neglected figure of Joseph.

Gerson's arguments in favour of Joseph's sanctification *in utero* are somewhat reminiscent of St Bernard of Clairvaux's famous remonstrance to the canons of Lyons on the subject of the immaculate conception of Mary. In order to promote the new feast day, the canons had appealed to the authority of a certain revelation in which, supposedly, the Virgin recommended the introduction of the new feast as a way to commemorate her parents, as prescribed by the fourth commandment ('Honour thy father and thy mother' (Exodus XX: 12)). Bernard had discarded such devotional claims, along with unproven revelations, as a possible justification for instituting a new feast day. Such arguments, he maintained, had not been proved by reason or attested by any ancient tradition (*novam inducendo celebritatem, quam ritus Ecclesiae nescit, non probat ratio, non commendat antiqua traditio*).[13] In this light, Gerson's own arguments read as an attempt to outwit Bernard's critique. In an earlier sermon, preached in Saint-Germain l'Auxerrois on 8 December 1401, Gerson refers explicitly to the Cistercian's reluctance concerning the instauration of the feast of the immaculate conception. Constructed on the famous verse from Daniel XII: 4 – 'Many shall run to and fro, and knowledge shall be increased' – Gerson's riposte is instructive with regard to his understanding of doctrinal development:

> Sometimes the Holy Spirit reveals to the Church and to the most recent doctors certain truths or expositions of the sacred scriptures which had not been revealed to their predecessors. That is what Gregory means by citing *Pertransibunt plurimi et multiplex erit sciencia Domini* (Daniel XII [4]).[14] Moses knows more

enim in officio Jerosolymitano de Joseph composito continetur et ex praemisso quadruplici principio sequi videtur' (Gerson, *Jacob autem genuit*, pp. 349–50).

[13] 'Sed profertur scriptum supernae, ut aiunt, revelationis, quasi et quivis non queat scriptum aeque producere, in quo Virgo videatur idipsum mandare et de parentibus suis, iuxta Domini mandatum dicentis: 'Honora patrem tuum et matrem tuam' [*Ex* 20, 12]. Ipse mihi facile persuadeo scriptis talibus non moveri, quibus nec ratio suppeditare, nec certa invenitur favere auctoritas' (Bernard of Clairvaux, *Epistola 174 ad canonicos lugdunenses, de conceptione Mariae*, in *Sancti Bernardi opera omnia*, ed. J. Leclercq, C. H. Talbot and H. M. Rochais (8 vols, Rome, 1974), vii. 391). On the subject of the immaculate conception, see M. Lamy, *L'immaculée conception: étapes et enjeux d'une controverse au Moyen-Age (XIIe–XVe siècles)* (Paris, 2000), pp. 52–3; also A. Wilmart, *Auteurs, spirituels et textes dévots du Moyen Âge latin* (Paris, 1932), pp. 202–4.

[14] 'Fallor si haec ipsa scriptura non loquitur: pertransibunt plurimi, et multiplex erit scientia. Sed haec eadem quae de abraham, moyse, prophetis et apostolis diximus, ex eiusdem scripturae uerbis, si possumus, ostendamus. Quis enim nesciat quia abraham cum deo locutus est? Et tamen ad moysen dominus dicit: ego sum deus abraham, et deus isaac,

> than Abraham; the prophets know more than Moses; the apostles know more than the prophets; and the doctors in their turn have added to what the apostles already knew. We can thus affirm that this truth, according to which Our Lady was not conceived in original sin, is one of the truths which have been recently revealed or declared. ... For this reason St Bernard reprimands the canons of Lyons in his letter, for they wanted to celebrate the feast of this conception too soon, just as if someone today wanted to celebrate the feast of a saint not yet canonized or consecrated by the tradition and authority of the Roman Church. However, things now are no longer as they were in Bernard's time, for truth has become clearer, such that we celebrate this solemn feast almost universally within the Roman Church. That is why we run fewer risks of incurring error by presuming to celebrate this feast, than not wanting to celebrate it.[15]

The allusion to Bernard's conservatism – which Gerson otherwise shared to a large extent – reveals the real issue underlying the chancellor's doctrinal innovations in the Constance sermon of 1416, for the central point of contention was not the use of Gerson's propositions by his adversaries for

et deus iacob, et nomen meum adonai non indicaui eis? Ecce plus moysi quam abrahae innotuerat, qui illud de se moysi indicat quod se abrahae non indicasse narrabat. Sed uideamus si prophetae plus quam moyses diuinam scientiam apprehendere potuerunt. Certe psalmista dicit: quomodo dilexi legem tuam, domine? Tota die meditatio mea est. Atque subiungit: super omnes docentes me intellexi; quia testimonia tua meditatio mea est. Et iterum: super seniores intellexi' (Gregorius Magnus, *Homiliae in Hiezechihelem prophetam*, ed. M. Adriaen (*CCSL*, cxlii, Turnhout, 1971), II, hom. 4, ll. 344–57).

[15] 'Le Saint Esperit revele aucunes foys a l'Eglise et aux docteurs darreniers aucunes veritez ou exposicions de la saincte Escripture lesquelles il n'a pas revelé a leurs predécesseurs. Ainsy le dit saint Gregoire super illo: *Pertransibunt plurimi et multiplex erit sciencia Domini*, Daniel XII [4]. Moyse sceut plus que Abraham, les prophetes que Moyse, les apostres que les prophetes. Et les docteurs ont adjousté oultre les apostres. Si pouons dire que ceste verité que nostre Dame ne fut point conceue en pechié originel est de celles qui sont nouvellement revelees ou declairees, tant par miracles qui se lisent comme par plus grant partie de saincte Eglise qui ainsy le tient' (Gerson, sermon *Tota pulchra es* [*Song of Songs* IV: 7], in *Oeuvres complètes*, vii, pt. 2, pp. 1057–80, at p. 1076); and 'Pour ce saint Bernart en l'espitre que il feist aux chanoines de Lyon [*Epist.* 174] les reprent, car trop hastivement ilz vouloyent celebrer la feste de ceste concepcion comme on devroit faire maintenant qui vouldroit faire la feste d'un saint non canonisé ou non acoustumé sans aucune autorité de l'Eglise romaine. Pour tant saint Bernart s'en raporte en la fin a ce que l'Eglise en vouldra ordonner. Mais maintenant autre chose est que du temps saint Bernart car a verité est plus esclaircie et se celebre la solennité presque universelement par toute l'Eglise rommaine et autre; par quoy il n'y a point de peril de conscience et de erreur coulpable ou de presumpcion celebrer ceste solennité mais trop plus a la non celebrer' (Gerson, *Tota pulchra es*, p. 1077). The same verses of the Book of Daniel are also quoted in the same sense by Vincent de Beauvais in the *Libellus totius operis apologeticus*, prologue to the *Speculum maius*, edited as *Préface au Speculum maius de Vincent de Beauvais: réfraction et diffraction*, ed. S. Lusignan (Cahiers d'études médiévales, v, Montréal and Paris, 1979), p. 116.

political ends,[16] but the acceptability of new religious beliefs and, more profoundly, the degree of latitude to be accorded to revealed truth. On what criteria of truth can the Church judge the acceptability of new objects of devotion? Is belief in them necessary for salvation in a way which would require the believer's unwavering assent?[17] In answer to these questions Gerson announced the composition of a brief treatise devoted to the normative classification of doctrinal discourse according to degrees of truth. A few months later, by the end of 1416, the *Declaratio compendiosa quae veritates sint de necessitate salutis credendae* laid down what could be rightly seen as the epistemological foundations and moral justification of doctrinal novelty according to Gerson.[1819]

The treatise establishes six degrees (*gradus*) of truth following a descending order of epistemic assent. The first three correspond respectively to orthodox doctrine as it is explicitly contained in the scriptures; as it is conveyed by the apostolic tradition; and the revelations received by certain individuals insofar as they have been confirmed by the scriptures or the Church. These truths, directly revealed by God, constitute the articles of faith and are therefore necessary for salvation. The following three degrees are logically deduced from the first and have only a probable status. The lowest of the three corresponds to truths which 'nourish the feeling of charity and devotion of the pious heart'. Such truths result from an exercise of 'estimation or pious belief' (*existimatio vel pia credulitas*) and escape the principle of bivalence of classical Aristotelian logic.[1920] Thus understood, pious truths are not required

[16] They did not result, however, in any formal condemnation. For Gerson's assertions regarding Mary's queenship, see *Jacob autem genuit*, pp. 346–9; and *Considérations sur saint Joseph*, p. 70. See also Lieberman, 'Pierre d'Ailly, Jean Gerson et le culte de saint Joseph, III', esp. pp. 39–47.

[17] 'Est igitur quaestio si de necessitate fidei tenenda est veritas nostra consideratione secundae. Et hoc est investigare sub generali regula quae veritas est certa fide et de necessitate salutis, quae de sola probabilitate, quae de pietate fidei et quae sit impertinens' (Gerson, *Jacob autem genuit*, p. 350).

[18] J. Gerson, *Declaratio compendiosa quae veritates sint de necessitate salutis credendae*, in *Oeuvres complètes*, vi. 181–9.

[19] See also Gerson, *De vita spirituali animae* (1402): 'Distinxerunt itaque in simili doctores ante nos quod veritas aliqua est pure de fide, aliqua solum pertinens ad fidem quae dici potest de pietate fidei, aliqua impertinens quae dici potest apocrypha' (*Oeuvres complètes*, iii. 137); *Collectorium super Magnificat*, tract. ix: 'Probabilia sunt insuper plurima de et super hac beata beatarum, quae sunt potius accipienda de pietate devotionis quam de fidei necessitate vel temeritate assertionis, ubi non suppetit auctoritas Scripturae cogens aut ratio convincens' (*Oeuvres complètes*, viii. 380); *De examinatione doctrinarum*: 'Nihilominus attendendum est multiplicem esse doctrinarum per Ecclesiam seu Concilium vice sua, approbationem. Quaedam enim approbantur, ut certitudinaliter, vere, necessarioque credendae; quaedam, ut utiles ad moralem religiosamque doctrinam, sine mictione falsitatis noxiae; non tamen

for salvation, but merely allowed by the Church.[20] Gerson's argument is founded on an Aristotelian principle formulated in the *Topics*: '[N]othing prevents certain false things from being more probable than true ones, for if two contradictory statements cannot be simultaneously true, they can nevertheless be simultaneously probable'.[21] Gerson concludes from this that 'nothing prevents us from piously believing something false' as long as we do not hold it with pertinacity. In other words, as Daniel Hobbins admirably put it, a pious belief is true if it is not entirely improbable: probability

sunt sic ut credantur obligatorie; sed dicuntur sive nominantur de pietate fidei' (*Oeuvres complètes*, ix. 459). See also *Josephina*, dist. II, vv. 747–50: 'Sed nec te Virgo beata/Septenni toto cum vicinis siluisse | Crediderim, sed eas de lege sacra docuisse | Quae ventura forent et quae credenda tenerent'; dist. III, vv. 875–6: 'Ex fas fuerit paucis deducere multa | Qualia non credi sed nec reprobare necesse'.

[20] 'in sexto gradu ... collocantur veritates illae quae tantummodo faciunt ad nutriendam vel fovendam devotionis religiosam pietatem, quae scilicet magis inducuntur ad inflammandum affectum quam ad instruendum intellectum, ubi pietas devota magis inspicitur quam veritas certa, ubi hoc unum reprobatur si adesset assertionis temeritas priusquam elucidaretur alio modo vel rationem certam ipsa veritas ... Cadit existimatio vel pia credulitas non super veritate vel falsitate sed tantummodo super probabilitate vel apparentia ... de talibus eligibilius est pie dubitare quam temere definire' (Gerson, *Declaratio compendiosa*, pp. 184–5). Cf. also *Religioso et bono viro*, the letter addressed by Gerson to Jean Morel on the subject of the *Vie d'Ermine de Reims* (Paris, 1408?), in *Oeuvres complètes*, ii. 94–5; and *De vita spirituali animae*, pp. 137–41.

[21] 'Unde, sicut dicit Aristoteles, nihil refert quaedam falsa probabiliora esse quibusdam veris, ita nihil refert quaedam falsa pie credi ... Sicut stat quodlibet contradictorium esse probabile et unum stat cum altero, non in veritate sed in probabilitate, sic diversis respectibus utrumque contradictorium credi potest cum fidei pietate dum tamen sit animus a pertinaci assertione alienus' (Gerson, *Declaratio compendiosa*, p. 184); also 'Didicisti quod duo contradictoria in veritate simul non stant, sed in probabilitate' (Gerson, *Collectorium super Magnificat*, p. 480); and 'Numquid non insania est concedere quod duo contradictoria sunt simul vera pro eodem instanti temporis licet non naturae' (*Ignem veni mittere*, letter addressed by Gerson to a Franciscan (Lyons, 1426), in *Oeuvres complètes* ii. 277–8). For Aristotle, see *Topics* VI, in Hamesse, '*Auctoritates Aristotelis*', p. 331; also *Metaphysics* IV, in Hamesse, '*Auctoritates Aristotelis*', p. 124. The same principle was later incorporated by Gerson in his treatise in favour of Joan of Arc, composed on 18 May 1429, a few days after the lifting of the siege of Orleans and shortly before Gerson's death. Intending to justify the pious belief in a politically controversial figure, the former chancellor claims that the probable nature of the reasons which lead us to believe in her are not contradicted either by evidence (*apparentiae*) or by the plausible conjectures (*apparentiae seu verisimiles coniecturae*) of the opposite party. The treatise is edited: D. Hobbins, 'Jean Gerson's authentic tract on Joan of Arc: *Super facto puellae et credulitate sibi praestanda* (14 May 1429)', *Mediaeval Stud.*, lxvii (2005), 99–155, at p. 146: 'Praeseupponendum est in primis quod multa falsa sunt probabilia. Immo secundum Philosophum non refert quaedam falsa probabiliora esse quibusdam veris, usque adeo quod duo contradictoria simul stant in probabilitate licet non in veritate'.

governs truth, thus leading Gerson to the notion of 'probable truth'.[22] In such cases the chancellor calls for the greatest prudence: if the doctrine in question is uncertain, it is advisable to doubt piously rather than to advance hasty conclusions.[23]

The same principle governs Gerson's attitude towards other cases of popular devotion, as can be seen in a famous letter he addressed in September 1426 to Jean Bassandi, provincial of the Celestines in Lyons. Bassandi had asked for the theologian's expert opinion on the *Arbor vitae crucifixae Iesu* of the Franciscan Ubertino de Casale, a work which had presumably caused interest mixed with mistrust on the part of monks otherwise fond of devotional literature.[24] The chancellor, then in exile in Lyons, developed a detailed critique against certain Christological tenets contained in the work of the Franciscan. He accused Ubertino of temerity, which he attributed to a lack of discernment between truths which are necessary for salvation and consequently require firm assent by faith; and truths which hold a merely probable status and therefore proscribe bold assertions. Without logically resulting from the scriptures, such 'pious propositions' (*propositiones de pietate fidei*) serve to edify charity and devotion insofar as they do not contradict the sacred text. Together with hagiographical legends and the opinions of the doctors of the Church, 'pious truths' include:

> devout meditations on what the gospel conveys regarding the acts of Christ and His mother, considering many things implicit in the way in which they could have acted; or what Jesus would have done with Joseph and Mary from His birth to the death of Joseph, as told in the epic poem the *Josephina*.[25]

[22] Hobbins, 'Jean Gerson's authentic tract on Joan of Arc', p. 116.

[23] 'Cadit existimatio vel pia credulitas non super veritate vel falsitate sed tantummodo super probabilitate vel apparentia … de talibus eligibilius est pie dubitare quam temere definire' (Gerson, *Declaratio compendiosa*, p. 185). See also the letter dated 1408 to Jean Morel, regarding the visions of Ermine de Reims (*Oeuvres complètes*, ii. 93–6, at p. 94).

[24] For an analysis of this letter, see I. Iribarren, 'Jean Gerson, spiritual adviser to the Celestines', in *Autorität und Wahrheit. Kirchliche Vorstellungen, Normen und Verfahren (XIII. – XV. Jahrhundert)*, ed. G. L. Potestà (Schriften des Historischen Kollegs, lxxxiv, München, 2012), pp. 159–78.

[25] 'Ceterum de opinione non temeraria sed probabili vel de pia credulitate, latius dici potest prout alibi [in *Declaratio compendiosa*] notavimus. Et hoc unum placet hic repetere quid sit pium credere aut quae propositiones de pietate fidei sunt censandae: omnes illae scilicet quae nec evidenter sequuntur ex contentis in sacra Scriptura, nec etiam patenter repugnant, et aedificant caritatem vel devotionem pii cordis temerarie nihil asserentis; tales sunt narrationes sanctorum Patrum, tales devotae recogitationes circa totum evangelii decursum erga Christum et matrem suam, considerando multa non explicita quemadmodum fieri potuerint, vel quid egerit Jesus cum Joseph et Maria ab initio usque ad mortem Joseph, qualiter processum est in Josephina carmine heroico' (J. Gerson, *De susceptione humanitatis Christi*, in *Oeuvres complètes*, ii. 269). In the *Collectorium super Magnificat*, tract. xii, Gerson lends to Mary a similar description of the *Josephina* (*Oeuvres complètes*, viii. 528).

As this passage reveals, the hierarchy of truths developed earlier in the *Declaratio compendiosa* underlies both Gerson's criticism against Ubertino's devotional audacity and his poetical composition of the *Josephina*. The connection between the two is not without importance. The growing interest in the character of St Joseph during the thirteenth century reached a climax in the fourteenth within Franciscan circles, in particular among the spirituals Peter John Olivi and Ubertino de Casale. Seeking to stress the importance of Christ's earthly life, these theologians had enhanced by extension the role played by his earthly father – not without betraying a certain Joachimite tendency which did not further the reception of their writings among ecclesiastical authorities. Although Gerson was no exception, his attitude towards popular devotion was not unequivocal. Indeed, the *Josephina* borrows extensively from the Franciscan tradition of devotional literature, notably the pseudo-Bonaventuran *Meditationes vitae Christi*. Like the latter, it seeks to guide the believer through the reading of the Bible and its various meanings; convey its message concerning Christian life and moral conduct; and provide spiritual consolation through devout mediation on concrete representations of Christ's childhood and passion.[26] From this perspective the *Josephina* could be read as an attempt to retrieve Franciscan devotion to St Joseph and channel it in favour of Church reform and political stability.

However, in attempting to reconstruct the story of the Holy Family through an exercise in biblical *amplificatio*, Gerson was skating on thin ice. A few verses of the *Josephina* testify to this:

> Our meditation ... does not advance any bold statements
> on what remains unknown, but moderately recurs
> to conjectures by means of topical arguments.
> Based on what is written, the spirit is capable,
> through a pious effort, of inferring what is unwritten.
> That is how a firm faith reveals what remains uncertain,
> what actually happened and what could have happened.[27]

[26] E.g., *Josephina*, dist. VII, vv. 1894–6: 'Deficit hic sensus, ratio stupet omneque mentis | Caligat lumen, dum te, vir, cernere tali | Conor in obsequio quid dicam nescio'. I. Fabre states that, 'un principe popularisé par la *devotio moderna* consiste à s'imaginer présent à la scène méditée, car c'est en partant de scènes imaginées que l'on s'élève plus facilement au-delà même de la méditation, de telles images étant tenues d'emblée pour contingentes et provisoires. Le rôle de l'imagination chez Gerson repose sur l'idée d'une dynamique exemplaire censée accoutumer l'âme contemplative à saisir la présence du mystère à travers un tissu symbolique' (I. Fabre, *La doctrine du chant du cœur de Jean Gerson. Edition critique, traduction et commentaire du 'Tractatus de canticis' et du 'Canticordum au pèlerin'* (Geneva, 2005), pp. 106–7).

[27] 'Nil super ignotis igitur meditatio nostra | Affirmet temere, sola suffecerit uti | Coniecturarum thopica ratione modeste. | Ex scriptis inferre potest non scripta pio mens | Cum studio, sic certa fides incerta revelat | Qualia sunt acta vel que fieri potuere' (*Josephina*,

Echoing Gerson's caveat in the Constance sermon, these verses contain the main features of the chancellor's 'grammar of assent' as stated in the *Declaratio compendiosa*: of merely probable status, the devotional *amplificatio* of the scriptural text is the result of conjectural arguments to which a minimum level of epistemic assent corresponds. Its principal aim is to foster the believer's affection, thereby precluding doctrinal temerity and hasty assertions. The concept of poetry as a narrative founded on what *might have* happened rather than on what actually happened comes from Aristotle's *Poetics*: '[T]he poet's task is not to tell how things really happened but rather to tell what could have happened'. That is why, Aristotle proceeds, poetry is 'more philosophical and of a loftier character than history, because poetry tends to give general truths while history tells particular facts. By general truth I mean the sort of thing that a certain type of man will do or say either probably or necessarily'.[28] The term 'philosophical' employed by Aristotle to qualify poetry takes us back to the principle stated in his *Topics*, cited by Gerson in his *Declaratio compendiosa*, as we saw above: '[I]f two contradictory statements cannot be simultaneously true, they can nevertheless be simultaneously probable'. 'If we deny this principle' – Aristotle adds – 'philosophy becomes impossible'.[29] Philosophy and poetics thus converge on the terrain of topical or conjectural reasoning as a mode of argumentation seeking credibility rather than certainty and as such eluding the scientific standards of evidence.

In this context conjectural reasoning represents a minimal criterion of certainty, serving to guarantee the acceptability of beliefs which, without contradicting the sacred texts, cannot be logically deduced from them. Conjecture thus becomes a truth-seeking tool when a superior level of certainty fails. Cicero's definition of divination is not dissimilar: '[I]t is the art of those who, having learned old things by observation, seek new things by conjecture'.[30] Conjecture proceeds by correlations between unusual phenomena and analogous ones already known: in order to

dist. III, vv. 855–60). See also the programmatic verses at the end of the Prologue: 'favete | Nostraque sit, facite pietas accepta Camene, | Ancillans fidei, nulli preiudica vero, | Multa probabiliter suadens, temeraria nusquam, | Apta peregrinum cor sursum attollere celis' (vv. 91–5).

[28] Aristotle, *De arte poetica*, ed. L. Minio-Paluello (*Aristoteles Latinus*, xxxiii, Brussels, 1968), ch. 9, 1451a36–10; also 1447a18–1448a27, 1448b4–23.

[29] Aristotle, *Metaphysics* IV, in Hamesse, '*Auctoritates Aristoteli*', p. 124; quoted by Gerson in *Declaratio compendiosa*, pp. 184–5.

[30] 'Est enim ars in eis qui novas res coniectura persequuntur, veteres observatione didicerunt' (Cicero, *De divinatione*, ed. T. E. Page, E. Capps and W. H. D. Rouse, with English trans. by W. A. Falconer (Cambridge, Mass. and London, 1927), p. 262 (I. xviii. 34)).

clarify the meaning of an unusual event, the interpreter relies on similar ones already attested in oral or written memory.[31] Similarly, the *Josephina* intends to elaborate a plausible narrative from what is implicitly contained in the scriptures, with reference to recorded traditions of biblical history or hagiographical models. An emblematic example of this kind of extrapolation from biblical narrative is the episode of the flight to Egypt, in which Gerson the poet imagines that, upon arrival, Joseph would prudently have attempted to conceal the identity of his wife. He draws his inspiration from a passage in Genesis in which the same behaviour is attributed to Abraham during his stay in Egypt.[32] These narrative mechanisms are not unusual in hagiographical literature, in which the deeds or features of one saint are often attributed to other saints. In the case of the Constance sermon, the doctrine that Joseph was sanctified *in utero* results from an extrapolation from the privilege granted to John the Baptist and traditionally accepted by the Church.

In an earlier treatise devoted to the spiritual promotion of St Joseph, the *Considérations sur saint Joseph* (1414), Gerson had defined the conjectural reasoning underlying devotional truths by the middle-French term *religieuse estimation*.[33] The choice of term is not arbitrary and takes us back to the Arab tradition of commentaries on the Aristotelian *Organon*. This tradition conceived rhetoric and poetics as part of logic, understood not as an *ars sermocinalis* (leading with language) but as an *ars ratiocinativa* (focusing on cognitive acts).[34] The result was a raising of the scientific standards of

[31] K. Park, 'Observation in the margins, 500–1500', in *Histories of Scientific Observation*, ed. L. Daston and E. Lunbeck (Chicago, Ill., 2011), pp. 15–44, at p. 18.

[32] *Josephina*, dist. II, vv. 411–24. Cf. Genesis XII: 11–13.

[33] 'Nous estudions prendre aucunes considerations particulieres selon *probables raisons ou arguments, morals et topiques*, comme appartient a tele matiere, et comme elle les peut souffrir et recevoir sans temeraire ou fole assertion; car en ce faisant, on edifie l'affection devote qui s'esmeut plus en considerations particulieres que universeles; et c'est ce que nous appelons en latin *pietas fidei*; nous le povons dire en francois: *religieuse estimation* … Et ceste consideration proffite a merveille pour entendre et concevoir … comment saincte Église use de leurs dis [des sains docteurs] en ses legendes et en ses chans' (Gerson, *Considérations sur saint Joseph*, p. 65). Cf. *Jacob autem genuit*: '*religiosa studiositas* plurima conquirere de castissima et sanctissima conversatione Joseph cum Maria, de confabulationibus suis divinissimis in loco peregrinationis suae super mysteriis nostrae redemptionis, super canticis ipsius Mariae, Zachariae et Simeonis; super his praeterea omnibus quae dicebantur de puero Jesu et quae videbantur in eo et quae revelabantur ab angelo; immo et quae felici experimento tu Maria didiceras' (*Jacob autem genuit*, p. 353) (my emphasis).

[34] E.g., al-Fārābī, *De scientiis, Al-Farabi über die Wissenschaften*, ed. F. Schupp (Hamburg, 2005), ch. 5; also Aristotle, *Rhetoric*, ed. B. Schneider (*Aristoteles Latinus*, xxxi, pts 1–2, Turnhout, 1978), I.1, 1355a14–18; Boethius, *De differentiis topicis*, trans. and notes E. Stump (Ithaca, N.Y. and London, 1978), bk. IV. On this subject, see, among a vast literature: *La*

evidence, thus opening the way to the notion of a moral kind of argument distinct from demonstrative syllogism. In this context the use of the term *aestimatio* (estimation) to describe the type of cognitive act characteristic of poetry is recurrent in Latin commentaries of the *Organon* in the thirteenth and fourteenth centuries. Based on a descending hierarchy of degrees of assent, Latin theologians ascribe necessary judgement to demonstrative reasoning; to opinion or belief (*opinio* or *fides*), in which one of the terms of the contradiction outweighs the other; to dialectics; to *suspicio* (suspicion) of the conclusion to rhetoric; and, finally, to *aestimatio*, to the poetical construction of a plausible literary universe seeking to influence the behaviour of the audience.[35] Gerson's use of the term *aestimatio* in the context of his promotion of St Joseph is indebted to this tradition and confirms the connection made previously between the principles governing his attitude towards lay devotion and his conception of religious poetry.

This analysis concludes with one last example of Gerson's strategy to justify devotional novelty by grafting it onto an existing tradition through probable arguments. In its doctrinal reconstruction of Joseph, the *Josephina* insists on the providential importance of Joseph's youthfulness. In order to exclude all suspicion of adultery by his pregnant wife (indeed, conception from an elderly man seemed improbable), a young Joseph was all the more

---

rhétorique d'Aristote: traditions et commentaires de l'Antiquité au XVIIe siècle, ed. G. Dahan and I. Rosier-Catach (Paris, 1998); J. Franklin, *The Science of Conjecture: Evidence and Probability before Pascal* (Baltimore, Md., 2001); K. Fredborg, 'The scholastic teaching of rhetoric in the middle ages', *Cahiers l'Institut du moyen âge grec et latin*, lv (1978), 85–105; P. O. Lewry, 'Rhetoric at Paris and Oxford in the mid-thirteenth century', *Rhetorica*, i (1983), 45–63; G. Dahan, 'Les classifications du savoir aux XIIe et XIIIe siècles', *L'Enseignement philosophique*, xl.4 (1990), 5–27; G. Dahan, 'Notes et textes sur la poétique au moyen âge', *Archives d'histoire doctrinale et littéraire du Moyen Âge*, xlvii (1980), 171–247; J. J. Murphy, *Rhetoric in the Middle Ages: a History of Rhetorical Theory from Saint Augustine to the Renaissance* (Berkeley, Calif., 1974); *Medieval Eloquence: Studies in the Theory and Practice of Medieval Rhetoric*, ed. J. J. Murphy (Berkeley, Calif., 1978); K. Eden, 'The rhetorical tradition and Augustinian hermeneutics in the *De doctrina Christiana*', *Rhetorica*, viii (1990), 45–63; D. Black, 'Traditions and transformations in the medieval approach to rhetoric and related linguistic arts', in *L'enseignement de la philosophie au XIIIe siècle: autour du 'Guide de l'étudiant' du ms. Ripoll 109*, ed. C. Lafleur and J. Carrier (Turnhout, 1997), pp. 233–54; W. F. Boggess, 'Aristotle's "Poetics" in the fourteenth century', in *Stud. in Philology*, lxvii (1970), 278–94; R. Copeland, '*Pathos* and pastoralism: Aristotle's *Rhetoric* in medieval England', *Speculum*, lxxxix (2014), 96–127, esp. at pp. 96–100. I am very grateful to Mary Carruthers for her valuable comments and references on this subject.

[35] E.g., Thomas Aquinas, *Expositio libri posteriorium*, in *Sancti Thomae de Aquino opera omnia*, ed. Leonine (multiple vols, Rome and Paris 1882–; 1989), i. 2. (I, 1); Albert the Great, *Super Ethica*, in *Natürliche Moral und philosophische Ethik bei Albertus Magnus*, ed. J. Müller (Beiträge zur Geschichte der Philosophie und Theologie des Mittelalters, Neue Folge, lix, Münster, 2001), pp. 325–58, at pp. 341–2 (I, 3).

likely to guarantee Jesus' legitimate birth (dist. V, vv. 1524–5; and dist. IV, vv. 1300–4). Following an idea which harks back to Augustine and is rather present in medieval religious imagination, Gerson considers that Joseph's role was crucial to deceiving the devil and thereby safeguarding the mystery of the incarnation.[36] In this respect he regrets the lasting influence of apocryphal accounts on iconographical representations of an old, slightly awkward Joseph, overshadowed by the imposing figures of Mary and the Child. According to the Paris chancellor, this tendency can only be explained by the fact that at that point in history the doctrine of Joseph's own virginity was not sufficiently established in the minds of the faithful. Indeed, the apocryphal literature had conveyed the image of Joseph as an old widower at the time he married Mary as a way of dispelling suspicion of any carnal knowledge between the two spouses.[37] As Gerson sees it, then, apocryphal accounts correspond to an embryonic stage in the development of doctrine, just like Bernard's position, alluded to earlier, regarding the immaculate conception of Mary. Governed by grace, the normative character of the new law requires gradual unfolding and adaptation in time, without thereby diminishing its perfect and definite character:[38] *non subito totam se monstrat gratia mondo* [the whole of grace does not manifest itself in a sudden way to the world] (dist. V, v. 1535). Convinced as they are now of the virginal nature of the union of Joseph and Mary – Gerson claims – the faithful are ready to embrace the new cult and see in Joseph the physically young, spiritually privileged spouse who corresponds to Mary's sinless conception. A passage from the *Considérations sur saint Joseph* offers, as it were, Gerson's final manifesto on doctrinal development:

> If someone argues that it would be introducing novelty in the Church, which would seem a danger and a temerity, for – they could add – our predecessors, who were so holy and wise, would have established such a solemn feast at their time had they considered it convenient: to this we could answer that God's providence accomplishes things by wise disposition, one after the other, even though he could have made them all at the same time. And we see this,

[36] 'Altera ratio [quod Joseph fuisse juvenem], fuit ad conservandam Mariae famam apud perfidos Judaeos et ad Incarnationis mysterium celandum demonibus; quae ratio cessasset prorsus si Joseph senex, frigidus et quasi maleficiatus palam apparuisset' (Gerson, *Jacob autem genuit*, p. 353). For Augustine, see sermon 263, *De ascensione Domini*: *muscipula diaboli, crux Domini* , in *Sancti Augustini Sermones post Maurinos reperti, Miscellanea Agostiniana*, ed. G. Morin (2 vols, Rome, 1930), i. 508.

[37] 'Vel ideo pingebatur senex ab initio nascentis Ecclesiae dum Mariae perpetua virginitas nondum ut modo radices fixerat in cordibus fidelium, ne suspicaretur carnale aliquid de Joseph et Maria' (Gerson, *Jacob autem genuit*, p. 353).

[38] On this subject, see E. Marmursztejn, *L'autorité des maîtres. Scolastique, normes et société au XIII*e *siècle* (Paris, 2007), esp. pp. 85–7.

> more to our purpose, as feast days have been successively instituted and the truths of faith successively preached. The feast of the Nativity of Our Lady was thus instituted a long time after the feast of her Assumption; and the feast for her Conception was recently established, and lately the feast of the Blessed Sacrament was instituted, as well as that of St Anne, and similarly for a number of other cases. For God wants our devotion to be turned first to one thing and then to another, as long as it is according to truth and following a good intention, since a holy novelty can be agreeable to him without reprehension.[39]

An epic reconstruction of St Joseph's *gesta*, the *Josephina* can also be seen in the light of the above analysis as a timely justification of new religious cults and, indeed, a far-reaching illustration of doctrinal boldness in the promotion of new institutional religious cults and beliefs.

[39] 'Et s'aucun dit que ce seroit introduire nouvelté en l'Eglise, qui sembleroit peril ou temerité, car c'est bien a savoir, dira aucun, que nos predecesseurs qui furent tant saints et saiges eussent pièca de leur temps ordonnee tele solennité se ce eust esté bien et convenablement fait, nous pouvons respondre que la providence de Dieu fait ses choses par saige ordonnance, l'une apres l'autre combien qu'elle les pourroit tout faire ensemble et nous le veons a nostre propos que les festes des sains et sainctes ont este successivement ordonnés et les verités de la foy successivement prachees. La feste de la Nativite Noster Dame fu faicte moult longtemps apres celle de son Assumption; puis on a fait nouvellement la feste de sa Conception et n'aguerez que la feste du saint sacrement fu instituee, et celel de sainte Anne, et ainsi de plusieurs telz cas; car Dieu veult bien que nostre devocion se torne puis en une chose puis en l'autre, mais que ce soit selond verité et bonne entencion, car sainte nouvelleté peut bien plaire sans reprehension' (Gerson, *Considerations sur saint Joseph*, p. 71).

Afterword

David d'Avray

The Franciscan university master and minister general Bonaventure (*c.*1217–74) once gave a talk about the 'order' of university study which, like this book, is an interpretative history of scholasticism.[1] He writes that there are four kinds of writing which are the object of study: first, the books of holy scriptures; second, the 'original [Patristic] texts' (*libri originalium*);[2] the *Summae* of the [university] masters (*Summae magistrorum*) are the third kind of writing; and the fourth are the writings of worldly teachings (*doctrina mundialium*) (*Collationes*, pp. 214–5). With the scriptures one must start with the literal sense, then go on to the 'spiritual' (symbolic/allegorical) sense. One must master the Bible as a whole (*oportet totum textum sacrae Scripturae habere in promptu*). To understand the literal sense of the scriptures properly, one must turn to the 'Fathers', who have had help from the holy spirit. Their writings too are difficult to understand, however; and some people studying them on their own have fallen into very many errors and heresies. Hence one needs to have recourse to the *Summae* of the masters, in which those difficulties are elucidated. Because these writings of the masters make much use of texts from the (pagan) philosophers (*verba Philosophorum*), it is necessary for the student of sacred scripture to hear lectures on and study the latter (*Collationes*, p. 216). Each kind of study has its danger. The *Summae* can mislead because the masters do not always understand the Fathers: for example, Peter Lombard (*c.*1100–60), though a great man, did not understand Augustine (354–430) in certain places (*Collationes*, p. 216). Moreover, (pagan) philosophy is full of dangers. It ought to be a preparatory study (*in scriptis Philosophorum transeundo studendum est*) (*Collationes*, p. 217). It does not work like that, however, 'because those who teach it [*professores*], even if not openly, nonetheless

[1] Bonaventure, *Collationes in Hexaemeron*, ed. F. Delorme (Bibliotheca Franciscana Scholastica Medii Aevi, viii, Ad Claras Aquas, 1934), pp. 212–22 (visio III, Collatio VII). Henceforth references will be given in the text.

[2] Later Bonaventure uses the phrase 'Sanctorum originalia' (*Collationes*, p. 216). All translations are my own.

D. d'Avray, 'Afterword', in *Individuals and Institutions in Medieval Scholasticism*, ed. A. Fitzpatrick and J. Sabapathy (London, 2020), pp. 269–76.

secretly read, copy and hide booklets [*quaternos*] of the philosophers like idols' (*Collationes*, p. 218).

This is meant to be a sort of syllabus but stands up well as a short history. Scholastic theology started with questions about the Bible and the 'Fathers' of the Church, who themselves seldom strayed far from biblical exegesis. Both sources of authority generated problems for anyone who read them in a spirit of intellectual enquiry, as did Peter Abelard, whose *Sic et non* juxtaposed authoritative texts which appeared to refute one another. 'Gratian's' *Decretum* (a theological as well as legal synthesis from the 1130s–50s; the inverted commas indicate scholars' uncertainty about the author or possibly the two authors) did the same.[3] The *Decretum* was itself a *Summa*, theological as well as legal; and the theological *Summa* of Peter Lombard, his *Sentences*, resolved the naked tensions emphasized by Abelard to make students think and set the parameters for a whole series of subsequent *Summae* in what would, by the early thirteenth century, become the university system as we still know it today. Logic and philosophical linguistics were at first the main problem-solving tools, but with the translation into Latin of the substantive philosophical works of Aristotle, Avicenna and Averroes, Bonaventure's 'philosophers' with their 'worldly teachings', the relation of these to theological data became a central preoccupation.

Bible, Fathers, *Summae* and pagan philosophy: Bonaventure's summary does considerable justice in a small compass to the intellectual movement with which this book is concerned. Dufal's chapter is all about the relation of the masters to the Fathers; and Kempshall focuses on the influence exercised by the greatest Latin Father, Augustine, on the historical writing of Nicholas Trevet, who chose the 'deliberate restatement of Augustinian restraint' over alternative approaches of which he was well aware. The *Summae* of the masters are at the centre of other analyses: Sabapathy's of Robert of Courson; Corran's of Peter the Chanter and Raymond of Peñafort and Linde's on Robert Holcot's commentary on the *Sentences*. Piron writes important pages on ideas from Peter John Olivi's rather loosely articulated *Summa*. Rolando of Cremona, the centre of Biller's chapter, also wrote a *Summa* (though it is only one of a range of sources used). Philosophy – non-Christian – is at the core of the contributions by Fitzpatrick (the ideas of Aristotle and Averroes were hugely important in the debate she studies) and Marenbon, writing about the celebrity arts professor Pomponazzi. Even in Iribarren's chapter on a poem about Mary and Joseph, in which one would not expect arts-faculty thinking or pagan philosophy, it is argued

[3] On 'Gratian' see the editors' note in their introduction.

that conjectural reasoning is used to justify devotional truths described in language which goes back to the Arab tradition of commentaries on the Aristotelian *Organon.*

Only the chapter by Melville resists easy insertion into Bonaventure's schema. It is true that it dovetails with the book as a whole because of its affinities with Piron's contribution. Both explore the same paradox: belief in institutions by misfits in the institutions of their time who felt inspired by God. Piron finds in Spiritual Franciscans a 'tendency to attribute a strong historical meaning to the Franciscan institution itself' which 'would develop especially among a minority group; and that this use would grow stronger the more they were marginalized and "de-institutionalized"'. Melville illustrates from the history of religious orders the paradox that charismatic leaders subversive of institutions had to institutionalize their movements. Peter John Olivi (*c.*1248–98), the man at the centre of Piron's article, had a conventional, 'scholastic' university training, even if from wholly Franciscan institutions; and can be counted among the writers of *Summae*, something which brings him into line with most of the thinkers discussed in the volume. However, Melville's contribution to the history of canon law and religious orders forces us to think about where we draw the boundaries around 'scholasticism'.

'Gratian' is Melville's starting point and, as already noted, there is a strong affinity between 'Gratian's' *modus operandi* and the technique of 'contrasting authorities' associated with academic theology from Abelard onwards. The excellent ideal-type of scholasticism which the editors borrow from the late Riccardo Quinto (1961–2014) fits academic canon law as well as academic theology, especially if one can understand 'truth value' to include truth about the state of the law:

(1) an 'objective' engagement with texts 'independent of the subjective conditions of the commentator' i.e. not primarily concerned with a 'subjective' personal, spiritual engagement – as in monastic texts;

(2) texts are subject to an analytical reading, with 'individual statements' compatibility established though dialectical means';

(3) the text's value comes wholly from its truth-value and not from its 'own' interest or purpose – to that degree it produces knowledge (*scientia*), 'an ensemble of propositions guaranteed by their conformity to an authoritative text, integrated yet in a new ensemble in which their legitimacy and reciprocal connection shines in an even clearer way.[4]

[4] R. Quinto, *Scholastica. Storia di un concetto* (Subsidia Mediaevalia Patavina, ii, Padua, 2001), pp. 416–7. See also the editors' discussion of the topic in their introduction and the comments by Emily Corran in her chapter at pp. 5, 222, 234.

That raises a question, however, for by no means all the texts studied in this volume fit that definition. Nor do they all fit other definitions of scholasticism which might plausibly be proposed (and which overlap a good deal with Quinto's): one could for instance define scholasticism as the systematic use of *quaestiones* to resolve problems and contradictions in authoritative tradition; or one could adopt Martin Grabmann's classic definition: the application of reason to revelation.[5] There is thus a surface contradiction between the contents of the volume and the definition of its subject endorsed by its editors. The editors themselves provide the conceptual tools to resolve the contradiction; and also to think in new ways about the relationship between 'ideas' and 'society', about which the introduction proposes some seminal ideas, going far beyond the conceptual frameworks for intellectual history which survive from the twentieth century.

What is the legacy of the twentieth century as far as frameworks for intellectual history are concerned? For the middle ages, a key role was assigned to 'the rise of towns and trade' by scholars far beyond the narrow circle of *Marxisant* historians: a diluted version of the 'socio-economic substructure/ideological superstructure' schema. Its typical *Annales* form was to point to homologies rather than a one-directional causal relationship. Out of the same tradition came the Jacques Le Goff (1924–2014) school of 'historical anthropology'; then 'scholastic anthropology' (the school of Alain Boureau which helped to form Piron and Dufal), working scholastic thought into its social setting in life. It focused on the penetration, into the actual content of high-level academic thought, of ideas underlying the social and political practice of their time; and perhaps also on scholastic thought which still seems relevant to understanding humanity. Also emanating from Paris were the theories of Michel Foucault (1926–84) of a dominant discourse in each age. From Cambridge came an emphasis on the immediate context of ideas as opposed to their long-term life. Meanwhile, most historians of scholastic texts have been primarily engaged in editions and high-quality description of content. None of this will provide an answer to the question of how to find a concept of 'scholasticism' which includes the rich variety in this volume without being impossibly vague. To this may be added the questions of how to integrate the intellectual and social aspects of scholasticism; and of where the field should go next.

[5] M. Grabmann, *Die Geschichte der scholastischen Methode* (2 vols, Freiburg, 1909–11), i. 36: 'Die scholastische Methode will durch Anwendung der Vernunft, der Philosophie auf die Offenbarungswahrheiten möglichste Einsicht in den Glaubensinhalt gewinnen' (the definition goes on to include bringing supernatural truth nearer to the thinking human intellect, synthesis and refutation of purportedly rational objections to Christianity (pp. 36–7)).

The introduction suggests solutions by drawing attention to Niklas Luhmann's brand of systems theory as a way to think about scholasticism; and offers an excellent short summary of his thought which need not be repeated. One way in which Luhmann (1927–98) differs from most previous anthropologists and sociologists is that he does not think in terms of 'the social system' so much as a myriad of systems and subsystems: any sequence of communications with boundaries is a social system. Scholasticism as defined by Quinto is a feature shared by a range of (but not all of) the subsystems within a loose, overarching system, something one might define *grosso modo* as the academic world of the central and late middle ages: universities and the institutions modelled on them (mendicant *studia*). The tradition of teaching the *Sentences* and writing *Summa* is a subsystem, as is the tradition of commenting on the works of Aristotle in texts and in the classroom. One could call scholasticism as defined by Quinto the scholastic method; and the over-arching system the world of scholasticism.

If social systems are sequences of communications within boundaries, we move beyond the world of texts. Textual arguments about excommunication, usury, rapine, vows, scandal and due process (Sabapathy); perfection (Piron); casuistical questions (Corran); or Holcot's interpretation of *Omnis utriusque sexus* (Linde) are just the – to us – most visible parts of ways of religious life, confessional conversations and tense disputes between friars and bishops. This volume is about a series of subsystems consisting not only of writings but also of oral teaching and debate and of ideas in action.

Even debates which are much more tightly defined can be re-conceived as social systems. Fitzpatrick's chapter on the 'unicity of substantial forms' makes this clear. She shows Franciscans and Dominicans locked in conflict over this apparently technical issue. (Actually, it was rather fundamental, as it involved questions about the continuity between an individual's body in life and after the resurrection.) Luhmann argues that conflicts can be highly integrated social systems.[6] Furthermore, the subject of the debate was more protean than its technical name might suggest. Dominican intellectuals who claimed to represent the position of Thomas Aquinas (1225–74) actually had different views.[7] It was the conflict as much as the content which makes this an identifiable subject of research. Furthermore, the conflict continued into the fifteenth century. It evolved into a debate about the status of Christ's blood and became relevant to popular devotion. The orders attacked each other vehemently

[6] N. Luhmann, *Soziale Systeme. Grundriß einer allgemeinen Theorie* (Frankfurt, 1984), pp. 532–5.

[7] A. Fitzpatrick, *Thomas Aquinas on Bodily Identity* (Oxford, 2017), pp. 175–82, 'Epilogue'.

and in public.[8] It was truly a 'conflict system' which had taken on a life of its own and moved into a new, popular arena.

A striking parallel is the argument about the immaculate conception of the Virgin: was she born free from original sin? As with the argument about bodily continuity before and after the resurrection, the conflict was about institutional identities and rivalries as well as belief. Broadly speaking, the doctrine of the immaculate conception was rejected by Dominicans and adopted by the Franciscan order, together with the Jesuits in the early modern period. The debate was fought out with scholastic intellectual weapons but also by mobilizing public opinion.[9]

This suggests a route for future research: the long-term history not of ideas as such, but of what might be called 'conversational threads': sequences of communication starting from the discussion of a specific problem or text, although evolving – as conversations (and arguments) do. The communication consists of oral teaching limited by tacit expectations as well as *quaestiones* in written *Summae*. The longer the sequence the better: these conversational threads can certainly be studied up to the Reformation, if not beyond.

This is different from the 'unit-idea' approach[10] because the conversations may shift their focus and change their character and even their content over time; and are not necessarily about one idea. For instance, 'ethics' in classical Greece, its boundaries marking it off from the religion of the Olympians with all their goings-on, can be seen as a conversation started by Sophists and continued by Socrates (469–399 BC) and Plato (*c.*429–347 BC). It embraced new themes with stoicism; slid into a Christian framework without losing the boundaries which marked off natural virtues from other religious duties; then started to part company with politics in Machiavelli's thought (1469–1527); and so on. This 'conversational-thread' approach would also be different from the study of the reception of an individual text or thinker. The sequence of communications could, in principle, consist only of authors replying to authors, but normally it will be more 'embodied'.

Take Augustine's idea of predestination. It takes off through controversy involving not just books but a council and popes. Opposition to it comes from John Cassian (*c.*360–after 430), working in a monastic social setting

[8] A. Fitzpatrick, 'Mendicant order politics and the status of Christ's shed blood', *Hist. Research*, lxxxv (2011), 210–27.

[9] The authoritative study is B. Gaspar, 'The immaculate conception 1100–1700: para-magisterial powers and their politics' (unpublished University College London PhD thesis, 2012).

[10] Usually represented, in polemics against it, by A. O. Lovejoy, *The Great Chain of Being: a Study of the History of an Idea* (Cambridge, Mass., 1936).

in which man did not seem so hopelessly sinful, as long as he thought about scripture enough. Ninth-century intellectuals revive the argument (Gottschalk, Hincmar of Reims). With John Wyclif (*c.*1330–84) the idea evolves into a union with his notion of an eternal Bible in the mind of God. From then onwards the debate spilled into the public sphere, where it had begun, with Martin Luther (1483–1546); John Calvin (1509–64); the Council of Trent (1545–63); Jansenism; Jacobus Arminius (1560–1609), etc. Between Gottschalk and Hincmar, and within the larger conversation about predestination, there is a more specifically scholastic conversational thread which one can trace through commentaries on Peter Lombard's *Sentences*. Research on the debate about predestination in commentaries on book 1, distinctions 40 and 41 can serve as a model for other investigations. Russell Friedman traces the debate up to 1320, distinctions 40–41 providing a thread to follow.[11] The subsequent exchanges have been more sketchily surveyed.[12] In the nature of the case, one would expect each to be responding to previous commentaries as well as to the original text.

Many other new questions could be asked about medieval scholasticism. A promising method, successfully applied to Duns Scotus by Michael Sylwanowicz, is to uncover deep presuppositions far below the surface of a master's work.[13] According to Sylwanowicz, Scotus had a much fierier, more dynamic idea of being than did Aquinas and a more generous notion of God. The approach could be applied to other thinkers. Again, one could

[11] R. L. Friedman, 'The *Sentence* commentary, 1250–1320. General trends, the impact of the religious orders, and the test case of predestination', in *Medieval Commentaries on the Sentences of Peter Lombard*, ed. G. R. Evans and P. Rosemann (3 vols, Leiden, 2002–15), i. 41–148, especially pp. 84–115.

[12] Research into this or other 'conversational threads' through *Sentence* commentaries is facilitated also by Rosemann's 2nd and 3rd volumes of *Medieval Commentaries on the Sentences* and F. Stegmüller, *Repertorium Commentariorum in Sententias Petri Lombardi* (Würzburg, 1947). Random examples are Hugolini de Urbe Veteri, OESA, *Commentarius in Quattuor Libros Sententiarum*, ii, ed. W. Eckermann (Würzburg, 1984), pp. 381–402 (he lectured in 1348–49: see Evans and Rosemann, *Medieval Commentaries on the Sentences*, i. 431); and Heinrich von Gorichem [= Henry of Gorkum], *In quatuor libros sententiarum* (Basel, 1498, repr. Frankfurt, 1967), Lib. 1, Di. XL and XLI (no page numbers). On Henry of Gorkum, whose commentary was produced at Cologne in the early 14th century, see J. T. Slotemaker, 'Henry of Gorkum's *Conclusiones super IV libros Sententiarum*: studying the Lombard in the first decades of the fifteenth century', in Evans and Rosemann, *Medieval Commentaries on the Sentences*, iii. 145–73. For traditional doctrinal history of the predestination doctrine, see W. Pannenberg, *Die Prädestinationslehre des Duns Scotus im Zusammenhang der scholastischen Lehrentwicklung* (Göttingen, 1954). My thanks to Michael Sylwanowicz for this reference. Pannenberg concentrated on Duns Scotus and his predecessors but provided a short 'Ausblick' on subsequent developments up to Luther (pp. 140–9).

[13] M. E. R. Sylwanowicz, *Contingent Causality and the Foundations of Duns Scotus' Metaphysics* (Leiden, 1996).

investigate the significant absences from the range of topics scholasticism characteristically covered in its initial phase and its thirteenth- and early fourteenth-century flowering. Negative facts matter. The whole theme of ecclesiology is left on the margins of scholasticism, for instance, though it was on the minds of theologians in the later middle ages. Canon lawyers thought about it systematically much earlier.

These two types of university intellectual and their respective paradigms should be studied together. The respective origins and methods of lawyers and theologians were similar: notably disputations and syntheses. Sociologically speaking, they were increasingly separate, however, and the same can be said of most of the scholars who study them today. To reconstruct the intellectual barriers of the middle ages some modern barriers need to come down.

The relationship of scholastic theology to preaching also needs systematic attention. The whole problem has been obscured by a tendency to characterize the preaching method of the mid thirteenth century on as 'scholastic'. That seems natural since these sermons were full of distinctions and authorities; but whereas scholastic theology proper used distinctions to resolve apparent contradictions between authorities, thirteenth-century sermons used them to unpack a topic – just as French students and scholars do in essays and lectures today (*les trois points* etc.) – and subsumed authorities under the parts thus divided, without any particular interest in contradictions between them. Furthermore, there are hardly any *quaestiones* in thirteenth-century sermons. Gradually, starting with a few exceptional cases in the thirteenth century and then, after that, less exceptionally, we meet *quaestiones* and genuine philosophical reasoning in sermons.[14] The stages of this and many other developments have still to be mapped, but no user of the present volume is likely to feel pessimistic about the future of the field.

[14] For unsystematic preliminary findings, see D. L. d'Avray, 'Philosophy in preaching: the case of a Franciscan based in thirteenth-century Florence (Servasanto da Faenza)', in *Literature and Religion in the Later Middle Ages: Philological Studies in Honor of Siegfried Wenzel*, ed. R. G. Newhauser and J. A. Alford (Binghampton, N.Y., 1993) pp. 263–73.

Index[I]

[I] Medieval names are indexed by first name except where prevalent modern usage makes this perverse (e.g. Peter Abelard under 'Abelard', not 'Peter'). Names have generally been anglicized. In a volume of this sort where concepts like institution, organization, etc. are pervasive it is difficult to strike a balance between excess and parsimony, but we have tried to do so.

CPSIA information can be obtained
at www.ICGtesting.com
Printed in the USA
LVHW101156220521
688071LV00003B/3

9 781912 702275